Abnormal Psychology

Abnormal Psychology

Timothy W. Costello, Ph.D.

Joseph T. Costello, Ph.D.

David A. Holmes, Ph.D.
Manchester Metropolitan University, UK
(adapting author)

HarperCollins*Publishers*

Adaptation (Abnormal Psychology: International Edition)
copyright © 1995 by HarperCollins Publishers Ltd, UK.

Abnormal Psychology, copyright © 1992 by Timothy W. Costello and
Joseph T. Costello.

Adaptation published by arrangement with HarperCollins Publishers, Inc,
USA.

This edition first published in 1995 by
HarperCollins College Division
An imprint of HarperCollins Publishers Ltd, UK
77–85 Fulham Palace Road
Hammersmith
London W6 8JB

David A. Holmes asserts the moral right to be identified as the author of the
adapted material.

British Library Cataloguing in Publication Data
A catalogue record for this book is available from the British Library

ISBN 0–00–499020–X

Typeset by Harper Phototypesetters Ltd, Northampton, England
Printed and bound by Scotprint Ltd, Musselburgh, Scotland
Cover design: The Senate

Contents

International Edition Preface

The new edition of *Abnormal Psychology* has been revised in three ways. This book is based on the most recent classificatory systems for mental disorders, the Diagnostic and Statistical Manual of Mental Disorder: Fourth Edition (DSM-IV) and chapter five of the International Classification of Diseases: Tenth Revision (ICD-10), both of which have been tested and used throughout the world. As well as being generally updated, it includes new material based on recent research, and a completely revised set of suggested readings. The book has been substantially altered to meet the requirements of a UK/European readership, whilst maintaining the clear presentation style of the original American text. In converting the material for the European reader, attention has been given to the differing approaches to abnormal psychology and the different mental health systems of these cultures, as well as to the specific changes needed in illustrative examples and suggested reading.

This book presents a descriptive and interpretative summary of the field of abnormal behaviour covering, in a systematic and comprehensive fashion, material usually taught in two-term courses in abnormal psychology. Students will find the contents clear and easy to assimilate and the organisation of the material will make for ease of revision and access to main points in preparation for examinations. To aid this process, each chapter is introduced in brief and ends in summary.

Although students of abnormal psychology will find this book of particular value in its balance between comprehensiveness and conciseness, it is also intended to suit a wider readership. When producing the previous edition, the original authors had in mind its usefulness not only to college students, but also to the general reader, as well as practitioners in the fields of personnel, teaching, law, social work, religion, nursing and the medical specialities. In making the revisions for this edition, the revising author hopes to have widened this readership further to include students of other disciplines such as health studies and the biological and social sciences, as well as psychology students at many levels.

The main text begins with an examination of the history and basic concepts and differing perspectives in abnormal psychology. Prior to examining the principal mental disorders, it describes the strengths and weaknesses of the main official systems for classifying these disorders, and the methods of client assessment and diagnosis. The book then describes each of the major psychological disorders identified in the two major classificatory systems, the USA based DSM-IV and the European based ICD-10 systems.

The major approaches to treatment are first outlined and then applied to the extent to which they are appropriate to each disorder. Cognitive, behavioural, biological, humanistic, existential and psychodynamic approaches to treatment are all critically examined. The book concludes with a separate listing of the psychiatric disorders as classified in the DSM-IV and ICD-10, an extensive glossary and an index.

In revising the original text for this edition, the current author has made every effort to preserve the intentions of the original authors. Where changes have been made in updating and converting the material for a more international market, the impact on the integrity of the original text has been minimised whereas the level and relevance of detail has been increased.

The revising author wishes to acknowledge the assistance of Martin Liu at HarperCollins, and his help, faith and encouragement. Special thanks also to Dee Fernley for correcting the early drafts and to Louise Radford for making the most efficient use of the word 'deadline'.

I would also like to thank all of my friends who left me alone during the crucial production period.

David A. Holmes
Manchester Metropolitan University, England (June 1995)

The Field of Abnormal Psychology

1

There is agreement between studies carried out in a number of countries that, at any one time, 10-20 per cent of the general population is suffering from a psychological/psychiatric disorder. The disorders range from relatively quiet symptoms that principally affect only the individual, to behaviour that seriously impinges upon the rights of others; from mild symptoms to more extreme and bizarre symptoms.

The 'average person' is vaguely aware of the problem, perhaps has experienced a mentally ill person in his or her family; but, for the most part, holds opinions about abnormal behaviour that are based on bits of information or erroneous reports. Common misconceptions about abnormal behaviour are that it is incurable or always inherited; that the mentally ill are dangerous; that abnormal behaviour is always bizarre; that mental illness come from weakness or will or immoral behaviour. Those statements are either totally false or apply in only limited ways. Apart from misconceptions, for many individuals, even the question, 'How does one distinguish between normal and abnormal behaviour?', is a puzzling one.

Abnormal psychology is that branch of psychology concerned with establishing criteria to distinguish abnormal from normal behaviour; describing the various types of abnormal behaviour; searching out the causes of abnormal behaviour; seeking means of treating it; and finally, with finding ways to prevent it. More formally, we can define abnormal psychology as the study, and ultimately the control, of behaviour which is not considered normal.

This chapter examines the basic aspects of abnormal psychology, and begins to answer the questions newcomers to its study often have in mind. How does one distinguish between normal and abnormal behaviour? How prevalent is mental illness? What causes these disorders? Why is professional help necessary? Where can such help be found? Who is professionally qualified to offer help?

What is normal? What is abnormal?

'Normal' and 'abnormal', as applied to human behaviour, are relative terms. Many people use these classifications subjectively and carelessly, often in a judgmental manner, to suggest good or bad behaviour. As defined in the dictionary, their accurate use would seem easy enough; normal – conforming to a typical pattern, abnormal – deviating from a given norm. The trouble lies in the word 'norm'. Whose norm? For what age person? At what period of history? In which of the world's many cultures?

Goodness as a criterion of normal

Equating normal with good behaviour and abnormal with bad behaviour also has its problems. Good or bad by whose values or standards? Under what circumstances? Is assertive behaviour bad because it is disconcerting, and complaint behaviour good because it is easy to accept? Is behaviour at variance with paternal practice bad, and model behaviour good? Is aggressive behaviour always bad?

Psychologists who work in the field of abnormal behaviour, usually referred to as clinical psychologists, have examined these problems and can offer more objective criteria.

Two basic but different concepts of normal and abnormal

Social science offers two ways of distinguishing between normal and abnormal. One emphasised by sociologists and anthropologists considers the question meaningful only as it applies to a particular culture at a particular time; abnormal is that which deviates from society's norms. The other, stressed more by psychologists, sets as the basic criterion the individual's well-being and the maladaptiveness of his or her behaviour.

Abnormal defined as deviation from social norms

The criterion of cultural relativism – that is, deviation from society's norms – provides an easy way of identifying abnormal behaviour. If behaviour differs in a significant way from the way in which others in the same society typically behave, it is abnormal. Cultural relativism bypasses the question of whether or not there are sick societies whose values are pathological, contravening, as they might, basic human rights. When such a sick society changes radically – as for example, German society did after World War II – does that make its previous behaviour abnormal and all the resistive, non-conforming individuals now normal?

Another problem faced by cultural relativists is the question of whether or not there are any types of abnormal behaviour, the observable symptoms of which cut across all cultures. Emil Kraepelin (1856–1926), whose *Textbook of Psychiatry*, published in 1923, provided a basis for classifying mental illness that is still used today, felt that depression, sociopathy (fixed patterns of antisocial behaviour) and schizophrenia were worldwide disorders, appearing in all cultures and societies.

There is no question that cultural factors colour the symptoms of any mental illness, nor is there question that some mental illnesses appear more frequently in some cultures than in others. But most psychologists question the usefulness of social acceptability as a meaningful criterion for distinguishing abnormal behaviour from normal behaviour.

Maladaptiveness as a criterion of abnormal behaviour

To reject cultural relativism requires that the individual or the society make a value judgement – one not necessarily defensible scientifically – that some values are intrinsically good. Most Western societies have made such a judgement, that the well-being of the individual is an important aim and that assuring the well-being of the individual assures the well-being of society. With that value in place, instead of acceptability by the society, behaviour that promotes an individual;s growth and well-being is considered normal behaviour and behaviour that maladaptively prevents that growth or significantly limits it, is considered abnormal.

Such a criterion does not do away with all subjectivity in evaluating the normality of anyone's behaviour, but it does put that decision in the hands of those who will use the objectivity of science to evaluate whether any given behaviour is adaptive and normal or maladaptive and abnormal. 'Well-being' here is given a broad definition: not merely 'survival', but 'growth and fulfilment', which are paths to self-actualisation.

The well-being perspective allows room for the conforming behaviour necessary for group cohesiveness *and* for deviant behaviour, since the latter may stimulate the society to re-examine itself and its goals, so long as it is not irreparably self-damaging. It includes a concern for the family's well-being and a mission to work to eliminate those social problems that can erode a society's well-being, such as racism, discrimination and poverty.

Specific criteria for judging maladaptive behaviour

Using maladaptiveness as a criterion of banormality has its own problems. It is a rare person whose behaviour is never maladaptive – who never becomes angry in a self-damaging way, who never takes one alcoholic drink more than is sensible, who never feels depressed or anxious. In evaluating the maladaptiveness of behaviour, psychologists take account of the frequency of the behaviour and the extent to which it impairs necessary functioning, especially in interpersonal relations and occupational pursuits. They also take account of severely stressful life situations that the individual may face, or catastrophic event he or she may have lived through. Those factors may cause a transitory spell of maladaptive behaviour.

Certain categories of behaviour suggest the presence of psychological disorders which may benefit from psychological treatment. All those disorders, in one way or another, are maladaptive in that they threaten the well-being of the individual. A description of them follows.

Long periods of subjective discomfort

Everyone goes through periods of psychological discomfort – worry about the severity of a loved one's illness; fearful anticipation of a challenging assignment;

aggrieved feelings after receiving criticism. But those feelings are transitory, and they are related to real or threatened events. When such feelings as anxiety and depression or frenetic behaviour persist, month after month, and appear to be unrelated to events surrounding the person, they would be considered abnormal and suggestive of psychological disorder.

Impaired functioning

Here again a distinction must be drawn between transitory inefficiency and prolonged inefficiency, between inefficiency caused by something that can be identified, and inefficiency over a prolonged period which seems to be inexplicable. Important examples that would be considered signs of abnormal psychological condition are as follows: frequent job changes without apparent justification or frequent loss of jobs; prolonged performance notably below the individual's potential, the most common examples of which are the very bright student who gets only low or failing grades or the brilliantly talented person who fails in one effort after another.

Bizarre behaviour

Here is not meant unconventional behaviour that is carried out for some reason that can be understood by others – for example, performances imposed on freshmen as part of an initiation rite or behaviour carried out to gain attention or to achieve notoriety. Older people will remember goldfish swallowing and flag-pole sitting. Silly, but most people understood the motivation. Today, unusually dramatic hairstyles may be another example of bizarre behaviour not considered abnormal in a clinical sense.

Bizarre behaviour, indicative of abnormality, has no rational basis, is unconnected to reality, and seems to suggest that the individual is disoriented. Such behaviour indicates serious mental illness. The psychoses (the most serious of mental disorders), to be described later, frequently bring on hallucinations (baseless sensations); the hearing of voices when no one is present, for example, or delusions, which are beliefs that are patently false, yet steadfastly held by the psychotic individual. An example is delusions of grandeur in which an individual may believe that they are an important historical character.

Disruptive behaviour

Disruptive behaviour means seemingly uncontrollable behaviour that regularly disrupts the lives of others or deprives them of their rights. Such behaviour is characteristic of several psychological disorders. The antisocial personality disorder to be described later has, as one of its principal characteristics, conscienceless and apparently purposeless, aggressive or exploitative behaviour.

These behaviours are maladaptive because they directly affect well-being by blocking growth and fulfilment of the individual's potential, or do so indirectly and in the longer term by seriously interfering with the well-being of others.

Prevalence of abnormal behaviour

In considering the extent of mental illness, a distinction is drawn between prevalence, which is the number of individuals suffering a mental disease at a given time, and incidence, which reports the rate at which a specified disorder appears in the population in a stated period of time. Incidence, for example, would report the lifetime risk of developing a specified mental illness for individuals grouped by age or sex. 'Associated risk factors' is a term used in reporting incidence, an example of which would be the lifetime expected occurrence of mental illness in individuals who have relatives with a mental illness.

Abnormal behaviour (or psychological disorder as we will frequently refer to it) brings unhappiness and discomfort to more than one in ten school-age children, around one in six of the adult population, and almost one in five of the elderly. The latter group are suffering an increase in the number of disordered individuals, especially with regard to the ten per cent with some form of dementia. The social costs of hospitalisation and mental health care, and lost income resulting from enforced unemployment and absenteeism are so high as to be inestimable. Although unknown this cost is believed to be rising, especially in the case of the elderly.

Prevalence of specific disorders

Later chapters will describe in detail the variety of psychological disorders which tend to affect greater or lesser proportions of the general population, depending on the specific disorder considered. Prevalence can further depend on the strictness of the criteria applied. For example, around 20 per cent of the population of England and Wales have a problem moderating their alcohol intake, making this one of the commonest disorders. However, only one per cent are recorded as having a serious alcohol problem. Some surveys of depression (of any form) provide estimates of 50 per cent of the population during their lifetime, making it more common than alcohol abuse. Again, using stricter criteria, about ten per cent of the population have a definite depressive episode in any one year. Episodes of schizophrenia are more clearly defined and affect approximately one per cent of the world's population during their lifetime.

Age and sex differences

There are both sex differences and age differences in the types of psychological disorders suffered. Although the two sexes suffer approximately the same levels of such disorders in general, they differ in the specific disorders to which they are prone. For example, the prevalence of alcohol problems for men is 25 per cent, but for women it is 15 per cent. However, women are more likely than men to suffer depression and anxiety. Illicit drug dependence occurs most frequently in the late teens to mid-twenties age group, whereas depression and alcoholism are commonest in those aged between their mid-twenties and mid-forties. Cognitive disorders are more prevalent among the elderly.

Principal factors causing abnormal behaviour

Here in this introductory chapter, we can take only a broad-brush approach to describing causative factors in mental illness. There are three important concepts for the student to grasp in considering the development of psychological disorders – stress, coping mechanisms and vulnerability. It is the interaction between those elements that will determine the development of mental illness. Detailed descriptions of causative elements can be found in chapters describing specific disorders.

Stress

Stress is a set of emotional tensions accompanied by biological changes (principally of the autonomic system; that is, sweating, heart pounding, blood pressure changes) caused by a threatened external event. In milder forms, it causes worry and fretfulness. The experience of some level of stress is a frequent event in everyone's life. When the stressing external event is extreme or prolonged, such as a serious car accident or an earthquake, or when it imposes prolonged frustration of an important human need or a bewildering conflict in which a decision is required, a major adjustive effort is required of the individual. That demand may push the individual into a breakdown of adaptive responses and cause the appearanced of abnormal behaviour. Whether that breakdown occurs at all, and whether it is mild or extreme, depends on the existence of previously learned adaptive behaviour or, in its absence, on the presence of a tendency to depend upon defensive coping mechanisms. Existing vulnerabilities predispose an individual to the possibility of mental disorder especially in stressful situations.

Coping mechanisms

Faced with a stressful event or set of circumstances, a person may rise to the challenge by directing behaviour primarily at dealing with the stressful event – that is, by task-oriented behaviour – or the person may become defensive and call on unconsciously operating coping mechanisms, which are commonly called defence mechanisms. A coping mechanism is defined as a process of changing the meaning or significance of an event to protect the self from psychic pain and/or psychological damage. Much maladaptive or abnormal behaviour is the result of defence-oriented, rather than task-oriented, behaviour.

Vulnerability

Whether or not individuals respond adequately to stress depends upon their vulnerability, or susceptibility to the development of psychological disorders. There are, of course, 'soft spots', or vulnerabilities, in the personalities of all people; but when they are significant or multiple, they can predispose the individual to break down and exhibit maladaptive behaviour.

A major cause of vulnerability is genetic predisposition, which can take the form of a maladaptive gene, or a deficiency or abnormality in the normal genetic composition and the way this is expressed during development. A person's vulnerability to disorders can be greater following injury, infection or other damage to the nervous system. Early life experiences that result from abnormal parenting or lack of adequate learning opportunities can also increase vulnerability to psychological disorder.

Why professional help becomes necessary

Despite expert opinion that psychological disorders (along with physical disorders) are most effectively treated at the earliest sign of significant emotional disturbance, many people, for one reason or another, delay treatment, deluding themselves that palliatives or self-help approaches will cure the illness. In most cases, it requires some relatively powerful influence to bring an individual to the therapist's office.

Troubled individuals finally enter therapy as a result of one or more of three kinds of influence: personal discomfort or distress, the pressure of relatives or friends, the demands of health, community or legal authorities.

Personal discomfort

Most people who seek professional psychological help are suffering from physical or emotional discomfort. Many discomforting, even frightening, physical symptoms stem from or are made worse by emotional disorders. Among them are asthma, ulcers and hypertension; among the physical symptoms are chronic fatigue, heart palpitations, stomach complaints, and pain. Often, the effective stimulus motivating the individuals is the family doctor, who has ruled out physical causes for a disorder and suggests that the person seek psychological or psychiatric assistance.

Emotional symptoms, particularly intense anxiety or spells of depression, may become so painful or alarming that they overcome whatever reasons the person may have had for delaying treatment. Many clinicians feel that a client must be experiencing notable psychic pain to persist with therapy and to respond to it.

The influence of family and friends

The behaviour associated with abnormal behaviour may be more painful to family members or friends than to the disordered individual. Examples are abuse of alcohol, assaultive behaviour, emotionally draining dependence, or exploitative behaviour. Sometimes, desperate to change things, family or close friends will bring pressure on the individual to seek help. That pressure may benignly be brought to bear in a 'heart-to-heart' talk, but strong methods are also used: threats by a spouse that he or she will leave, or by a parent that the house will be locked against the individual unless treatment is sought. Previously supportive friends may simply desert the individual.

The kind of pressure used to induce the individual to enter therapy will, of course, have an effect on the individual's responsiveness to treatment, sometimes causing an indifferent attendance at therapy sessions with little emotional improvement; or, in other situations, causing panic-stricken demand that the therapist do something to help.

The influence of health, legal and other community authorities

Psychological disorders can produce behaviour that is so antisocial, disruptive or self-harming as to call the individual to the attention of the community authorities, a health or social worker to whom the individual or their family has become known, a member of the clergy who tries to help, or, in an increasing number of cases, the police or other legal authorities. With this kind of intercession, the pressure to receive therapy is great. How that pressure is brought to bear will also have an effect on the individual's attitude towards therapy.

Specialists who provide help

In later chapters, we will consider the variety of help, called therapies, available to those with psychological disorders. The first step in that process is an assessment of the individual's condition. That process leads to a diagnosis, which enables the clinician to fit the psychological troubles of the individual into a specific category of mental illness. That diagnosis gives the clinician an initial understanding of some of the elements in the individual's illness and enables the clinician to plan a course of treatment.

There are four professions that provide helping services, either as a team or, more frequently, individually. They are psychologists (usually clinical psychologists), psychiatrists, psychiatric nurses and social workers. The academic and experiential training they receive, although different for each of the professions, prepares them to offer psychological help in a skilled and responsible fashion. Beyond that primary group of mental health professionals, there are other professionals and para-professionals who offer specialised ancillary services, but not psychotherapy. They ordinarily work in association with psychiatrists or psychologists.

Psychologists

These professionals, who are trained to make assessments and provide psychotherapy, fall into three categories: clinical psychologists, educational psychologists and counselling professionals. Clinical psychologists begin as psychology graduates who have gained sufficient clinical experience to be accepted onto a two-year clinical psychology MSc course (a few four-year PhD courses exist) which qualifies them to practice. An educational psychologist will be a psychology graduate with a further year's training to teach, obtaining a Post

Graduate Certificate in Education (PGCE). This is followed by four years teaching experience after which an educational psychology MSc is studied before the person is qualified to assess children in a clinical sense. Counsellors are usually psychology graduates with additional counselling training. However, some have only counselling training, limiting their applicability in a clinical setting.

Clinical psychologists specialise in working with those who suffer psychological disorders, whereas counsellors may see less disturbed individuals and also usually work with school children with problems which may stem from learning or emotional difficulties.

Psychiatrists

Psychiatrists are qualified medical doctors who have specialised in psychiatry during their training. They undergo further training to qualify for membership of the Royal College of Psychiatrists (in Britain) then work towards gaining consultant status. Only a medical doctor, and thus a psychiatrist, can write prescriptions for medication, undertake other biological forms of therapy or admit an individual as an inpatient.

Psychoanalysts may be psychiatrists, psychologists or other professionals who have also completed an authorised course in psychoanalysis such as that offered by the British Psychological Society (BPS). An essential element of this training is the candidate's own personal analysis. Of the few psychoanalysts working within the National Health Service in Britain, most are psychiatrists.

Psychiatric nurses and psychiatric social workers

Nurses can specialise in psychiatric care during their training and additionally qualify as psychiatric nurses. Further training can qualify them for more specialist roles, for example that of community psychiatric nurse. Graduates in social work, or who complete a post-graduate (or direct entry) social work course, can also receive specialist training to deal with patients and their relatives as psychiatric social workers. Some social workers in Britain can have approved social worker recognition giving them particular responsibilities under the Mental Health Act.

Other professionals and para-professionals

A number of other professionals are increasingly involved with the handling and care of the psychologically disturbed. With increasing numbers of patients in the community, General Medical Practitioners (GPs), paramedics, and even the police have frequent psychiatric patient contact. In addition, a growing number of specialist therapists can be found in psychiatric hospitals and health centres, for example, occupational, art and music therapists.

Settings in which mental health therapists work

An increasing number of psychiatrists, psychologists, and even social workers, work in private practice, either singly or in groups or teams. Clients or patients can be referred to them by GPs, social or health services, or by former clients. Some agencies keep 'recommended lists' of these. All other things being equal, the Yellow Pages section of the telephone directory is not a suitable source for finding a clinician.

Other mental health professionals practise in outpatient settings which are often attached to hospital psychiatric units or behavioural medicine units. They may also be found working from Community Mental Health centres or a more general GP's Health centre. Less conventional services may be on offer in centres for 'alternative medicine'.

SUMMARY

Abnormal Psychology is that branch of psychology that establishes criteria distinguishing normal from abnormal behaviour, describes the various types of abnormal behaviour, searches out the cause of it and seeks to find means of treating or preventing it.

Psychologists see maladaptive behaviour, that is, behaviour that interferes with the individual's well-being and psychological growth, as the over-riding criterion for diagnosing abnormality. They do not consider behaviour that deviates from society's norms as necessarily a sign of abnormality.

There are four principal criteria for considering behaviour maladaptive: long periods of personal discomfort; impaired social, educational or occupational functioning; bizarre behaviour; disruptive behaviour.

In assessing the problem of mental disorder, social scientists speak of prevalence (the total number of individuals in a specific category suffering a mental disorder) and incidence (the rate at which mental disorders, usually of a particular type, will occur in a specified population during a stated period of time).

The principal factors leading to psychological disorders are stress, failure to learn adequate coping mechanisms, and vulnerability (such as genetic or organic predisposition or deficiencies in the early stages of development).

People seek professional help because of personal discomfort, the urging of family or friends, and the influence of health, legal or other community authorities.

There are four professional groups that offer help to victims of psychological disorder. They are psychologists, psychiatrists, psychiatric nurses and psychiatric social workers. They are assisted by other professional groups such as counsellors or occupational therapists (patients may also be cared for by para-professional workers such as psychiatric nursing assistants).

FURTHER READING

Audit Commission. 1986. *Making a Reality of Community Care*. London: HMSO.

Block, S. & Chodoff, P. (Eds). 1991. *Psychiatric Ethics* (2nd ed.). New York: Oxford University Press.

Chester, P. 1972. *Women and Madness*. Garden City, N.Y.: Doubleday.

Jones, J. 1988. *Experiencing Mental Health*. London: Sage Publications.

Kaplan, B. (Ed). 1964. *The Inner World of Mental Illness*. New York: HarperRow.

Kiesler, C.A. 1982. Public and Professional Myths About Mental Hospitalization. *American Psychologist* 37: 1323–1339.

Leff, J. 1989. *Psychiatry Around the Globe; a Transcultural View*. London: Gaskell Books.

Manzillier, J. & Hall, J. 1991. *What is Clinical Psychology?* Oxford University Press.

Offer, D. & Sabshin, M. 1991. *The Diversity of Normal Behaviour*. London: Basic Books – A division of HarperCollins.

2 | History of the Problem of Abnormal Behaviour

The problem of mental disorder is probably as old as humankind. Recorded history reports a broad range of interpretations of abnormal behaviour and methods for correcting it, which have generally reflected the degree of enlightenment and the religious, philosophical and social beliefs and practices of the times. It is not surprising that earlier efforts to deal with the problem were fraught with difficulties and that the evolution of a science of abnormal psychology has been painfully slow. This has been the case for two reasons.

First, the very nature of the problems caused by abnormal behaviour has made it a 'thing apart', arousing fear, shame and guilt in the families and communities of those afflicted. Hence, the management of the mentally disordered has been turned over to the state and the church, which have been the traditional guardians of both group and individual behaviour. Second, the evolution of all the sciences has been slow and sporadic, many of the most important advances having been achieved only against great resistance. While this has been more typical of abnormal psychology than of other disciplines, the difference is only relative. In reviewing the historical account that follows, one should not be too critical; although it is true that in earlier times the abnormal person was misunderstood and often mistreated, the lot of the 'normal' individual was not much happier.

Primitive period

Archaeological findings suggest that some types of mental illness must have been recognised as far back as the Stone Age. Skeletal remains from that period reveal that attempts were made to relieve brain pressure by chipping away an area of the skull. Though the procedure was similar to the operative technique now known as trephining, there is a serious question as to whether it was based on any knowledge of brain pathology. It seems more likely that the operation was performed in the belief that, in this way, an avenue of escape was provided for 'evil spirits'. Our knowledge of primitive 'psychiatry' does not go beyond speculations suggested by such skeletal remains.

Pre-classical period

Although primitive superstitions persisted into and beyond the Classical period, history shows that attempts were being made before the 'golden ages' of Greece and Rome to find a more rational approach to the understanding and treatment of the mentally disordered.

In the Orient

About 2600 BC, in China, some forms of faith healing, diversion of interest, and change of environment emerged as the chief methods for treating mental disorders. By 1140 BC institutions for the 'insane' had been established there, and patients were being cared for until 'recovery'. In the writings of physicians in India around 600 BC there are detailed descriptions of some forms of mental disease and epilepsy, with recommendations for kindness in treatment.

In the Middle East

Egyptian and Babylonian manuscripts dating back to 5000 BC describe the behaviour of the mentally disordered as being due to influences of evil spirits. Aside from the practice of trephining (opening the skull), treatment was restricted almost exclusively to the ministrations of priests and magicians. Biblical sources indicate that the Hebrews looked upon mental illness as a punishment from God and that treatment was principally along lines of atonement to Him.

Classical period

As in all areas of scientific and social thought, in the era of classical Greece and Rome, important strides were made toward a more reasonable and humane treatment of the mentally ill, and the first glimmer appeared of a medical approach to the problem.

In Greece

Some of the more significant assumptions of Greek thought have been confirmed by modern research, and much of the terminology of modern psychiatry (as, indeed, of medicine and science in general) is a legacy from this period. The humane, rational approach to mental illness that emerged during this era was due largely to the findings of the following men.

Pythagoras (circa 500 BC)

Before 500 BC, priest-physicians combined suggestion, diet, massage and recreation with their more regular prescriptions of incantations and sacrifices, but in all treatment, the guiding motive was appeasement of good or evil spirits. However, Pythagoras was the first to teach a natural explanation for mental illness. He identified the brain as the centre of intelligence and attributed mental disease to disorder of the brain.

Hippocrates (460–377 BC)

The 'Father of Medicine' held that brain disturbance is the cause of mental disorder. He emphasised that treatment should be physical in nature, urging the use of baths, special diets, bleeding and drugs. Hippocrates taught the importance of heredity and of predisposition to mental illness. He related sensory and motor disturbances to head injuries. Anticipating later ideas, he also thought that the analysis of dreams can be useful in understanding the patient's personality.

Plato (428–347 BC)

This Greek philosopher manifested keen insight into the human personality. He recognised the existence of individual differences in intelligence and in other psychological characteristics, and he asserted that man is motivated by 'natural appetites'. To Plato, mental disorder is partly moral, partly physical and partly divine in origin. He described the patient–doctor relationship in the treatment pattern, he believed that fantasy and dreams are substitute satisfactions for inhibited 'passions', and introduced the concept of the criminal as a mentally disturbed person.

Aristotle (384–322 BC)

Aristotle accepted a physiological basis for mental illness, as taught by Hippocrates. While he did consider the possibility of a psychological cause, he rejected it, and so strong was his influence on philosophical thought that for nearly two thousand years, his point of view discouraged further exploration along these lines.

Alexander the Great (356–323 BC)

Alexander established sanatoriums for the mentally ill, where occupation, entertainment and exercise were provided practices. These approaches were also continued during later Greek and Roman periods.

In Rome

The Romans, for the most part, continued to follow the teachings of the Greek physicians and philosophers in their treatment of mental illness. Greek physicians, the most outstanding of whom were Aesclepiades, Aretaeus, and Galen, settled in Rome, where they continued their studies and teaching.

Aesclepiades (124–40 BC)

This Greek-born physician and philosopher was the first to differentiate between acute and chronic mental illness. He developed mechanical devices for the comfort and relaxation of mental patients; he opposed bleeding, restraints, and isolation in dungeons. Whereas his predecessors had considered both delusions and hallucinations under one heading ('phantasia'), Aesclepiades differentiated between the two.

Aretaeus (first to second centuries AD)

Aretaeus was the first to suggest that mental illness is a psychological extension of normal personality traits. He believed that there existed a predisposition to certain forms of mental disorder. One of his original thoughts (placing the seat of mental disease in the brain and the abdomen) foreshadowed the psychosomatic approach to medicine.

Galen (AD 129–199)

Galen's contribution to medical science, though of great value in one respect, served to retard development in another. Like Hippocrates, who lived seven centuries earlier, he gathered and organised an enormous amount of data concerning mental and physical illness and conducted studies in the anatomy of the nervous system and its relation to human behaviour. He recognised the duality of physical and psychological causation in mental illness, identifying such varied factors as head injuries, alcoholism, fear, adolescence, menopausal changes, economic difficulties and love affairs. On the other hand, like many others of his time, he permitted his concern with teleology (having to do with purpose in nature) to cloud his scientific conclusions. He felt impelled to assign specific divine or astrological influences to this or that organ of the body. Since his prestige was great, for centuries after his death, progress was encumbered by controversies over the metaphysical aspects of his contributions and, thus, independent thinking in the medical sciences was delayed until well into the eighteenth century.

In Arabia

The last faint echo of the efforts of the classicists to conquer the problem of mental disorder was heard not in the West, but in Arabia, where Avicenna (AD 980–1037) and later, his follower, Averrhoes (AD 1126–1198), maintained a scientific approach to the mentally ill and urged humane treatment. Elsewhere, as we shall see, a return to primitive notions prevailed.

Medieval period

With the dissolution of the Graeco-Roman civilisation, learning and scientific progress in Europe experienced a grave setback. Ancient superstitions and demonology were revived and contemporary theological thinking did little to discourage the 'spiritual' approach to the problem of mental illness. Exorcism (expelling an evil spirit) was considered imperative; accordingly incantations were regarded as a legitimate adjunct of medicine. Even the application of perfectly rational techniques had to be accompanied by the pronouncement of mystical phrases.

The best physicians of the time were given to the use of amulets. Alexander of Tralles (AD 525–605), for example, who stressed the importance of constitutional factors and related them to specific types of mental disorder, and who studied frontal lobe injuries and noted accompanying changes in behaviour, treated colic by the application of a stone on which an image of Hercules overcoming the lion was carved.

The dancing mania

At intervals from the tenth to the fifteenth centuries, the dancing mania, also referred to as 'mass madness' in which large groups of people danced wildly until they dropped from exhaustion, was seen in Europe. In Italy, the condition was called 'tarantism' because the mania was thought to be due to the bite of a tarantula spider. Elsewhere in western Europe, the mania was called 'Saint Vitus's dance'. It is difficult to say whether these seemingly epidemic manifestations have been greatly exaggerated in the telling. It has been suggested that a large number of people may have been suffering from various forms of chorea. Fear of this unexplained disorder may have risen to a mass suggestibility and hysteria which mounted unchecked and which subsequently have been recorded as a single clinical entity.

Witchcraft: belief in demonology

The period from the fifteenth to the eighteen centuries comprises a sorry chapter of history with respect to the fate of the mentally ill. Their afflictions were generally ascribed to possession by the devil, and treatment, consisting chiefly of attempts to 'cast out the demon', was hardly distinguishable from punishment. The 'Black Death' (bubonic plague) had ravaged Europe in the fourteenth century, and the resulting depression and fear rendered many people highly susceptible to the ministrations of witchcraft. The humane, scientific approach to the mentally ill (for that matter, to all illness) was indeed at a low ebb.

Late in the fifteenth century, the plight of abnormal people was intensified by the publications of Malleus Maleficarum, 'The Hammer of Witches which destroyeth witches and their heresy as with a two-edged sword', by Henry Kraemer and James Sprenger, of the Order of Preachers. Their book, appearing in 1484 and fortified by an approving papal bull of Pope Innocent VIII, was to be the handbook of inquisitors for 200 years. The bull authorised inquisitors to proceed according to the regulations of the Inquisition. Ecclesiastical courts ferreted out persons thought to be 'possessed of the Devil'; the unfortunates were then turned over to civil authorities to be tortured or executed. Kraemer and Sprenger met some early resistance from cooler heads in the church and community but soon won support from people already imbued with fear of witchcraft; their crusade caught fire and thereafter spread throughout both Roman Catholic and Reformed centres in Europe. So widely held was the belief in witches that the persecution of wiches continued off and on for the next three centuries. Even as far afield as America, such notorious trials for witchcraft as those of the 'Salem witches' (Massachusetts 1692) took place. In England the penal laws against witchcraft ended in 1736, but trials in isolated parts of the British Isles continued into the nineteenth century.

Institutional care of the mentally ill

Symbolic of the kind of institutional care afforded the mentally ill during the late medieval and early Renaissance periods was that seen at 'Bedlam' (the name is a contraction of Bethlehem). As early as 1400, the monastery of Saint Mary of Bethlehem in London began caring for 'lunatics'; in 1547, the monastery was officially converted into a mental hospital. Because of the inhumanity of the treatment there, 'Bedlam' has come to stand for anything that is cruel in the management of the mentally disturbed.

But this era was not entirely without examples of tolerance and mercy. The shrine of Saint Dymphna at Gheel in Belgium (established in the fifteenth century) not only lent solace to thousands of afflicted persons who visited there, but also grew gradually into a 'colony' dedicated to the care of the mentally ill. Its work still goes on, and the Gheel is regarded as the model for similar colony plans elsewhere.

Renaissance period

Although the mentally disturbed became engulfed in the morass of superstition and inhumanity, in certain countries of Europe voices were raised in the cause of reason by enlightened men of religion, medicine and philosophy. Their efforts during this period can well be described as 'lights in the darkness'.

In Switzerland

Paracelsus (Theophrastus von Hohenheim, 1493–1541) rejected demonology, recognised psychological causes of mental illness, and proposed a theory of 'bodily magnetism', a forerunner of hypnosis. Like Hippocrates, he suggested the sexual nature of hysteria. However, like so many otherwise reasonable men of his time, he laid great store by astral influences, assigning to various planets control over specific organs of the body.

In Germany

Heinrich Cornelius Agrippa (1486–1535) fought against hypocrisy and blood-thirsty application of the edicts of the Inquisition. A scholar and later advocate of the city of Metz, Agrippa was persecuted and reviled for his views, and died in poverty. Johann Weyer (1515–1588) was a physician who studied under Agrippa. In 1563, he published a scientific analysis of witchcraft, rejecting the notion of demon causation in mental illness. His clinical descriptions of mental disorders were remarkably concise, uncluttered with opinions and theological illusions. Weyer is regarded by some as the 'Father of Modern Psychiatry'.

In England

Reginald Scot (1538–1599) published a scholarly, painstaking study, *The*

Discovery of Witchcraft: Proving That the Compacts and Contracts of Witches and Devils Are But Erroneous Novelties and Imaginary Conceptions. James I ordered the book to be seized and burned, and published a refutation of Scot's views.

In France

Saint Vincent de Paul (1576–1660) urged a more humane approach to the mentally ill. He emphasised the fact that mental disease differs in no way from bodily disease. In the hospital which he founded at Saint Lazare, he put into practice what he held to be a basic Christian principle, namely, that we are as much obliged to care humanely for the mentally ill as for the physically ill.

Eighteenth to Twentieth Centuries

The transition from the demonological to the scientific approach to mental illness was not accomplished overnight. In France, for example, capital punishment for convicted 'sorcerers' was not abolished until 1862. The first general trend towards specialised treatment of the mentally ill probably came in the wake of the social, political, economic and scientific reforms that characterised the latter half of the eighteenth century.

In France

Soon after the Revolution, Philippe Pinel (1745–1826) removed the chains from the inmates at Bicêtre and provided pleasant, sanitary housing along with walkways and workshops. Later, at Salpêtrière, he introduced the practice of training attendants. Jean Esquirol (1772–1840) continued Pinel's work; through his efforts, ten new mental hospitals were established in France.

In England

William Tuke (1732–1822), a layman and Quaker, interested the Society of Friends in establishing the York Retreat in 1796. Through his urging, special training was instituted for nurses working in this field. John Conolly (1794–1866) founded a small medical association for the wide acceptance of non-violent measures in the treatment of the mentally ill.

In Germany

Anton Muller (1755–1827), working in a hospital for mental diseases, preached humane treatment of the insane and protested against brutal restraint of patients.

In Italy

Vincenzo Chiarug (1759–1820) published his 'Hundred Observations' of the mentally ill and demanded humanisation of treatment of the deranged.

In Latin America

The first asylum for the 'insane' in the Americas was San Hopolito, opened in about 1570 by Bernadino Alvarez in Mexico City, but it is difficult to say whether it was really more than a place of confinement. Elsewhere in Latin America, the earliest mental hospitals began to appear in the 1820s. As late as 1847, visitors to Mexico and Peru reported that 'lunatics' were displayed for the amusement of the populace, who paid for the exhibition (as had been done at Bedlam three centuries earlier).

In the United States

In Philadelphia, the Blockley Insane Asylum was opened in 1752. The only other institution for the mentally disturbed in the United States before the nineteenth century was the Eastern State Lunatic Asylum in Virginia, opened in 1773.

Benjamin Rush (1745–1813) encouraged the growth of humanitarian treatment of disturbed individuals and the study of psychiatry in the USA. A great deal of reform in the care of the mentally ill resulted from the lifelong campaigning of Dorothea Dix (1802–1887), a New England schoolteacher who had been horrified by the conditions prevailing at the time. In Utica the Association of Superintendents of American Institutions for the Insane was formed in 1846, which evolved into the American Psychiatric Association of today.

In the Western World: national and international efforts

The mental hygiene movement spread throughout the Western world. During the first half of the twentieth century, a variety of national and international organisations were established to aid in the development of improved facilities for the mentally ill. In recent decades, there has been a trend towards public acceptance of both humanitarian and scientific approaches to the problem of mental abnormality. This new attitude has been reflected in the activities of world organisations such as the World Health Organisation, UNESCO, and the World Federation for Mental Health, as well as in those of innumerable national and local public and private agencies. (For a discussion of modern treatment approaches, see chapter 6.)

The modern era: developments in psychiatric thought

The development of psychiatric thought and the subsequent contributions to the understanding of mental abnormality between the eighteenth and twentieth centuries may be summarised under two headings: organic interpretations and psychological interpretations.

Organic interpretations

The importance of brain pathology in the causation of mental illness was recognised by Albrech von Haller (1708–1777), who sought corroboration of his beliefs through postmortem studies. In 1845, William Griesinger (1817-1868) published his *Pathology and Therapy of Psychic Disorders*, in which he held that all theories of mental disturbances must be based on brain pathology. The psychiatrist Henry Morel (1809–1873) attributed mental illness to hereditary neural weakness. Valentin Magnan (1835–1916) investigated mental illness occurring in relation to alcoholism, paralysis and childbirth.

Perhaps the most influential figure in psychiatry in the latter nineteenth and early twentieth centuries was Emil Kraepelin (1856–1926). In 1883, he published a textbook outlining mental illness in terms of organic pathology, in particular the disordered functioning of the nervous system, a point of view which oriented his approach to the general problem of mental disturbances. He described and classified many types of disorders and provided a basis for descriptive psychiatry by drawing attention to clusters of symptoms. Kraepelin evolved a theoretical system that divided mental illness into two large categories: those due to endigenous factors (originating within the body) and those due to exogenous factors (originating outside the body). His classification remained substantially unchanged until a few years after World War I. Kraepelin made notable contributions to psychiatry, but his approach to mental illness was that of an experimentalist, and, consequently, he studied disease processes as entities in themselves rather than as the dynamic reactions of living individuals.

In 1897, Richard von Krafft-Ebing (1840–1902), a Viennese psychiatrist, disclosed experimental proof of the relationship of general paresis (a psychosis) to syphilis (see chapter 16). In 1907, Alois Alzheimer established a link between brain pathology and senile psychoses. In 1917, Julius Wagner-Jauregg (1857–1940) inoculated nine paretic patients with malaria, with consequent alleviation of their condition. These and other discoveries during the early twentieth century lent strong support to believers in the organic approach to mental illness.

Psychological interpretations

Despite the achievements of the organically-oriented investigators very little progress was being made in treating mentally disordered patients. As early as the first decades of the eighteenth century, vague and uncertain theories (eg. mesmerism) had postulated psychological causation.

Mesmerism

The development of a psychological interpretation of mental illness can be traced from the early works of Anton Mesmer (1734–1815). Mesmer developed and applied a technique he called 'animal magnetism'. He attributed his cures to the control and alteration of 'magnetic forces' which he believed to be the causes of mental disease. Although Mesmer's work was discredited by a distinguished panel of experts in Paris in 1784, John Elliotson (1792–1868), an English physician, used mesmerism in surgery.

Another physician, James Braid (1795–1862), studied the process and concluded that it was a purely psychological phenomenon of which the chief characteristic was suggestion, and in 1841 he termed the process 'hypnosis'. Ambroise-August Leibeault (1823–1904) and Hippolyte-Marie Bernheim (1840–1919), two French physicians practising at Nancy, investigated the influence of suggestion in inducing a hypnotic state. They concluded that both hypnosis and hysteria are due to suggestion. Jean-Martin Charcot (1825–1893), a French neuropsychiatrist, disagreed with them, believing that hypnosis was dependent upon physiological processes as well as upon suggestion. He insisted that persons capable of being hypnotised were hysterical.

The development of psychoanalysis

The foregoing observations laid the groundwork for the accomplishments of the psychologically oriented scientists: Janet, Breuer, Freud and others.

Pierre Janet (1859–1947) developed the first psychological theory explaining neurosis. Using hypnosis as the investigating technique, he did extensive research on hysteria, and his work did much to attract attention to the psychological point of view in mental illness.

In Vienna, Josef Breuer (1842–1925) in 1880 successfully treated hysteria with hypnosis and observed that the release of pent-up emotion resulted in the removal of symptoms. This discovery served as a point of departure for the development of psychoanalysis. However, in Vienna, a colleague of his, Sigmund Freud (1856-1939), who was a physician and neurologist, was less successful with hypnosis and thus worked out the 'cathartic' method in which free association and dream interpretation are used to uncover dynamic and unconscious material. Freud's technique and his theory are the cornerstones of the psychoanalytic school.

The differences in the organic and psychological points of view that were present in the early history of abnormal psychology continue to form the backdrop to this field of scientific endeavour. The question of the relative importance of organic and psychological factors in the causation of mental illness remains unanswered.

SUMMARY

Psychological disorders, expressing themselves in a variety of maladaptive behaviour patterns, different, to some extent, from one time period to another and from one culture to another, have beset men, women and children for as long as we have any record of humankind's existence. Interpretations of those disorders and ways of caring for the psychologically-disordered have, over the centuries, rested on superstition, religious beliefs, the speculations of philosophers and, to some extent, on common sense and compassion.

The earliest record of any physical mode of treatment is found in the skeletal remains of primitive humans, which reveal holes made in certain skulls from the prehistoric period, presumably to release evil spirits within.

In the earliest periods for which we have historical records (about 2600 BC), faith healing, diversion of interest, and change of environment emerged as the chief methods of treating mental disorders. In Egypt and Babylon, manuscripts dating back to 5000 BC attribute mental disorders to evil spirits. In India, around 600 BC, medical records describe some forms of mental disorder, including epilepsy.

During the Grecian classical period, Hippocrates, the 'Father of Medicine', held that brain disturbance was the cause of mental disorder. While Plato considered mental disorder partly moral, partly physical and partly divine in origin, Aristotle followed Hippocrates and shaped medical thinking for centuries to come by attributing mental disorder to physiological influences.

During the medieval period, with the dissolution of earlier civilisations, ancient superstitions and demonology were revived to explain the abnormal behaviour of the disordered. Remnants of that way of thinking about mental disorder continued to be influential until the late seventeenth century, when 'witches' were still burned at the stake in some countries.

The foreshadowing of the modern approach to mental disorder appears during the Renaissance period in the work of exceptional individuals in the major countries in Europe.

The social, political, economic and scientific reforms accelerated by the Industrial Revolution in the late nineteenth century introduced radically new ways of understanding and treating the mentally disordered. Pinel in France, for example, removed their chains; William Tuke, an English Quaker, introduced psychological training for nurses working in the field; in North and South America, psychiatric hospitals were established; and in the United States, Benjamin Rush, the 'Father of American Psychiatry' published the first psychiatric textbooks.

Among other advances during this period in understanding the nature of mental disorder were Krafft-Ebing's experimental demonstration that general paresis was caused by the syphilis spirochete and Alzheimer's establishment of brain pathology as a senile mental disorder, which has since been named Alzheimer's Disease. In the early twentieth century, Wagner-

Jauregg inoculated nine paretic patients with malaria and thereby provided a treatment for the disease. Those findings lent strength to an organic interpretation of mental disorders. Kraepelin generalised that point of view by providing a systematic classification of mental disorders which he attributed to a malfunctioning of the brain.

Recognition of the influence of psychological elements in causing mental disorders can be traced to Mesmer, who considered that 'magnetic forces' caused mental disorders; James Braid, in examining Mesmer's work, concluded that the influences he described were psychological in nature, largely the result of suggestion provided in a hypnotic-like trance. That finding was elaborated upon by Liebeault, Bernheim and Charcot, who concluded that both hypnosis and the mental disorder then called 'hysteria' were caused by suggestion.

Building on those insights, Pierre Janet developed the first psychological theory explaining neurosis. In 1880, Breuer successfully treated hysteria with hypnosis. That early work blazed a path for the profound insights of Sigmund Freud, whose work is described in chapter 4.

FURTHER READING

Allridge, P. 1970. Hospitals, Madhouses and Asylums: Cycles in the Care of the Insane. *British Journal of Psychiatry* 134, 321–334.

Campbell, D. 1926. *Arabian Medicine and Its Influence on the Middle Ages.* New York: Dutton.

Fine, R. 1979. *A History of Psychoanalysis.* New York: Columbia University Press.

Goffman, E. 1961. *Asylums; Essays on the Social Situation of Mental Patients and Other Inmates.* Harmondsworth: Penguin Books.

Goldberg, D. 1967. Rehabilitation of the Chronically Mentally Ill in England. *Social Psychiatry,* 2, 1–13.

Hare, E. 1958. The Origin and Spread of Dementia Paralytica. *Journal of Mental Science,* 105.

Hunter, R & Macalpine, I. 1963. *Three hundred years of psychiatry, 1535–1860.* Oxford University Press.

Jones, K. 1954. *Lunacy Law and Conscience 1744–1845.* London: Routledge & Kegan Paul.

Jones, K. 1972. *A History of the Mental Health Services.* London: Routledge & Kegan Paul.

Lader, M. 1979. *A History of Psychiatry.* SKF Publication.

Prins, H. 1987. Understanding Insanity: Some Glimpses into Historical Fact and Fiction. *British Journal of Social Work,* 17, 91–98.

3 Behavioural, Cognitive and Biogenic Perspectives

Abnormal psychology has evolved a great deal since the relatively primitive interpretations of abnormal behaviour offered in past centuries. Close inspection of this growth reveals that this area of psychology is not a single entity but a number of schools of psychology. Although these differing schools, or perspectives, in psychology share the same objectives, they differ and sometimes conflict over methods and explanations. Some approaches enjoy prominence at times when they are emerging or are in agreement with the spirit of the time, or Zeitgeist. The psychodynamic approach began when biological discoveries in abnormal psychology were in their infancy, whereas today, original psychoanalytic theory seems crude in the face of the sophisticated methods of contemporary biopsychology. However, behavioural approaches did not find favour in abnormal psychology until half a century after their discovery and, although they are very common today, are still seen as lacking in consideration for the individual's feelings and thoughts, especially from the more recent humanistic, existential and cognitive approaches.

It is not reasonable to expect a complete explanation of the causes of abnormal behaviour, or to treat a disorder, by viewing the behaviour through a single psychological perspective. In recognition of this, most clinicians working in the field take an eclectic approach, selecting from each perspective the insights that increase understanding and the methods that lead to effective treatment for individual problems. The authors of this book have also adopted an eclectic approach in presenting all the major perspectives and considering each in relation to the different disorders. The three perspectives covered in this chapter have come to overlap one another a great deal in recent times. This is evident in the formation of hybrid approaches such as cognitive neuroscience and the cognitive–behavioural perspective on treatment. However, in order to gain a clear picture of each of the major approaches they will be considered individually in chapters 3 and 4.

A series of conditioning experiments by the Russian physiologist, Ivan Pavlov (1849–1936), provided John B. Watson (1878–1958) in the 1920s with the basis for the first major statement of behaviourism: Psychology is a purely objective, experimental science that needs introspection as little as do chemistry and physics. Watson was able to give scientific strength to his statement by demonstrating that a highly subjective human experience, fear, could be produced by the objective, measurable process of conditioning. Watson's campaign to establish behaviourism as the only scientific method of psychology was directed primarily against psychologists who were using introspection to identify mental states as a source of particular human reactions. Some of his criticism brushed off on the methods of psychoanalysis.

Pavlov and Watson were interested in the causal effect of what preceded a response. Edward Lee Thorndike (1874–1949), in his animal studies, instead asked a reverse question: What are the effects of what follows a response on the likelihood of its recurrence? He expressed his findings as the Law of Effect, which states simply that rewarded responses are strengthened, and unrewarded responses are weakened. B.F. Skinner (1940–1990), in years of carefully quantified research, refined Thorndike's Law of Effect and renamed it the 'Principle of Reinforcement'.

In turn, the exclusively stimulus–response framework of behaviourism and reinforcement theory aroused the opposition of a group of psychologists, who contended that what effect a stimulus–response connection produced was dependent upon the mediation between stimulus and response of mental events or cognitions. They stated that, for example, thoughts or expectations, which themselves had been learned from past experiences, gave interpretation or meaning both to the stimulus and to the response. For cognitive psychologists, it is the subjective meaning given to external events and their consequences that share the influence of both the stimulus and the response.

This chapter first describes classical (or respondent) conditioning and then operant (or instrumental) conditioning, two of the principal ways through which behaviour is changed or learned. Both classical and operant conditioning function through the mediating influence of cognitive activities. The details of that mediating effect make up the cognitive perspective on human behaviour. The chapter goes on to examine the rapidly developing area of the biological perspective in abnormal psychology. This is commonly referred to as the 'medical model', and covers an area of overlap between psychology and the biological sciences.

The behavioural perspective

Behaviourists trace all human behaviour to a limited number of biological drives (hunger is one) which are extended through subsequent conditioning experiences. Both respondent conditioning and operant conditioning are most easily understood through the experiments of Pavlov (classical conditioning) and Skinner (operant conditioning).

Classical (respondent) conditioning

In the latter part of the nineteenth century, Pavlov published the first account of classical conditioning. His work earned him the Nobel prize. It was to have a dramatic effect on developments in the then-young science of psychology. As with many great scientific discoveries, Pavlov's work began with his scientific curiosity about a casual observation. He had noticed that when he merely walked into the room to feed a laboratory dog, the animal began to salivate. For Pavlov, this signalled that the animal had come to attach a reflex action, salivation, previously triggered only by taking food into its mouth, to a neurologically unrelated stimulus, his presence.

Fascinated by this observation, Pavlov then conducted a series of experiments that provided the first scientific basis for the behaviouristic perspective.

Pavlov's experiment

What Pavlov called the conditioned stimulus (CS) – a bell – was sounded just prior to the animal's feeding. Food, the unconditioned stimulus (US), elicited a flow of saliva, the unconditioned response (UR). After several repititions of that sequence, the animal had 'learned' to connect the sound of the bell (the conditioned stimulus) to the now-conditioned response (CR). Respondent conditioning can be diagrammed simply, as follows:

Food (US) Saliva (UR)
Sound (CS) Food (US) Saliva (UR)

repeated several times, which soon led to:

Sound (CS) Saliva (CR)

Significance of Pavlov's experiment

Pavlov's animal was responding to a pleasant US ie food, but this form of conditioning works regardless of the animal's (or human's) liking of the stimulus. Responses, particularly autonomic responses, including those related to such emotional experiences as fear and anxiety (for example, rapid heartbeat and increased perspiration) can be readily conditioned. The behavioural perspective emphasises the possibility that fear and anxiety may be initially brought about by such conditioning experiences. In the behavioural perspective, many disordered emotional responses, such as irrational fears (phobias), can be cured by reversing the process of classical conditioning (see chapter 7).

The importance of classical conditioning, in the veiw of behaviourists, is that all emotions, preferences and even values in later life develop from conditioning of the Pavlovian type; that is, the associating of a neutral stimulus with an emotion being felt by the individual. In time, with a sufficient number of those couplings, or even with one coupling when the emotion is an intense one, the now-conditioned stimulus develops the power to elicit the emotional response. For example, if a person were mugged and physically assaulted on Avenue X, the next time he or she walked through the street the emotion experienced in the attack would again be experienced, perhaps less intensely. In this way classical conditioning produces a broad range of both pleasant and distressing emotional experiences. The latter, if intense, can be the cause of phobias or anxiety attacks. With this possibility in mind behaviourists have developed a number of treatment techniques to promote the extinction of abnormal emotional reactions.

Basic principles of classical conditioning

Two of the simplest principles operating in classical conditioning were identified by Pavlov in his experiments.

The first is acquisition of response. Acquisition is the learning of a response based on the contingency (the timed togetherness) between a conditioned stimulus and an unconditioned stimulus, for example, the sequence of sound and food in Pavlov's experiment. Experience teaches that it usually takes from three to four pairings to acquire a conditioned response.

The second principle is extinction, which is the loss of the conditioned stimulus's potential for eliciting the previously conditioned response. Extinction is produced by repeatedly presenting the conditioned stimulus (eg. sound) but no longer following this with the unconditioned stimulus (eg. food). The length of time required for extinction varies with the strength of the original conditioning experience.

There are two other principles operating in classical conditioning, which were identified in work following Pavlov's original experiments. The first is stimulus generalisation: once an individual has been conditioned to one stimulus, he or she may make the same response to other similar stimuli. For example, a child who, in a frightening experience, has learned to fear dogs, may come to fear other animals; or, in the behavioural perspective, a child who has been conditioned to respond with hostility to a parent may show less intense but nevertheless noticeable hostility to other people of the same sex as the parent.

The remaining principle, stimulus discrimination, is almost the reverse of generalisation; that is, that through a proper sequence of stimuli, a person can be taught to discriminate, for example, between two quite similar sounds. This will take place when a person experiences an electric shock following a high-pitched sound, but no shock when hearing a sound lower in pitch.

Operant conditioning

Following the lead of Thorndike, Skinner initiated a lifelong research effort to study the principles governing the effect on future behaviour of what follows a particular response. Those principles he named 'operant conditioning'.

Significance of operant conditioning

Behaviourists hold that it is through operant conditioning, as a result of reinforcement following specific responses, that children acquire skills such as walking, reading and craft or athletic competencies, and learn ways of behaving to satisfy their needs, both to gain what they consider desirable and to avoid what they consider undesirable.

It is the combination of respondent and operant conditioning that fleshes out the individual's efforts to adjust to circumstances: classical conditioning influencing preferences and creating needs; operant conditioning influencing the way an individual goes about satisfying them.

Basic principles of operant conditioning

The basic elements in the Skinnerian form of conditioning are operants (the animal's actions) that can be strengthened by positive reinforcement (a reward) or weakened by punishment. Punishment must be distinguished from what is called negative reinforcement. In negative reinforcement a punisher or aversive experience (usually an electric shock in animal experiments) is removed as a consequence of the action (or operation) of the animal or individual. This increases the likelihood of that action or behaviour being repeated. Punishment is an aversive event (eg. being sent to one's room) produced by an action of the individual; it may have effect on the behaviour that caused the punishment but the effect is unpredictable. For example, the punished behaviour may persist, but in covert fashion to escape punishment; or the punished behaviour may be displaced by even more unacceptable behaviour. A punishment may act as a negative reinforcer when the punishment is removed. For example, a child may be sent to his or her room for unruly behaviour. Once in the room, the child picks up a book and reads quietly. When the mother comes upstairs to invite the child to rejoin the family, the act of reading is reinforced, and the probability of its recurrence is increased.

Acquisition and extinction.   Acquisition and extinction are produced differently in operant conditioning from the way they are in classical conditioning. A response in operant conditioning is acquired when it is followed by a positive reinforcer a number of times. Extinction occurs when the response is unreinforced over a period of time. The time it takes to extinguish a response will vary with the schedule of reinforcement.

Schedules of reinforcement.   Skinner's research revealed an extremely important aspect of operant conditioning, the scheduling of reinforcement. Scheduling does not work with classical conditioning procedures. The schedule of reinforcement referred to so far has been continuous reinforcement, that is, each response is reinforced leading to rapid learning and extinction. The more economical partial reinforcement comes in a number of forms, or schedules, which may slow down learning but can also dramatically increase the time taken to extinguish the response. Ration schedules can be *fixed*, ie reinforcement only occurs after a fixed number of responses, or *variable*, in which reinforcement occurs randomly, but to a pre-arranged average number of responses. Interval schedules are similar but it is the length of time that is fixed or variable, during which at least one response must be made before reinforcement is given at the end of the interval.

Gambling is a good example of partial reinforcement schedules in humans, and the associated problem of addictive gambling provides a good illustration of how difficult it is to extinguish partially reinforced behaviour. Experimental schedules used with pigeons have produced thousands of responses for only one reinforcement but this has to be attained in stages by a process of shaping the behaviour.

Shaping.   A significant process in operant conditioning, one that is especially valuable in treatment, is shaping. The shaping process can be compared with the children's game of 'you're getting warmer', a comment which serves to guide the child to a hidden object. In operant conditioning, when the goal is to teach a complex response, any response the individual makes in the direction of the complex response, even a meagre one, is reinforced. An example is one of Skinner's early studies. His goal was to teach a pigeon to peck at the centre of a target hung on an interior side of its cage. The sequence of reinforcement was as follows: any movement towards the correct side of the cage (in the children's game, equivalent to the comment, 'you're getting warmer'), then any movement towards the target, then any pecking behaviour in the direction of the target, then any pecking behaviour directly on target. To encourage the pigeon to continue to move towards the goal, any appraoching response was reinforced only until a response more directed at the target occurred. That response was then reinforced. This process of shaping, which has been used to teach animals extremely complex skills, also is useful in teaching skills to human beings, especially children.

Modelling

A widely influential form of learning, modelling, is subsumed under the rubric of behaviouristically viewed learning. Children soon learn to imitate the behaviour of parents and, later in life, of other admired persons. Part of the basis of this relies on vicarious reinforcement, that is seeing others rewarded for a behaviour may make one more likely to imitate the behaviour, as we will refer to later in the work of Albert Bandura. For a developing child, the process of modelling involves other behavioural influences. Positive attitudes and emotional feelings towards parents develop, in the first instance, as a result of classical conditioning. Early in the life of the infant, the image of mother precedes the receiving of food, which is accompanied by the relief of hunger tensions. Repetition of that sequence soon allows only the image of mother to produce a pleasant feeling. Once that loving attitude towards mother (and later, towards father) exists, operant conditioning takes over. As a parent expresses approval of a child's modelling efforts, those efforts are reinforced, and the probability of their recurrence is increased. In time, only a child's awareness that it has successfully modelled a parent's behaviour or that of another admired person is reinforcement enough to cause the behaviour to persist.

The cognitive perspective

Discontented with what they considered the simplistic SR (stimulus–response) explanation of human behaviour, cognitive psychologists have done much to re-establish a place for the organism. Their research has indicated that memories, beliefs and expectations (characteristics of the organism, the individual) serve as a mediating influence between stimulus and response, and influence the kind of connection the individual will make to the stimulus. Cognitive psychologists write the old formula as follows: stimulus–organism–response (SOR).

In the cognitive perspective, there are four overlapping interpretations of how cognitive elements influence an individual's behaviour. Categorised by the principal author of the interpretation, they are as follows.

Bandura: expectations

For Albert Bandura (as he indicates in research published in 1977 and 1982), the important cognitive influence on behaviour is the individual's expectations, which may be thought of as beliefs or hopes of what a particular response will bring. Bandura divides expectations into two types: outcome expectations, expectancies that a given response will lead to a certain outcome; and efficiency expectations, expectancies that one will be able to carry out the response effectively. Such expectations can be the product of earlier experiences including those of childhood, though some may be more immediate, such as those following vicarious learning (referred to above). Bandura's social learning approach combines cognitive and behavioural aspects such as expectancies and vicarious learning.

Atkinson: decision theory

John W. Atkinson, a decision theorist, presents his point of view by asking how an individual will make a decision to do anything, to make any response. Faced with a situation requiring a decision, before taking action, Atkinson states, the individual will weight two elements. One he calls *utility* or *subjective* value to be gained by taking the action. The second is the probability of the individual possessing the capacity to be successful in carrying out the action. Those are essentially the elements of Bandura's thesis, but Atkinson uses the language of decision theory.

The cognitive elements identified are no doubt shaped, or at least influenced, by the basic processes of conditioning, classical and operant, which have occurred during the early childhood years and as a result of later experiences, especially those of an interpersonal nature, elements that are an important consideration in the psychodynamic perspective. In other words, the strict behaviouristic and cognitive perspectives must both be taken into account in understanding an individual's behaviour.

Mischel: five cognitive variables

According to Walter Mischel, a cognitive psychologist, there are five variables that influence an individual's response to a stimulus: competencies, encodings, expectancies, values and plans (Mischel, 1973; 1979)

Competencies

The individual acquires a number of technical and social skills through learning. The level of those skills will help determine the individual's response in a particular situation. Suppose a colleague, in a public situation, responds to one's statement by saying, 'No, you're absolutely wrong there'. If an individual has developed the trait of assertiveness, that individual will respond in one way; if not, in a quite different way.

Encodings

All human beings perceive and categorise experiences in a particular way, perhaps even uniquely. The categories they create cause them to sort new experiences into one or another of those categories. An individual's response reflects the category into which he or she has sorted the situation. Political categories, for example, are an important source of coding for some individuals. How a person responds to a Conservative chancellor's budget will be significantly affected by that individual's political affiliation, and by the degree of significance political values have in his or her thinking.

Expectancies

Here Mischel joins Bandura. Previous experience teaches us all to expect (hope, fear) certain outcomes from particular types of behaviour. Those expectations influence significantly how an individual will respond.

Values

Very early in life, individuals learn to prize or value certain social, religious and artistic causes or points of view. Modernists in art would respond in one way to a friend's invitation to visit a Rembrandt exhibition, and in quite a different way to an invitation to the Museum of Modern Art. On the other hand, the value they assign to friendship might cause them to accept either invitation.

Plans

Most individuals start each day with some plan as to how they will spend it, detailed and formal or loose. The plan decided upon will influence their decision to enter into situation A or situation B. The decision will hinge, no doubt, on how much either will disrupt their plans. Plans can also be made as to how we intend to spend the next few years of our life; for example, in completing a law degree. Unless a proposed alternative is very attractive indeed, long-term plans will determine our response.

Attribution of causality

The individual's thoughts about what causes the things that happen – that is, to what he attributes causality – will also influence behaviour. Julius B. Rotter's theory of internal or external control (1973) provides a good example. People's beliefs can be measured on the Rotter Scale and be placed on a continuum that extends from beliefs that nothing they do counts (external control) to a conviction that they are master of their own fate, and that what they do counts a great deal (internal control). Given an opportunity to work hard for a promotion, it is easy to guess how those two different beliefs will influence behaviour. Another major type of attribution is the conviction either that the world and its people are hostile, or that, in general, they are neutral or benign. Behaviour in a wide range of situations will vary accordingly. Early life experiences do much to shape the nature of one's beliefs about why things happen, good things and bad things.

The biogenic perspective

The brain is the most complex system we know of. Its intricate function controls or monitors all our behaviour. A small abnormality of brain structure or function can produce either very subtle or profound and tragic consequences for the individual so affected depending on the type and location of the abnormality. Modern medical technology has advanced our understanding of these processes vastly in recent years. However, there are factors which limit this progress. One obvious factor is the complexity, delicacy and interactivity of brain structure. A wide variety of differences in behaviour can be produced by small changes in the brain which are difficult to detect or localise. The brain is also able to adapt or change to some degree as a consequence of psychological pressure on the individual (eg. stress). For some professionals this creates a 'chicken and egg' situation with regard to biogenic causes of psychological disorder ie are they a consequence or cause of changes in the brain? Another problem for biogenic perspective is that experimental investigation is difficult on ethical grounds. Much research is carried out on animals and, apart from the fact that such research is ethically questionable, the results are not always transferable to humans on whom these experiments could not be performed. It may be accepted by most people, including the patient, that their brain be examined when they have a disorder. However, a healthy individual could not be expected to have their brain altered in order to see if they become disordered.

A number of professionals in the area of abnormal psychology, usually psychiatrists, hold the view that all psychological disorders are physical illnesses for which the physical cause has yet to be found. History has generally supported this view as a number of psychological conditions have been found to be the secondary effects of physical illnesses, for example, the psychological effects of syphilis described below. Further support for the biogenic view comes from the success of the more sophisticated drug treatments currently available for psychological disorders. However, the consensus among researchers in the field of abnormal psychology is that some disorders are clearly of a biological origin and others have a definite biological component, with the possibility that other disorders could be of a purely psychological origin.

The medical model

The biogenic perspective is closely associated with the medical model of psychological disorder. This model assumes that mental illnesses can be classified and treated in the same way as physical illnesses, thus gaining the advantage of having a relatively simple framework in which to locate the patient and their disorder. Unfortunately the very nature of mental disorders makes this a far less precise system when put into practice, leaving the medical model open to criticism of its methods and efforts to push atypical cases into ill-fitting categories. Within the medical model or biogenic perspective, causes of psychological disorder are sought from those of physical illnesses eg. infection, genetics, chemical imbalance (neurochemistry) and faults in neuroanatomy. The biogenic way of defining and explaining a particular disorder also adopts this standardised approach.

A first step in the biogenic approach to a new disorder is usually to identify a syndrome, that is, a collection of diverse symptoms which co-occur in one patient in sufficient numbers to diagnose the disorder. Some of these symptoms may be more important to the diagnosis than others.

Once the syndrome has been identified and its symptoms described in detail, the search for causes is begun, the etiological phase. Here, as has been previously indicated, four sources of hypotheses for the cause of the illness are considered: infection, genetics, chemical imbalance and neuroanatomy. Once etiology has been established, the next step is either to attempt to find ways of preventing the illness, which in modern medicine is a first priority, especially in illnesses deemed to be untreatable, or to search out methods of treatment for those who already suffer the illness. That approach, with appropriate adaptations for mental illnesses, is taken by those with the biogenic perspective. The medical model also sets a pattern for non-medical professionals, principally psychologists, in their studies of mental illness, even though they may bring a different perspective to the problem.

Infection as a cause of mental illness

The first mental illness to be associated with infection was paresis, now recognised as the result of long-term infection by the syphilis spirochete. The syndrome-establishing phase was initiated in the latter part of the seventeenth century by Thomas Willis. He grouped together dullness of intellect and forgetfulness with the later development of stupidy and foolishness. Jean Esquirol added mental deterioration and paralysis, with death soon to follow. A.L.J. Boyle later brought the process to its conclusion by describing its symptoms in detail and identifying them as a separate disease, which he labelled 'general paresis'.

It was decades before the specific cause of the illness was discovered, and still later that a reliable method of testing for syphilis was developed and a method of treating it was found. In more recent years, a viral infection early in life has been suggested by Timothy Crow as a possible cause of schizophrenia in later life.

Inherited genes as a factor in mental illness

'Bad seed' as a nineteenth-century derogatory term for defective genes has long been connected in the lay mind with certain kinds of abnormal or unacceptable behaviour: alcoholism, criminal behaviour, and other forms of 'immoral' behaviour. In the twentieth century, science has vigorously pursued the nature of genetic influence, if any, on abnormal behaviour. There are three principal methods of doing so: studying the families of those with pathological mental symptoms, twin studies, and adoptee studies. This section considers each briefly.

Family studies. Science can now approximate the percentage of common genes in family members of varying degrees of closeness. It is, for example, estimated that siblings have in common 50 per cent of their genes, aunts and uncles 25 per cent, and cousins 12.5 per cent. That knowledge provides one method of testing the influence of heredity on the development of mental disorders. Starting with a patient with a diagnosed mental disorder, research can seek out relatives who vary in their closeness to that individual and count the number of family members of each degree of relationship showing signs of the same illness. A correlation between consanguinity and the illness, other factors being equal, suggests a hereditary influence.

Just that kind of research was undertaken with a group of schizophrenic patients. The results unquestionably indicated that the closer the relationship to the schizophrenic individual, the higher the incidence of the disease. Such a study does not prove the certain influence of hereditary factor as a cause of schizophrenia, since common environmental conditions among the relatives could not be ruled out as a causative factor. It is nevertheless strongly suggestive of a relationship.

Twin studies. The scientific reasoning in twin studies can be tighter than in family studies since monozygotic twins (identical twins developed from a single fertilised egg) have the same genes and are said to be the same genotype. Their physical characteristics, and presumably their mental characteristics, are almost identical. They are to be contrasted with dizygotic, or fraternal, twins, developed from two separate eggs, fertilised at the same time. They are no more alike than any two siblings.

A twin study requires that a sufficient number of monozygotic and dizygotic twins with one or both twins suffering a particular mental disorder be identified. The concordance rate – that is, the percentage of times both twins have the same illness – is studied. Such studies of schizophrenics reveal, for example, that the identical twins show a concordance rate three to five times as high as non-identical twins. The finding provides a very strong argument for a hereditary effect on the development of schizophrenia.

Adoptee studies. When one schizophrenic identical twin has been adopted and raised apart from his or her co-twin, since the hereditary factor is identical but environmental influences can be assumed to be different, the situation provides a critical test of the possible hereditary influence on development of the disease. Since concordance rates, despite environmental differences, are high, such studies provide the strongest evidence for the hereditary transmission of a tendency towards schizophrenia, not as absolute as the inheritance of eye colour, for example, but quite strong.

Biochemical imbalance as a cause of mental illness

An excess of deficiency in one or another chemical element in the body has also been studied as a possible cause of mental illness. It is again one of the psychoses that provides evidence to support the hypothesis. Research suggests, for example, that schizophrenic patients suffer from the excessive action of the neurotransmitter dopamine in the brain. Neurotransmitters are the 'chemical messengers' in the brain, communicating between brain cells, or more properly, neurones. This finding is supported by the known action of drugs used to treat some of the symptoms of schizophrenia, known as neuroleptics. Their main effect on the brain is to block the action of dopamine and it is this action that would appear to be effective in reducing schizophrenic hallucinations and delusions. Further to this, a drug treatment for Parkinson's disease (a degenerative disorder of the brain) is L-dopa, which increases the amount of dopamine available in the brain. Excessive doses of L-dopa have been associated with some schizophrenic symptoms in these patients, perhaps confirming the association of dopamine action and certain schizophrenic symptoms.

Neuroanatomy as a causative factor in mental illness

It has been established for some time that the dementias and other mental disorders that commonly occur in the elderly mainly result from changes in the higher levels of the brain, affecting memory and other functions. These areas tend to weaken before the lower levels of brain function that support the basic biological functions. Here, abnormalities in the structure of the brain can be related to loss of normal mental functioning. Other forms of brain abnormality have been related to schizophrenia-like symptoms, earning these the name of 'organic psychoses'. Some researchers believe that abnormal brain structure could provide an explanation of some forms of schizophrenia, although the evidence for this is difficult to establish clearly.

Intensive studies of one family with a high incidence of manic-depressive psychosis provided a possible example of how genetic factors and chemical factors interact to effect mental illness. In the instance of the family studied, a genetic weakness seemed to produce biochemical changes in the brain, thus suggesting that it is the combination of defective genes producing a biochemical imbalance that tends to cause the development of manic-depressive psychosis.

SUMMARY

There are seven perspectives or models that different psychologists use in defining human behaviour as normal or abnormal. They are the psychodynamic view, which emphasises the importance and interactive influences of childhood and later interpersonal experiences; the behavioural perspective, which stresses the role of learning, particularly conditioning experiences, both classical, first demonstrated by Pavlov, and operant, which is the basis of reinforcement theory created by the research of Skinner; the cognitive perspective, which gives a central place to cognitions (expectations, beliefs, values, plans made) in determining what response an individual will make in confronting life situations; the humanistic perspective, which considers most important the individual's self-concept and his or her potential for growth; the existential perspective, which focuses exclusively on the individual's present life and the difficulty of living authentically in the modern world. Becoming increasingly important in abnormal psychology is the biogenic perspective, which attributes much abnormal behaviour to biological anomalies – for example, defective heredity.

One helpful way to make use of the various perspectives is to take an eclectic point of view, which recognises that no one perspective can explain all mental illness or provide effective therapy. Most mental illness results from, or takes on characteristics influenced by, causative elements featured in various of the perspectives. For example, biogenic factors may create a predisposition which is made worse by interpersonal problems, conditioning experiences, or ineptly learned coping mechanisms. The individual's self-concept will be an important variable in the prognosis of the illness, as will capacity to deal with problems presented by modern society.

FURTHER READING

Bandura, A. & R. Walters. 1963. *Social Learning and Personality Development.* New York: Holt, Rinehart and Winston.

Carlson, N. 1994. *The Physiology of Behaviour* (5th ed). London: Allyn & Bacon.

Crow, T. 1994. Prenatal Exposure to Influenza as a Cause of Schizophrenia. *British Journal of Psychiatry*, 164: 588-592.

Ellis, A. & Young, A. 1988. *Human Cognitive Neuropsychology.* London: Lawrence Erlbaum Associates.

Frith, C. 1992. *The Cognitive Neuropsychology of Schizophrenia.* London: Lawrence Earlbaum Associates.

Gottesman, I. 1991. *Schizophrenia Genesis: the Origins of Madness.* New York: Freeman.

Hergenhahn, B. & Olson, M. 1993. *Introduction to Theories of Learning* (4th ed). Prentice Hall.

Kazolin, A. E. & G. T. Wilson. 1978. *Evaluation of Behaviour Therapy: Issues, Evidence, and Research Strategies.* Cambridge, MA: Ballinger.

Martin, G. & Pear, J. 1992. *Behaviour Modification* (4th ed). Prentice Hall.

Plomin, R. 1994. Genetics and Experience. *Current Opinion in Psychiatry*, 7: 297-299.

4 Psychodynamic, Humanistic, Existential and Sociocultural Perspectives

Clearly, the more empirical approaches to psychological disorder described in the previous chapter have flourished during their historical development. Such perspectives have led to scientifically measurable forms of therapy. The psychodynamic approach of Sigmund Freud represented a less scientific, but highly influential school of thought, which began before behaviourism and is still widely practised in countries such as the USA. In contrast to the previously described perspectives, this approach lays greater emphasis on the subjective feelings and insights of patients and therapists. This tradition continued as the school evolved in the wake of advances in its own and other fields, paving the way for the more recent humanistic and existential schools. All these perspectives consider the way the individual interacts with others, often looking at early relationships. The sociocultural perspective also considers the external forces acting on an individual as a result of their social and cultural context.

This chapter examines the psychodynamic perspective traceable to Freud's work in psychoanalysis and will also consider deviations from it by the neo-Freudians and the humanistic and existential schools. This will be followed by an examination of the influence of the social environment as viewed by the sociocultural perspective.

The psychodynamic perspective

This perspective has been referred to as the psychodynamic, psychoanalytic or 'analytic' school, or sometimes, confusingly, as the 'psychotherapeutic approach'. Psychodynamic refers to the theoretical approach within general psychology, whereas psychoanalysis is a treatment approach based on this theoretical approach. Psychotherapy is misleading in this context as it actually refers to any form of psychological therapy. Although chapter 2 describes the beginnings of the psychodynamic approach in the work of a number of individuals, its establishment can be attributed to Sigmund Freud's clinical and theoretical writings in the late nineteenth and early twentieth centuries, which have been sustained, if modified, by the neo-Freudians and ego-psychologists.

Basic concepts of the psychodynamic perspective

Key to an understanding of the perspective is an understanding of the word 'psychodynamic'. From the dictionary comes this definition: 'an emphasis on the interaction of the various psychic or mental forces that influence behaviour'. Psychoanalysts and other psychodynamic theorists make that definition more specific: 'the interactions of the psychic forces and processes developed during childhood that influence adult thinking, motives and behaviour'.

Almost universally, members of the psychodynamic school identify three basic concepts underlying the psychodynamic perspective: psychic determinism, unconscious motivation, and the role of childhood experiences.

Psychic determinism

Psychodynamic theorists believe that although we have a sense of freely choosing what we will think about, desire and do, much of our behaviour, as a matter of fact, is determined for us, or at least strongly influenced by, earlier life experiences.

Unconscious motivations

Motivational forces operate, to a considerable degree, at an unconscious or, at most, preconscious level. The psychodynamic theorists hold that the full basis for significant behaviour, especially for motivation, is largely unknown to the affected individual. This belief significantly influences psychotherapeutic techniques, which are discussed in later chapters.

Childhood experiences

The individual is most vulnerable to influences from the environment during the early years of life. For this reason, most, but not all, psychodynamic thinkers believe that critical dynamic forces influential throughout the lifespan of the individual are developed during the early years of childhood. This principle of the psychodynamic perspective also has an important influence on treatment approaches, especially on psychoanalytically-oriented treatment.

Sigmund Freud: psychoanalytic theory

Because of the originality of Freud's thinking and his continuing influence on modern psychological thinking and practice, this chapter gives special attention to the details of his psychoanalytic theories.

There are four principal aspects of psychoanalytic theory: the three levels of consciousness; the structural components of the human mind; psychosexual development; the defence mechanisms.

The three levels of consciousness

Freud described three levels of consciousness: perceptual consciousness, the preconscious, and the unconscious.

Perceptual consciousness. At any moment, the individual attends to – that is, is consciously aware of – only a small number of items or events. This awareness Freud called the perceptual consciousness. An example of the perceptual consciousness follows: an individual may be aware of the content of a book he or she is reading, yet hears the phone ring, and perhaps with less sharpness, is aware of the person sitting across the table.

The preconscious. This level of consciousness comprises those events or facts not in the centre of attention, yet readily retrieved from memory: an experience in class yesterday, a forthcoming appointment, luncheon fare two hours ago.

The unconscious. The largest mass of memory of past experiences, impulses and data lies at the unconscious level. There are two types of unconscious material: the first are those that have been forgotten, for whatever reason; the seocnd those that, because of conflict and the anxiety they produce, are repressed and actively excluded from consciousness. Ordinary forgotten events, such as the exact price paid for last year's textbook or a difficult-to-understand theory in chemistry, gradually fade out of memory and have little subsequent influence on personality. But repressed items live on and show up in a variety of covert ways: dreams, fairly well-disguised fantasies, slips of speech, motivated recall under hypnosis or drugs and, for some people, in a variety of psychological disorders. From the psychodynamic perspective these forces have a great deal of influence in the development of psychological disorders, although this is contested by other schools of thought.

The structural process of the human personality

The human personality in psychoanalytic theory is structured by three kinds of dynamic and interactive processes. Freud makes clear that they are neither objects nor places, but ways in which personality expresses itself. The three are the id, the ego and the superego.

The id. The word 'id' comes from the original German word, 'es', meaning 'it' by way of Latin, which translates 'it' as id. Formally defined, it is that division or process of the psyche or personality associated with instinctive impulses and demands for immediate satisfaction of primitive and essentially biological needs.

According to Freud, this energy comes from one of two basic instincts within the id, one of which he named 'eros'. The energy derived from the eros is libido. The other major instinctive force within the id is 'thanatos', or the death instinct, to which Freud and his disciples have attributed only a small role in affecting human behaviour.

In the first few weeks of life, all the organism's activities motivated by the id process, instinctive and biological, seek immediate and uninhibited gratification. As maturing takes place, the libido, the id's source of energy, provides life-furthering power and the driving force for later activities that are part of psychological growth and biological survival. The id process operates raw and unrestrained under the demand of the pleasure principle, which seeks immediate gratification of impulses and immediate reduction of tension. A comparison frequently used is that the id behaves like an extremely spoiled child. This primitive irrational process is labelled 'primary process thinking'.

The ego.   Under the influence of the id process, individuals know no limits to what they will do, and thus would eat whatever they please, express aggression indiscriminately, and find sexual satisfaction without social or moral limitations.

Ego, from the German word 'ich', by way of the Latin word ego, means 'I'. The ego is that part of the self that operates to some extent at a conscious level, most immediately controls behaviour, and is most in touch with the real world. The ego allows expression of the id but only in ways that meet the requirements of reality, and thus it operates in accordance with the reality principle.

Freud uses the example of horse and rider to describe the possible interactions between the ego and the id. He puts it in these words: 'The horse supplies the locomotive energy, while the rider has the privilege of deciding on the goal and of guiding the powerful animal's movements. But only too often, there arises between the ego and the id the not-precisely-ideal situation of the rider being obliged to guide the horse along the path by which it (the id) itself wants to go.'

The ego process can begin to function in this way only when children's maturing reaches the point at which they can use reason to allow thought, memory, evaluation and planning to control behaviour. The individual under the influence of the ego process behaves in a way to minimise negative results from the influence of the id. The increasing control of behaviour exacted by the ego process is a maturing form of behaviour and is called 'secondary process thinking'.

The superego.   The superego loosely resembles the conscience. It comprises values, ethical standards and concepts of what is right and what is wrong, almost all of which have been acquired from parents. The superego is formed out of the child's resolution of the Oedipal or Electra complexes (to be described later).

The superego, like the id, develops with only limited relation to reality. Typically, instead of allowing reality to provide boundaries for its development, it aims for an ego ideal which sets unrealistically high standards for the suppression of id impulses.

With the development of the superego, some time around the age of six or seven, the child's personality expresses itself under the influence of three forces: the id, made up of pleasure-seeking impulses, all unconscious; the ego, the only one of the forces in direct contact with reality; and the superego, the strong voice of conscience.

Psychosexual development

Freud divided the child's personlity development into five stages: oral, anal, phallic, latency and genital. In each of the first three stages, the pleasure-seeking behaviour of the id is associated with an area of the body – the mouth, the anus and the genital region, which have been called erogenous zones. As the child goes through each of these three phases, it faces conflict between personal demands for gratification and the restrictions of reality – for example, the child is asked to give up the nipple or bottle, but still desires its satisfactions; toilet training places limitations on anal satisfactions; during the phallic phase (notice the masculine emphasis Freud gave this process), the child is taught that any attention paid to the genital area is 'naughty'. The latency period is a period of respite, giving the child a time of quiet and freedom from sexual tensions of the earlier periods. How the child resolves the conflicts and frustrations of the early three phases shapes the adult personality, particularly in psychosexual areas of life.

Freud's use of the words *sex* and *sexual* can lead to misunderstanding of what he meant by the pleasures to which he attaches those words. The words have broad application to any pleasurable psychic feelings, as well as to genital intercourse and fantasies about sex.

The oral stage. At birth, the child is equipped to suck the nipple or the bottle reflexively and thus is, from the beginning, naturally equipped to obtain food and find oral pleasure. As the neural system matures, the child is able to do much more with his mouth, mouthing objects, biting, chewing, rolling food around in it. The child soon develops special feelings for a number of objects – a pacifier, a security blanket to suck on or chew, his or her thumb, and many more. The psychologically significant conclusion Freud drew was that experiences with these early oral satisfactions shape later personality traits. For example, a child whose oral needs are not adequately satisfied may turn, later in life, to overeating, heavy smoking, or even alcoholism. Such traits as tenacity, disruptiveness or acquisitiveness may, according to psychoanalytic thinking, be shaped by early oral experiences. The first year of life marks off the oral stage.

The anal stage. During the second year of life, the child's id strivings for pleasure focus on the anus. All of a sudden, toilet training becomes an important influence of later personality traits. Early in life the child finds pleasure in retaining and expelling the faeces and in the reduction of the tensions that accompany bowel movements.

Those representatives of reality, parents, insist on surrounding anal activities with rules. The confrontation is a sharp one, and the frustration imposed, and the resulting testing of will with parents, can be a more disturbing one even than weaning. The discipline of voluntary control of pleasurable impulses is a first-time experience for the two-year old. How parents approach this training activity will, Freud states, have a significant effect on later personality traits. Too strict a regimen, for example, can lead to what has been called the anal personality, characterised by stinginess, obsessiveness and excessive concern with cleanliness. Too little control can lead to tolerance of mess and sloppiness. When overconcern with the experiences of a particular psychosexual phase develops, Freud speaks of the freezing of development, to which has been given the name 'fixation'.

The phallic stage. During this third phase of the child's psychosexual development, between the third and fifth or sixth year, the child seeks pleasure from stimulation of the genitalia, expressed in much relatively innocent masturbatory behaviour. The child is soon again confronted with another first-time demand, that he or she give up pleasures that are not reflexively produced but brought on by voluntary stimulation of the child's own body. This confrontation does much to direct children's attention to their own body. With the focus, self-identity, a sense of independence and wilfulness lead to a kind of narcissistic preoccupation.

The phallic stage is of special importance because during it, the Oedipus complex develops. How children resolve that complex will affect, in significant ways, their sexual adjustment in later life.

The story of King Oedipus, originally a Greek legend, has become a part of the mythology of most countries of the Western world. King Oedipus, after a great struggle, finds that in that struggle he has killed his father and married the Queen, his mother. Crushed by grief and guilt, Oedipus gouges out his own eyes. Freud uses that metaphor to describe the young boy's psychosexual experiences towards the end of the phallic stage. The metaphor for girls is the Electra complex, the story of a daughter who avenges her father's death by killing her mother and her mother's lover.

During the Oedipus complex in the later part of the phallic stage, the young boy has an incestuous desire to keep possession of the mother, and sees the father as a more powerful competitor for the mother's attentions. The boy thus fears the father and, not realising that his guilty thoughts about the mother are his alone and not available to the father, he also fears that the father may take away the physical focus of his attention, at this the phallic stage, producing castration anxiety. That anxiety, under normal circumstances, is resolved as the incestuous impulses are repressed and kept unconscious. In accomplishing this, the boy, instead of continuing to fear a war with his father, joins the 'enemy' in a process of identification through which the boy internalises (makes part of himself) the values and sentiments of the father and incorporates them into his own behaviour, even to the external mannerisms of his father.

According to Freud's theory, girls experience a similar set of consequences in the form of the Electra complex, although this is less clear and has been treated with scepticism by followers of Freud. As a girl comes to realise that she has been born without a penis, penis envy develops. That envy seems to impel her towards incestuous desire for her father. Freudian psychoanalysts would say her reasoning is that if she cannot have her own penis, she can make up for that loss through possession of her father. Her response to the guilt and fear aroused in her by her forbidden wishes is to declare peace with her mother and to identify with her.

The period of latency. Once the Oedipus and Electra complexes are resolved at the age of six or seven, the child's sexual impulses become latent. The libido seems at rest, and the narcissistic preoccupation with self disappears as the child turns to the outside world. During this period, there is time for learning and the acquiring of social and technical skills that serve as steps towards maturity.

The genital stage. With the arrival of puberty, the adolescent experiences a new stirring of sexual impulses, but not now directed narcissistically towards his or her own body. The child's interests are now aroused by other people. The child has arrived at the foothills of maturity. Altruistic love and tenderness gradually prepare the individual for mature sexual behaviour. Dependence moves toward independent resourcefulness, and the ability to master work skills. However, unresolved conflicts from earlier stages may emerge from latency to disturb the processes of the genital stage.

Anxiety and the defence mechanisms

Freud distinguished three kinds of anxiety. Realistic anxiety, which modern psychology calls fear, arises out of the presence of danger in the real world. That danger may result from a physical hazard – for example, military combat or being trapped in a burning building. But it may also be psychological in nature – for example, tensions resulting from real-life frustration or irresolvable conflict. Neurotic anxiety, in Freud's thinking, arises out of concern that unconscious impulses, particularly sexual and aggressive ones, will gain the upper hand in a conflict between the id and the ego. Moral anxiety arises out of concern that behaviour will violate one's personal standards of conscience (a conflict between the ego and the superego). The experience of anxiety (any one of the three types described by Freud) is a disquieting trial, from which the individual attempts to escape, often through the use of defence mechanisms.

Defence mechanisms are the unconscious attempts of individuals to protect themselves from threats to the integrity of the ego or self and also to relieve the tension and anxiety resulting from unresolved frustrations and conflicts. All people employ these self-deceptive measures to some extent, attempting in this way to maintain their self-esteem and soften the impact of failure, deprivation, or sense of guilt. It must not be assumed that defence mechanisms invariably signify abnormal personality structure. Such mechanisms frequently result in gains for the individual using them; their reactions may be a constructive form of adjusting. Excessive dependence on defence mechanisms to block out significant aspects of the individual's personality indicates abnormal modes of adjustment. The principal defence mechanisms are described below.

Compensation. Using this mechanism, individuals devote themselves to a given pursuit with increased vigour in an attempt to make up for some feelings of real or imagined inadequacy. The compensation may be direct or indirect. Direct compensation refers to the generation of an intense desire to succeed in an area in which one has experienced failure or inadequacy. The classic example is the effort of Demosthenes to become an outstanding orator because of his early childhood speech disabilities; the very existence of this frustrating handicap provided the motivation to work more intensely to overcome it. Indirect compensation consists of the effort to find success in one field when there has been failure in another. This is seen in the vigorous efforts frequently made towards social achievements by students who fail to make their mark in academic circles or on the athletic field. Overcompensation is compensatory effort which is made at the expense of a well-rounded and complete adjustment to a variety of life's demands.

Denial. In this mechanism, an individual avoids painful or anxiety-producing reality by unconsciously denying that it exists. The denied reality may be a thought, a wish or a need, or some external object or condition. Denial may take a verbal form in an occasional statement that something is not so, or in a compulsively repeated formula which is resorted to as a means of keeping the thought, wish, etc., out of consciousness. In an extreme form, such a denial may result in complete loss of contact with surrounding reality.

Displacement. This is a mechanism in which pent-up emotions are redirected towards ideas, objects or persons other than the primary source of the emotion. Displacement may occur with both positive and negative emotions. For example, feelings of love which cannot be expressed openly towards a married member of the opposite sex may be displaced towards a child of that person. Another way in which displacement may be shown is by changing the channel of expression for the emotion. For instance, physical aggression may be inhibited but expressed verbally.

Dissociation. Here is a defence mechanism in which a group of mental associations are separated or isolated from consciousness and operate independently or automatically. The end result may be a splitting of certain mental content from the main personality or a loss of normal thought–effect relationships. Examples are amnesia, development of a multiple personality (see chapter 9) and somnambulism (sleep-walking).

Fantasy. In this mechanism, daydreaming or some form of imaginative activity provides escape from reality, with satisfaction obtained through imagined achievements or, occasionally, even martyrdom of some sort. A certain amount of daydreaming, especially in the earlier years of life, must be regarded as normal. As a preparation for creativity, fantasy is not only desirable but even essential. But fantasy becomes a dangerous and sometimes disturbing mechanism if it is consistently preferred to reality and is indulged in as a method of problem-solving.

Identification. In using this mechanism, the individual enhances his self-esteem (or believes he or she is doing so) by patterning behaviour after another person. This may be done in fantasy or in real life. Employed in moderation, identification may be both helpful and stimulating, and it frequently leads to superior achievement. Used to excess, it may deny the individual gratification of his or her own personality needs.

Internalisation. Those who employ this mechanism take into their own psychological makeup the values, beliefs or ways of thinking of another person, frequently a parent or other admired figure.

Projection. Individuals using this mechanism protect themselves from awareness of their own undesirable traits or feelings by attributing them to others. In its function of self-deception, this mechanism is particularly harmful to healthy personality development since it blocks self-insight.

Rationalisation. This is a common mechanism in which individuals justify inconsistent or undesirable behaviour, beliefs or motivations by providing acceptable explanations for them. A 'sour grapes' reaction, in which one denies wanting what one has failed to obtain, is a common example.

Reaction formation. This is a mechanism in which impulses that are not acceptable to consciousness are repressed (kept unconscious) and in their stead, opposite attitudes or modes of behaviour are expressed with considerable intensity. For example, overprotestations of sincerity or of willingness to help may often mean the very opposite. Scrupulosity (overconcern about the morality of one's behaviour) may stem from unacceptable desires.

Regression. Confronted by anxiety, threat or frustration, an individual retreats to an earlier and psychologically more comforting level of adjustment. Mild regression is seen in the return of an older child to babyish mannerisms upon the birth of a sibling. The infantile behaviour of some psychotics (see chapter 13) is an expression of extreme regression by Freudian thought.

Repression. Here the individual prevents dangerous or intolerably painful or guilt-producing thoughts or impulses from entering consciousness. Repression is essential for the existence and operation of all the other defence mechanisms. It should be distinguished from suppression, which is the conscious control of unacceptable impulses, feelings and experiences.

Sublimation. Here unconscious and unacceptable desires are channelled into activities that have strong social approval. The unacceptable desires, in Freudian theory, are sometimes sexual in nature, and their expression may be sublimated as creative effort in music, art and literature. Other areas of life that provide avenues for sublimation are social welfare, teaching and the religious life.

Undoing. In this defence mechanism, individuals symbolically act out in reverse (usually repetitively) something they have done or thought which is unacceptable to them. Through this behaviour, they strive to erase the offending act or thought and with it the accompanying sense of guilt or anxiety.

Breakdown in defences

The function of a defence mechanism is to maintain the integrity of the ego and thus to keep the individual in a state of psychological equilibrium. When the stress is too great for the personality to resist, defences are weakened and the personality begins to disintegrate. This process is called decompensation. In decompensation, individuals may at first attempt to use other measures. They may, for example, pass from superficial rationalisation to severe projection. The decompensation may produce a panic state of anxiety as the individual is confronted with the breakthrough of unconscious material. From a Freudian psychological point of view, the final stages of decompensation for some individuals may be florid psychotic reactions.

Overview of Freudian concepts

When Freud first presented his work it was seen to challenge the established approaches of the day, meeting with criticism and resistance. Although it seems less radical, even quaintly old-fashioned today, his approach is still the focus of a great deal of criticism and debate, even from within the psychodynamic schools of thought. Some of these criticisms are addressed below, followed by the concept of what is seen as normal and abnormal development from a Freudian perspective.

Limitations of Freud's work

Freud's development of psychoanalytic theory suffers two critical limitations. In the first place, the structure he outlined, the development states described, and the conflicts experienced are largely unverifiable – a criterion for all scientific work. Beyond that, modern study disputes many of Freud's statements about infancy and childhood.

Critics have challenged his emphasis on the sexual drive, especially the idea of sexual urges in childhood, and drawn attention to some of Freud's less reputable ideas and colleagues.

Secondly, Freud's professional experience was severely limited in the kinds of contacts he had with human behaviour. Except for his own family experiences, he spent no time studying the behaviour of infants or children. Even his clinical practice was limited to the kind of clients he had opportunity to study. They were principally upper-class men and women in early and middle age and were all drawn from the highly-stylised Viennese culture. Both limitations narrowed his views as to the nature of all the influences operating on the human being's psychological development. As a result, later psychoanalysts and others with a psychodynamic point of view have modified significantly his theories about human development.

The Freudian concept of normal development

Freud taught that both normal and abnormal individuals were subject to irrational forces. The personalities of both normal and abnormal individuals are formed, according to Freud, out of childhood experiences occurring before the age of six. They differ only in the nature of those experiences and in the effect that they have had on the formation of personality.

The essential distinction betwen normal and abnormal for Freud was in the balance achieved by normal individuals in the influence of id, ego and superego. There is, in the normal individual, greater strength in the gatekeeping function of the ego.

The Freudian concept of abnormal development

For Freud, the neurotic individual (one suffering from what is now called anxiety-based disorder) is one in whom spells of overwhelming anxiety have created the need to become overdependent on personality-warping defence mechanisms. Damaging early childhood experiences are the source of anxiety. The result is severe impairment in functioning and the development of severely uncomfortable symptoms.

From a Freudian point of view, psychosis (described in later chapters) develops from a severe weakening of the ego, either from extreme underdevelopment in early life or from later life experiences. The result is a breakdown of the personality's defence system, with resultant overpowering anxiety as id forces become dominant. Associated with this development is loss of orientation, incoherence of speech, and delusions and hallucinations in which voices are heard issuing destructive demands.

Early dissonant voices

Although Freud's original concepts evoked considerable opposition from contemporaries, his work also attracted a number of influential students. Many critics liken the Freudian psychodynamic school to a religious movement rather than a scientific school of thought. In these terms, two of the earliest disciples who studied under Freud, but who later disagreed with his teachings were Carl Jung and Alfred Adler. In later years, other clinicians with an initial Freudian perspective made their own lasting contributions to perspectives on human development, each characteristically different from Freud's. Below we examine briefly the contributions of Jung and Adler, and then the later contributions of Harry Stack Sullivan, Karen Horney, Erik Erikson and Melanie Klein.

Carl Gustav Jung (1875–1961)

Among the voices dissonant from Freud's, Carl Jung stands alone because although accepting the Freudian unconscious, he added to it the existence of a collective unconscious. It comprises a variety of archetypes, or universal ideas, with which we are born. The child does not have to learn fears of darkness, fire or death, for example; he is born with those predispositions. Jung moved away from the concept of libido with its emhasis on sexual energy and hypothesised the existence of a spiritual instinct. He gave much more emphasis than did Freud to the importance of religion, mythology, mysticism and the occult.

Alfred Adler (1870–1939)

Adler departed from orthodox Freudian teaching in three important directions. He disagreed with what he felt was Freud's undue emphasis on libido, and substituted for it an aggressive drive for dominance. He also placed much less emphasis on early childhood experiences, believing instead that psychological difficulties had their roots in immediate social context surrounding the individual. To attain maturity, the individual must, Adler taught, give up his self-absorbed power struggle and focus on service to others. In moving away from the biological emphasis of Freud, Adler accented the importance of self and gave it a creative function which enabled the individual to work out his lifestyle.

In popular thinking, Adler is perhaps best known for his concept of the inferiority complex, a feeling of inadequacy which stirs up compensatory strivings for power and dominance.

Later modifications of Freudian views

Clinicians independent of Freud but psychoanalytically trained suggested further modifications to orthodox Freudian thinking. Four examples of these are Karen Horney, Harry Stack Sullivan and Erik Erikson in the USA and Melanie Klein in England.

Karen Horney (1885–1952)

In her influential book, *The Neurotic Personality of Our Time*, Horney presented what was perhaps her most significant modification of Freudian theory. Here she presented the case that neurosis was a response to the values of industrial society, which pressed for competition and materialism, leaving the individual with anxieties about aggression and an overweening interest in seeking affection, but an incompatible inability to express affection.

Behind this propositon there was her understanding of the nature of neurosis, which was, for her, the result of having to face a hostile world. Its cause lay in bad parenting, whether too strict or too indulgent, negligent or too concerned, which led to neurotic strategies of adjustment, such as helplessness, hostility or isolation.

Harry Stack Sullivan (1892–1949)

Sullivan's contributions to the newly developing psychodynamic/psychoanalytic perspective were twofold: the importance he assigned to the self concept, and his willingness to use psychoanalytic therapy in the treatment of psychotics, an approach that even Freud considered of little value. Sullivan believed that personality could not develop apart from the social context in which it operated and is perceived. He defined psychological disorders as those that occurred in social relationships. The self concept, he stated, evolves principally out of the appraisal of the self by others. When those appraisals are hostile, the individual blocks them out of consciousness by denial. When this warping of reality in the self concept becomes extreme, Sullivan believed, psychological disturbance, neurosis or psychosis results.

Sullivan was the first to claim success in using analysis with young schizophrenic patients. In Britain analysis would not now be considered for psychotic patients and much of Sullivan's success with such patients in the USA can be attributed to his non-confrontational supportive clinical style rather than his theoretical approach. Sullivan's style in therapy has become a part of the modern psychodynamic perspective in America.

Erik Erikson (1902–1990)

Erikson brought to psychoanalysis a strong anthropological orientation, which gave his concepts a heavily social emphasis and also a more hopeful point of view than Freud's. He saw personality development as taking place in eight stages. At each stage, there was a challenge to be faced, largely psychological in nature. As individuals face each challenge successfully, they work out what Erikson called their ego identity, an integrated, unique and autonomous sense of selfhood. Each stage offers the individual a chance to eradicate earlier damaging experiences. Personality formation does not end with childhood, but continues on through the adult years. In influencing personality, Erikson added the influence of teachers, advisers, friends and others to that of parents.

Melanie Klein (1882–1960)

Born in Vienna, Klein moved to Britain from Germany and became a major influence on the British analytic movement, as was Freud's daughter, Anna. Although both women focused on child analysis, examining the significance of play and fantasy as methods of expression, there was a certain amount of personal and professional conflict between the two. Klein examined the child's earliest relations and objects, with the child attributing them with the responsibility for the emotional responses they evoke ie 'good objects' give pleasure and 'bad objects' give pain. Kleinian analysis gives special significance to the child's uncertain relationship with its earliest object, the mother's breast, which can give and withhold milk, causing tension. Klein also believed children to have an innate sexual understanding and aggressiveness and emphasised primitive mental processes which were named 'introjection', 'projection' and 'splitting'. In relating to the mother the child 'splits off' the bad images associated with painful experience and 'projects' them outside, whereas good feelings or images are 'introjected' inside. In being concerned with early instinctive drives, Klein was considered to expand on 'Id psychology'.

An overview of the psychodynamic perspective

As the individual theorists whose contributions we have just described, beginning with the concepts of Jung, have moved further and further away from the emphasis of Freud, the importance of interpersonal relationships has become a central feature of the psychodynamic perspective. For the student desirous of understanding the modern psychodynamic interpretation of abnormal behaviour, a good summary statement is the following:

'Abnormal behaviour can best be understood by studying the individual's past and present relationships with other people. Begin by assigning principal weight to the child's interpersonal relations with parents, and then continue on through the life of the person's interpersonal relations with siblings, grandparents, teachers, early and current friends. It is that set of relationships that offers the best understanding of his or her personality and any pathology that may be present.'

Humanistic and existential perspectives

With theoretical roots extending, for the humanistic group, back to William James (1842–1910), Gordon Allport (1897–1967) and Gardiner Murphy (1895–1979), and for the existential school, back to nineteenth century philosophers Søren Kierkegaard (1813–1855) and Martin Heidegger (1889–1976), and with only slight connections to psychoanalytic ways of thinking about human behaviour, two separate groups of theorists, working individually, have developed ways of looking at the human personality, normal and abnormal, that can conveniently be discussed under the headings, the 'Humanistic Approach' and the 'Existential Approach'.

The humanistic approach is best represented by Abraham Maslow (1908–1970) and Carl Rogers (1902–1987). The existential perspective is described in the formulation of Rollo May (born 1905) and the literature of Ronald Laing (1927–1989). Both schools, humanism in America and existentialism in Europe, grew out of major social changes that seemed to dehumanise humankind (the technological society) and to devalue human life (the million-person slaughter of World War I). Both trends seemed to these theorists only to be growing in strength with Hitler, Stalin, World War II, and nuclear bombs. The emphasis of the humanistic perspective is to re-establish a belief in the basic strength of the human psyche, its goodness and great potential for growth; the concepts emphasised by existentialists are choice, the search for meaning, authenticity and social obligation. Existentialists identify, as a central anxiety-producing problem for humanity, the 'nothingness' and 'non-being' which death brings to everyone.

The humanistic perspective

The two outstanding proponents of a humanistic way of thinking about human adjustment efforts, Abraham Maslow and Carl Rogers, made the main focus of their perspective a principal concern not with pathology but with helping the average individual to move from being merely normal and mediocre toward full self-actualisation.

Abraham Maslow

Maslow, working independently of Rogers, described in his hierarchy of human needs the aspirations humanistic psychology holds out for the developing individual. That hierarchy served, so to speak, as a map, providing guidance on the path to maturity.

The individual's life in Maslow's hierarchy is a progression from the lowest, yet fundamental, needs – physiological and safety – through the psychological needs of self-esteem and love/belongingness to the highest achievement of self-actualisation. Each level of need must be met before the individual moves to the next highest. Environmental influences, especially within the family, that block this progress – for example, neglect, rejection, oversolicitousness or authoritarianism – are the negative forces that individuals must be helped to understand and to overcome in order for them to move towards self-actualisation. That form of development is a continuing process through the life of the individual. Its strands are fulfilment of mission, a deeper understanding of capacities and personality, and a more fully integrated unity of personality.

Carl Rogers

Rogers developed an almost revolutionary new form of psychotherapy, which he described in his book, *Client Centered Therapy*, published in 1951. His theory of personality development was fully described in his 1966 publication, *On Becoming a Person*. Rogers places the self concept at the centre of personality. Through this concept, the individual organises the world, decides what is good or bad for growth, and moves toward self-actualisation in terms dictated by the self. Whether or not the individual accepts this valuing process is a result of the interaction of the organism (the sum total of the individual's perceptions of the world) and the self-awareness of one's own identity. When the two begin to come together, the individual moves towards 'self-actualisation'.

To have this happen requires that the individual, in the developing years, experiences positive regard. Life sets conditions on what forms of behaviour will be well regarded. In a happy environment, the child incorporates these into the self as conditions of worth. When those conditions are extreme or overdemanding, individuals redefine themselves to exclude any behaviour or desire tabooed by the conditions set. The individual is thus prevented from being a fully-rounded, wholesome person. Taught by parents to be docile and sweet at all costs, a person may never be able to feel the anger that can be a normal human outlet. Anxiety is aroused by the unconscious tensions created by that abnormal inhibition. The individual resorts to defensive behaviour, the process of self-actualisation is stopped, and symptoms of abnormal behaviour develop.

It is the nature of client-centred therapy to remove this blockage through the individual's own efforts by surrounding the client in therapy with warmth and unconditional expressions of regard, in the course of which the therapist reflects back acceptingly the feelings expressed by the client. In this way, the need for thwarting defensive behaviour is reduced, and the person can move towards integrating the organism's perceptions and those of the self and thus be free to move towards self-actualisation.

The existential perspective

Although the vocabulary used by Rogers is notably different from that found among existentialists, the processes they describe leading to healthy growth instead of pathology and unhappiness have certain striking similarities. Rogers identified the organism and the self; the existentialists speak of 'existence', which is the given, the world in which the individual finds himself or herself and the 'essence', what the individual makes of the world by the choices he or she makes. The latter point is succinctly made by Sartre: 'I am my choices'. Both schools place responsibility for fulfillment and happiness on the individual, but also credit him or her with the strength to assume that responsibility. In making choices, the individual is driven by the need to find meaning and value in life. Rollo May describes this as the person's effort to provide a stable foundation on which the centre of existence can be preserved. Not inconsistent with Rogers' understanding of maladjustment is May's contention that in the face of internal or external threats, essentially anxiety, individuals shrink the world that they admit into existence. May states, 'That shrinking is a way of accepting non-being in order that some little being may be preserved'. The goal in existential therapy is to help individuals to find a way of accepting a fuller world that is uniquely theirs, with the responsibility and loneliness that goes with it.

There is a pessimistic tone in the philosophy of existentialism, a feeling of alienation or spiritual death, brought on by a vast amoral and technological society that seems to have no place for the individual. The point of living on, existentialists say, is to combat the anxiety of existence in such a world, with the feelings of nothingness it creates, by directing our choices to give significance to our lives. One way of doing so is to recognise our social obligations in an indifferent world.

These aspects of the existential perspective fitted well within the writings of the so-called 'anti-psychiatrist', Ronald Laing. His existential approach to the explanation and treatment of some schizophrenic patients' conditions became a cornerstone of the 'alternative psychiatry' movement which evolved during the alternative-culture youth movement of the 1960s. One outcome of this was the opening-up of psychiatry and psychology to criticism by the public at large, especially with regard to medical treatments. These criticisms are no longer considered to have much practical value but are often referred to in purely academic debate.

The sociocultural perspective

Study of the influence on personality and abnormal behaviour of the surrounding social and cultural environment is a relatively recent development. Such a study has been largely influenced by the disciplines of sociology and anthropology, which emerged as independent fields only in the early twentieth century. The sociocultural perspective that developed as a result of the growth in importance of those two disciplines has two quite different aspects. One might be called cultural, largely having to do with differences in mores, family life, social pressures and religions that are prevalent in different regions of the world. The other has to do with the effect of differences in social, educational and economic levels existing among sectors in the same cultural area (intracultural factors), for example, in large urban communities. This section will consider both aspects separately.

Cultural influences

The field of study of social anthropologists is study of the ways in which people living in separated sections of the world carry on their daily routines, set up interpersonal structures, including sex and marriage, and develop ethical codes. Anthropologists compare one culture with another and attempt to draw conclusions about reasons for the different styles of life and the effects of those different styles on the individuals affected. A principal interest is to contrast various world cultures with the Western American culture. Anthropological studies are handicapped by weakness of scientific controls and difficulties in quantifying results of their efforts. Nevertheless, significant and widely influential conclusions have been drawn from their studies, which are usually conducted during a period of residence in the community under study.

Three principal conclusions about abnormal behaviour can be drawn from their research, each of which is a facet of the sociocultural perspective.

Criteria of mental disorder

People who cannot control their own behaviour, cannot assume basic roles in society and cannot even care for themselves in a prudent fashion are considered mentally disordered in all cultures. Interpretations of causality may vary, but acceptance of the fact of mental illness is universal.

Culture-bound patterns of mental illness

Apart from universally recognised mental illness, some types of abnormal behaviour seem to be tied to a particular culture. For example, anorexia nervosa is a disorder occurring mostly in women, in which there is such a predilection for staying thin that the individual loses almost all appetite for food. This seems to occur mainly in Western societies, perhaps due to the body shape ideals there, although it may be that it is simply less detectable outside the West.

Emil Kraepelin first used the term 'comparative psychiatry' in 1904 to represent the study of the differences between cultures in terms of such disorders. At this time the major comparisons were between Europeans and non-Europeans.

Patterns of child-rearing practices

Societies in the West tend to believe that their child-rearing practices are universal: how infants are nursed and toilet trained and when; who primarily takes care of the children; when children are considered adults. Anthropological studies suggest that quite the opposite conclusion is closer to the truth. Even among Western cultures, child-rearing practices vary. And as child-rearing practices differ in significant ways, one can expect different patterns of normal behaviour in the adult population and different symptom patterns in abnormal behaviour.

It should be noted that child-rearing practices can differ between socioeconomic groups within the same culture. In Britain for example, those middle-class (or above) parents with sufficient income will send their children to private residential schools at a relatively young age. This is not the case with the lower socioeconomic groups, who do not traditionally expect to send their children away from home or have the financial ability to do so.

Intracultural factors

Urban versus rural differences

There are correlational studies showing a co-variance (two factors tending to vary together) between the presence and absence of psychosis and urban versus rural residence within the same large culture. In many countries there are more cases of psychosis reported in urban as opposed to rural societies. On the surface this would appear to indicate that a more urban environment causes an increased risk of psychosis, indeed, some studies reveal that greater levels of psychological disorder are found in urban societies undergoing rapid change. However, there are alternative explanations. Medical facilities may be better and people more willing to report their problems in urban areas. Rural families may be more willing to care for their ill relatives at home or, in the absence of such care, the psychologically disturbed may drift into the bigger cities in the same manner as the homeless unemployed. In modern Britain the number of psychiatric patients living on the streets of big cities is a cause for concern for the mental health services.

Influence of deprivation

Epidemiological studies (surveys) indicate higher incidences of mental illness in those areas where there is also a higher incidence of impoverishment, discrimination and illiteracy. It is not difficult to understand that the misery of living under those conditions places a heavy burden on the individual's resources for healthy adjustment, and such conditions can be seen as a cause, but *only a contributory cause*, of mental illness. That analysis is supported by the fact that more impoverished individuals, for example, escape mental illness than suffer from it.

However, it has also been established that in most cultures there is a 'downward drift' of mentally ill patients towards the more deprived areas and lower socioeconomic groups.

Mental illness as a product of sociocultural influences

A more strongly stated aspect of the sociocultural perspective describes mental illness as the product of social ills. This view is supported by the observation that during times of economic recession, and consequent social pressures, admissions to mental hospitals tend to increase. That fact presents a strong argument, at the least, for the position that widespread economic setback, affecting many people, pushes some of them, perhaps only those with pre-existing disposition or genetic weakness, into severe mental illness.

Mental illness as a social institution

The most forthrightly stated position in the sociocultural perspective describes mental illness as a myth. One of its most ideologically convinced advocates (Thomas Szasz, 1961) holds that mental illness is a socially convenient myth used to explain away people who do not live according to society's norms. Such deviations from norms, it is said, are expressions of 'problems in living' in society as it is now constituted. Adherents to this view ask the question, 'How does society decide which deviants from its norms are mentally ill?' And why do individuals so labelled accept the label? The answer they themselves provide is that 'Deviant behaviour is quite common, and for the most part, it is transitory; some deviant behaviour, for a variety of unsatisfactory reasons, is labelled mental illness. Once so labelled, an individual has no choice but to behave in accordance with a socially prescribed role because society powerfully rewards such behaviour. Although such a person is denied the reinforcements of the sane – a career, a respected position in the family – they are provided with other rewards: the tender, loving care given to a sick person.'

SUMMARY

Although they express their positions in differing words, adherents of the three perspectives described in this chapter – psychodynamic, humanistc and existential - agree on basic propositions: that human motivations have unconscious roots; that a significant difference between unconscious motivations and what the individual believes motivates behaviour will cause maladaptive behaviour; that the struggle between unconscious motives and the controls an individual imposes on behaviour causes anxiety which the individual protects against through defensive behaviour, which often constitutes the substance of the abnormal individual's disorder. Impulses and feelings that the individual cannot accept are repressed (in the psychodynamic perspective) or screened out (in the humanistic and existential perspectives). An overarching similarity among the three perspectives is recognition of the complexities produced in the individual's behaviour by the dynamic interaction among opposing forces operating within the individual's psyche (the individual's functioning mind).

The psychodynamic perspective stemming from the early work of Freud, but much modified by those who came after him, has, as its central theme, the significance of unconscious conflicts originating in childhood. It sees abnormal behaviour as the development of maladaptive symptoms unconsciously used by the individual as a defence against the intolerable anxieties aroused by the childhood conflicts, the influence of which persists into later life. In orthodox Freudian theory, those conflicts grow out of a tension between biologically-based psychosexual impulses, the pleasurable expression of which is inhibited by limitations set by reality.

Adherents to psychodynamic deviations from Freud substantial enough to be thought of as a different perspective moved away from his biological orientation and gave less weight to the id and more significance to the ego or self. They all but dismissed the significance of early psychosexual development and focused on the broader concepts of interpersonal relations. They considered important not only interpersonal tensions of early life, but characteristics of the individual's present life. The anxiety at the root of abnormal behaviour was considered traceable not only to psychosexual conflict but also to conflicts about aggressive behaviour, feelings of inadequacy, and the difficulty of establishing satisfying interpersonal relations. Room is made for the pressures on the individual from the society itself.

The humanistic and existential perspectives developed separately and outside the mainstream psychoanalytic thinking. Both give heavy emphasis to the individual's own responsibility for self-fulfillment and assign, as a principal cause of abnormal behaviour, the failure to accept oneself, which failure interferes, in the humanistic perspective, with self-actualising efforts, and in the existential perspective with failure to develop authenticity, which is a way of living one's full personality.

The pressures placed on the individual by their cultural and social environment are accounted for in the sociocultural perspective, placing the dynamics within the person into the external context of that person.

FURTHER READING

Boyers, R. & Orril, R. (Eds). 1972. *Laing and Anti-Psychiatry*. London: Penguin Books.

Brown, D. & Pedder, J. 1991. *Introduction to Psychotherapy* (2nd ed). London: Travistock/Routledge.

Brown, J. 1964. *Freud and the Post-Freudians*. London: Penguin Books.

Dryden, W. & Feltham, C. (Eds). 1992. *Psychotherapy and its Discontents*. Open University Press.

Fernando, S. 1991. *Mental Health, Race & Culture*. Macmillan Education Ltd.

Gay, Peter. 1986. *The Bourgeois Experience: Victoria to Freud*. Oxford University Press.

Kohon, G. (Ed). 1986. *The British School of Psychoanalysis*. London: Free Association Books.

Leff, J. 1994. Cultural Influences on Psychiatry. *Current Opinion in Psychiatry*, 7: 197–201.

Maslow, A. H. 1971. *Farther Reaches of Human Nature*. Escalem Institute Book Publishing Program, New York: Viking Press.

May, R. E. Angel, and H. S. Ellenberger. (Eds.). 1958. *Existence: A New Dimension in Psychiatry and Psychology*. New York: Basic Books.

Rogers, Carl R. 1989. *Carl Rogers: Dialogue, Conversations with Martin Buber, Paul Tillich, B. F. Skinner, Gregory Bateson, Michael Polanyi, Rollo May and Others*. MA: Houghton-Mifflin.

5 Assessment and Classification

In their initial contacts, clinicians set out to appraise the severity of a client's illness, strengths and weaknesses the individual brings to therapy, earlier life history, and the characteristics of the client's interpersonal life. That appraisal is formally labelled 'the assessment process'. It may be a relatively informal procedure undertaken by the therapist in the early sessions of therapy; in many settings, particularly in hospitals or outpatient clinics, it may be an extensive process conducted by a team, including a psychiatrist, psychologist, social worker, and often a physician to conduct a thorough physical examination. A variety of techniques are used, each related to the special competence of a team member.

The principal outcome of the assessment process in abnormal psychology is the development of what some psychologists refer to as the dynamic formulation of the client's problem. This may be formalised in a comprehensive case history which contains informative summaries of all material gathered in the assessment process. The case history describes the current situation and its history, and also proposes hypotheses about the causes of the maladaptive behaviour, and presents a diagnosis drawn from an officially approved classification system.

Assessment, then, is a scientific process that observes and describes significant aspects of a client's behaviour. That description is used as a basis for predictions about future behaviour of the client which, in turn, provides the information and hypotheses for making decisions about a programme of treatment. In that regard, questions considered might be, What type of therapy is indicated? What is likely to be the outcome? How long a term of treatment can be predicted? What should the characteristics of the therapist be?

The assessment process is also used for making decisions other than those related to therapy. A variant of the assessment process is used in making personnel decisions, for example, is Ms Jones likely to be an effective sales manager for product division A? In vocational guidance, the basis of recommendations to the client is data gathered in an assessment procedure that measures interests and aptitudes. A simple assessment procedure can be used by universities in some countries as part of their admission procedure.

After considering the characteristics of a good assessment, this chapter considers four components of a comprehensive assessment: the physical examination, observation of the client's behaviour, the interview and the psychological test.

The chapter concludes with a description and evaluation of the two major classificatory systems. The first of these is the International Classification of Diseases (ICD) now in its tenth edition (ICD-10) by the World Health Organisation, the second is the Diagnostic and Statistical Manual (DSM) by the American Psychiatric Association which is in its fourth edition (DSM-IV). Both of these systems are widely accepted and used for the classification of psychological disorders.

The characteristics of a good assessment

There are two major characteristics of a good assessment: its reliability and its validity. Of lesser but notable importance are such practical considerations as the cumbersomeness of the procedure and the time it takes to complete.

Reliability

The degree to which an assessment consistently gives the same results is the measure of its reliability. The higher the reliability, the more likely it is that repeated assessments will arrive at the same conclusion, measure or diagnosis. Reliability says nothing about what is being measured; it speaks only to the dependability of the measure. The reliability of an assessment procedure or of a psychological test can be determined in three ways: internal consistency, test–retest consistency, and interjudge consistency.

Internal consistency

The method of internal consistency answers the question, Do different sections of the test appear to measure the same thing? For a psychological test, the method correlates one part of the test against scores earned on a different part of the test. If the correlation is high, the test is considered reliable. In the clinical assessment, a comparison might be made between conclusions drawn in the interview, from observations, and from the psychological test. Clearly, where the components of the assessment measure entirely different things then this form of reliability would not be appropriate.

Test–retest consistency

Will a second administration of the assessment device, conducted independently of the first, lead to the same judgements? If concordance is high, the assessment device would seem to be reliable. This method is most often used to test reliability of psychological tests; it is rarely used in the clinical assessment.

Interjudge consistency

How likely is it that a test or assessment prcedure, when scored or interpreted by different judges, will yield the same result? This mode of testing reliability, sometimes referred to as 'inter-rater reliability' (reliability derived from comparison between different raters), has been used in the work carried out to establish the ICD-10 and DSM-IV classificatory systems. In that effort, the question asked was,

When different clinicians use the diagnostic criteria set up in the manual, to what extent do their judgements correspond? The field testing of these systems will be referred to later in this chapter.

Validity

The validity of a test or procedure is an indication of the degree to which it measures what it purports to measure. Does an intelligence test measure what is generally considered to be intelligence? Does a personality test truly measure, for example, the trait of extroversion? Some psychologists would question whether or not traits, such as characteristic ways of responding in all situations, can indeed be demonstrated.

A test or procedure may be highly reliable without being valid. For example, the daily temperature can be measured with a high degree of reliability; it is not, however, a valid indicator of whether or not the sun is out. A test cannot be valid if it is not reliable. Validity may be evaluated in at least three ways: descriptive validity, construct validity and predictive validity.

Descriptive validity

Descriptive validity is a measure of how accurately a score, diagnosis or interpretation describes the current behaviour of those who have been assessed. For example, a valid intelligence test should have a high degree of accuracy (not 100 per cent) in indicating a child's academic performance in elementary school. With respect to psychiatric diagnoses, when it comes to descriptive validity, there is a problem. Individuals with different diagnoses may show identical current symptoms, for example, a manic depressive and those with certain types of anxiety-based disorder may exhibit both low self-esteem and depression. And those with an identical diagnosis may currently show quite different behaviour. Of two individuals with a diagnosis of anxiety-based disorder, one may have somatic symptoms, and the other may not. The difficulty can be cleared up as the diagnosis is made more precise; one diagnosis might be somatoform disorder, the other phobic disorder.

A psychiatric diagnosis is not a statement of the individual's characteristics but a statement of the individual's typical pattern of behaviour. There will always be an overlapping of individual symptoms among different diagnoses. If a diagnosis accurately describes the overall pattern of an individual's behaviour, as it usually does, it meets the criterion of descriptive validity.

Construct validity

By the word 'construct' we mean the actual thing being measured. Rather than asking if we are validly diagnosing autism, construct validity tests whether autism itself is a valid construct. Construct validity is usually assumed from a consistency across the related measures used in testing for the disorder which is strengthened by agreement between different measures of the same construct (convergent validity) and disagreement between the measurements of different constructs (discriminant validity). This is generally carried out in the course of establishing the disorder. However, in the case of some disorders such as schizo-phrenia there tends to be recurring doubt as to whether it is a single disorder or not. Problems of construct validity such as these are addressed when each edition of a classificatory system is compiled and adjustments made if necessary after careful examination of current evidence.

Predictive validity

When a test, assessment procedure or diagnosis accurately predicts future behav-iour, it meets the criterion of predictive validity. In abnormal psychology, the clinician is interested in predicting the course of the individual's illness, that is, its prognosis: the likelihood of recovery, in response to what form of treatment in how long a period of time.

There is an asymmetrical relationship between reliability and validity, ie that which is valid should be reliable but that which is reliable may not necessarily be valid. However, poor reliability can undermine attempts to measure predictive validity, especially when this involves diagnosis and assessment. Poor agreement between a number of clinicians at diagnosis and assessment, ie reliability, will clearly lead to poor predictive validity in the cases concerned. Thus, one of the aims of modern classificatory systems is to improve agreement between clini-cians on the diagnoses made using these systems. In this way, the improvements that have been achieved for the ICD-10 and DSM-IV should increase the predic-tive validity for diagnoses based on them. The increases that have been achieved for the ICD-10 and DSM-IV should thus increase the likelihood of higher predic-tive validity for diagnoses based on them.

Problems of assessment

There are three major types of influence that tend to bias the assessment process and negatively influence the end result, or diagnosis. They are characteristics of the clinician, especially the theoretical perspective he or she holds; the setting in which the diagnosis is made; and the purpose for which a diagnosis is made.

Characteristics of the clinician

Such basic characteristics as the age, race and gender of the clinician may influ-ence the rapport between clinician and client, especially when there is a notable difference between the two. The result can be difficulty in communicating on the part of the client, or even a selectivity in what the client will be willing to discuss. A formal and austere approach by the clinician may have the same effect.

A principal barrier to accuracy of diagnosis is the personal biases of the clini-cian and the clinician's theoretical perspective. Both will influence the weight clinicians will assign to the components of the assessment process, for example, a particular clinician may be expert in one of the psychological tests and give more weight to it than to the total picture drawn by other components of the assessment. Clinicians may have a tendency to see psychological weaknesses more quickly than psychological strengths. A clinician with a strongly biogenic perspective may tend to favour diagnoses with a physiological or neurological basis.

Influence of the setting

A clinician in a mental health setting may be quicker to pick up a mild anxiety-based disorder than a clinician working in a psychiatric hospital who is accustomed to seeing mostly seriously disturbed patients. The theoretical orientation of senior staff may also influence the interpretations of those working under them.

Purpose for which a diagnosis is made

Psychiatric assessments are undertaken for a variety of purposes. The principal one is to plan a course of treatment. Such a purpose is least likely to bias judgements made. But assessments may be sought for other purposes, for example, criminal cases, private medical insurance or for an employment medical. In such cases the clinician may be influenced by the possibly competing needs of the client and those requesting the assessment.

The components of the assessment process

This section examines the four principal components of the assessment process: the physical examination, the interview, observation of behaviour and psychological tests.

The physical examination

The physical examination has as its purpose an evaluation of the individual's general health and the discovering of any physical/medical/neurological factors that may be influencing the individual's behaviour. It is not always required as part of a psychological assessment.

The medical check-up

Basic to the physical examination is a medical check-up, in which a physician takes a medical history from the patient and checks the major systems of the body. That examination will ordinarily include an electrocardiogram to test the heart, measurement of blood pressure, a blood chemistry test, palpation of various parts of the body, and a lung X-ray. The examination may have been done before the patient seeks psychotherapeutic help, especially by those suffering from somatoform disorders or hypochondria. It is especially important when addictive or organic disorders are suspected.

Specialised procedures

More advanced and highly technical procedures may be ordered for special purposes. Some of these are as follows:

1 The electroencephalogram (EEG), in which electrical activity in the brain cells is picked up by electrodes attached to the scalp and recorded in oscillating patterns that are called brain waves. The EEG is used to help detect tumours or brian injuries that may be affecting the individual's behaviour.

2 The computerised axial tomography (CAT scan). This procedure uses a computer analysis of X-ray beams directed across areas of the patient's brain or other bodily parts. The CAT scan quickly and precisely provides information about brain injuries.

3 A more recently developed technique, the positron emission tomography (PET scan) adds to the data provided by a CAT scan, a measurement of the body's metabolic processes after a compound (such as glucose) is metabolized by the brain or other organs of the body. Thus the PET scan can monitor brain activity and in this way can record areas of abnormally high or low activity, and thus can also pinpoint sites in the brain that produce epileptic seizures, or locate brain damage or tumours.

In addition to physical measures, there are a number of psychological test batteries which can provide a comprehensive assessment of the 'soft signs' (ie psychological signs) of neurological abnormalities but these are very lengthy to administer. For example, the Halsted–Reitan Battery can take six hours and is probably the most comprehensive; other tests such as the Luria–Nebraska Neuropsychological Battery take less time and are also less costly. There are also a large number of quicker, more specific sub-tests for the various aspects covered by the batteries of tests. All of these tests infer neurological function from the cognitive, psychomotor and sensory functions they actually measure.

The assessment interview

A face-to-face conversation, in which the clinician seeks information about the client/patient's complaint, typical behaviour, life circumstances and early history, is the most commonly used assessment procedure. During the interview the clinician observes the patient's appearance and non-verbal aspects of their behaviour that may indicate signs of disorder and which can be added to the information gathered verbally from the patient. The clinician may even reflect on their own reaction to the patient and the reasons for that reaction. The interview with the client may be supplemented by interviews with family members, teachers, ward attendants, or others knowledgeable about the client. In many psychiatric situations, it is the only assessment made as the clinician uses the first few sessions to appraise the client. For relatively minor adjustments, or emotional or interpersonal problems, such an approach is efficient and accurate enough to meet the client's needs. Nevertheless, such a relatively unstructured use of the interview has been criticised as too unreliable for arriving at a scientific diagnosis. Research suggests that there is basis for criticism. There have been several attempts to improve the unstructured interview. Three are briefly reported here: the structured interview, the computer-assisted interview, and the self report.

The structured interview

In the structured interview, a series of previously prepared questions, asked in a fixed order, encourage the client to describe what he or she did in a variety of life situations. This assures full coverage, in the client's own language, of critical behaviour patterns. Follow-up research using the interjudge method of testing reliability indicates a notable improvement in agreement on a diagnosis when this approach is used.

The computer-assisted interview

Computer-assisted interviewing, although not yet widely used, is a new approach to assessment. There are a growing number of computer programs that allow clients, adults and children, to answer the structured interview questions using the computer keyboard. This provides a very standardised procedure by removing the differences that may exist between clinical interviewers. The advantage claimed is that pertinent information is gathered more fully than would be the case in a less formally conducted interview. In addition to the saving in cost and clinician time, Farrel, Stiles-Camlair & McCullough (1987) favourably compared computerised assessments with those carried out by clinicians, but found that although clients found it easier to answer questions via the computer they preferred to see the clinician in person.

One criticism of the use of the computer is that it mechanises a process that is and should be highly interpersonal. The absence of rapport between computer and client could limit the candour and completeness of the interview process.

The self report

The self report, in which the client writes answers about his or her own behaviour to standardised questions or responds to a problem checklist, is less mechanised than the use of a computer, but it still minimises the interpersonal aspect of the process. When the self report is followed by a personal interview, as it usually is, the danger of mechanising the process is reduced.

Clinical observation of behaviour

Observation of the client's behaviour in natural and typical family and interpersonal situations is a rich and accurate source of information. The disadvantage, of course, is that it is expensive and time-consuming. It is usually more practical to observe children in the classroom – especially valuable when the problem is school-related – and to observe psychiatric patients in a hospital setting.

To extend the process to other situations, the assessor can design role-playing situations among family members or with the partners in a marriage. The clinician sets the stage, usually around a communication problem or around a topic on which there is disagreement. While not as absolute as field observation, the role-playing approach does reveal nuances of the problem about which the client may not be conscious and therefore is unlikely to report in an interview. A rating scale can be used to standardise recordings of the observation. The rating scale usually allows the clinician to indicate not only the existence of the behaviour, but also its frequency.

As mentioned previously, information can be added to these arranged observations by noting the behaviour of the client during interviews and during the administration of psychological tests.

Psychological tests

A principal means of assessing behaviour, which is almost always administered and interpreted by a psychologist, is the psychological test. Tests are of two types: ability or performance tests, of which the principal type is the intelligence test; and personality tests. Among the ability tests are those that assess functioning in a variety of cognitive and psychomotor areas, a procedure that is useful in determining the presence of brain damage and locating it. Although it is lengthy, the Halsted–Reitan Battery is commonly used for this.

Intelligence tests may be entirely verbal, but most individually administered tests (the type used most frequently in clinical settings) combine verbal and performance items. Personality tests are of two types: projective tests, which offer the testee an unstructured way of responding, and objective tests, which limit the client's answers to yes or no or a choice from multiple choice items. Since the tests are principally in the province of the psychologist, this section provides detailed descriptions of them.

Intelligence tests

The concept of the intelligence test, and the first intelligence test, were developed in 1905 by Alfred Binet, a French psychologist, who introduced the test into French schools to screen children for higher education. Although there are many intelligence tests, those used in the clinical setting are likely to be the Wechsler Scales which have an adult version and two children's versions, or the revised Stanford–Binet, which can be used on children from two years of age to superior adults.

The Stanford–Binet. The Stanford-Binet is the oldest standardised intelligence test, and until the Wechsler Scales were developed, it was the standard individual test for use with children. It now shares that distinction with the Wechsler Scale for children. Although there is an adult section of the Stanford–Binet, the Wechsler Scale is used commonly for testing adult intelligence. The Stanford–Binet and the Wechsler Scale for very young children are used for testing children younger than five years of age.

The Stanford–Binet and the Wechsler Scales provide scores that can be directly converted into an intelligence quotient. Statistical procedures fix the mean IQ at 100. From an intelligence quotient, an individual's performance can be given a percentile rank in the general population. For example, an IQ of 130 places an individual in the upper five per cent of the population.

The Stanford–Binet organises such tasks as recognising objects in a picture, remembering a series of digits, defining words, and completing sentences in a logical way, into age groups. In administering the test, which requires considerable training, the psychologist may begin testing at a level just below the child's chronological age. If the child passes all items (thus establishing a basal age), the test proceeds to older levels until a level is reached at which the child fails all items (the ceiling age). In scoring the test, the psychologist adds to the basal age the credits for all other passed items. It is that score that is converted into an IQ.

The Stanford–Binet requires a programme of supervised training for anyone planning to use it and takes from two to three hours to administer, score and interpret. The latter requirement limits its usefulness in many clinical settings.

The Wechsler Scales. The Wechsler Adult Intelligence Scale (WAIS-R), used here to illustrate types of item content, consists of six verbal scales and five performance scales, which yield a verbal and a performance IQ. The subscale totals can be combined to provide a total IQ score.

Typical verbal items are word definition; identifying similarities in paired words, eg. cat–dog versus tree–house: general information; and mathematics. Performance items include assembling pieces of a jigsaw-like object, putting coloured blocks together to match an exposed picture, and transcripting a code. Performance items are timed. Each type of item presents a scale of items from very easy to difficult. The score is the number of credits earned for each item, plus credit for speedy performance.

The other two Wechsler scales are the WISC-R – the Wechsler Intelligence Scale for Children, with a range from six years of age to superior adult, and the Wechsler Preschool and Primary Scale of Intelligence (WPPSI) for younger children.

Evaluation of intelligence testing
There are four principal weaknesses or limitations of intelligence testing, and three significant strengths.

Weaknesses or limitations.
1 They are time-consuming to administer.
2 In many clinical situations, the problem presented may not require a precise measure of intelligence. Frequently, indications from the client's job or educational level may provide an adequate indication of intellectual level.
3 Intelligence is not, as Wechsler himself has pointed out, an existing thing as is, for example, one's heart rate, which can be directly measured. It has to be inferred from the officially correct answers which the testee is able to report on an intelligence test. With this limitation in mind, some psychologists define intelligence as whatever intelligence tests measure.
4 The charge has been made that intelligence tests assume a common middle-class cultural background, and measure the individual's response to that background. Impoverished children and many ethnic minority children, for

the most part, come out of a very different cultural background. Yet what happens to them, how they are classified for future education opportunities, and what careers are recommended to them, all depend on a measuring device that might not be fair to them.

Some tests, such as the Raven's Progressive Matrices have been designed to be 'culture free'. The Raven's test does not involve language but makes its estimate of intelligence from the ability to place a missing design in a series, and still has a high level of agreement with other tests of more diverse skills.

Strengths.

1 During the administration of an intelligence test, the psychologist has rich opportunities to observe the client's behaviour as they respond to an unfamiliar and challenging situation. Such anxiety-producing situations are normally faced in everyday life. Does the client respond with apprehension and anxiety? Does the client invest adequate effort and try hard? Are there notable mannerisms? Does the client try too hard? Is success all-consuming? Are there speech defects or idiosyncracies, or visual or hearing impairment?

2 Apart from the overall score, the intelligence test analysis details the client's cognitive functioning and lists strengths and weaknesses. In addition, the test may reveal the earliest indication of possible brain damage.

3 Finally, intelligence tests measure, fairly accurately, the likelihood of the individual's potential for success in the educational system. Even though that may not be a full measure or definition of intelligence, it is a forecast of likely success in an arena in which a child or adolescent will spend a great deal of time, and in which success is a principal gate-opener.

Personality tests

The two types of personality test, projective tests and objective tests, are a significant part of the assessment procedure and are typically administered and interpreted by the psychologist. This section will examine in detail the Rorschach Test and the Thematic Apperception Test (TAT), both of which are still used.

There are many established personality tests such as the 16PF Questionnaire (Cattell, 1965) or the Eysenck Personality Inventory (Eysenck & Eysenck, 1964) commonly in use. However, these have not been adapted for more specialised clinical use; for example, they are not used to measure personality disorder. The Minnesota Multiphasic Personality Inventory (MMPI) by Hathaway & McKinley (1943) also measures personality but has had various scales derived from it for specific clinical use, for example, Morey and colleagues (1987) have adapted part of the scale for personality disorder measurement. The MMPI will be described in more detail below as an example of an objective test.

The Rorschach. Herman Rorschach, a Swiss psychiatrist, created this test in 1912. It consists of ten cards, each having on it an ink blot such as might be made by folding in half a sheet of paper on which a blot of ink has been left. The ink blots, as a result, are all symmetrically balanced; they range in colour from black to grey to bright, vari-coloured designs. There are three phases to the test:

1 A card is held up by the psychologist, who asks clients what they see there. After the clients respond, they are asked, can they find anything else?
2 After the ten cards have been exposed, the psychologist asks clients, what was it about the card that caused them to see what they reported?
3 The test is then scored in accordance with a manual of detailed instructions. Aspects of the test scored are: goodness of fit (form); content of response (eg. animal, human figure); the use of the whole ink blot, a major detail, a small detail, the use of texture; attribution of movement.

It is that pattern of scoring that the psychologist uses to arrive at a description of the underlying personality characteristics, motivations, conflicts, level of intelligence, and possible psychoses or brain damage. When, for example, a client principally uses a small detail of a blot and avoids major parts of the card as a whole, a possible interpretation is that the client has difficulty in facing central issues and might tend to become bogged down in detail or trivia, a characteristic that might be related to such diagnoses as obsessive–compulsive personality disorder or one of the anxiety-based disorders.

A major criticism of the test is the low interjudge reliability reported for interpretations of the test and the paucity of information about its validity. Despite those criticisms, the test continues to be much used, although psychologists have come to use it less often during the past 20 years.

Although this essentially psychodynamic approach to testing has fewer practitioners these days, a small number of psychologists still use the Rorschach test, although they would admit to the difficulties of scoring and interpretation in its use.

New impetus may be given to the use of the Rorschach by the development of Exner's computer-generated interpretations for certain Rorschach scores. In using that approach, clinicians can depend upon interjudge reliability of intrepretations, if there is initial agreement about scoring, about which there is little criticism.

Thematic Apperception Test (TAT). Like the Rorschach, the TAT offers the client a series of relatively ambiguous pictures to interpret. Developed by Henry Murray in 1935, the TAT uses up to 30 cards upon which there are pictures of one or more people whose activities are not entirely clear. Clients are asked to make up a story about the picture with three parts which answer these questions: What has occurred before the picture? What is happening in the picture? How will the story end? What are the people thinking, feeling, doing?

The stories are then scored subjectively and impressionistically, or in accordance with a formal scoring system. Despite the existence of a number of scoring and interpretation systems that assess client needs, perceptions of reality and typical fantasies, psychologists most frequently use their own method of qualitatively and quantitatively assessing the significance of the client's stories.

Among the factors considered to provide leads to the client's personality characteristics, unconscious motivations, and conscious concerns are: the style of the story – length and organisation and any frequently occurring themes – for example, retribution, guilt, parent domination; who are the primary characters; and interpersonal and sexual concerns suggested by the stories.

Here, again, as with the Rorschach, there is caution in the clinical field about reliability and validity. Although the test is time-consuming, it is still occasionally used in assessment. The reason for its survival probably lies in the fact that it can access a patient's unconscious motivations and preoccupations, especially useful in forensic (criminal) assessments.

Objective personality tests. The Minnesota multiphasic personality inventory. As mentioned previously, there are many personality tests in use around the world but the MMPI has proved to be one of the most frequently used in the area of clinical practice and abnormal psychology research. The test is essentially a self report, in which clients answer true or false, agree or disagree, to 550 statements.

Typical of the statements are the five listed below, taken from the test form published by Hathaway and McKinley in 1951:

1 I go to a party every week.
2 I forgive people easily.
3 I often feel as if things were not real.
4 Someone has it in for me.
5 I sometimes enjoy breaking the law.

The MMPI has been subjected to more research scrutiny than any other personality test. That research can be categorised as follows:

Original validation studies. The original questions were adminstered first to a large, representative sample of individuals and several groups of psychiatric patients. All statements were then subjected to an item analysis (with items clustered into identifiable groups). This enabled the authors to discover which items differentiate among the several groups, that is, which differentiated the normal population from psychiatric patients, and which differentiated one disorder from another in the psychiatric population.

The study enabled the authors to develop ten scales, each of which assesses tendencies to respond in deviant ways, similar to the ways in which patients with known psychiatric disorders respond. In presenting its graphic summary to the clinician, the psychologist plots, on a graph, scores earned by the client on the ten scales, to be compared with a mean score on each scale for the normal population.

Thus, at a glance, the clinician can see, from the profile, in which areas the individual deviates significantly from normal. That evaluation does not necessarily establish a diagnosis, but it does suggest the characteristically deviant behaviour of the individual under study.

Subsequent validation. In the past, MMPI has been criticised for its dated language, circa 1950. Fourteen per cent of the items have now been changed to bring them up to date. Additional scales have been validated and are now part of the test. Two forms of the original test have been developed, one for adults and the other for adolescents.

Critique of the MMPI. Despite the endorsement suggested by its widespread use, criticism of the test appears in the psychological literature. The most basic criticism is that the test is a more valid indicator, not of an appropriate diagnosis, but of the degree of overall disturbance experienced by the individual, that is, whether or not the client is mildly disturbed or deeply disturbed. The more the individual scores deviate in a negative direction from the normal profile, the more severe is the disturbance. It should be noted that even that finding, apart from any indication of diagnosis, is a significant contribution to the assessment process.

A second criticism is that response sets which a person brings to a personality testing situation may warp the accuracy of the answers. Clients, it is said, tend to give socially desirable answers, but they also have an 'acquiescent set', causing them to agree with statements proposed. These two sets would have opposite effects. For example, to the statement, 'I sometimes tell lies', a socially desirable set would motivate a 'no' answer, an acquiescent set would stimulate a 'yes' answer.

In answer to that criticism, it should be pointed out that three scales in the test tend to control the response set. They are as follows:

1 The L scale, which assesses the tendency to claim excessive virtue, that is, a tendency to answer too often in a socially desirable way.
2 The F scale, which assesses a tendency to acquiesce too often and to report psychological problems inaccurately.
3 The K scale, in a reversal of the F scale, measures a tendency to see oneself in an unrealistically positive way, that is, for example, to acquiesce to the statement, 'I have never had any nightmares'.

Clearly, no personality test can ever be expected to be 100 per cent accurate in its measurement, and especially not a test which relies on the subjective judgement of the client. Thus, the more widely used tests need to be regularly updated and themselves subjected to rigorous evaluation. In the case of the MMPI, Butcher and colleagues (1990) have produced a revised version, the MMPI2. Although this is still undergoing evaluation, this re-standardised and up-dated version is claimed to be a considerable improvement by its authors, addressing a number of issues, for example, the appropriate representation of differing ethnic groups in the items.

Diagnosis and the classificatory systems

One significant outcome of the assessment process is to provide a diagnosis that fits the individual into a category of psychiatric disorder that is recognised by an official classification system. In addition to the selection of an appropriate disorder from the system, it is useful to have information on the current state of the patient, including any co-occurring disorders, physical conditions, current stresses and their ability to cope. This information is usually made available during the assessment procedure enabling the clinician to produce a formulation for that patient. The formulation is a picture of the particular patient and how they may vary from others with the same diagnosis, whereas the diagnosis itself is a more rule-based procedure tending to generalise amongst patients in the same category. Some classificatory systems incorporate rating scales which provide some of this information as part of their administration. The American based Diagnostic and Statistical Manual of Mental Disorders (DSM) is such a system, having a multi-axial ranging system, which will be described later. The other major classificatory system is the International Classification of Disease (ICD) system, a more internationally based system covering physical and mental disorders, which will also be described. (See chapters 20 and 21 for a more detailed listing of these two systems.)

Strengths and weaknesses of the diagnostic process

There is psychological value in attaching a diagnosis to a client/patient, but there are also costs. Both are described below.

Value of a diagnosis

A diagnosis places a client/patient into a group of other individuals with a known disorder. The diagnosis says that the symptoms and patterns of behaviour of this client/patient are similar (not identical) to those of other individuals who have been diagnosed as suffering from the named disorder. The most immediate value of that decision is that, at this stage of development in abnormal psychology, we have learned much about the prognosis of the various disorders (their predicted future course, if untreated) and about which therapies are likely to interrupt that prognosis.

A second value is that, for a limited number of mental disorders, there is knowledge of specific causes of the disorder in which case a diagnosis can be helpful in planning treatment. For other illnesses for which specific causes may not have been identified, certain other factors, sometimes (unfortunately) general, have been related to the illness. That knowledge can also be helpful.

Diagnostic categories can provide a scientific framework within which to conduct research. Such research into these established categories can provide information useful to the treatment process. For these purposes it is sometimes necessary to use a more exacting diagnostic procedure such as the Diagnostic Interview Schedule (DIS, Robins *et al*, 1981). Such a procedure is useful in research as it can be used by non-clinicians (with training) and assists differential diagnoses, or the careful distinguishing between two classifications with similar symptoms.

Criticisms of the diagnostic process

There are a number of criticisms of the diagnostic process, some of which are detailed below. The general uncertainty of the process, the problem of labelling, the implication that labelled individuals are qualitatively different and the assumption that a diagnosis is an explanation allied to the medical model, are only some of the possible criticisms of the process.

The problem of uncertainty

Unlike the diagnosis of some physical disorders, psychological conditions are sometimes very difficult to define precisely. Modern classificatory systems and assessment procedures have helped to remove much of this uncertainty. However, the difficulties that existed prior to their development persist in the opinions of some professionals. Early studies such as that of Rosenhan (1973), and of Passamanick and his colleagues (1959) highlighted the difficulties in validly diagnosing schizophrenia at that time, implying that a 'medical diagnosis' was not flexible enough to deal with the individual human qualities involved in mental distress. It is in order to rectify this history of diagnostic inconsistency that the ICD and DSM systems have been modified and individual criteria for disorders reviewed on a regular basis.

The problem of labelling

A diagnostic label stereotypes clients/patients and tends to bias the way in which clinicians, and society in general, tend to regard them. It may, for example, blind the clinician to the individual's abilities and resources for growth and self-fulfilment, which could be of significance in a programme of treatment. There is also danger that, to some extent, a diagnosis may become a self-fulfilling prophecy: once classified, the individual is expected (some may fear that he or she is even encouraged) to behave in ways consistent with the diagnosis. In more extreme cases normal behaviour can be re-interpreted as abnormal following the application of a diagnostic label.

The problem of qualitative difference

Calling individuals phobic, obsessive–compulsive, histrionic or dependent personalities holds at least the suggestion that they are in a class by themselves, that is, that they are a different kind of human being. On the contrary, those with psychological disorders are not different in kind, but rather have carried certain kinds of behaviour to such an extreme as to place them on the far end of a continuum, with many gradations along the way, from ideally adjusted to severely maladjusted.

The problem of believing a diagnosis is an explanation

A diagnosis, by itself, although helpful, without the support of a well-developed case history, does little to help explain what caused the illness or what treatment will cure it. As helpful as the diagnosis may be in the clinical process, its presence is open to the possibility that clinicians will tend to think about it in stereotyped ways, thus ignoring the fact that the person is a human being, different from other human beings, and entitled to be treated as such.

The ICD and DSM classificatory systems

Emil Kraepelin, a psychiatrist, developed the first useful classification system for mental disorders in the latter part of the nineteenth century. Although features of his classification system continue to influence recent developments, his approach to mental illness was based on a mainly organic view of the field. Following the medical model, he tended to believe that similar groups of symptoms (a syndrome), labelled with the same diagnosis, would result from similar causes, respond to similar treatment, and that the illness would follow a similar course during treatment. Although Kraepelin's approach has been criticised for not sufficiently accounting for social and environmental factors, there are still those who share his view today.

Kraepelin's classification system formed the basis of the first editions of the fifth chapter of the ICD (WHO, 1948) and DSM (APA, 1952) systems, which have only recently lost his familiar structure. The ICD system by the World Health Organisation (WHO) is in its tenth version, ICD-10 (WHO, 1992), and the DSM system by the American Psychiatric Association (APA) is in its fourth version, DSM-IV (APA, 1993) although there was an interim revision in 1987, DSM IIIR, which greatly paved the way for the DSM-IV.

The ICD system is part of a very large and detailed classificatory system of all disorders. The DSM system differs from the ICD system in that it has been deliberately developed to give clear operational rules in making diagnoses, a concentration on reliability in clinical practice. Both systems give very detailed lists of options for each disorder (which have been summarised when reproduced in chapters 20 and 21).

Characteristics of the ICD-10

The classification of psychological disorders in ICD-10 only concerns the fifth chapter in the manual produced by the World Health Organisation, which has 458 categories of psychiatric disorder under ten main headings (an abbreviated listing of the ICD-10 can be found in chapter 21). Several versions of the ICD-10 have been prepared for more specific purposes, for example, a version more suited to research work and another for clinical settings. Abbreviated versions of the system are available and various assessment schedules or diagnostic interviews have been based on it. The Composite International Diagnostic Interview (CIDI) is based on both the ICD-10 and DSM IIIR systems.

In the one hundred years since its inception, the ICD system has been revised and evaluated a great number of times, especially with regard to agreement between clinicians from different nationalities. From the sixth edition (ICD-6, 1948), psychological disorders were added as its fifth chapter and thus included in subsequent evaluation. Okasha and colleagues (1993) found their reliability figures higher for the ICD-10 than for either its predecessor the ICD-9, or the older version of the American DSM system DSM IIIR. Other field trials in 39 countries have found the ICD-10 clinical guidelines suitable for widespread international use as well as having good reliability, but already points have been identified for improvement in the versions to follow (Sartorious *et al*, 1993).

The ICD-10 is expected to remain in use for around 20 years, twice as long as its predecessors, in order that some stability be introduced into the teaching and practice of its use. One aspect of the construction of the current version which should prolong its life has been the aim of compatibility with the DSM and other systems. This has been a common aim in the most recent revisions of classification systems, giving the international community of professionals more similar language. There are some persistent differences, a notable example being the retention of the term 'neurotic disorder' in the ICD system, a term which is absent from the DSM-IV and only appears in parentheses in the DSM III. To some extent this exemplifies the original distinction between the systems, in that the term 'neurosis' implies a theoretical aetiology whereas the DSM uses 'anxiety disorder' which is a more descriptive, atheoretical term. Collaborating professionals from both systems have had the task of minimising, if not eradicating, such differences.

Characteristics of the DSM-IV

Following the production of the ICD-6, the American Psychiatric Association produced the first edition of the American system, DSM I, in 1952. The most recent edition, DSM-IV (1993), is in a multi-axial form, that is, patients are rated on each of five independent scales, or 'axes'. Students of abnormal psychology are mostly concerned with the first two of these axes, which contain all of the categories of psychological disorders, the majority being in axis-1. The other axes are important in gaining a clearer picture of the patient's condition, rating their medical and environmental problems, and their ability to cope.

The diagnostic dimensions of the DSM-IV axes

- Axis-I lists all mental disorders and the criteria for rating them, except personality disorders, which can often be found in addition to axis-I disorders.
- Axis-II contains only personality disorders, which are considered as life-long conditions independently of the disorders on axis-I.
- Axis-III lists any general medical conditions that may be present and thus could influence the mental state of the patient.
- Axis-IV contains a checklist of psychosocial and environmental problems of varying types and severities.
- Axis-V contains a Global Assessment of Functioning Scale (GAF Scale) which enables the clinician to rate the patient's current and best potential level of adaptive functioning or coping.

Although the patient can be rated on each axis independently of the other four, the information provided by each axis can have a great deal of bearing on the interpretation of the other ratings. For example, the initial selection of generalised anxiety disorder from axis-I may be modified in the light of diabetes mellitus recorded on axis-III. This is because hypoglycaemia, a symptom state of diabetes, can be a biological cause of anxiety.

As mentioned in the previous section, the American DSM is a descriptive system avoiding implied aetiology in its classifications. Although it achieves this aim to a greater extent than its ICD partner, it can still be criticised on similar grounds. Shon Lewis (1994) has pointed out that both systems use the term 'organic' in such a way as to imply that organic causal factors are not involved in the rest of the classifications. The fact that the American system has removed a number of other suggestions of aetiology but not this one, may reflect an underlying bias towards the psychodynamic as opposed to the biogenic perspective in American abnormal psychology.

SUMMARY

The assent process seeks to evaluate and include in a case history the client's illness, strengths and limitations, life circumstances, early history and current interpersonal relations.

The principal means of conducting the assessment process are as follows:

The physical examination, which may include such advanced medical procedures as the electroencephalogram, the computerised axial tomography (CAT scan), and the positron emission tomography (PET scan).

The interview, which may be largely informal and unstructured. Recent adaptations of the simple interview are a structured interview with a comprehensive list of questions for use by the interviewer, and a self report, completed by the client, for which a computer program has been developed.

Psychological tests, including intelligence tests. The most commonly used are the Wechsler Scales for use with adults and children, and the Stanford–Benet, with a range from age two to superior adult; and personality tests, which may be projective (ambiguous stimuli onto which the individual projects his or her own interpretations) or objective (providing a list of statements with which the individual may agree or disagree). The more familiar projective tests are the Roschach ink blot test and the Thematic Apperception Test (a series of pictures about which the client invents a story). A widely-used objective personality test is the Minnesota Multiphasic Personality Inventory, which in its full form, uses 550 questions to provide a ten-scale personality profile.

The assessment process develops a dynamic formulation of the client's disorder and provides a diagnosis drawn from an official diagnostic system such as the World Health Organisation's ICD system (ICD-10) or the American Psychiatric Association's DSM system (DSM–IV).

FURTHER READING

American Psychiatric Association. 1993. *Diagnostic and Statistical Manual of Mental Disorders, DSM-IV*. Washington DC.

Anastasi, A. 1988. *Psychological Testing* (6th ed). Prentice Hall Macmillan.

Clare, A. 1980. *Psychiatry in Dissent* (2nd ed). London: Routledge.

Goldber, D., Benjamin, S. & Creed, F. 1994. *Psychiatry in Medical Practice* (2nd ed). London: Routledge.

Lewis, S. 1994. *ICD-10:* A Neuropsychiastrist's Nightmare? *British Journal of Psychiatry*, 164: 157–158.

Maruish, M. 1994. *The Use of Psychological Testing for Treatment Planning and Outcome Assessment*. London: Lawrence Earlbaum Associates.

Patel, V. & Winston, M. 1994. Universality of Mental Illness Revisited: Assumptions, Arifacts and New Directions. *British Journal of Psychiatry*, 165: 437–440.

Peck, D. & Shapiro, C. 1990. *Measuring Human Problems*. Chichester: John Wiley.

Robins, L. N. & J. E. Helzer. 1986. Diagnosis and Clinical Assessment: The Current State of Psychiatric Diagnosis. *Annual Review of Psychology*, 37: 409–432.

Sartorious, N., Kaeber, C., Cooper, J. *et al.* 1993. Progress Toward Achieving a Common Language in Psychiatry. *Archives of General Psychiatry*, 50:115–124.

World Health Organisation. 1992. *The ICD-10 Classification of Mental and Behavioural Disorders: Description and Diagnostic Guidelines*. Geneva: World Health Organisation.

6 Behavioural, Cognitive–Behavioural, Biogenic and Psychodynamic Forms of Therapy

In most countries in the world, between two and five per cent of the population will visit some form of mental health agency for help with a psychological problem. Many of these will then undertake a programme of therapy which could involve only three or four visits for psychotherapy or a single course of physical therapy (eg. drug therapy), but in some cases could lead to therapy lasting for years.

What will they experience? The number of therapies available makes this a difficult question to answer. In 1989 Holmes & Lindley acknowledged over 300 types of psychotherapy and this number can be assumed to increase with the passage of time. Unfortunately, research testing of the comparative effectiveness of the various therapies has not kept pace with their growth. Almost all of these therapies can be grouped into one or other of the perspectives in this chapter, some therapies only differing very slightly from one another.

Most clinicians will select a mode of treatment consistent with their perspective on human behaviour. They will set therapeutic goals, follow procedures, and schedules and terminate treatment in ways consistent with that perspective. But increasingly, clinicians are adopting an eclectic point of view and, to some extent, adopting psychotherapeutic approaches from one or another of the ideologies in a way that best suits the needs of the client.

Differing therapies may have different goals. Some therapies set their goal as a change in the patient's behaviour or physical/emotional state, whereas others aim to encourage insight into, or coherence of, the personality on the part of the patient. Therapists may see their therapy as a precise science or closer to a skilled but flexible art.

Therapies may prioritise differing areas of human functioning in approaching their goals. The target area may be the behaviour of the patient, their emotional reactions, the way the patient thinks, their physiological state, or the ways in which they cope with their problems. Although each of these areas may be important, some therapeutic approaches may measure their success by improvement in only one of them. The degree and extent of the disruption caused to the patient's life by the abnormal behaviour is a concern for all therapists.

The style of interaction between patient and therapist can be characteristic of the therapeutic approach. This can vary from the passive intimate interaction with the psychoanalyst or counsellor to the behavioural therapist actively driving a patient around town for hours during flooding *in vivo* therapy. The choice of therapist where this is in the patient's control, can be difficult given that the patient can be distressed at this time.

After dealing with these general introductory issues, this chapter will describe the characteristic features of the main types of therapy that are available and some evaluation of these approaches. Behavioural therapy is one of the commonest treatments for psychological thinking patterns of the patient and in cognitive–behavioural therapy thoughts are considered as internal behaviours susceptible to similar rules of change to those in behaviour therapy. Biogenic therapy tends to be the domain of psychiatrists as it represents the treatments of the medical model. Group therapy, or multiple therapist situations, will also be described. Finally, the psychoanalytic and humanistic therapies represent a less scientific approach in which the client gains insight into their own feelings and motivations.

Differences in the goals of therapy and the therapeutic interaction

Therapies differ in their goals and styles of interaction, usually as a consequence of therapists' differing theoretical perspectives.

Behavioural, cognitive and biological approaches are considered to be scientific by the professionals who adopt them. This objective viewpoint is reflected in the goals and methods of therapy. Behaviourists see faulty conditioning as the cause of abnormal behaviour, and thus their goal is a change in this behaviour, which is achieved by means of classical or operant conditioning techniques. Cognitive therapists aim to change the faulty thinking patterns, replacing unrealistic aspirations and fears with more adaptive ways of perceiving themselves and the world. This is often approached in a cognitive–behavioural way by treating the faulty thoughts as if they were behaviours to be changed. In either case the therapist is treating the change to adaptive thinking as an objective and measurable process. The psychiatrist with a medical or biogenic approach would probably consider their approach the most scientific, reducing psychological distress to its related physical aspects. The goal of therapy here is to rectify a physiological fault by direct physical intervention such as surgery or, more commonly, to alter the physical processes by drug therapy or sometimes by electro-convulsive therapy. Perhaps as a result of these therapies being seen as scientific and objective, they tend to give less consideration to the sense of self or unconscious motivations of the patient playing a part in their illness as would be the case with the psychoanalytic or humanistic approaches.

The psychodynamic perspective considers the influence of childhood experiences on current behaviour and emotional state. For the psychoanalyst this process is mediated by repressed experiences producing unconscious motivations and their goal is to allow the patient to gain conscious insight into their repressed feelings, actively working through these rather than a process of passive recognition. The goals and methods of psychoanalysis are not scientific, nor are they objectively measurable. Although the humanistic and existential therapist examines less remote influences on the patient's state, their goals of insight and a positive sense of self are achieved by using intuition and empathy rather than by any form of scientific method. In common with the psychoanalyst, these therapists would see their approach as an art-form rather than a science, with insight as their goal rather than any objectively verifiable and predictable outcome.

Which therapy?

In some countries such as Britain, the choice of therapist is usually made by a General Practitioner who will refer the patient to a specialist he or she thinks appropriate in the same way as would happen for specialised heart treatment. In other countries where there is only private health care, and increasingly in Britain, the choice is up to the paying client. This creates a number of dilemmas for the client which will be briefly covered here.

Some knowledge of what the therapy entails, its aims and effectiveness for the client's disorder will be required. This is best gained by consulting a trusted professional, such as their GP, as gaining the knowledge to make the decision could adversely affect the client's condition by delaying treatment. Further to this, providing a choice may seriously mislead the client. To take a simplified example, a client with problems arising from an undetected brain tumour may 'choose' to see a psychoanalyst as they find the analytic process more pleasant and have a fear of medical treatments, clearly the wrong basis for the decision. Hopefully this would be a rare event, with the analyst referring the patient back for medical examination, but this may be after a damaging delay.

The best treatment for the disorder may not be as obvious as in the above example. There may be more than one treatment that is appropriate for some disorders, so which therapy is best? Anxiety can be treated by anti-anxiety drugs or desensitisation by a behavioural therapist. The psychoanalyst would argue that these therapies avoid confronting the cause of the anxiety which he or she would try to address. The behaviourist would argue that the behaviour is the problem and nothing further underlies that. The arguments are endless, but studies such as those of Gordon Paul tend to find that behaviour therapy has the highest success rate whereas psychoanalysis has little effect on its own above that of chance recovery, at least in the short term. Drug therapy could be said to merely mask the symptoms of disorder, but this may be essential with some disorders such as schizophrenia. Thus there is no simple answer to this question, except to state the eclectic view that different treatments should be employed to the extent that they are useful and not to the exclusion of others.

Carl Rogers, an exponent of the humanistic perspective, would claim to get a positive response from the client as a consequence of the warm empathic approach of this form of therapy. Whether this is the case or not, the expectations of the client and their attitude to the therapy and therapist can make a difference to the outcome of the process. It is thus important that the best is made of the client's motivation for the therapy to succeed. With this in mind, there are some cautionary rules for clients below.

Some cautionary rules for prospective clients

1 Don't continue working with a therapist whose personality traits are unacceptable to you.
2 Be wary of therapists who urge you to behave in ways that go against your religious, moral or ethical standards. A therapist who makes sexual advances of any sort is behaving unprofessionally and destroying any possible effectiveness of treatment.
3 Try not to hold back information from your therapist.
4 Don't hesitate to ask questions or to raise objections to what a therapist is doing or proposing.

Behavioural therapies

Behavioural therapies are the most successful of the psychotherapeutic approaches and form the treatment of choice for a number of conditions such as phobias or sexual disorders. Elements of the behavioural approach have been incorporated into many other therapies and hybrid therapies have emerged from this, notably cognitive–behavioural therapy. The practice and variety of cognitive–behavioural therapies has expanded greatly in the last 20 or so years.

As described in chapter 3, the behavioural perspective focuses on the behaviour of the individual in a scientific or empirical way. In clinical practice this focus usually involves specific behaviours rather than the 'global' state of the client. Within the behavioural therapies there is variation. At one extreme radical behaviourism considers all behaviour, whether adaptive or maladaptive, to be the product of conditioning and therefore treatable by this means only. Towards the other end of the 'behavioural continuum' approaches such as those of the cognitive–behavioural therapist acknowledge other influences on behaviour including such elements as free will. At both positions on this continuum, therapists would agree that faulty learning can be treated by the clinical application of conditioning techniques.

Basic principles of behavioural therapy

The basic principles of conditioning used most freuqently in behavioural therapy are the following:

1 Reinforced behaviour is strengthened and likly to recur.
2 A stimulus regularly paired with a second stimulus that elicits a response will come to elicit the same response.
3 Behaviour that is not reinforced will tend to disappear from the individual's behavioural repertoire.

4 Any response that removes an unpleasant or hurtful condition will be strengthened.

5 Reinforcements of the components of a desired response in a way to move the individual towards that response will eventually make that response a part of the individual's way of behaving.

6 Although infrequently and warily used, punishment following a response will cause an undesired response to disappear, but may produce other undesirable consequences.

These principles can be sub-divided in two different ways. One way is to consider behaviour therapy as pertaining to classical conditioning applications and behaviour modification to the application of operant conditioning principles. Another way is to consider the removal of unwanted behaviour on one hand and the instigation or increase of desirable behaviour on the other, involving either classical or operant techniques in either case. In practice, faulty or maladaptive learning is normally reduced first and then adaptive behaviour, or behaviour incompatible with the unwanted behaviour is encouraged. Consequently this is the order in which the different types of behavioural therapy will be described here.

Specific types of behavioural therapy

There follow brief descriptions of widely used behavioural therapeutic techniques with examples of behaviour they seek to modify.

Extinction by removal of reinforcers

Undesirable behaviour is sometimes taught by situations in the environment that reinforce the behaviour in an unplanned way by means of operant conditioning. A common example in many homes is that of the child throwing a temper tantrum, which is unwittingly reinforced by the child becoming the centre of everyone's attention, especially that of the parents. Once the parents leave the room or totally ignore the tantrum, thereby no longer reinforceing it, the temper tantrum subsides. If that practice is followed regularly, temper tantrums disappear or, at least, become less frequent.

Dependency or helplessness in adults can be reinforced by giving in to it; conversely, it can be reduced if the person appealed to – a spouse, an older child or a friend – can be taught to refuse to comply with the pleas for help in a compassionate way.

A particular form of the technique of extinction has been labelled 'time out'. Principally used with children, the behavioural technique is to place the child in a completely neutral setting,where there are no reinforcements to be found, when the undesired behaviour occurs. Compassion for the child demands that the isolation be relatively brief and that the place of removal is not frightening to the child.

Extinction by systematic desensitisation, flooding and implosion

There are three basic techniques for reducing maladaptive anxiety responses (autonomic nervous system activity) and the consequent avoidance of the feared stimulus or situation. They rely on the principles of classical conditioning and are successful with disorders such as specific phobias, eg. acrophobia, an irrational fear of heights leading to the avoidance of everyday situations such as climbing open staircases. These techniques have in common the goal of making the client less sensitive to the stimulus that causes the avoidance response. They are systematic desensitisation, flooding, and implosion. In each of them, there is exposure to the very stimulus producing the avoidance response for which treatment has been sought. The exposure may be to the actual situation, to a vivid representation of it, or to the client's imagining it.

Systematic desensitisation. Joseph Wolpe created a procedure for reducing anxiety preceded by specific anxiety-causing situations, for example, glass-fronted lifts for the acrophobic. The procedure is based on the principle of reciprocal inhibition in the autonomic nervous system, that part of the nervous system which is responsible for our involuntary alertness when in danger, and conversely our ability to relax and recuperate when not in danger. Clearly we cannot be relaxed and alert at the same time, thus being in 'relaxing' states tends to make being anxious difficult or even impossible. Staying relaxed is an obvious anti-anxiety state but eating or being assertive are also reciprocally inhibitive of anxiety. The three stages in Wolpe's procedure illustrate this principle.

Wolpe first trains the client in relaxation. He uses any of several methods, including the occasional use of hypnosis and drugs. Once the client has learned to relax, the therapist encourages the client to describe a number of anxiety-producing situations, ranging from those that cause mild anxiety to those producing extreme anxiety. These situations create a scale of increasing levels of anxiety known as Subjective Units of Discomfort (SUD) scale. This has two uses: as a reference scale for the client's level of anxiety and as the stimuli set for the next step in the procedure. With the client fully relaxed, the third step is to have the client imagine the previously identified anxiety-producing situations, beginning with the least disturbing and gradually working up to the most disturbing. Because of the incompatibility of feeling safely relaxed and anxious at the same time, the client is gradually desensitised to the unpleasant stimulus, and the maladaptive response is extinguished.

Flooding and implosion. Here the principle of extinction by the non-reinforcement of a negative, undesired response is used. But no gradual approach is allowed. Instead, the client is exposed to the prolonged presence of the feared stimulus or to a vivid representation of it. Implosion is similar to flooding, except that feared stimuli are vividly imagined by the client at the direction and encouragement of the therapist. Maintaining the response at a high level is important as this 'exhausts' the autonomic response, making the client unable to feel anxious whilst still in the presence of the feared stimulus. This is obviously more difficult to maintain in a client who is imagining the stimulus, but there are advantages to the implosion method. The client can 'practise' the technique between therapy sessions, thus increasing the likelihood that the client would actually confront the anxiety-producing situation in real life. Repeated many times in a calming situation, the techniques reduce the anxiety attack and the maladaptive response of avoiding the previously feared situation.

Flooding has been particularly effective in controlling obsessive–compulsive behaviour. For example, if the compulsion is hand washing to avoid contamination, the client is actually 'contaminated' and prevented from washing, an activity which, in the past, had been reinforced by a reduction in anxiety. The client, in time, comes to discover that there is really nothing to fear and therefore no compulsive behaviour is required to remove it.

Flooding and implosion, because of their simpler but just as effective procedures, have, to some extent, replaced systematic desensitisation as the treatment of choice for some forms of anxiety disorders. One significant disadvantage is the intensity of anxiety experienced early in treatment. For that reason, some therapists are reluctant to use either flooding or implosion.

Aversion therapy

Instead of using removal of reinforcements as a means of modifying behaviour, aversion therapy pairs undesirable behaviour with an aversive after-effect. It has been found useful in problems of impulse control, for example, alcohol abuse or cigarette smoking. Here the stimulus associated with the undesirable activity (eg. alcohol) is paired with a noxious stimulus (eg. an emetic) using the process of classical conditioning. Deviant sexual behaviour can also be reduced using a comparable technique. In such cases, it is sometimes the deviant response which is paired with the aversive stimulus, which in the case of a voluntary response would be governed by the rules of operant, rather than classical, conditioning. It can be easily understood that full cooperation from the client is required for the use of aversive therapy.

Covert sensitisation

An occasional substitute for aversive therapy is to have the client imagine, rather than experience, the unpleasant consequences of maladaptive impulsive behaviour. The client is directed to pair the image of the undesired behaviour with vivid images of unpleasant consequences, for example, imagining the revolting and possibly dangerous consequences of getting drunk.

Positive reinforcement

The most ethically desirable method of modifying behaviour is the reinforcement of desirable behaviour, usually by means of operant conditioning. However, since therapy is principally sought to eliminate desired behaviour, the major challenge to using that method is eliciting the desired behaviour in the first place. Often the desired behaviour is incompatible with the undesired behaviour – this can be termed a 'differential reinforcement of incompatible behaviour' (DRI) schedule. A 'differential reinforcement of other behaviour' (DRO) schedule is where any behaviour but that which is undesirable is reinforced, which has the operant effect of suppressing the undesirable behaviour by omission of reward. There are four recognised techniques for initially promoting desirable behaviour: shaping, modelling, assertiveness training and biofeedback.

Shaping. When an individual seems unable to make a desired response instead of a maladaptive one, or when the desired response is a complex one, the client can be gradually led in the right direction by shaping his or her behaviour, that is, by reinforcing any response, no matter how slight, that moves the client towards the targeted goal, which is any behaviour that approximates the desired response. For example, where an autistic child (see chapter 18) avoids any interaction with other children, behaviour as simple as turning in the direction of another child sitting in the room would be reinforced every time the child does so; a step towards the other child, as it occurs, would next be rewarded, until finally, the child has reached the point of standing in front of the other child and making eye contact with him or her. As the process is repeated, the initial rudimentary responses are no longer reinforced and only those responses which most nearly resemble the desired response are reinforced until the target is achieved. The procedure does work to produce rudimentary social behaviour, which, once engaged in, can produce its own reinforcing effects.

Modelling. Observing the successful efforts of others and then modelling one's behaviour on theirs is a very common human learning experience. It begins early – one-year-olds imitate the behaviour of an older sibling or parent – and continues throughout life, for example, the amateur golf player imitating the stance of the golf professional. We all model our behaviour on that of parents, teachers, friends, and particularly in adolescence, on movie and television stars.

It is just as easy to imitate good behaviour as bad behaviour, adaptive behaviour as maladaptive behaviour. This fact has turned the attention of psychologists to modelling as a form of treatment. The positive reinforcement that motivates modelling is two-fold: anticipated success in enjoying what another person seems to be enjoying, and the self-satisfaction of modelling the behaviour of an admired person.

Its use in therapy is ordinarily easy to arrange: the admired therapist demonstrating his or her lack of fear of snakes; allowing the client to watch a group of children enjoying the antics of a dog; in a controlled setting, surrounding a child with children who are modelling desired behaviour. Assertiveness training (to be discussed below) offers positive modelling experiences for adults.

Assertiveness training. A well-known and widely used technique for encouraging shy or submissive people to assert themselves, assertiveness training can be viewed as both a desensitising technique and a shaping procedure. The trainer, or group leader, might begin by stating the goal of the training, describing non-assertiveness as a common but handicapping trait, and assuring the group that active participation is voluntary. A next step is to get someone to volunteer to act out a very mild expression of assertiveness. The trainer might suggest a possible situation. After the performance, the encouraging comments of the trainer serve as reinforcement. Other volunteers are drawn into role-playing assertiveness in a variety of situations. The participants are then directed to attempt a real-life demonstration of an assertive position.

Three positive influences are operative in assertiveness training; positive reinforcement, the desensitising effect of engaging in behaviour that is gradually made more assertive, and the modelling effect of peer behaviour. Assertiveness training is a useful therapy when maladaptive anxiety is due to a lack of self-assertiveness. However, the treatment has little relevance for phobias involving non-personal situations.

Biofeedback. The essential element in biofeedback is immediately reporting back to a person any changes in autonomic activity, such as heart rate, blood pressure, changes in skin temperature, or galvanic skin response. Those are all associated with emotional responses and are involved in anxiety attacks and phobic reactions.

Until the early 1960s, voluntary control of autonomic responses was not thought to be possible. With the development of sensitive electronic devices that could accurately measure such physiological responses, it was soon discovered that they could be modified by such learning procedures as respondent and operant conditioning. With that discovery came the possibility that the unpleasant subjective experiences associated with heightened autonomic responses could be controlled by the process of what has been called biofeedback. The procedure is itself a rather simple one, although it requires the use of elaborate and expensive equipment. Autonomic responses are carefully measured, and the measurements are converted into visual or auditory signals which are quickly fed back to the client, who is then encouraged to use the signals in an effort to reduce the undesired autonomic response. The goal of treatment is to teach the client to control internal responses that may intensify the emotional responses associated with anxiety or panic reactions.

This goal has been achieved with biofeedback, although it is more difficult to maintain the improvement if the client depends on the specialised apparatus as opposed to practising the well-learned positive responses. However, modern biofeedback devices have become cheaper and more portable, enabling patients to take them home or, in some cases, purchase their own from high street chemist shops. Biofeedback techniques are still in their infancy.

Overview of behavioural therapy

Behaviour therapy is a widely-used and effective form of therapy based on sound theoretical principles and is the treatment of choice for a number of disorders, especially the anxiety disorders. It is also an empirical approach to therapy, being relatively easy to apply in a precise way and having a predictable outcome for the client.

Despite its effectiveness, the behavioural approach has its critics. In focusing on one aspect of behaviour at a time, behavioural therapy would appear to leave the client 'cold' ie with little insight into their problem and no treatment of them as a whole person. In practice this is not usually the case, with the client receiving constant explanation, encouragement and counselling from the therapist, with the possibility of involving other professionals to supplement this treatment in the manner of the eclectic approach. Psychodynamic school critics claim that behavioural therapy only treats the symptoms and not the cause of the disorder, leading to symptom substitution, ie, another symptom appearing to replace one that has been behaviourally removed. Behaviourists argue that there is no underlying cause, and that there is no scientific evidence for symptom substitution. Although the evidence from studies would tend to support the behaviourists' case in this debate, an eclectic approach to therapy would suggest that some harmonisation of these differing therapies may enhance the effectiveness of each in isolation.

Cognitive and cognitive–behavioural therapy

As early as 1950, Dollard and Miller, themselves both possessing strong behaviouristic leanings, had proposed that cognitions (previously excluded from psychological research by behaviourists) were as much events subject to psychological study and modification as were actions. They, in effect, proposed changing the stimulus–response formula to one including the organism with all its idiosyncratic cognitions in the formula, making it an SOR (stimulus organism response) arrangement.

Not until 1965 was this followed up in any systematic way. At that time, other behaviourists argued that S-R connections were not automatic, that what cognitions the individual brought to the situation influenced interpretations given to a stimulus and placed particular values on one response as compared with another response. Chapter 3 discussed those in detail. Examples of important cognitions that might influence what response an individual makes to a given stimulus are expectations, plans and competencies.

This new approach has frequently been called cognitive–behavioural therapy as a result of its being drawn from both behaviourism and cognitive psychology. However, the therapies in this area are probably best thought of as lying on a continuum, reaching from radical behaviourism at one extreme through cognitive–behavioural therapy to pure cognitive therapy (with little reference to behavioural change) at the other. Thus, the therapies in this area can be very similar, or quite different, depending on the degree to which the client's cognitive processes are given priority in the specific approach. The examples of therapeutic approaches briefly described below are representative of cognitive behavioural therapy in approaching behaviour-change by altering cognitions. These are the therapies of Albert Ellis, Aaron Beck and Donald Meichenbaum.

Albert Ellis: rational–emotive therapy

Ellis bases his therapeutic approach on what he calls the irrational beliefs individuals bring to situations that cause them to respond maladaptively. An example is the belief that one should be competent, intelligent and achieving in all situations. The client with such a belief sees depression-causing failure in many situations in which success should never have been expected, ie, in which expectations of successful performance were irrational.

Ellis's treatment is aggressive confrontation. After discovery of the client's principal irrational beliefs, Ellis bluntly spells out the irrationality of the belief and directs the client to minitor behaviour dictated by such beliefs and correct it. Between therapy sessions, the therapist encourages the client to behave in ways contrary to one or another of his or her irrational beliefs.

Ellis's proposed theory was so radical a departure from the well-established therapies that it was first looked upon scornfully by many clinicians. However, despite the discouraging start, one 1976 survey reported rational–emotive therapy to be one of the more widely used therapies.

Aaron Beck: cognitive–behaviour therapy

Close in theory to rational–emotive therapy, Beck's therapeutic methods are notably different. His methods are based initially on Beck's theory of depression, which he thought to be the result of irrational self-devaluation, an irrationally pessimistic view of one's life expectancies, and an irrationally gloomy view of the future.

The job of the therapist in Beck's approach is to draw out the client's defences of the unidentified irrational beliefs by Socratic questioning and, in that way, help the client perceive their irrationality. Beck's soft approach gradually allows clients to reach their own conclusions about the irrational nature of their beliefs. Beck has reported success in using his method for treatment of depression, anxiety and phobias.

Donald Meichenbaum: self-instructional therapy

The unique feature of Meichenbaum's therapy is self-talk. Behaviour, he believes, is influenced by what people say to themselves, before, during and after their actions. For example, a nail-biter, unhappy with the habit and unable to break it, might habitually self-talk in these words: 'There I go again. I'll never be able to stop.' Once the therapist is able to discover a self-talk pattern such as that one, he or she attempts to change it from a self-defeating to a coping way of talking. Meichenbaum gives this example: 'There I go again. Just this one nail. Then I'll stop . . . I knew the treatment wouldn't help me. I just can't control myself. Cut it out. You always make excuses for yourself. Take a slow, deep breath. Relax. Just think of sucking my finger in front of everybody. What a picture.' Clients are trained to practise encouraging self-talk on their own. The technique is useful not only in therapy but in everyday use to build up confidence. Nowadays it is possible to spot international sportsmen and women engaging in positive self-instruction at critical moments in their performance.

Overview of cognitive–behavioural therapy

Within the limits set by its goal, ie, a change in specific behaviour, research indicates positive outcomes for all three therapies described here. Control of depression has been particularly promising. The technique tends to focus on specific aspects of thought and behaviour and could be said to overlook the client's insight into their broader personality. As previously mentioned in the case of behavioural therapy, the therapist will in practice counsel the client beyond the confines of the immediate therapy, to some degree minimising the effects of any such limitation.

Again in common with behavioural therapy, cognitive–behavioural therapy may tend to act and have an effect within the confines of its own approach only. That is to say, the therapy may be delivered at the level of the client's thought processes in order to change them and the subsequent behaviour based on them. However, improvement in the client's thought patterns may not be reflected in their actual behaviour, their feelings or physical responses in the situations under scrutiny. Thus it may be useful to evaluate progress in each of these dimensions following a course of treatment. Cognitive-based therapies have tended to minimise the importance of the emotions in their approach.

Although it is a more recent approach, cognitive–behavioural therapy's successes are likely to encourage its growth in both therapeutic practice and theory development.

Biogenic therapies

Treatment of mental illness by direct alteration of bodily states has a long history. Even prehistoric people drilled holes into the skulls of those judged abnormal to allow evil spirits to excape. Long after that, primitive practices continued: purging the body of substances thought to cause mental disorder by laxatives; bleeding, which continued through the eighteenth century as a common medical practice for physical and mental illnesses.

Successful treatment of mental disorders has trailed far behind effective treatment of physical illness. But as bodily functions have become better understood, and as science has learned the effect of surgery, drugs, and even electricity on those functions, progress in treating physical disease has led, in the twentieth century, to increased physical treatment of mental disorders.

Virtually all the effective biogenic treatments of mental disorders were discovered by accident, often whilst pursuing the treatment of an unrelated physical disorder. Early biogenic treatments were very crude, often incurring a great deal of damage along with their therapeutic effects. In their defence, they were mostly developed for very severe and disabling disorders, for which there was no existing treatment, just a very bleak prognosis. Modern techniques, based on far greater knowledge of the underlying physiological processes, are greatly refined, minimising any side effects, and are used sparingly where physical change may be permanent. This is not to say that they carry no dangers, especially if over-zealously used.

One form of convulsive therapy – electroshock, as distinguished from insulin coma shock – is an effective form of therapy for severe depression. But the most progress in biogenic forms of treatment has come from developments in the field of pharmacology (the study of drugs and their effects on the body). Pharmaceutical drugs in current use aim at producing physiological changes that affect specific symptoms of mental illness. They have proven strikingly effective in the treatment of anxiety-based disorders, mood disorders, and for some symptoms of schizophrenia.

This section describes briefly electroconvulsive therapy, psychosurgery, and four types of drug treatment: antianxiety drugs, drugs for psychotic symptoms, antidepressant and antimanic drugs. All described treatments are administered in a medical setting.

Electro-convulsive therapy

Coma, induced by the administration of increasing dosages of insulin, a procedure that brings on shock and coma from an acute shortage of glucose (sugar) in the blood, was introduced in 1932. It was a drastic form of biogenic treatment with significant physiological complications, some fatal, but was nevertheless used widely in the treatment of schizophrenia until the end of the thirties, when it gradually faded away as a treatment because of a high rate of relapse and a relatively high fatality rate.

Beginning in 1938, electrically induced convulsions gradually became the preferred form of convulsive type therapy. Following a short period when electroshock was used to induce convulsions in schizophrenics, its use was shifted to the severely depressed.

Electroconvulsive therapy (ECT) is a very controversial treatment owing to the nature of its procedure and accounts of its use as a punishment, especially in popular fiction. In the early treatments the shock given was so severe and unchecked that bones were broken during the convulsions. The modern treatment contrasts with this in that the minimum voltage is used to cause a convulsion (which could be as mild as the arching of a toe) and the patient is given a muscle relaxant to prevent accidental injury. Although some patients are anxious about consenting to it and there have been some reports of memory loss, a number of clinicians consider it a treatment of choice for some patients with severe depression, especially where the use of drugs is less appropriate. Though not the best of motives, the cost-effectiveness of the treatment has led to an increase in its use for some disorders in recent years.

Psychosurgery

The first human psychosurgery was carried out in 1890 by Gottlieb Burckhardt. It was not considered successful, but in 1936 Egaz Moniz reported more promising results using a crude form of leucotomy. For a 20-year period (1935 to 1955), prefrontal lobotomy, which involved the destruction of precisely defined and minute parts of the brain, was a frequently used treatment for severe psychoses. While the operation did eliminate or reduce the most disturbing symptoms of the patients and thus made them more manageable, it also brought many of them to mere vegetative existence. Modern techniques have vastly minimised the extent of surgery needed to produce a therapeutic effect, and improved accuracy has been possible with the advent of the stereotactic methods (X-ray guided probe in the brain) and its computerisation. Even with these more refined procedures, and the greater knowledge of brain function, it is still difficult to remove unwanted behaviour or sensations by psychosurgical techniques without simultaneously creating unwanted side effects. The discovery of psychoactive drugs has reduced the need for psychosurgery and limited it to severe or stubborn cases of disturbance.

Drug therapies

The language of the brain is neurochemical, so it would seem logical to influence its malfunction by chemical means. Since its discovery, drug treatment has been the commonest form of therapy for mental disorders (and probably still is). Until recently, barbiturates (eg. Tuinal) and benzodiazepines (eg. Valium) were prescribed to vast numbers of people around the world for the relief of anxiety and to promote sleep. Discovery of the potential for dependency in the use of these particular medications has restricted their issue and initiated a search for less addictive replacements. The process of evolving new, more specific drugs is accelerating with time aided by three-dimensional computer modelling, which enables a hypothetical drug to be tested for 'fit' with models of the brain molecules before its manufacture. This progress is only slowed down by the careful testing of the new drug in clinical trials. We will look briefly at four areas where drug therapy has been particularly useful: anxiety (anxiolytics), schizophrenia (antipsychotics), depression (antidepressants) and bipolar disorder (antimanic/antidepressants).

Anxiolytics

Anxiety is a very common symptom in a number of psychological disorders and drug treatment provides immediate relief from the physical feelings and arousal resulting from anxiety. In some cases the anxiety does not recur and the therapy can be discontinued. In other cases there are psychological or environmental factors producing the anxiety which have to be addressed before drug treatment can be discontinued. More problematic are those patients where the anxiety is chronic, self-perpetuating or its cause cannot be removed, in which case long-term pharmacotherapy may be the only way of coping with the condition. In times of financial restraint and increased numbers of patients to deal with, a clinician may resort to long-term drug therapy by default with only a token gesture towards uncovering the source of the anxiety. Its use as a 'therapy of convenience' has often resulted in drug therapy being poorly regarded in the public eye.

Since the progressive disuse of barbiturates, there have been three main pharmacological treatments for conditions of anxiety: antidepressants, beta-blockers, and bezodiazepines and their newer replacements. Antidepressants will be dealt with in the relevant section below, although it is worth noting that their anxiolytic effect occurs outside of depression. As is the case with antidepressants, beta-blockers require a time of use before they become effective and so are not suited to short-term use. In addition, care has to be taken when discontinuing beta-blockers, especially if there are signs of heart problems in the patient. As referred to above, the benzodiazepines provided a revolution in the biogenic treatment of anxiety until their potential for dependency was realised during the last decade. Given their widespread use, the search for replacements has created a sense of urgency amongst the drug manufacturers. Low-dose neuroleptics (see the section below) have been used, but have their drawbacks. Some new alternatives such as buspirone show promise, but until a safe replacement is found, benzodiazepines will still be cautiously prescribed. The controversial antidepressant Prozac has also been used for anxiety disorders such as obsessive–compulsive disorder.

Antipsychotic drugs

Those drugs which control psychotic symptoms are referred to as antipsychotics, neuroleptics or major tranquillisers interchangeably. The tranquillising effect was originally a side effect of the use of such drugs for their antihistamine (anti-allergy) value. The French surgeon Henri Laborit then utilised these drugs for the purpose of calming patients prior to surgery. It was subsequently thought that the same calming effect may be useful for schizophrenic patients. The first of the group of drugs, termed phenothiazines, was synthesised. This was called chlorpromazine and was tested on individuals with schizophrenia, anxiety disorders, mania and depression. Although it calmed patients with the other disorders, it had a profound effect on the hallucinations, delusions and confusion suffered by schizophrenic patients and provided a much needed breakthrough in a disorder which was very difficult to manage. As with most drug therapies however, there were side effects such as involuntary muscular movements (similar to those in Parkinson's disease), other non-Parkinsonian movements or dyskinesias, dryness of the mouth and excessive sedation at higher doses, complicating their long-term use. The powerfully tranquillising effect of these substances at high doses leaves them open to abuse in controlling difficult patients, which has led to the term 'chemical strait-jacket' among the critics of pharmacotherapy.

More sophisticated antipsychotic medications were (and still are being) developed for both short- and long-term use, the latter being necessary in the case of schizophrenia where patients may be put on maintenance (or prophylactic) medication to prevent relapse during periods of recovery (remission). Clozapine, a relatively new but atypical (differently acting) antipsychotic drug, has fewer of the side effects of the usual medications for schizophrenia, but needs careful medical monitoring itself.

For around a third of the cases of schizophrenia, these medications are of limited value. These 'drug-resistant' cases include many of the patients with negative symptoms of schizophrenia (see chapter 12), making it difficult for them to be settled in the community at large. For many patients, the ability to function outside institutional care is entirely due to these medications, although this situation can be abused in the interests of economy by discharging patients prematurely. Patients discharged thus are very vulnerable, unlikely to continue medication and often form the core of the inner city homeless.

Antidepressant drugs

There have been a number of treatments for depression or unipolar mood disorder. Amphetamines had to be withdrawn for this purpose as they were open to abuse for their euphoric and sustained alertness effects and their highly addictive nature. MAO-inhibitors (eg. imipramine) inhibit the action of the enzyme monoamine oxidase, which breaks down certain neurotransmitters or brain chemicals. The net result of this is to increase the amount of the neurotransmitters, mainly noradrenaline and serotonin, available to the brain, producing the antidepressant effect. However MAO-inhibitors react adversely in the presence of other substances found in foods such as cheese and the combination can result in dangerous side effects.

Tricyclic-antidepressants (eg. tranylcyronize) repeat the re-uptake of these same neurotransmitters into the ends (or synapses) or neurones (brain cells), again increasing their availability and antidepressant effect. Although they have uncomfortable side effects, the tricyclic antidepressants do not have the dangerous reaction to food inherent in the MAO-inhibitors. Newer, 'second generation' drugs have also been developed for depression such as Buproprion. Another such drug is fluoxetine, which is marketed under the trade name 'Prozac' and has been associated with controversy following reports of side effects. These side effects have not been scientifically verified and Prozac has very rapidly become the most commonly prescribed psychoactive medication.

Antimanic/antidepressants

Bipolar disorder is a mood disorder which includes episodes of depression and extreme elation or mania. The treatment of choice for this is drug therapy with lithium, usually in its salt form as lithium carbonate. As this is available in its generic form and cannot be patented, its use has in the past been limited by the lack of profit incentive for the drug companies involved. The therapeutic effect is thought to stem from the working of ionic transport processes at the surface of neurones, ie a slowing of electrochemical systems. The drug needs careful medical monitoring especially in view of the fact that lithium is primarily a maintainence medication with the patient often taking it indefinitely. There is little tolerance in the dose levels of lithium and the initial dose and further adjustment also requires great care.

Lithium is effective for both the manic and depressive episodes in bipolar disorder but not so effective for unipolar depression, emphasising the distinction between the two disorders. Although the drug helps about 70 per cent of sufferers, some patients prefer to remain unmedicated due to the side effects of this medication, especially where the mania is not so severe, ie hypomania.

Other additions to the antimanic medications are carbamazapine and valproic acid.

Overview of biogenic therapies

The basic argument against biogenic therapies uses the analogy of the TV set. If there is something wrong with the programme, eg. an offensive newsreader, should one attempt to fix this by removing wiring or electrical components from the set, especially where this is a permanent 'treatment'? Modern drug, electrical and surgical procedures have tended to undermine this argument showing the human brain to be very different from the TV set with a far greater relationship between the 'hardware' and the 'program'. The permanent nature of many biogenic therapies remains a problem, especially where this is unavoidable as in maintenance medication. To this end, it is hoped that the increasing sophistication of the relatively crude biogenic methods may soon be a match for the highly complex brain systems that seem to be at fault.

Future developments in biogenic therapies will almost certainly include the controversial but expanding area of genetic counselling. This is where the genes responsible for some disorders can be identified in an individual and then allowing them the informed choice as to whether they should take the chance of possibly passing the disorder on to another generation.

Psychodynamic therapy

Considered by its exponents as more of an art form than a science, psychodynamic therapies are global in their expected outcome. Nowadays psychoanalysis is little used in some countries such as Britain, certainly in its original Freudian form, but in countries such as the USA it is a flourishing form of therapy and has many new variants on the orthodox Freudian method. Many of these new variations are so similar as to bring their independent existence into question, and as a consequence their exponents tend to over-emphasise their distinguishing characteristics. As a result of their limited use in modern therapy, both orthodox Freudian and post-Freudian approaches will be described only briefly in this chapter.

Freudian psychoanalysis

Orthodox Freudian psychoanalysis rests on Freud's psychodynamic theorising, assuming that a patient's current problems are repressed conflicts stemming from their childhood adjustments to others, usually their family. Freud, in a passive role, allowed the patient to consciously access these conflicts by the slow process of free association of ideas, guided principally by their unconscious gravitation towards the repressed experiences. In this method, the analyst's role is mainly that of interpreter whereas in the methods of those following Freud, the role is increased to include actively guiding the patient.

The setting and techniques of analysis

The traditional setting is a quiet room free of distraction with the client relaxed on a couch facing away from the therapist, who sits quietly taking notes for the majority of the time, only occasionally providing an interpretation of the client's words. This process may last years, usually at the rate of three one-hour sessions a week and involves the Freudian techniques of free association, dream analysis, analysis of resistance and analysis of transference.

In free association the client is directed to say whatever comes into their consciousness and in doing this not hold anything back, however bizarre, painful or insulting it may be. In time, the experienced analyst should be able to form a meaningful picture of the repressed feelings of the client from their seemingly random utterances, based on their unconscious connections which may be unique to the client. In guiding their understanding of the way in which the original conflict is influencing their current behaviour via some defence mechanism, the analyst enables the client to confront their problem without repression, sometimes a painful episode (rather than the 'sudden cure' portrayed in fiction).

In dream analysis Freud assumed that ego defences were weakened in sleep, allowing some expression of repressed material but in a symbolic, masked form. Freud examined the client's description of their dream, its manifest content, and looked for the unconscious meaning in the symbolism, its latent content. For example, a large menacing monster over a small child may symbolise their fear of an overbearing father. The dream's manifest content can form the basis for free association.

The analysis of resistance refers to the examination of the client's unconscious motivations when analysis is disrupted by the client cancelling sessions, drying up or suddenly feeling 'well'. When such disruption occurred following good progress Freud assumed the client to be defensively resisting further progress as this would involve painful experiences, usually a strategic step in the analysis with the degree of resistance indicating the degree of importance. Here the significance of the therapeutic alliance is evident as the analyst needs to explain the hidden motivations to the client.

One important aspect of the relationship between client and therapist is examined in the analysis of transference. Transference is where the client introduces the characteristics of a previous, and usually significant, relationship into the way they relate to the analyst. For the analyst, the transferring of emotions and interactions to them from the client's early life (sometimes referred to as transference neurosis) is a significant step in the analysis process and requires working through before further investigation is attempted.

Post-Freudian psychodynamic therapies

Orthodox Freudian analysis is rarely found nowadays, even in the USA. Modern psychodynamic therapists have moved from Freud's theoretical stance and modified his analytic method. However, the essential framework they use is as dependent on Freud's original work as the post- and neo-Freudian's theories were.

Post-Freudian theorists have given their names to these newer styles of analysis. Thus we have Jungian analysis complete with his theoretical distinctions from Freud, de-emphasising Freud's biological and sexual underpinnings and introducing Jungian concepts such as archetypes into the interpretation process. In the same way Adlerian analysis and Kleinian analysis emphasise power and very early relations, respectively. Modern psychodynamic theory gives greater prominence to the ego, with emphasis on how its conscious and rational function can be used to help the client back to normal adjustment, especially in terms of the client's interpersonal relations.

Modern psychodynamic therapists have also altered the process of therapy in some ways. The process is briefer, involving fewer sessions over a shorter period of time, thus the analysis is more focused with the therapist taking a more active role in leading the client, the lack of passivity being emphasised by the abandonment of the couch. Specific goals (eg. symptom relief) may be set, for which time frames are arranged and the focus for exploration is more likely to include the client's current life and interpersonal relations.

Overview of psychodynamic therapy

Although many clients pursue psychodynamic therapy in the USA, and there are respected centres in other countries such as the Tavistock clinic in Britain, psychodynamic theory and practice has not fared well in studies evaluating it, or comparing it with other therapies. There are a number of criticisms of the approach: the lack of scientific foundation; conflict between schools of analysis; its exclusiveness in relation to suitable clients.

Karl Popper asserts that a scientific theory should be capable of being tested or refuted and psychodynamic theory fails in this respect. The methods of analysis rely on intuition and insight, and are thus not open to scientific scrutiny with their success being judged in terms of their own analytic framework. Where theoretical approaches differ, these differences can be seen to undermine the psychodynamic perspective. In other words, if there is a valid psychodynamic approach then its fundamental principles should not vary from therapist to therapist. Psychoanalysis is an expensive and time-consuming process, which is only generally suitable for younger, verbally fluent clients who can afford it. This exclusivity applies today as it did in Freud's time when his clients tended to be wealthy, middle-class and female.

The psychoanalytic school has been criticised further, in that studies have found it less effective than other therapies, giving little improvement above that of non-analytic meetings, or in some cases, no treatment at all over a period of time. However, it is difficult to experimentally examine the outcome of psychodynamic therapy owing to the timescale involved.

Client-centred, existential and gestalt therapies

There are three therapeutic approaches which are distinct from the other forms of therapy both in terms of their practice and any theoretical basis. These are client-centred (humanistic based) therapy, existential therapy and gestalt therapy. They all share the aims of a 'global' outcome with the client achieving insight into the causes of their problem by becoming aware of repressed and unconscious material. Both client-centred and existential therapies also share the aim of encouraging self-actualisation in the client, in which they realise their potential to influence their own destiny. In addition to their perspectives (see chapter 4), these three therapies differ in their practice.

Client-centered therapy: the humanistic approach

Client-centred therapy has evolved from an original treatment described by Carl Rogers in 1950. He initially called it nondirective therapy. In subsequent publications, he has developed parallel developments to his therapeutic approach, a conceptual framework for it, the humanistic perspective. Rogers now prefers to call his approach person-centred therapy, thereby suggesting the equal standing of the two individuals involved in the therapeutic endeavour. A principal emphasis in the therapy is to create a profound and intensely personal relationship between therapist and client. To accomplish this, there are two principal thrusts made in therapeutic effort: helping the client to experience the therapist's unconditional regard, and the therapist's efforts to achieve empathy with the client in order to see the world as he or she does.

Unconditional positive regard

The most fundamental conviction giving direction to centred therapy is the belief that people are basically good even when they are doing 'bad' things. It is, Rogers would say, because they have not received unconditional positive regard from significant people in their lives that they do 'bad' things. Unless the therapist first attempts to meet the client's needs for positive regard, the client remains defensive and will not let down his or her psychological guard to relate honestly to the therapist. Unconditional acceptance of the client is the most important message a Rogerian therapist initially attempts to deliver.

Empathy with the client

Once the therapist feels that the message of unconditional positive regard has been felt by the client, the therapist uses his or her skills to relate to the client so empathically as to share the client's world as the client, in the security of the therapist's positive regard, reveals it. To move the client towards insight, a client-centred therapist listens intently to what the client is saying, and then reflects back their understanding of feelings expressed, conflicts and frustrations experienced, and goals envisioned. In that way, the therapist helps the client to clarify and know life experiences for what they are, and eventually to accept and deal with them.

Existential psychotherapy

The treatment practices of this school can best be described by stating the two major conceptual propositions of the existential perspective (discussed more fully in chapter 4). The first is that human beings are free to make their own choices but they must assume responsibility for the consequences of those choices. Their problems are of their own making and only they can undo them. The second proposition has been labelled 'the ontological context,' the 'here and now', the individual's 'lived world'. The therapist's goal in promoting insight is to focus on that world, to clarify it, and to confront the client with the problem of dealing with it. Existential therapeutic practices are whatever will bring into focus and clarify for the client those two determinants of the individual's problems.

The approaches of existential therapists and the techniques used vary from therapist to therapist. Two techniques used by Viktor Frank (1905–), a founder of the existential mode of therapy, illustrate the wide range of existential therapeutic practice that characterise existential therapy.

Paradoxical intervention

Here clients are encouraged to include, even to exaggerate, their symptoms – for example, to eat a gluttonous meal when overeating is the problem. The point is to drive home the individual's freedom of choice, even to choosing the very behaviour he or she considers the most undesirable.

Dereflection

This odd term refers to the second of Frank's therapeutic techniques, in which the client's attention is directed away from his or her symptoms, and then the therapist helps the client to visualise how much richer life could be, how much more enjoyment there could be, if the client was not so preoccupied with his or her symptoms.

To the extent that those exercises lead clients to take responsibility for what they do, they become conscious of what they are doing with their lives, more aware of their choices and values, with the possibility that their lives will then become more open, honest and meaningful; or, in existential terminology, more authentic.

Gestalt therapy

Drawn from a major German school of psychology, gestalt therapy emphasises the wholeness of the human being. It combines insight and behavioural change components, and requires, to begin with, that the client identify significant emotional conflicts of the past and then that the client act those out in a role-playing way. Clients are encouraged to be as vivid, even violent, as possible, stopping only at physical attack except, for example, such minor assaults as kicking over a chair or banging on a table.

Frederick (Fritz) Perls (1893–1970), the founder of gestalt therapy, maintains that in identifying an early emotional crisis and acting it out with strong feeling, clients will confront their feelings, assume responsibility for them and gradually control them. The ultimate goal of gestalt therapy is to integrate past disruptive feelings into a wholeness of personality – healthier, more spontaneous, open and honest – and, in that way, less maladaptive.

Overview of the humanistic, existential and gestalt therapies

Two principal criticisms have been levelled against these therapies: their failure to base therapeutic approaches on a fully developed and integrated view of the human personality, and a certain 'airiness' about what their goals in therapy are. They have also been criticised for the great variability in the approaches they take to therapy, but clients range so widely in the nature of their problems, their motivations and the circumstances of their lives, that diversity in treatment techniques might be considered more of a strength than a weakness.

The humanistic approach is less subject to those criticisms since Rogers has systematically developed a theory of personality that is widely respected. In order to submit his approach to outside evaluation, he has been one of the first to tape his therapy sessions for discussion and evaluation by peer groups.

On the positive side, these newer therapies have had an influence on the practice of more traditional psychodynamic approaches, especially in terms of the positive self-regard encouraged in the client. In addition, they have paved the way for the diversity of therapies in existence today and in this way helped the eclectic approach to therapy to evolve. However, it must be emphasised that although the majority of therapists have the well-being of the client as their primary aim, not all such diverse therapies or therapists are suitable for all clients and there have been occasions where therapy has worsened the client's condition.

Multiple-person therapies

One of the most distinctive developments in psychological treatment is multiple-person therapy. It takes a variety of forms. The most common of them are group therapy, peer group therapy, family therapy and marital counselling.

Group therapy

Simply defined, group therapy is the assembling of a group of people with psychological problems for the purpose of discussing their problems under the guidance of a professionally trained leader, usually a psychologist. Within that framework, group therapy can take a variety of specific forms determined principally by the theoretical perspective of the leader and the kinds of problems the participants bring.

Irwin Yalom identified a number of benefits that group therapy can offer. Groups can establish family-like relationships as well as a sense of belonging, enabling new ways of relating to others to be learned. Information exchange helps the individual to place their individual problem into context and to recognise that they are not alone in their plight. Participants can express feelings openly in this environment and have the opportunity to model their behaviour on others in the group.

A further development of this setting is to consider the dynamics of the group interaction as a form of psychoanalysis. The psychoanalyst S H Foulkes founded the Group Analytic Society in London in 1952, the *Group Analysis* journal in 1967 and was instrumental in the establishment of the Institute of Group Analysis in 1971. Foulkes looked at the dynamics of the group at different levels such as 'current adult relationships' or 'archetypal universal images' (taken from the work of Jung).

In each of these cases a professional therapist (or more than one therapist) is present to guide the group but, as in the next example, this is not always the case in multiple person therapy.

Peer group therapy

Some of the benefits of professionally-led groups can be found in peer groups, a group of individuals with similar problems – substance abusers, for example – who come together to give each other social support and possible guidance in solving problems. One widely known and well-thought-of peer group is Alcoholics Anonymous. The group is distinctive, since its operation is based on a number of strongly held beliefs: once an alcoholic, always an alcoholic; no one can strop drinking without help; in offering that help to others when called upon, one helps oneself. The programme is widely supported by former alcoholics who have benefited from it and by many clergy of all faiths. In treating alcoholism, most therapists consider the benefits of AA as supplementary to, rather than a replacement for, other treatments.

Family and marital therapy

A family with children or a childless couple can be thought of as a group with a structure, roles that are enacted and communicated among members, good or bad. Where any of those elements are warped – for example, a family structure with a domineering head, a scapegoat role for one of the children, or contradictory messages from parents, or sometimes from the same parent – problems will develop. Both family and marital therapy, with the help of a neutral outside person, attempt to bring maladaptive practices out into the open and effect changes in them.

A variety of techniques has been found useful in family and marital counselling. Two examples are: the communication approach, in which an effort is made to identify and discuss covertly contradictory messages used by one or more members of the family or marital group; and paradoxical intention, in which a family member will be encouraged to role-play offensive behaviour that has been identified and to learn how it affects other members, who are encouraged to react to it. An emphasis in marital therapy is dialogue between the two members, with an attempt to motivate each to express their feelings about what is wrong with their ways of talking to each other.

SUMMARY

A vast number of therapies are potentially available to the many clients seeking psychological help. Some of these therapies are very different in their approach whilst others are merely variants on the same theme. Although some therapies may be favoured above others, clinicians are increasingly taking an eclectic approach, in considering a number of perspectives and adopting a flexible range of therapies.

Therapists from the various schools of thought will also differ in the methods and goals set in their corresponding therapies. Behavioural, cognitive and biogenic approaches adopt a scientific approach with a specific, objective goal, ie, a change in the patient's behaviour or physical state. Psychodynamic, humanistic and to some extent multiple person therapies tend to resemble an applied art form with the more global aim of the client's insight into their problem.

Although individuals with problems are frequently having to choose from a range of private therapists as health services increasingly come under commercial control, the majority of these decisions are still made by the family doctor on behalf of the patient. The family doctor and hospital clinician are good sources of advice in this, as a client may be swayed by concerns for comfort rather than effectiveness. Regardless of the choice the client's rights within treatment should be respected, including their right to question the methods and discontinue if they wish.

Behavioural therapy is an action-orientated therapy with the goal of effecting specific behaviour change; it is therefore considered specific, not global, in its focus, and is looked upon as an applied science in its methodology. Seven aspects of behavioural therapy and three types of cognitive–behaviour therapies have been considered in this chapter.

EXTINCTION OF UNDESIRABLE BEHAVIOUR. Here is a form of behavioural therapy in which any reinforcement of the undesired response, no matter how subtle or indirect – for example, merely paying attention to it – is eliminated. A common form is 'time out' in which, for example, a misbehaving child is placed in a neutral situation and isolated from all social reinforcements of the undesired behaviour.

EXTINCTION BY SYSTEMATIC DESENSITISATION. Used principally to reduce anxiety or phobias, the goal here is to gradually allow the individual to experience graded levels of tension-producing stimuli under highly relaxed and protected circumstances until the individual becomes desensitised to the stimuli. Flooding and implosion are variants of this therapy.

SHAPING. To encourage an individual to move towards more complex but desirable social skills, for example, the therapist reinforces any behaviour that moves the individual in the desired direction.

MODELLING. This is a simple therapy in which a situation is created to allow the client to observe examples of the desired behaviour and to imitate them.

ASSERTIVENESS TRAINING. This is a group form of therapy in which an overly-inhibited individual is taught to be more assertive, that is, to be more demanding and expressive, by verbal instruction, protected trials, and then relatively safe real-life trials, which are later reported to the group.

BIOFEEDBACK. To learn to control varoious physiological responses that support undesired symptoms – for example, anxiety – the therapist arranges equipment so that the client can immediately get feedback on such physiological responses as pulse rate and blood pressure and then, while watching the feedback data, the client is directed to lower the physiological response.

In cognitive-oriented therapy, faulty ways of thinking, such as 'everyone must like me', that would lead to maladaptive submissive behaviour, are first identified and then corrected. Such thinking includes unrealistic expectations, impossible plans, and feelings of inferiority about one's competence. There are three principal cognitive therapies.

RATIONAL–EMOTIVE THERAPY. Developed by Albert Ellis, the therapy first identifies irrational beliefs. The therapist, in a confrontational fashion, then points out in multiple ways how irrational the belief is.

Aaron Beck instead uses a soft and gentle form of changing irrational beliefs. He employs a Socratic questioning method to reduce the grip of the irrational belief on the individual's behaviour.

Donald Meichenbaum encourages clients to take a self-instructional approach. He directs them to talk to themselves in ways that attack the false beliefs or encourage desired behaviour.

There are two principal forms of biogenic therapy. The most widely used is drug therapy. Drugs are now available to reduce anxiety, psychotic symptoms, depression and manic behaviour. All have at least a short-term effect on the undesired symptoms, but are most effectively used when accompanied or followed by psychotherapy. A second form of biogenic therapy, convulsive therapy, is occasionally used to treat severe and persistent depression.

Biogenic therapies are increasingly being used as scientific advances have led them away from their crude, sometimes brutal, pasts towards a more sophisticated, better targeted future. A number of drugs are available for the effective treatment of anxiety, psychotic symptoms, depression and manic-depressive behaviour, although there are problems with the long-term use of these, particularly with regard to a drug's side effects. Although little is understood of how electro-convulsive therapy brings about its therapeutic effect, it is very useful in treating some forms of depression, especially where other therapies have failed. A more drastic biogenic intervention is psychosurgery, which is essential in the case of some neurological conditions, but should be considered carefully for others, where there may be less permanent alternatives.

Psychodynamically-orientated therapy stems from the work of Freud and involves the client talking to the therapist, usually about early life experiences. This approach is little used in Britain but is still flourishing in the USA. The methods used include free-association, dream analysis, and analysis of resistance and transference. It is a lengthy and expensive treatment in its original form, but newer techniques developed by neo-Freudians and others have moved towards a briefer, more therapist-guided approach.

In client-centred, existential and gestalt therapies the client's way of regarding themselves, their freedom of choice and the integration of their past experiences and present selves respectively become the foci for therapy.

Much therapy takes place in a one-to-one relationship between client and therapist. In recent years, a variety of multiple-person therapies have been developed. The two principal types are peer group therapy, which may be led by a professionally trained leader or carried on by the clients themselves, as in Alcoholics Anonymous and family/marital therapy, in which all members of a family group are seen in therapy, both as a group and individually.

FURTHER READING

Abraham, K. & Kulhara, P. 1987. The efficacy of Electroconvulsive Therapy in the Treatment of Schizophrenia. *British Journal of Psychiatry*, 1512: 152–155.

Ayllon, T. & Azrin, N. 1965. The Measure and Reinforcement for Behaviour in Psychotics. *Journal of the Experimental Analysis of Behaviour*, 8: 357–383.

Bandura, A. 1969. *Principles of Behavior Modification*. New York: Holt, Rinehart and Winston.

Beck, A. T. 1976. *Cognitive Therapy and the Emotional Disorders*. New York: International University Press.

Bohart, A. & Todd, J. 1988. *Foundations of Clinical and Counselling Psychology*. London: Harper & Row.

British Psychological Society 1991. *Code of Conduct, Ethical Principles and Guidelines* (March). Leicester: BPS.

Clarkson, P. & Pokorny, M. 1994. *The Handbook of Psychotherapy*. London: Routledge.

Dryden, W. & Aveline, M. (Eds). 1988. *Group Therapy in Britain*. Milton Keynes: Open University Press.

Ellis, A. & R. A. Harper. 1975. *A New Guide to Rational Living*. Englewood Cliffs: Prentice Hall.

Grant, L. & Ness-Evans, A. 1994. *Principles of Behaviour Analysis*. HarperCollins.

Kruk, Z. & Pycock, Cl. 1983. *Neurotransmitters and Drugs* (2nd ed). London: Croom Helm.

Meichenbaum, D. 1977. *Cognitive-behavior Modification*. New York: Plenum.

Norcross, J.C. 1986. *Handbook of Eclectic Psychotherapy*. New York: Brunner/Mazel.

Rogers, C.R. 1986. *Client-centred Therapy*. London: Constable.

Schneidter, K & May, R. 1995. *The Psychology of Existence*. London: McGraw-Hill.

7 The Anxiety Disorders (Anxiety Neuroses): Anxiety Observed

Unwanted or excessive anxiety is one of the commonest conditions that brings an individual to seek therapy. Estimates suggest that between 10 and 20 per cent of the population suffer this condition at any one time.

Because of their prevalence and the suffering caused by them, much effort has been expended in attempting to understand the nature of these psychiatric illnesses. That understanding is not only necessary for the work of psychologists and psychiatrists, but is also of practical value in such other professional fields as medicine, social work, teaching, the ministry, and police work. These professionals are often asked to help those who suffer the disorder. It is also of usefulness in giving the healthy person insight into his or her own fears and occasional attacks of anxiety.

Beginning with a discussion of fear and anxiety in the context of disordered states, this chapter continues with an explanation of the differences in the classification of anxiety disorders (neuroses) in the ICD-10 and DSM-IV systems. It then describes four types of anxiety disorder; phobic disorder, post-traumatic stress disorder, generalised anxiety disorder, and obsessive–compulsive disorder, their symptoms and how widespread they are. Causal factors and therapeutic approaches are examined in chapter 9 after all the anxiety-related disorders have been described.

Fear and anxiety

Fear and anxiety are disturbing emotional states that occasionally beset the normal individual but appear more prominently and with more disruptive effects in the lives of those with anxiety disorders .

The two states overlap one another to a great extent and the subjective experience of them is very similar, as is their physiological basis. However, anxiety is seen as more abstract and less controllable than fear, as fear is usually closely associated with feared objects or situations, whereas anxiety can be context-free.

Fear

Fear has been considered to have four elements or dimensions which interact but can sometimes vary independently of one another. These are the cognitive, physiological (or somatic), emotional and behavioural components. The cognitive element refers to thoughts about feared or embarrassing events or entities, often exaggerating the client's inability to cope. The physiological element concerns the activity of the autonomic nervous system, which reacts to fear by preparing the body to 'fight or flee' the situation, increasing blood flow and respiration, preventing digestion leading to a 'knotted feeling' in the stomach and other somatic (bodily) reactions. These physical changes are interpreted by the individual as an emotional element of the fear which may be experienced as tearfulness, queasiness, apprehension, or even sexual arousal in some cases. The behavioural element of the process concerns the action taken by the individual which may be to confront or escape the situation. A more problematic action in disorders is that of maladaptive behaviour leading to the avoidance of the feared state.

Normal fears

The experience of fear in the face of real or threatened danger is a normal and healthy experience. Walking through a dangerous neighbourhood late at night will arouse some fearfulness in almost everyone. A construction worker atop a skyscraper may experience fright in the face of a strong wind. Few men in combat have escaped fear.

Abnormal fears

Fear is an abnormal response when there is no real or possible danger, and when most people would not be frightened, that is, when the fear is irrational. Examples of such fears are fright at the approach of a leashed dog or the presence of a cat rummaging in the rubbish. The abnormality of the fear is more certain when the fearful response takes an extreme form and severely limits the individual's life activities. Such fears are called phobias and are known to the phobic individual to be irrational.

Anxiety

Although anxiety has the same four elements as fear, it is to be distinguished from it. In anxiety, the cognitive element is vague and intellectually unfocused. Instead of awareness of a clear and known danger, the individual feels a generalised apprehensiveness. The predominating thought is that 'something terrible is going to happen to me'. In some cases the sufferer has no physical entity to escape or blame for their anxiety, or the source of the anxiety is benign and cannot justify their reactions.

The emotional and somatic elements of anxiety are similar to those of fear but usually more intense. An anxious response is maladaptive; yet short periods of anxiety can occur in the normal person. When anxiety is severe, persistent and disruptive of normal life activities, it signals an anxiety disorder.

The classification of anxiety disorders (neuroses)

ICD-10, the current version of this classificatory system refers to neurotic, stress-related and somatoform disorders and contains the classifications listed in Table 7-1. These include the DSM-IV items referred to in Table 7-2 under the heading of anxiety disorders and also those items described in the next chapter under the separate DSM-IV headings of somatoform and dissociative disorders. Thus the one group of disorders in ICD-10 is represented by three separate groups in DSM-IV.

In earlier versions of these diagnostic systems the word neurosis was used in the description of the earlier forms of these groups but has been eliminated from DSM-IV. This was a deliberate move away from any implication of causality for the disordered, placing the emphasis on the grouping of symptoms instead. The thinking behind the change in the DSM system was that 'the neuroses' grouping of the earlier systems assumed that anxiety was the basic symptom of each of these symptom groupings. However, observable anxiety is relatively absent from the somatoform and dissociative disorder groupings and has to be inferred from the somatic and evasive symptoms presented in these. Thus there is a distinction in the DSM system, intended to make it more objective and reliable, which is now partly reflected in the ICD system (in that 'neurotic' only refers to the anxiety disorders within the grouping).

TABLE 7.1 ICD-10 Classification of neurotic, stress-related, and somatoform disorders

Agoraphobia
Social phobias
Specific phobias
Panic disorder
Generalised anxiety state
Obsessive–compulsive disorder
Post-traumatic stress disorder
Adjustment disorders
Dissociative (conversion) disorders
Somatisation disorder
Hypochondriacal disorder
Persistent somatoform pain disorder

Table 7.2 DSM-IV Classification of anxiety disorders

Panic disorder
   Without agoraphobia
   With agoraphobia
Agoraphobia (without panic disorder)
Specific phobia
Social phobia
Obsessive–compulsive disorder
Post-traumatic stress disorder
Acute stress disorder
Generalised anxiety disorder
Anxiety disorder due to general medical condition

Phobic disorders

A phobia is a persistent fear reaction to some specific object or situation. The fear is disproportionate to the likelihood of danger. Some phobias, even though maladaptive, may have minimal influence on a person's activities: for example, a snake phobia will not much trouble a city dweller and hardly needs treatment. Other phobias may completely disrupt a person's life.

Types of phobia

There are four types of phobia: agoraphobia, panic disorder, social phobia and specific phobia. These are the most prevalent of the anxiety disorders and one of the commonest groups of psychological disorders overall, especially amongst women but less so in men.

Agoraphobia and panic disorder

These two disorders can be found to co-exist in patients. Such a co-existence of disorders is often referred to as 'comorbidity', and each can be found without the other. In a number of cases, comorbidity is a result of one disorder making the patient more susceptible to the other.

Agoraphobia. Far and away the most common phobia is agoraphobia (fear of the marketplace). The principal symptom is a fear that a panic attack will occur when the individual is in a crowd, in an open space, when travelling, or even on the street. The fear may be present without such an attack ever having materialised. A common concern is that away from home, there will be no one to help should the feared attack occur.

Agoraphobia is the most disabling of all the phobias; in many cases, the individual is unwilling to leave home, even to go out into the street. Agoraphobia individuals have more other psychological problems than those with other phobias: panic-proneness although in a 'safe' situation, depression, and anxiety. The phobia, in extreme cases, may be a lifelong illness, may occur intermittently, or may remit spontaneously.

Panic Disorder. Panic disorder is defined as an unexpected panic attack which is not provoked by the individual's being the centre of attention (which would classify it as a social phobia). The symptoms are multiple and terrifying, although usually lasting only a few minutes. Typical symptoms during the attack are shortness of breath, heart palpitations, profuse sweating, dizziness, and wild fear of dying or going insane.

Individuals suffering panic attacks are thought to be prone to 'catastrophic misinterpretation' of their physical reactions. For example, they may interpret their rising heart rate etc. as a sign of an impending panic attack, heart attack, or even death, consequently bringing about just such an escalation of their symptoms, in the manner of a self-fulfilling prophesy. Often such an attack seems to follow a disturbing life experience such as an enforced job change.

There is some evidence that agoraphobia and panic disorder may be genetically linked.

Social phobias

The exclusive concern of the social phobic is being seen or watched. Thus, they would avoid or worry about eating in restaurants, performing a job chore while being watched, speaking or performing in public. They avoid crowds because they may be watched critically. All of these experiences produce an acute sense of embarrassment and the urge to escape.

Social phobias most frequently develop in adolescence. Onset is gradual. Later on, the disorder may produce serious disruption in the life of the individual, causing him, for example, to give up job after job for fear of being watched. In social phobias, unlike agoraphobia, the individual usually experiences no other psychological disorder.

Specific phobias

The specific phobia (formerly simple phobia) most closely approximates the formal definitions of a phobia. It is a fear of a specific object or situation. Frequently it is a fear many normal people also feel, such as fear of darkness, heights, spiders, snakes or disease. The sufferer's response, however, is extreme. In the case of dog or cat phobias, for example, the fear response can make a normal life difficult or impossible.

Specific phobias fall into three categories: animal phobias, particularly dogs, cats and snakes, but also occasionally birds and insects; injury or disease phobias, also called nosophobia; and inanimate object phobias, such as heights. closed-in spaces (claustrophobia), aeroplane flights, storms or darkness.

In all the specific phobias, the individual goes to extreme lengths to avoid the source of fear. In nosophobia, for example, the phobic, although in apparent good health, worries constantly about contracting the feared disease. As a result, his or her behaviour is irrationally defensive as the individual constantly looks for symptoms and scrupulously avoids contacts that he or she imagines may cause the disease.

Prevalence of phobias

Agoraphobia, which accounts for half of the phobias, afflicts three to six per cent of the population. Panic disorder, with or without agoraphobia, affects one per cent of the population. Social phobias constitute about 10 per cent of all phobic reactions, occurring more frequently among women than men. Mild and unreported cases of stage fright, a form of social phobia, are probably much more prevalent. Although some estimates suggest that specific phobias only account for a small percentage of all phobias, fears of specific entities are commonly found amongst the non-clinical population. Most of these individuals' reactions are not as severe as those of the phobic, and of those that are severe only a small number present for treatment. The majority of them occur in women, and they often begin early in childhood.

Reactions to stress; acute stress disorder and post-traumatic stress disorder

What distinguishes acute stress disorders (formerly adjustment disorders) and post-traumatic stress disorders from phobic disorders is that the former are reactions to an actual undesirable and usually recent or ongoing event; the latter are fearful anticipations of an undesirable and unlikely event. Phobias grow out of fear, an anticipatory emotion; acute stress disorders and post-traumatic disorders grow out of stress, the consequence of a trying situation to which the individual is attempting to adjust. The phobic says 'something will happen to me'; the individual with a stress disorder says 'something has happened to me'.

Stressors

Stressors are adjustive demands made on the individual by such events as missing an important engagement or an argument with a spouse. But life also requires adjustive demands to very serious events: divorce, death of a loved one, and even such catastrophic events as military combat or natural disasters.

Adjustive demands imposed by stressors

Stressors impose one or another of three types of unpleasant psychological states to which the individual must adjust: frustration, conflict and pressure.

Frustration

When an obstacle, either external or internal, stands in the way of an individual's goal-striving, or when the individual can find no suitable goal to focus on, frustration results. External obstacles are unavailability of satisfying employment or rejection in a romantic pursuit; internal obstacles (characteristics of the individual) may be incompetence, physical handicap or handicapping personality traits.

Frustration causes anger, feelings of inadequacy, and self-deprecation. When prolonged, it can elicit the fight-or-flight reaction.

Conflict

Everyone's life is occasionally beset by conflict, minor or major. There are three patterns of conflict: approach–avoidance conflict, a situation in which the individual has reason both to approach a goal and to avoid it – a desirable goal has an undesirable consequence, such as an early marriage, which might necessitate giving up a university education; double-approach conflict, in which an individual seems doubly blessed in having to choose between two equally desirable goals – two attractive job offers, for example (although a happy type of problem, the stress in making a decision can be trying); and double-avoidance conflict, a problem of choosing between the devil and the deep blue sea. A poignant example is that of the elderly individual who must have a painful and risky operation or continue to live with a painful and debilitating medical condition.

The stress of conflict causes troubling thoughts, fits and starts of activity, and, if prolonged, emotional exhaustion.

Pressure

Life, especially for young people, can be full of pressure: to do well at school, to get a job, to 'shape up'. Sometimes the pressure is from parents; at other times it may be self-imposed. Surprisingly, the latter may be the more stressful. Later on, life may bring other pressure; from a spouse, from the demands of a job, from pressure to care for elderly parents.

Factors affecting severity of stress

The severity of stress is judged by its disruptive effects on the individual's behaviour. Disruptive effects are determined by characteristics of the stressor, the psychic make-up of the individual, and by the social supports available to him or her.

Characteristics of the stressor

Duration, cumulative effect, and multiple stressors all increase the extent of the disruption. A second day of a nagging headache is disruptive indeed. Mounting stress can lead to a breakdown. One stressor after another is bound to weaken the individual's capacity to adjust. Some values in life are especially meaningful; an attack on them can be extremely stressful.

The individual's experiences and expectations

Vulnerability and the presence of positive coping mechanisms are key to understanding the likely disruptive effects of stress. A lifetime of unrewarding experiences, negative interpersonal relations or frail health can make an individual especially vulnerable, even to relatively minor stress. The coping techniques life has taught an individual are critical. A problem-solving approach reduces the negative impact of stress; the very effort of doing something helps. If the experiences of an individual lead them to assume that they are helpless to effectively reduce the stress, then this 'learned helplessness' can produce apathy in the face of future stressors. The short-term benefits of defensive behaviour may provide some relief for immediate symptoms but may also lead to greater complications in the long term.

Social supports

Never are helpful relatives or friends more appreciated than in times of stress; to talk with, to suggest options, and to provide tension-relieving social activities. Group support, although less personal, can provide helpful resources. Support can be found in social and religious groups, and professional help from counselling, social and other services.

Reactions to stress

There are three principal reactions to stress: task-oriented behaviour, defensive behaviour, and, ultimately, decompensation.

Task-oriented behaviour

The secure and confident individual, taught by earlier life experiences to be resourceful, will direct efforts towards a goal in a task-oriented way, meeting the adjustive demands of the stressor, yet protecting himself or herself from mental distress, or behavioural disorganisation.

Typical task-oriented responses include objectively appraising the situation, developing possible options, selecting one and observing its impact on the stress. The more secure the individual, the more flexible the individual, the more willingness there will be to change behaviour in response to feedback obtained from its effect. If attempting to change the situation won't work, a person may shift to making personal changes. Examples are lowering one's expectations or changing goals, changing the natures of one's emotional responses in interpersonal situations, becoming less demanding or critical, or leaving the situation altogether to seek other satisfactions, eg. divorce in an impossible marriage.

Defence-oriented behaviour

Defensive behaviour has both short-term positive effects and long-term maladaptive effects. Expressive defensive behaviour, such as crying, repetitive talking or mourning behaviour, has the short-term effect of releasing tension, and also, perhaps, gaining sympathy. But as time goes on and no effort is made to attack the problem, the individual seeks escape in one or another of the defence mechanisms. Principal mechanisms are denial of unacceptable reality ('things are not really that bad'), repression, in which painful thoughts or feelings are excluded from consciousness, sometimes only temporarily, by resorting to a frenzy of unimportant but distracting activities; or regression to earlier, less mature and less demanding forms of behaviour – for example, setting up babyish or at least childish, forms of dependency, and in that way escaping responsibility for solving the problem.

Defence mechanisms do offer protection from the most extreme demands of the stressor, but they are, in the long run, maladaptive because they are self-deceptive, distort reality, and deflect problem-solving effort.

Decompensation

The most seriously disruptive reaction to stress is decompensation. When the stressor situation is extremely demanding or prolonged – a siege of combat duty or being held captive as a hostage or in a concentration camp, for example – any adaptive capacities of the individual may be overwhelmed. Efficiency is lost, vulnerability to other stressors is increased, somatic disorders develop, and complete exhaustion makes any self-sustaining effort impossible. Decompensation is considered in biological and psychological terms and can also be seen in the behaviour of the sufferer.

Biological decompensation. The general adaptation syndrome of Hans Selye is widely used as a model to picture the course of biological decompensation under extreme stress. He pictures three phases of that reaction: the alarm phase, during which the body's resources are called into action and all the body's physiological defences against assault are alerted; the stage of resistance, a prolonged period when the biological resources of the individual work at maximum level to reduce the stress; collapse results when the body's resources are exhausted. The consequence is disintegration, and if outside help is not provided, death.

Psychological decompensation. The psychological analogue follows exactly the stages of biological decompensation except that psychological, not biological, resources are used. In the alarm stage, the individual is alert and mobilises 'mental' energies. Emotional arousal, tension and sharpened sensory power lead to the initiation of coping responses. The stage of resistance intensifies task-related or defensive behaviour. If stress continues unabated, the individual's mental resources are expended. Individuals vary in the length of time that that process will take. When decompensation does take place, psychological collapse matches biological collapse.

Behavioural decompensation. The behavioural reaction to stress is an overt display of the psychological reaction. During the alarm stage the individual indulges in a number of behaviours in the hope that something will be adaptive. Failure to produce a form of behaving which is successful and not merely defensive leads to inactivity paralleling the exhaustion of psychological and biological decompensation. This experience of ineffectiveness can then lead to inactivity in the face of future events, eliminating the possibility of then producing an adaptive response. This is what was referred to earlier as 'learned helplessness'.

Acute stress disorder, adjustment disorder and post-traumatic stress disorder

DSM-IV lists three stress-related disorders: acute stress disorder, post-traumatic stress disorder (PTSD) and, under an independent heading, adjustment disorder. The previous edition, DSR-IIIR, listed adjustment disorder in place of acute stress disorder and this is also true of the current ICD-10 system. The distinction made in the earlier version included the assumption that the stressful event in adjustment disorder was within normal experience and for PTSD was outside of normal experience (eg. an earthquake). This distinction is difficult to make objectively and in DSM-IV differentiation of acute disorder and PTSD can be made more objectively by reference to the duration of the symptoms, whereas adjustment disorder is now listed as a separate heading in DSM-IV. As all three disorders are still current each is briefly described in this section.

Acute stress disorder

Most people who undergo a stressful event show some symptoms of stress: crying, restlessness, sleep disruption, feelings of hopelessness, perhaps with depression; there may also be erratic reckless behaviour which may be anti-social. If the symptoms persist for two days but no longer than four weeks, a diagnosis of acute stress disorder can be made, with more persistent symptoms indicating a diagnosis of PTSD. Some individuals are found to be more vulnerable to these symptoms than others, who may cope with the event with little or no stress reaction. Thus for vulnerable individuals, pronounced reactions to stress within the normally expected duration, irrespective of the type of stressful event, can be categorised as acute stress disorder.

Adjustment disorder

Adjustment disorder refers to a reaction (within three months) to an identifiable stressful event resulting in the kind of symptoms listed above. In the case of adjustment disorder, the precipitating event is within the range of normal human experience, although its duration may be longer than normal, and the impact magnified by having more than one event at the same time eg. a death in the family co-occurring with moving home. As with acute stress disorder, some individuals seem to be more vulnerable than others. The symptoms of adjustment disorder are expected to remit when the stressor has passed or the sufferer achieves a more adaptive level of adjustment, with or without therapy.

Both acute stress disorder and adjustment disorder are considered to be of limited duration and although common, exact prevalence figures are difficult to ascertain.

Post-traumatic stress disorder

Diagnosing PTSD rests on two essential elements: the occurrence of a catastrophic stressor in the past history of the individual and a characteristic pattern of symptoms.

Stressors associated with PTSD

These are experiences that do not occur to the average individual: military combat, rape, being held hostage, captivity in a concentration camp or natural disasters such as flooding or earthquakes. Almost everyone would show significant signs of distress following any of those experiences. The condition is PTSD if three highly specific symptoms occur.

Characteristic symptoms

The three symptom patterns are as follows:
- Reliving the event, which may take the form of recurrent nightmares, sharp periodic recollections of the event or feeling as though the event was recurring.

- Numbness to outside events or withdrawal from such events.
- Cognitive and emotional symptoms, such as memory impairment, inability to concentrate, feelings of guilt about those who did not survive, exaggerated startle response, and avoidance of activities that stir up memories of the trauma.

Prevalence

In recent years, the extent of PTSD symptoms suffered by those who experienced traumatic events during the two world wars is being recognised. Retrospective diagnoses such as these are an indication of the difficulties involved in estimating the prevalence of PTSD and, in addition, studies suggest that few victims of such traumatic events escape any such symptoms. Although some individuals would seem more susceptible to PTSD, reports of these events have clearly shown that some stressors can produce symptoms in otherwise normal individuals.

The reports vary depending on the nature of the catastrophe (human-made catastrophes cause a more severe response), its duration, and the criteria used in the determination of the presence of symptoms.

Here follows some representative figures on prevalence: in a night-club fire in which 500 persons died, more that 50 per cent of the survivors required treatment for severe shock; one study reports that about 70 per cent of those with prolonged combat experience in the Vietnam War experienced PTSD. Among survivors of concentration camp captivity, 90 per cent still experienced disturbing symptoms 20 years later.

Reactions to three specific types of catastrophe

Natural disasters, rape and military combat tend to produce somewhat different patterns of response.

Natural disasters. Psychological reports of reactions to earthquakes, tornadoes and similar disasters outline three phases through which victims move, in what they have called the disaster syndrome. The stages are these: the shock phase, which is characterised by numbness and immobility (in extreme cases, there may also be memory loss and disorientation); the stage of suggestibility, in which victims are passive and submissive to the directions of rescuers; the recovery phase, in which most victims begin to function more efficiently and to be more rational about their plight.

Amongst those who do not recover in this way, there are early symptoms of a more lasting PTSD disorder, perhaps because of vulnerability created by earlier life experiences. A striking and lingering symptom among many victims of natural disaster is a sense of guilt about their own behaviour and their survival, and the deaths of others, especially loved ones.

Military combat and concentration camp captivity. Although these experiences are equally gruelling, except for duration, typical reactions differ. In military combat breakdown, the prime symptom is depression and apparent physical exhaustion. Among concentration camp victims, there are marked personality changes: heightened irritability, the stealing of food and other comforts from other victims, and pandering to the enemy. One study characterises the reactions as debility, dependence and dread. Guilt reactions are prominent in both types of catastrophe.

Rape. The reaction to rape, although the experience is an individual one and not a mass experience, is increasingly being categorised as PTSD, with the addition of the special label, 'rape trauma syndrome'. Reactions fall into two quite different patterns. About half the victims respond expressively with crying, sobbing, fear and anxiety; the other half show a first response that is highly controlled, with a calm exterior masking the underlying turmoil. The calm is soon followed by periods of terror in which the victim relives the dreadful experience and experiences symptoms typical of PTSD. One-quarter of the women victims continue to show stress symptoms years after the rape. Sexual dysfunction, as might be expected, is a long-term problem. A beneficial activity in relieving symptoms seems to be involvement with the women's movement or with rape crisis centres.

Obsessive–compulsive disorder

The primary symptoms characterising obsessive–compulsive disorder are preoccupying yet unwanted thoughts (obsessions) and repetitive, irresistible and undesired behaviour (compulsions). Both types of behaviour in mild form commonly appear in the general population. Though maladaptive, they do little harm.

In severe form, they are disruptive of ordinary life activities and are often associated with depression.

Normal obsessions

Examples are persistent thoughts, sometimes unpleasant, about an upcoming event, a longed-for experience, a repeated melody that cannot be cleared from consciousness or a persistent thought that harm will come to a loved one. They are irritating and maladaptive but not pathological.

Normal compulsions

Examples are repeatedly checking to see that a door has been locked or a stove turned off, or that the baby is safely asleep. The superstitious and repetitive behaviour of batters and bowlers in a professional game of cricket is a good example of compulsive behaviour which results from the past reinforcement of this repetitive behaviour.

Normal compulsions, for the most part, occur only sporadically. Although they are bothersome, they cause no major disruption in the individual's life.

Pathological obsessions

Pathological obsessions do not easily pass away, they are not easily controlled, and they significantly disrupt the individual's life. Their content is often unacceptably sexual or hostile and violent.

Pathological compulsions

These are most often of one of two types: a checking ritual or a cleansing ritual. They are not the occasional rituals of many normal people but use hours of the day in compulsive behaviour. In the checking ritual, the individual may go from checking all the doors to checking all the windows, repeating the process again and again in fear that he or she may have missed one. In the cleansing compulsion, the sufferer seems driven to engage in some cleansing activity to get rid of contamination or to prevent it. It most often takes the form of hand washing, which may, in extreme cases, take place a hundred or more times a day, every time an object has been touched.

Other symptoms of obsessive–compulsive disorder

With both obsessions and compulsions, the individual finds no satisfaction in either the thoughts or the actions. In the former case, the person's helplessness in driving the thoughts out of his or her mind is depressing; with compulsions, the individual is continuously fearful about the result of not carrying them out.

In the most extreme cases of obsessive thinking, the individual does not listen to what other people are saying; their words are lost in the obsession. With compulsions, the individual can do little else during the day except to carry out the compulsion and is thus prevented from living a normal life in the family or at work.

The compulsions of this disorder should be distinguished from 'compulsive eating' or 'compulsive gambling'. In those activities, the individual finds satisfaction (even though of an abnormal sort) in the activity itself. In the obsessive–compulsive disorder, the compulsion is forced on the individual to avoid the tension of *not* carrying it out.

Prevalence

The rate of obsessive–compulsive disorder seems to vary very little between nationalities. Prevalence of this disorder in its fully developed form has been found to be very low, less than three per cent of psychiatric referrals or between one and two per cent of the general population. However the symptoms of the disorder can be frequently found in other disorders such as mood disorders.

It is more common among women. Onset is usually in adolescence or early adulthood, though it may develop in childhood.

Generalised anxiety disorder

In all the anxiety disorders (or neuroses) described so far, there is anxiety with some object, activity or event and the individual sufferer then tends to employ destructive or self-defeating defensive behaviour to reduce the pain of anxiety, at least in the short term. In generalised anxiety, the central symptom is the anxiety itself, persistent (for at least a month) and unfocused. It is sometimes labelled 'free-floating anxiety'. It may be centred in one or two aspects of the individual's life – for example, school grades or career prospects – but it usually cuts across all the individual's life adjustments.

Symptomatology

There are four sets of specific symptoms: physiological, apprehensiveness, hypervigilance, and scanning behaviour.

Motor symptoms

Here the muscles of the body adopt a posture of timidity. The brow is furrowed, muscles are tense and achy, the face is strained. There is a pronounced startle reaction, jumpiness and fidgeting.

Physiological symptoms

Accompanying the external motor symptoms are internal bodily changes, such as dizziness, heart pounding, frequent urination, hot flushes, and cold and clammy hands or feet.

Apprehensiveness

The individual ruminates and worries about possible impending calamities: a school exam will be failed, a parent will become ill or die, something dreadful will happen.

Vigilance and scanning

The individual seems always to be on edge, looking for trouble that rarely, if ever, comes. As a result, there is a distractability, loss of capacity to concentrate, and difficulty in falling asleep.

A secondary problem that frequently develops is overuse of alcohol or anxiety-reducing drugs. These are activities which, in the long run, can be more damaging than the anxiety.

Prevalence

Possibly because many individuals somehow manage to live with this disorder without seeking psychological help, except in occasional conversations with the family doctor, little is known about its prevalence, age of onset or sex differences in the occurrence of the illness.

SUMMARY

Estimates indicate that the anxiety-based disorders (those described in this and the following chapter), together constitute the most prevalent form of psychiatric illness. Exact prevalence of the disorders is difficult to ascertain as only a small proportion of the many sufferers present themselves for treatment, but estimates are usually of the order of 10–12 per cent of the adult population. DSM-IV no longer mentions the term 'neurosis', a term that has been used in this context since the days of Freud, dividing these 'neuroses' into anxiety, dissociative and somatoform disorders. Nevertheless, because of the explanatory value of the concept of neurosis and its broad familiarity, most psychologists continue to use the term.

This chapter has described the disorders categorised in the diagnostic manual under the heading, anxiety disorders: phobic disorder (including panic disorder), in which the central anxiety characterising all of those disorders is expressed in an irrational fear; post-traumatic stress disorder, in which a variety of debilitating symptoms develops as the direct result of a catastrophic event; obsessive–compulsive disorder, in which the core anxiety is masked by tensions associated with the individual's obsessions and compulsions; and generalised anxiety, in which a disruptive, unfocused apprehensiveness is the predominating symptom.

FURTHER READING

Edelmann, R. 1991. *Anxiety: Theory, Research and Intervention in Clinical and Health Psychology*. Wiley.

Grant, L., H. L. Sweetland, J. Yager and M. Gest. 1981. Quality of Life Events in Relation to Psychiatric Symptoms. *Archives of General Psychiatry*, 38(3): 335–339.

Hollander, J., Zohar, J., Marazzitti, D. & Oliver, B. 1994. *Current Insights in Obsessive–Compulsive Disorder*. Wiley.

Meyer, C. B. and S. E. Taylor. 1986. Adjustment to Rape. *Journal of Personality and Social Psychology*, 50: 1226–1234.

Rapee, R. 1991. Generalised Anxiety Disorder: A Review of Clinical Features and Theoretical Concepts. *Clinical Psychology Review*, 11: 419–440.

Snaith, P. 1991. *Clinical Neurosis* (2nd ed). Oxford University Press.

8 Somatoform and Dissociative Disorders: Anxiety Inferred

The anxiety-based disorders discussed in this chapter are still grouped with those of the previous chapter in the ICD-10, where the older heading neurotic disorder is preserved. The DSM-IV system has removed this term, presenting these disorders on axis 1 under three headings: anxiety disorders (discussed in the last chapter), somatoform and dissociative disorders. The separate heading of factitious disorder is also described here owing to its similarity to the somatoform disorders. The DSM system emphasises the symptomatology rather than the aetiology of these disorder groups. The title of this chapter indicates that anxiety is to be inferred because there are few, if any, overt signs of anxiety in these disorder groups and psychodynamic approaches have traditionally inferred it from the symptoms presented.

Somatoform disorders

A sharpened focus on some bodily function, with the development of physical symptoms or complaints without an organic basis, is the common characteristic of the somatoform disorder. Dysfunctions produced by the symptoms range from specialised sensory or motor disability through preoccupation with, and symptom formation in, any bodily function, to hypersensitivity to pain. There are five somatoform disorders listed in DSM-IV: conversion disorder, hypochondriasis, somatisation disorder, pain disorder and body dysmorphic disorder. Factitious disorder is a separate heading but will also be described briefly in this chapter.

Conversion disorder

Conversion disorder was originally known as hysterical neurosis (conversion type), a reminder of its place in Freud's clinical writings, and is still referred to as 'hysterical conversion' by some practitioners.

This disorder almost always develops in a setting of extreme stress, eg. military combat or the death of a loved one. Its course is usually dramatic and short-lived. While symptoms are present, the individual may be severely handicapped; and in unusual circumstances, the primary symptoms may persist for a prolonged period, causing atrophy or contracture of the muscle groups involved.

Symptomatology

The primary symptom is a loss or alteration in physical functioning without a detectable organic basis. Despite the seriousness of the physical disability, the individual commonly reacts with a relative lack of concern, an attitude which has been named, 'la belle indifference'.

Common forms of the primary symptoms are paralysis, fits or seizures, aphonia (loss of speech), blindness, or amnesia. Of significance in the conversion disorder is the secondary gain (side benefit) that results from the disability: the primary symptom is a defensive reaction enabling the individual to escape from or avoid a psychologically stressful situation without the need to admit to responsibility for doing so.

The primary symptom is beyond the individual's control and is not seen by the person as related to the stressful situation which is being avoided. There may be a grey area in which awareness of the secondary gain (including insurance payments or court settlements) tends to worsen or prolong the symptoms.

For convenience, the primary symptoms are grouped into three categories: sensory symptoms, motor symptoms and visceral symptoms.

Sensory symptoms. These include anaesthesia, excessive sensitivity to strong stimulation (hyperesthesia), loss of sense of pain (analgesia), and unusual symptoms such as tingling or crawling sensations.

Motor symptoms. In motor symptoms, any of the body's muscle groups may be involved: arms, legs, vocal chords. Included are tremors, tics (involuntary twitches), and disorganised mobility or paralysis.

Viceral symptoms. Examples are trouble with swallowing, frequent belching, spells of coughing or vomiting, all carried to an uncommon extreme.

In both sensory and motor symptoms, the areas affected may not correspond at all to the nerve distribution in the area.

Caution in diagnosis

Because conversion disorder can simulate almost every known physical ailment, care must be taken to exclude any organic basis for the disorder. Support for the psychological basis of the disorder can be found in such criteria as these: an attitude of indifference to the symptom; a lack of correspondence between the known symptoms of a particular disease and the individual's complaints; the disappearance of the symptom under hypnosis or narcosis (drug-produced sleep); or suggestibility of the individual in responding to the therapist's efforts to control or change the symptom.

Prevalence

Although conversion disorder, along with hypochondriasis and the dissociative disorders of amnesia and multiple personality, are given much notoriety in news stories, on television and in films, they are, as a group, much less prevalent than other anxiety-based disorders and seem to have been more prevalent in past years than they are today. Only about five per cent of all the neurotic disorders fall into this category today. Onset is usually early in life, but may occur at any time. It is usually triggered by a severely stressful event.

Hypochondriasis

In conversion disorder, the individual develops a functional disorder (psychologically caused) and is indifferent to it; contrariwise, in hypochondriasis, the hypochondriac has no real physical disability or illness but is nevertheless preoccupied with and worried about ordinary bodily functions, eg. heartbeat, bowel movement, minor sores, blemishes or coughs. The individual reads into the sensations of normal bodily functions the presence of a feared disease.

Symptomatology

The individual magnifies small irregularities in bodily functions and expresses concern about the general state of his or her health. He or she may shift from one bodily system to another or focus on one major system, eg. persistent concern about a heart condition. There is much doctoring as the individual goes from one doctor to another after being told that there is nothing wrong. Hypochondriacs find pleasure in criticising doctors and explaining to family and friends why the doctors are wrong.

Those with hypochondriasis experience some impairment in interpersonal relationships and in job performance. But often, except for frequent job changes, the illness is limited to years of doctoring and endless descriptions of symptoms with no other impact on functioning. In extreme cases, however, the individual may become a lifetime invalid and take to bed with a complete collapse of independent activity.

Prevalence

The ailment is frequently seen by family doctors, but because of the individual's resistance to accepting a psychological interpretation of the illness, the disorder carries over to rejecting any referral to a mental health facility. Onset is any time from adolescence to the forties. Hypochondriasis affects men and women equally.

Somatisation disorder

Although listed as a separate disorder in the DSM-IV somatisation disorder very much resembles hypochondriasis, with only nuances distinguishing the two.

Symptomatology

The primary symptom in somatisation disorder is multiple complaints of physical ailments over a long period of time, beginning before the age of 30. By this age, DSM-IV requires this history of complaints to include at least: four pain complaints at different sites in the, body, two gastrointestinal symptoms, one sexual symptom and one pseudoneurological symptom.

One strong difference between hypochondriasis and this disorder is in the attitude the individual has to the physical disorder. The hypochondriac fears there might be a physical disorder, yet seems to hope that the doctor will find it upon examination. In somatisation disorder, the symptoms of physical disorder are believed to be real, and the individual is convinced of its existence and worried about it. There may also be dramatic reactions to this strongly-held belief: submission to unnecessary surgery, threats of suicide, or seeking release in substance abuse.

Perhaps understandably, given his or her belief in the presence of serious illness, the individual is frequently depressed and finds difficulty in living an orderly existence.

Prevalence

Prevalence is difficult to establish as the disorder was only distinguished from conversion disorder in DSM-III, but around one per cent of females seem to be affected. The figure for males is unknown as they are rarely diagnosed as having the disorder although a greater number conform to the criteria. This sex bias may be partly a legacy of its original title of 'hysteria'.

Pain disorder

The primary – indeed, the only – symptom in pain disorder (except when other psychiatric disorders are also present) is severe and prolonged pain in the absence of a physical basis for it. Diagnosis may be difficult, since extensive medical testing may be necessary to rule out an organic basis.

Certain psychological cues may be helpful in clarifying the functional (psychological) nature of the illness: a conflictful or stressful event preceding the experience of pain, the existence of secondary gain if pain is present, or the individual's persistent need of attention. A history of past physical injury or illness, which no longer accounts for the pain, may nevertheless provide the patient with justification for complaining.

No reliable figures on prevalence are available, although reports from family doctors suggest that it is a frequently seen disorder. It is again more common among women than men.

Body dysmorphic disorder

Most individuals believe that some part of their body is less than perfect, and may even take some action to alter this by exercise or, in extreme cases, by surgery. In body dysmorphic disorder this concern over a single body part is wholly disproportionate to any 'imperfection' and it is usually the case that as such the defect is imaginary. Facial features are the usual focus of attention and remedies are repeatedly appealed for, including multiple attempts to receive plastic surgery. The preoccupation with the body part leads to a great deal of distress and distraction producing disruption in the individual's life.

The inclusion of body dysmorphic disorder with the somatoform disorders has been considered controversial and the disorder seems to be subject to cultural variation. As a consequence of these factors and its recent inclusion, exact prevalence figures are not available.

Factitious disorder

Factitious disorder is a separate heading in DSM-IV but the symptoms are similar to those of the somatoform disorders. Individuals with this disorder deliberately present with physical or psychological symptoms for which there is no actual basis. Unlike conversion disorder, factitious disorder 'patients' are consciously aware of the lack of underlying pathology. In another DSM-IV item, malingering, there is some advantage to the patient in presenting fake disorders, but in factitious disorder the only goal seems to be maintaining the role of a sick person. These disorders are also similar to Munchhausen's syndrome, where the patient actively seeks medical treatment (eg. surgery) by faking symptoms.

Dissociative disorders

The DSM-IV lists four varieties of dissociative disorder: dissociative amnesia, dissociative fugue, dissociative identity disorder (formerly multiple personality disorder) and depersonalisation disorder. In the ICD system the heading 'dissociative (conversion) disorders' is used, indicating more overlap with the concept of conversion disorder. Although dissociative disorders receive attention from the media, they are relatively uncommon diagnoses.

They have in common an attempt by the individual to escape from a significant personal problem or responsibility by severing, forgetting or distancing himself or herself from the core personality.

Dissociative amnesia

Amnesia is inability to recall or identify one's past experiences or identity. It may result from a variety of pathological brain conditions. When it develops as a response to extreme psychosocial stress, it is labelled dissociative amnesia.

Common examples of such stressful situations are: living through a catastrophic event such as an earthquake, a personally experienced threat of death or major injury, the need to escape an unacceptable impulse or an unbearable life situation; for example, facing a bankruptcy or other financial calamity.

Symptomatology

Symptom formation in dissociative amnesia may follow any one of four different patterns: localised amnesia, selective amnesia, generalised amnesia, and continuous amnesia.

Localised amnesia. In this pattern of psychogenic amnesia, the individual fails to recall all details of a particular event, usually one that is traumatic. An example would be failing to recall all the circumstances of an atrocious rape. Localised amnesia is the most common form of psychogenic amnesia.

Selective amnesia. Following closely behind localised amnesia in prevalence is selective amnesia. Here the individual blanks out certain details of a traumatising experience. An example of this would be the uninjured survivor of an accident in which the rest of their family perished being able to remember making funeral arrangements but selectively unable to remember discussions with other family members about the funeral.

Generalised and continuous amnesia. The least common forms of psychogenic amnesia are generalised amnesia, in which the individual may be unable to recall the details of an entire lifetime, and continuous amnesia, in which the person 'forgets' everything subsequent to a specific time or event, including the present.

Prevalence

Dissociative amnesia of the first or second type is a fairly common initial response to catastrophic events. When it results from more common stressful experiences which most people are able to overcome, it is an example of disordered functioning.

Dissociative fugue

Although listed in the DSM-IV as an independent clinical syndrome, a fugue is simply a type of generalised amnesia in which the added feature is a flight from family, problem and location, and the creation of a new identity which may be maintained for days, weeks or months, and even for years. The individual's behaviour during fugue states of limited duration may be very casual, such as going from one cinema to another without being able to recall where he has been. An uncommon pattern is for the person to create a whole new life.

Dissociative identity disorder

The most dramatic of all the dissociative disorders is dissociative identity disorder, in which there is the occurrence in the same individual of two or more personalities, each of which is able, for an interval in the person's life, to live a stable life and to take control of the person's life, although not necessarily in a mentally healthy way.

Symptomatology

In dissociative identity disorder the individual acts out one or another of coexisting personalities. In a famous case of Dr. Prince, there were 17 different personalities, each quite different from the others. One personality may be the governing or good personality, and another full of unacceptable and immoral impulses. There may be complete or partial amnesia during the existence of other personalities, or a pattern in which whatever becomes known to the principal personality (but to that person only) is known to all other personalities (asymmetrical amnesia). There have been a number of notorious cases of feigned multiple personality, with the purpose in mind to evade criminal culpabilty. One means of detecting the feigned disorder is the likelihood in such cases that the amnesia is symmetrical, ie what is known by any of the 'individuals' is known by all.

Impaired functioning or illegal behaviour may occur in a form that depends on the number and characteristics of the personalities assumed.

Prevalence

Much has yet to be learned about dissociative identity disorder. There is no certainty about even its prevalence. In past decades, only two hundred known cases were listed – not a very significant number among the millions afflicted with other neurotic disorders. During the late eighties several psychologists have reported larger numbers. These reports come only from the United States and are thought by some psychologists to be the result of suggestion under hypnosis or therapy. More recently, increased diagnosis of dissociative identity disorder has been reported in a number of countries including Britain. This may be due to an increased awareness of the disorder amongst clinicians and less scepticism about symptoms when they are presented. Onset is frequently reported in late adolescence and among young adult females often with a history of abuse in childhood.

Depersonalisation disorder

Mild feelings of depersonalisation or feelings of being someone other than oneself or of not being able to control one's movements are common human experiences, to more that 30 per cent of young adults. When the symptom is recurrent and impairs social or occupational adjustment, the person is said to be suffering from depersonalisation disorder.

Symptomatology

The disorder is characterised by a change in the person's perception of self and in the way self-identity is experienced. Strange feelings about the size of arms and legs abound, and the individual has a sense of looking at his or her body from a distance, sometimes described as floating above the body and looking down at it. Despite the extreme distortion of self-awareness, the individual's reality-testing function remains intact, and there are no delusions or hallucinations. The sufferer may experience difficulty of recall and a loss of awareness of time going by.

Other people may be seen as mechanical or dead. Others, or the self, may be described as existing only in a dream. The individual often worries about going insane.

Feelings of depersonalisation are frequently accompanied by spells of dizziness, depression and obsessive thoughts.

Prevalence

Onset is sudden, rarely occurring after mid-life but symptoms linger, disappearing only gradually. The disorder is extremely rare: no sex differences are reported.

Causal factors in anxiety, somatoform and dissociative disorders

These DSM disorder classifications are found under the single heading 'neurotic, stress-related and somatoform disorders' in ICD-10, which implies that some factor unifies them. Most approaches see a maladaptive reaction to anxiety as the central causal feature of these disorders. This reaction, or neurotic behaviour, is usually an inefficient way of dealing with the demands of life or an unusual/stressful experience, in the absence of normal coping mechanisms. The neurotic behaviour will then become exaggerated as its ineffectiveness at reducing anxiety becomes more evident.

The principal causes of neurotic behaviour

The five perspectives on the cause of neurotic behaviour referred to here each emphasise differing factors in the history of the problem. Each perspective is more or less useful as an explanation depending on the specific disorder under consideration. The behavioural perspective makes the fewest assumptions in the cause of neurotic behaviour, focusing on faulty learning experiences. The psychodynamic view incorporates a somewhat elaborate explanation of how the behaviour arises from early negative interpersonal experiences and is an integral part of maladaptive defence mechanisms. Biogenic approaches view life events as secondary to a biological (usually genetic) predisposition to neurotic behaviour. Cognitive–behavioural approaches see maladaptive thinking processes as the origin of the behaviour and the humanistic–existential approach sees neurotic behaviour as the product of blocked personal growth.

Where an approach assumes a predisposing vulnerability, the onset of the disorder is often assumed to be triggered by some stressful event.

The behavioural/learning perspective; faulty learning

This perspective considers three possible paths to the development of neurotic behaviour: failure to learn adaptive coping mechanisms; learning anxiety through conditioning experiences; or learning neurotic patterns by observation or modelling.

Failure to learn adaptive coping mechanisms. Faced with parents such as those described in the following section and the consequent feelings of inadequacy and insecurity that they elicit, a child judges himself or herself to be incompetent and fails to make an effort to learn adequate coping mechanisms. Failure or the expectation of failure leads to mounting anxiety and the possibility of disordered behaviour as a defence.

Learning anxiety through conditioning. The two forms of conditioning, classical and operant provide different explanations of how neurotic behaviour originates. Classical conditioning provides the most plausible (and parsimonious) explanation of anxiety disorders, especially phobias. In these, an action, object or event comes to be associated with an inappropriate fear response. This associated fear produces anxiety on subsequent encounters with the feared stimulus leading the sufferer to avoid it. As a consequence the sufferer becomes sensitised to this stimulus and this is often generalised to similar stimuli. The behaviourist J B Watson demonstrated this process in what would today be considered an unethical study.

He associated fear with a rat in a young child with no such existing fears by making a loud noise whenever the child reached for the animal. The child went on to develop a specific phobia for rats which was generalised to other furry creatures.

In avoiding the feared stimulus, the sufferer feels relief at not experiencing the associated anxiety, negatively reinforcing the avoidance behaviour by a process of operant conditioning. This provides an explanation for the 'neurotic paradox', or the paradoxical way in which fears strengthen rather than dying out as a result of the process of extinction. Operant conditioning also provides its own explanation of neurotic behaviour creation in that negative reinforcement increases the frequency of the initial response. This would be the case with obsessive– compulsive disorder where the compulsive behaviour maladaptively provides short-term relief from the anxiety provoked by the obsessive thoughts.

Observation and modelling. A criticism of avoidance learning is its failure to take account of cognitive activity, such as images and verbal self-statements, which may operate in the absence of concrete stimuli for anxiety. It leaves no room for learning anxiety by observation of others or modelling the behaviour of parents. Observation of a horrifying experience involving someone else or the model of a worrying, fretful parent can be carried over into a child's life and serve as the basis for anxiety.

The psychodynamic perspective; damaged interpersonal relations

Stemming from the early work of Freud but going beyond it, the psychodynamic perspective gives great weight to the causal effect of such early life experiences as deprivation, parental oversolicitude and seductiveness, and paternal authoritarianism. It explains the development of neurotic symptoms as a defence against the anxiety produced by the later effects of such paternal treatment.

Early deprivation. Emotional or physical neglect by parents can cause a child to feel unwanted and unworthy. Those feelings generate anxiety in the face of normal exigencies in life. Sometimes such deprivation takes the form of coldness and intellectualisation in paternal attitudes which lack any nurturing warmth, even though perfunctory care is provided.

Oversolicitude and seductiveness. When a parent blocks the develpment of independence and self-confidence through overbearing supervision and control, worries fretfully about the child, or disturbs the child by seductive physical or emotional behaviour, the child falters in developing adequate coping behaviour required for adjusting to life's ups and downs, with resultant anxiety when those trials appear.

Authoritarianism and dictatorial parental behaviour. Dogmatic behaviour in setting absolute and detailed rules, or rigid standards and demands for submissiveness and total compliance, can cause one of two reactions: rebellion, which brings its own problems, or anxiety aroused by the hostile thoughts and aggressiveness, covertly felt, in an overly submissive child. Unable to contain the anxiety the child's reaction may take the form of inhibitory tensions which forbid involvement in ordinary life activities. With those satisfactions lost, the next step might very well be the development of an anxiety disorder.

The biogenic perspective

The biogenic perspective has attempted to throw light on two issues with regard to the etiology of these disorders.

The issues as to why some people develop the disorders when others undergoing the same experiences do not would seem to indicate a weakness or predisposition which is likely to be of a genetic or physiological nature. Evidence for this is stronger for some neurotic disorders than others. An inherent sensitivity of the autonomic nervous system or some neurotransmitter systems could predispose that individual to anxiety disorders including panic disorder and generalised anxiety disorder. However, the results of studies of the inheritability of these disorders are not clear cut: although some support a genetic factor, other studies fail to agree with these results.

A further issue is that of the physical mechanism by which the disorder's symptoms are expressed, and thus the area of physiology that may be abnormal in individual sufferers. In generalised anxiety disorder for example, the action of the neurotransmitter noradrenaline is thought to be implicated in this way.

The biogenic approach has been found less useful in the explanation of dissociative disorders. However, among the somatoform disorders, conversion disorder symptoms tend to occur on the left side of the body, indicating some brain hemisphere difference in the disorder.

The cognitive–behavioural pespective

The cognitive–behavioural perspective is increasingly being adopted as it is more flexible than the strictly behavioural approach, but makes fewer assumptions than the psychodynamic approach in accounting for internal processes. In this approach, the anxieties felt by a client are the result of maladaptive thinking patterns, usually those which exaggerate fears and can lead to an over-reaction to events or objects, as in the exaggerated unsubstantiated fears suffered in obsessive–compulsive disorder. Another good example of a cognitive origin of neurotic behaviour would be the 'catastrophic misinterpretation' of bodily sensations put forward in the explanation of panic disorder. It is the distorted cognitive element which mediates between perception and the initiation of action that lies at the centre of the cognitive–behavioural explanation of anxiety-based disorders.

The humanistic–existential perspective; blocked personal growth

The humanistic perspective shares with the psychodynamic view a concern about the individual's early interpersonal experiences which, it states, may limit the individual's capacity for self-actualisation and growth. It is, according to this school, that discrepancy between the individual's damaged self-image and the ideal self envisioned by the person that causes anxiety and the move towards neurotic behaviour.

The emphasis in the existential perspective is on the concept of authenticity. Individuals suffering anxiety disorder, it is stated, are uncomfortable living with the gap that exists between the true self and the self which the adjustment to society demands. It is this conflict, no doubt stemming back to vulnerability produced by early life experiences, which produces the anxiety and ultimately the psychological disorder. Others accept the personality mask imposed by society, forgetting their real selves. In so doing, they avoid the troubling anxiety.

Therapeutic approaches to anxiety, somatoform and dissociative disorders (neurotic disorders)

Chapter 6 provides a detailed description of the various treatment approaches to psychiatric illness. Here only brief reference is made to those that are found useful in treating the above disorders.

Therapeutic effectiveness in treating neurotic behaviour

Examining and statistically analysing 81 controlled studies of the results in treating neurotic individuals, one major research study reports that the treated individuals were more functional (met their responsibilities) than 80 per cent of untreated individuals with the same level of illness. The relapse rate after treatment was slight.

Basic considerations and goal of therapy for neurotic disorders

The choice of a particular therapy is to some extent dictated by the specific disorder being treated, as for each diagnosis and individual's level of functioning, some therapies are more effective than others.

Increasingly, the eclectic approach to therapy is being adopted, in which methods from any of the main perspectives are used by the therapist to suit the individual's needs; for example, a programme of behavioural treatment may be supplemented by more psychodynamic or humanistic approaches. In eclectic approaches the immediate aims of therapy, such as elimination of symptoms, improved function and increased insight, may be more important than theoretical perspective in determining treatment choice.

Specific treatment approaches to neurotic disorders

Specifically and briefly, each of the five perspectives offers particular treatment techniques.

The behavioural perspective

The techniques of systematic desensitisation flooding and, in the case of obsessive–compulsive disorder, response prevention, are the treatments of choice for the anxiety disorders, being far more effective than other approaches.

The cognitive–behavioural perspective

Therapies of this perspective have become very useful supplements to other therapies, especially drug and behavioural therapies. The usefulness of them on their own is dependent on the specific disorder in question.

The biogenic perspective

The evidence for a genetic role in these disorders is not sufficient to consider genetic counselling (with a view to preventing the passing on of genetic traits). Although drug therapy is the most commonly used therapy for anxiety disorders, this should only be thought of as a temporary measure whilst behavioural or other therapy is employed to remove the neurotic behaviour. In more extreme cases of anxiety, somatoform and dissociative disorders, electro-convulsive therapy or even psychosurgery may be resorted to.

The psychodynamic perspective

Although the value of this approach in the form of psychoanalysis is difficult to substantiate in many areas, it is most effective in dealing with dissociative disorders, and to some extent conversion disorder. It is often the treatment of choice in unifying the different personalities in dissociative identity disorder.

The humanistic–existential perspective

Therapies such as client-centred therapy can help individuals face up to their feelings and expectations, perhaps becoming better able to cope with situations causing anxiety. Although a useful supplement, these therapies are less able to deal with more extreme symptoms.

SUMMARY

The DSM-IV no longer classifies the psychological disorders described in the preceding two chapters as neuroses. Instead, it groups them into three major syndromes (clusters of syndromes). They are the anxiety disorders (which have been described in chapter 7), somatoform disorders, and dissociative disorders. The term 'neurotic' has been retained in ICD-10 to head a single disorder grouping, which includes most of the items in the three DSM groupings.

The primary symptoms of conversion disorder is a loss or alteration in physical functioning – for example, blindness or paralysis – without a detectable organic basis. In hypochondriasis, the individual has no real physical disability, but nevertheless is preoccupied with and worried about ordinary bodily processes. The primary symptom of somatisation disorder (which may be easily confused with hypochondriasis) is multiple complaints of physical ailments over a long period of time, a set of symptoms that cause the individual to go from doctor to doctor, seeking confirmation of his or her complaints. Pain disorder causes severe and prolonged pain in the absence of any physical basis for it. In body dysmorphic disorder, a physical feature, usually part of the face, is a source of disproportionate dissatisfaction and intensive corrective surgery may be sought. Factitious disorder is a separate heading in DSM-IV where individuals consciously present physical symptoms without a physical basis and without any apparent gain or purpose other than medical attention.

The dissociative disorders include dissociative amnesia, dissociative fugue, dissociative identity disorder and depersonalisation disorder. All those disorders have in common an attempt by the individual to escape from an unpleasant life situation by forgetting or distancing himself or herself from the core personality. In dissociative amnesia, the individual loses memory for some aspect of previous existence. The amnesia may be selective or general. In fugue, the individual not only 'forgets', but also creates a new life, escaping from the old life. In dissociative identity disorder (formerly multiple personality disorder), there is in the same individual, the occurrence of two or more personalities, each of which controls the individual's behaviour for some period of time.

Depersonalisation disorder causes a loss of self-identity and strange feelings about the victim's body and his or her relation to other people. The suffering individual may feel as though existence is a dream.

FURTHER READING

Bass, C. & Benjamin, S. 1993. The Management of Chronic Somatisation. *British Journal of Psychiatry*, 162: 472–480.

Fahy, T. 1988. The Diagnosis of Multiple Personality Disorder. A Critical Review. *British Journal of Psychiatry*, 152: 597–606.

Kellner, R. 1985. Functional Somatic Symptoms and Hypochondriasis: A Survey of Empirical Studies. *Archives of General Psychiatry*, 42: 821–833.

Pilowsky, I. 1989. Illness behaviour and neuroses. *Current Opinion in Psychiatry*, 2: 217–224.

Snaith, P. 1991. *Clinical Neurosis*. Oxford University Press.

Stern, R. & Drummond, L. 1991. *The Practice of Behavioural and Cognitive Psychotherapy*. Cambridge University Press.

Thigpen, C. H. & H. Cleddey. 1957. *The Three Faces of Eve*. New York: McGraw-Hill.

9 Psychological Factors Affecting Physical Condition and Eating Disorders

Before the arrival on the philosophical front of scientific rationalism, the topic of this chapter, the effect of the psychological on the physical, would have been labelled a mind/body problem. Pre-scientific humanity, led by its philosophers and religious leaders, considered mind and body to be independent entities.

The dichotomy for the two was an easy concept for primitive humans. It provided an explanation of death. There was the body, but it was lifeless. Its spirit, or soul, had left it. It was dead. That way of thinking about body and mind became a part of the Judeo-Christian religious beliefs. The concept dominated religious thinking throughout the Middle Ages and was formally elaborated in the thirteenth century in the scholastic philosophy of Thomas Aquinas, who was an influential interpreter of Christian thought in medieval Europe.

In philosophical, apart from religious, thought, Plato created a complete dichotomy between body and mind. The 'rabble of the senses', which he equated to bodily processes, was a different order of being and knowing from the world of ideas, created out of the thought processes, and unchanging.

Other philosophers were even more extreme in their thinking: for example Berkeley, the eighteenth-century Irish philosopher and idealist, maintained that everything was mind. Whatever existed, existed in the mind only.

Rene Descartes removed the mind/body problem from religious thinking and constructed a dual way of thinking about the two. Early scientists Galileo and Newton provided the kind of early scientific thinking that brought medicine and psychology to their modern interpretation of mind/body relationships. The two put philosophical and religious thinking aside as not within their province. Their thinking blazed the way for modern theory, which considers that body and mind function as a unit.

The fact that psychological factors can lead to physical disease has been recognised in previous editions of the DSM classification system and this is also true of ICD-10 which lists the heading 'physiological dysfunction associated with mental factors', where sexual disorders are also included. In DSM-IV, the link is less clear, with the implication that predisposing psychological factors should not be listed as psychological disorders. However, they are still an important influence on health and will be described in this chapter. Eating disorders are a new separate heading in DSM-IV and will also be described here, although they could equally logically be considered with substance-related disorders.

Interactions between psychological and physical functioning

We have seen, in the history of abnormal psychology, that at least by 1883, with the publication of Emil Kraepelin's textbook on psychiatry, recognition of the influence of somatic (bodily) changes on mental activities was commonplace. The important effect of organic conditions on particular mental disorders had been recognised well before Kraepelin; but his broadened interpretation of those influences give additional emphasis to their presence.

The acceptance of influence in the opposite direction, that is, the mind influencing physical disease, was a much later concept. There were exceptions: for years, observant physicians had noted the cause-and-effect relationship, for example, between physical ailments, such as high blood pressure and ulcers, and worrying and chronic emotional tension. Conditions known as psychosomatic disorders had been introduced gradually into classifications of medical diagnoses.

But it was not until the 1960s that a much-broadened way of thinking developed about the influence of psychic factors on bodily processes. During that period, physiological psychologists, aided by the development of sensitive electronic instruments that could precisely measure physiological responses such as blood pressure, pulse rate and bodily temperature, demonstrated that those responses, once thought to be involuntary, could be brought under voluntary control. This work was very influential in establishing that psychological effort could affect autonomic system responses such as heart rate.

That research generated speculation that perhaps psychological influences also operated, even in cancer and infectious disease. There are reports in the psychological and medical literature that make it unwise to dismiss those speculations out of hand. In 1991, for example, carefully controlled, parallel studies conducted in Pitttsburgh in the United States, and in Salisbury, England, led to the conclusion that high levels of psychological stress could almost double a person's chance of catching a cold. Apparently the stress lowers bodily resistance to viral infections. While much more work needs to be done with those particular physical disorders, in recent years, a dozen or more illnesses – for example, coronary heart disorders, ulcers, asthma and migraine headaches – have been related to psychological causation. They were first labelled as psychosomatic illnesses; then the Diagnostic and Statistical Manual listed them separately as psychophysiological disorders. The current DSM-IV no longer specifies these on axis 1, but under 'other conditions that may be a focus of clinical attention' the heading 'Psychological factors affecting medical condition' allows the inclusion of psychological factors that may influence the medical conditions rated on axis III. These physical conditions include ulcers, asthma, headaches, hypertension and coronary heart disease. In the case of eating disorders, these are specified on axis I of the DSM-IV and for these obesity or emaciation would be listed on axis III.

Models of psychological–physical interaction

Science today knows that the brain is the bodily organ that controls both bodily activities and subjective events, such as cognitions and feelings; but what biological processes does the brain command to produce the interaction between mind and body? We examine two models that suggest how that interaction takes place: the diathesis-stress model and the general adaptation syndrome.

Diathesis–stress model

The diathesis–stress model states that human disorders, both physical and mental, result from the presence of a diathesis, or predisposition for developing a particular disease, for example, tuberculosis or schizophrenia. The diathesis, or vulnerability, may result from genetic deficiencies from earlier physical disease, for example, whooping cough in infancy. That predisposition is provoked by a stressor, that is, a disturbing bodily invader, in the case of a physical disorder, or a disturbing early-life emotional experience, in the case of a psychological disorder. Here we will be applying the model to psychophysiological disorders, which may be defined as disorders in which the psychological events, such as cognitions, and feelings, contribute to the development of physical disorders or diseases. The stressors on which we focus in this discussion are distressing emotional experiences.

The damage caused by a stressor acting on a vulnerability is dependent upon the coping mechanisms available to the individual. Those mechanisms are outcomes of positive earlier experiences: for example, favourable parent/child relationships or positive learning experiences when facing earlier stressful situations. To put it more succinctly, psychologically healthy individuals ordinarily deal with stress in ways that do not trigger physical vulnerabilities to produce a psychophysiological disorder.

The general adaptation syndrome

Seyle's adaptation model does not deal with causal factors, but rather describes the sequential way in which the individual psychologically and physically responds to stressful events. He identifies three stages of the organism's response to a stressor event. The first stage is the alarm phase, which arouses the individual's defences, either psychological defences or the defensive reactions of the autonomic system, which in general prepare the body for action. The second stage is the stage of resistance, in which all the resources of the individual are employed defensively. If they succeed, there is no third stage; but if they are inadequate, a third stage of collapse is reached, called decompensation, in which the tensions produced by the stressor cannot be reduced, and there is the likelihood that those tensions will now combine with a vulnerability in the body, and a psychophysiological disorder will develop. Once developed, the disorder may remain as a lifetime weakness of the individual that flares up whenever stressor events threaten.

By integrating those two models, we can, at least hypothetically, outline the development of a psychophysiological disorder. Examining the specific ways in which stressors affect the individual will further clarify the etiology of those disorders.

The role of stress in psychophysiological disorders

In chapter 7, we examined the influence of stressors on human behaviour. Stressors can range from catastrophic events to highly personal events – divorce, for instance – which arouse the body's autonomic system and, in turn, its immune system.

Autonomic reactions to stress

Walter Cannon, very early in the history of what was then called psychosomatic illness (1936), postulated that in order to survive, our primitive ancestors had need of bodily reactions that would respond to the life-and-death struggle of their daily lives. Cannon called that process 'the fight-or-flight' pattern. He identified the autonomic nervous system as the mechanism that prepared the individual to make either of those responses.

The autonomic system responds to external events that threaten the individual by initiating a whole series of physiological changes, Seyle's 'alarm reaction'. These changes increase the individual's capacity to respond to external danger, either to fight or to flee. The autonomic nervous system increases breathing and heart pumping in order to increase the body's oxygen supply, causes flushing, which brings a supply of blood to the musculature, increases the blood sugar for increased energy, causes pupillary dilation for increased acuity in seeing, and increases the flow of neurotransmitter secretions to increase the speed of reactions.

All of those physiological changes aided primitive humans in their 'fight' to survive. The effects of those changes were consumed in the battle or race that ensued; but for civilised humans, most of whose threats are not physical but the emotional tensions of intangible psychological situations, those autonomic changes are not helpful or even relevant, and only intensify apprehensiveness and anxiety. There is no way to directly reverse this arousal and its physiological consequences. These stressful states of physiological activity, especially where repeated or prolonged, may eventually adversely affect one or several organs of the body.

They affect most often those individuals who are vulnerable, possibly for genetic reasons. With the body weakened in that way, the individual's immune system may be called into action.

The immune system

The body's alarm reaction, in itself, does not cause infection or disease, but may, over time, reduce the body's defences by impairing the functioning of the immune system. The components of the immune system are the blood, thymus, bone marrow, spleen, and lymph glands. The system is a complex one, and there is much yet that medical science has to learn about its functioning. We focus here on a critical element, the white blood cells.

The white blood cells of the immune system recognise and destroy pathogens that have invaded the body, such as bacteria, viruses, fungi and tumours. Their massive presence in the lymph system and the bloodstream is indicated by the importance and complexity of the work done by the white cells. In the healthy individual, there are over one thousand billion cells.

We do know there are two types of white blood cells, lymphocytes and phagocytes. Their composition and function are somewhat different, but their combined functions are to detect and destroy antigens (invasive agents in the body) or foreign cells. Any impairment of the functioning of the immune system will reduce its ability to protect the body against disease-causing elements or damaging tissue growth. For example, the cancerous disease leukaemia reduces the white cell count and therefore weakens the body's resistance to other diseases. The frightening effect of AIDS is basically its attack on the body's immune system, which leaves the body defenceless against a multitude of antigens, some of which can prove fatal.

Physical effects of psychological stressors

One explanation of the way in which psychological tensions cause or contribute to the development of physical disease is that some physiological changes of the psychologically intense alarm reaction may impair the effective working of the immune system. It is known, for example, that in the alarm reaction, there is a release into the bloodstream of such neurohormones as catecholamine, cortical steroids, and endorphins, each of which, in different ways, lowers the efficiency of the white blood cells in their defensive work. The effect is a vulnerability to what are now called psychophysiological disorders.

There is abundant evidence that stressors, some of them present sooner or later in the lives of all of us, will reduce the effectiveness of the immune system and create a vulnerability to physical illness. The research literature cites the following examples: for husbands and wives, the intense grief at the death of their spouses seems to produce a measurable lowering in the activity of the immune system; and development of a chronic active stage of tuberculosis seems to be more likely when the individual is an unhappy person.

The influence of psychological factors on physical health is also demonstrated in 'positive' ways. People who are happy in their interpersonal relationships and content with the work they do seem to develop an immunity to certain physical diseases; for example, respiratory infections such as colds. If they are not totally immune, they at least recover more quickly.

Mediating influences on the effects of stressors

Distressing events are part and parcel of the human condition. They occur more frequently to some than to others; their severity varies, and some stages of the life cycle seem more vulnerable than others. But regardless of those variables, there is abundant evidence, from research on the problem, and even from casual observations of the resilience of some people we know, that stressful events need not lead to physical disorders. What are the critical factors that control that effect?

To illustrate that range of possibilities, we examine three influencing factors of many that have been suggested in the research. They are life-style, what has been called 'explanatory style', and certain personality traits.

Life-style

Aspects of how one chooses to live one's life have been related to the development of psychophysiological illness. People differ in what they eat, how much they eat, and in their manner of eating. Powerfully persuasive evidence points to the damaging effect of smoking; lung cancer is only one of the fatal diseases it causes. On the other hand, physical exercise is suggested as a healthful aspect of life-style by all health experts.

More subtle factors are also part of life-style: one's impatience to get things done, temper flare-ups, strongly conflicting attitudes or needs. Those traits have been identified with the 'Type A' personality, which is also associated with coronary illness.

J. H. Knowles, in an editorial in *Science* (1977), describes a healthy life-style: if no one smoked cigarettes or consumed alcohol, and everyone exercised regularly, maintained optimal weight on a low-fat, low-refined carbohydrate, high-fibre diet, reduced stress by simplifying their lives, obtained adequate rest and recreation, drank fluoridated water, followed the doctor's orders for medication and self-care if disease was detected, and used available health resources, we would all live healthier and happier lives.

Sadly, it will take more than reading that paragraph to produce any converts.

Explanatory style

People differ in the way in which they explain life's events: consequently, they also differ in what they expect from life. Explanatory styles have been sorted into two principle types: the pessimistic and the optimistic. Individuals who have developed a pessimistic outlook see events as a part of the way things are, or as the result of what they seemingly are always doing. We are, they conclude, surrounded by bad happenings.

Individuals with a pessimistic explanatory style unfortunately are creating their own fate in that attitude. For example, they are, as a group, at greater risk of illness and infectious disorders as well as those that are more apparently related to emotional tensions, such as ulcers.

Martin Seligman put forward the concept of 'learned helplessness' (see Chapter 11) in which there is expectancy that an individual who lacks control over events will not only be more depressed than one who feels in control of events, but also be more susceptible to physical illness. This is similar to hopelessness as a personality trait described in the next section.

Peterson and Seligman (1988) in a longitudinal study found that pessimistic explanatory style at the age of 25 predicted poorer health at age 45 than for those who were more optimistic. Thus, both optimism and a sense of control in the way one explains life's events can have a significant effect on one's physical health.

Optimistic as opposed to pessimistic style has also been found to affect the outcome for breast cancer patients in terms of survival.

Personality traits

One group of psychologists, focusing on a trait they called 'hardiness', studied a group of executives in high-stress jobs. They found that three aspects of the trait identified stress-resistant individuals, those in whom stress produced minimal health changes: openness to change (the most powerful variable), a sense of involvement or commitment to their jobs, and feelings of being in control of their lives.

Hopelessness is a trait very different from hardiness, although both could be related to the learned helplessness model of Seligman mentioned above, in terms of sense of control and helplessness and all being factors in the vulnerability to illness.

The persistence and severity of diseases as different as cancer and influenza have been related to depression or feelings of hopelessness. Studies of residents of nursing homes suggest that survival rate after placement in a nursing home is related to the amount of control the individuals felt they had over what happened to them. That feeling of control enhances the attitude of hopefulness which the individual develops about future events.

Psychological factors in specific physical disorders

Mounting evidence such as that which we have reported indicates that mind and body act as a unit. Here we examine the effect of psychological facts in triggering, or in contributing to, specific disorders. Although there are many specific psychophysiological disorders, this section reports on those that have been researched most extensively.

Coronary disease

An exciting event on the psychosomatic front was the arrival of the concept of the 'Type A' personality. In 1974, in a book of that title, Friedman and Rosenman described the concept, and they were able to relate that personality type to heart disorders. The concept caught on with many health-conscious people and also elicited research activities among medical and psychological professionals.

Friedman and Rosenman described Type A personalities as aggressive, competitive, hostile (at least unconsciously), feeling pressured by time, and always striving to succeed. They also described Type B individuals as relaxed, and opposite in many ways to Type A personalities. Diagnoses of the personality types are made either on the basis of a stress-type interview or by a self-administered questionnaire.

On either type of assessment, Type A personalities are likely to admit such things as eating too fast, being too active, needing to slow down, setting work deadlines or quotas, and being irritated at interruptions in their work. Type B answers are at the opposite pole to those responses.

Two levels of research have been directed at the Type A concept:

1 Prospective studies predicting risk of heart attack from a personality assessment.
2 Research attempting to pinpoint what it is in a Type A personality that increases risk of cardiac disease.

Predicting coronary heart disease from personality assessments
This section describes the three best-known and carefully-researched studies of the relationship between a heart attack and personality type.

The Western Collaborative Study (Rosenman, 1975). The researchers tested first personality type, then followed 3,200 males and monitored their medical status for the next eight years. They found that Type A personality types had more than twice as many heart attacks as did those men who had been judged to be Type B.

The Framingham–Massachusetts study (Haynes, 1980). In a population of 1,600 male and female white-collar workers, who had been classified as Types A or B, the researchers found three times as many cases of coronary heart disease among Type A men and two times as many among Type A women than among Type B men and women.

The Belgian Heart Disease Preventive Program (Shekelle, 1985). Two thousand men in good health, as determined by a physical stress test, were rated on a Type A/Type B scale and followed for five years. The results were similar to the earlier studies. The men on the Type A side of the scale had almost twice as many cardiac symptoms as did those on the Type B end of the scale.

Characteristics of the type A personality that cause coronary heart disease
Findings such as those just summarised have challenged research psychologists to find precisely what it is about Type A personalities that makes them high risks for heart disease. They have pursued most vigorously two characteristics: hostility and response to being helpless in an apparently hopeless situation.

Hostility. Several researchers have followed a lead provided in the writings of the psychoanalytically oriented Franz Alexander, who related high blood pressure to the way in which individuals dealt with their aggression. They found that when hostility was felt but not expressed overtly, the frequent result was high blood pressure, inhibited hostility and a Type A personality, and it is now thought that those relationships play a significant role in causing the coronary reactions in the Type A personalities.

Helplessness. Later research seems to suggest that the significant element producing the pathology is not the hostility itself but a sense of helplessness that is felt when hostile individuals cannot express their feelings. It is not the helplessness of the depressed individual that researchers associate with Type A personalities; it is a much more covert helplessness than that.

David Glass, in his 1977 publication, *Behaviour Pattern Stress in Coronary Disease,* describes what he believes to be the underlying principle of the Type A personality: a lifelong struggle to control a world that is threatening. Many of the traits most often assigned to Type A – competition to be best, time pressure to get things done, hostility at interference with work – seem to be expressions of that unconscious struggle.

Glass's research design to test his hypothesis is both interesting and convincing. His subjects were first sorted into two groups – Type A and Type B. Glass confronted both groups with a set of unsolvable problems to guarantee that each group would have a failure experience. Later in the experimental situation, he asked both groups to work on another set of problems with easier solutions. He then observed the reactions of both groups to each set of problems. The Type A personalities could be identified by the way in which they responded to his experimental design. In response to a task that had been made highly salient for subjects, they:

1 Responded with initial vigour to the challenge. That response changed to desperation when they found that they could not control the situation, that is, solve the unsolveable problems.
2 Faced with that sense of helplessness, they totally gave up. That despair interfered with their attempts to solve the easier problems, confronting them once again with failure.

Type B subjects were disappointed but did not surrender in such a complete way. They proceeded to solve the second set of problems easily and with less emotional stress.

Glass concluded that the sequence of attempting to control, then giving up, then trying again, tends to produce in Type A individuals the physiological changes – for example, heightened blood pressure – that put them at high risk for a heart attack. His findings have been supported by research of quite a different design in which there were definite indications that when an individual's need for power – that is, desire for control – was inhibited, this factor often was predictive of hypertension later in life.

McClelland (1979) found greater levels of hypertension among a group of middle-aged individuals, who had been rated many years earlier as having a high need for control which had been frustrated, leaving them feeling 'helpless'. Again, the importance of control of events put forward by Seligman can be seen to be a constant element in the psychological factors affecting physical condition. However, what constitutes control for type A individuals is not always clear in experiments where such subjects appear to refuse opportunities of control in the experimental procedure. This has been explained by Evans and colleagues in 1984 as an attempt by the Type A individual at control over the entire situation, including the experimenter, by not complying with what was expected of them in the experiment.

The emergency reaction and type A personality

Pulling together all of the evidence that relates coronary heart disease to psychological influences, psychologists now point to what has been described as an 'emergency' reaction which, in the face of threat, raises heart rate and increases blood pressure. We have described already the sense of helplessness which Type A individuals feel more frequently than others; and because they feel helpless, they also feel more threatened than others. It is this relatively continuous emergency reaction, with persistently rapid heart rate and high blood pressure, that wears out their heart muscles and causes the coronary disease.

That hypothesis also suggests a prescription for Type A patients (and for others) of regular exercise. Reasonably taxing exercise does indeed raise pulse rate and blood pressure, but only while exercising. However, it also strengthens the heart and the vascular system so that the individual's heart and blood pressure are lowered, which is just what type A people need most!

Peptic ulcer

Acid indigestion is a frequent complaint of many adults, with the result that entire chemist shelves are lined with over-the-counter preparations intended to ameliorate it. None of them, however, remove the cause of stomach acidity; they merely alkalinise the acidity of the stomach's content, treating the symptoms only. But what causes the excessive flow of acid into the stomach, that in time erodes the lining of the stomach or duodenum (the first part of the small intestine), creating a craterlike, open and painful sore?

First reported in the early part of the nineteenth century, when it was more prevalent in women than in men, ulcers now affect more than twice as many men as women. Although having an ulcer is a fairly common and treatable condition, thousands of people still die from this each year.

Causes of an ulcer

A variety of factors are implicated in the creation and maintenance of ulcers. Some overt biological factors such as acidic food, alcohol consumption and smoking, clearly increase the possibility of an ulcer. However, not all individuals who indulge in these develop ulcers, so other factors must either predispose some individuals or interact unfavourably with diet compared to those who do not develop them. Areas that have been investigated are biology, stress and personality.

Biological factors. A predisposition to ulcers can be inherited in the form of genetic differences in the physiology of the digestive system and its reactivity, and also differences in behavioural style. The physiological processes which lead to an ulcer, an increase in gastric acid and pepsin (a digestive enzyme) and a reduction in the production of the mucus which protects the stomach, could be genetically biased toward ulcer generation. Ulcers also improve with antibiotic treatment, which suggests that a bacterial process may be predisposing some individuals to ulcers. Although genetics and disease processes may play a larger part in the development of the various types of ulcers than previously thought, the stress–diathesis model would seem to be appropriate here also. In other words biology may select the individuals who will react to stress by developing an ulcer.

The stress–diathesis model.   Relatives of ulcer sufferers are three times as likely to develop them as non-relatives. It is also the case that ulcers are more common in peacetime than in war and that very busy air traffic controllers suffer more ulcers than those who are not so busy. Thus both precipitating stress and a diathesis towards ulcers is involved, but the exact nature of the influence of stress is unclear.

In 1958, John Brady and his colleagues reported the initial studies of stress in 'executive monkeys'. In these studies, monkeys that had control over (could switch off) electrical shocks developed more ulcers than those receiving the same shocks with no control over them (a yoked experimental control animal). One unfortunate aspect of this experiment was that the 'executive monkeys' were assigned to this role on the basis of their pre-existing frequency of 'switch-pressing' behaviour. Thus some initial difference between the two monkey groups may have led to differing ulcer rates rather than 'executive stress'. In a better-designed experiment with random assignment of rats to the two conditions, Weiss (1971) found fewer ulcers in the 'executive rats' than in those that had no control over the shock. Although this fits better with the idea that uncontrollability of stressful events leads to disease. It is difficult to generalise from animals to humans in this, especially as they differ in types of ulcers.

Personality types.   Clearly, biological factors and uncontrollable stressful events lead to ulcer formation, but are there styles of personality which may also predispose individuals to this disorder? Perhaps there was something in the habitual responses of Brady's executive monkeys that led them to both be selected for that group and develop ulcers.

Early psychological explanations of ulcer-proneness were couched in psychodynamic terms. Although there is little surviving support for this approach, the concept of repressed dependency needs from childhood influencing susceptibility is still referred to among clinicians in the USA.

Essential hypertension

Essential hypertension refers to damaging high blood pressure which is assumed to have no obvious physical cause (ie, 'essential'). This assumption is somewhat misleading as there are almost always some physical factors involved in hypertension such as alcohol consumption, salt intake or obesity. These factors are similar to those involved in coronary heart disease, for which hypertension itself is usually a predisposing factor. In up to 90 per cent of cases of hypertension however, such factors are not the main cause of the hypertension and the cause is assumed to be psychological. This figure should be treated with caution as even in the absence of obvious physical factors it would be unwise to assume the absence of biological influences as there is a probable genetic element in addition to less detectable physical influences.

Psychological factors in hypertension

As with ulcers, early psychological explanations of hypertension proposed psychodynamic factors such as repressed anger and inhibited power needs. Although there is little likelihood that early life events such as these directly lead to hypertension, there is clear evidence that the continuous stress on the cardiovascular system in individuals who overcontrol their anger does increase the risk of this condition.

Other stressful factors have also been found to increase blood pressure such as overcrowding and occupational stress. Usually stressors are temporary and one would expect the effects to disappear or be reversible in the absence of stress. The relatively permanent effects on blood pressure may be brought about by some of the physiological responses of the body to stress and elevated pressure becoming long-lasting changes in the body's physiological systems. Possible changes of this sort may be the prolonged constriction of peripheral blood vessels or capillaries, the kidneys not excreting salt and water normally, or lessening ability to control the activity of the autonomic nervous system. Thus a causal route from psychological stressor via physiological change to hypertension can be traced.

Other physical disorders affected by psychological factors

A significant, and some say growing, number of physical disorders, in addition to those already described, have been characterised as psychosomatic. These include asthma and recurrent headaches, and we have also included the two disorders anorexia nervosa (failure to eat enough) and bulimia (excessive eating binges followed by vomiting), which DSM-IV lists as eating disorders on axis 1. In the following section, any psychological factors influencing these disorders will be examined.

Asthma

Asthma attacks occur when there is a narrowing in the bodily passages that allow oxygen to enter the lungs and carbon dioxide to be exhaled. This disorder of the respiratory process causes coughing, wheezing, and often a degree of breathlessness that leads to gasping for air and extreme apprehensiveness. The attacks may last from under an hour to one or two days. Three per cent of the general population suffer from some level of severity of the disease. It develops often in childhood, and one-third of all asthmatics are under the age of 16. Death rates for asthma have been relatively low until recent years when there has been a dramatic increase in both incidence and mortality. Possible reasons for this will be discussed later.

There is evidence that the earlier the disorder occurs, the longer it lasts. For example, it was found that when the disease developed before the age of one year, 80 per cent of the children were found to still have the disease five years later; when the age of onset was five years, that percentage dropped to 20. Two-thirds of asthmatics are male.

Incidence of biogenic and psychological types of asthma. In those cases of asthma in which the allergies are to specific irritants, such as pollen, dust or dandrufflike sheddings of animals, or when the attacks follow such serious respiratory illnesses as pneumonia or whooping cough, psychogenic factors cannot be considered to be primary causes, although they may be contributory. In a large study in Wales, Rees (1964) found that in 30 per cent of cases, psychological factors had no part to play, whereas in 37 per cent they could be considered the main cause, and in 63 per cent only a contributing factor. Subsequently, Rees concluded that asthma was clearly the product of a number of causes. At this time he did not consider air pollution, which has become an area of concern in relation to a number of disorders including asthma, and only identified psychological, ineffective and allergic influences. The psychological factors identified by Rees were frustration, anger, depression and anticipated pleasurable excitement, all of which lead to anxiety and tension which, in turn, adversely affect the functioning of the respiratory system.

The factors so far identified – psychological factors, allergic reactions, infection and pollution in the air – could be said to have all become more prevalent with time (though infection is debatable), and thus the recent dramatic increase in asthma cases cannot be tied to any one of these factors.

In other efforts to find a specific cause of asthma, scattered studies have suggested childhood depression or family conflict as important etiological elements in some cases. Studies have reported such psychological findings as:

1 Once the disease has occurred, asthmatic children can be highly suggestible to elements in the environment that are proposed as causes of asthmatic attacks.
2 Asthmatic children are sometimes capable of using their asthmatic condition in an attempt to control parental behaviour.
3 Asthmatic children are no more 'neurotic' than are other sickly children; for example, cardiac children.

Overview of psychological effects on development of asthma. Summarising the research evidence, we can conclude that it hardly supports the widespread notion that asthma is always psychosomatic in origin. Nor is there much evidence, such as has been found in other psychophysiological ailments, that there is a personality type that predisposes a child to the illness. Stress or emotional tensions trigger an asthma attack when the disease is already present. No convincing evidence exists that personality traits play a significant etiological part in asthma.

Anorexia nervosa and bulimia

These two troubling eating disorders, with symptom patterns that are the very opposite of each other, are nevertheless linked, by specialists in the field, as cyclical reactions which are caused by the same underlying psychological disorder. Some professionals in the area consider bulimia to be a secondary phase of anorexia; others see these as separate disorders. The DSM-IV also lists them as separate disorders.

Anorexia. In anorexia, the individual eats too little and borders on a starvation diet.

Onset of the principal symptoms often occurs at the time of a critical life change, such as going to college, becoming engaged, or beginning a new job. Those experiences are hardly limited to anorexic females, and for that group, no especially anxiety-producing features of their life 'crisis' have been identified. The reaction sometimes is an extreme continuation of early dieting efforts; but here, again, ordinary dieting is no basis for the extreme reactions of the anorexic individual.

In studies of the interpersonal relationships of anorexic women, it is reported that they are frequently perfectionists in their standards and tend to be hypercritical of their mothers, using such adjectives as 'intrusive' and 'domineering' to describe them; but no control groups are available to assure us that those views are not common in normal young women of that age group. Carson *et al.*(1988), in their analysis of the illness, caution about giving credence to those criticisms since, as they say 'Mothers frequently respond in that way to the self-starvation of their children.'

Another aspect of upbringing which has been linked to anorexia is the importance and emphasis on food created by the parents (usually the mother). Where food is used as a comfort for emotional upset or a reward for some behaviour, then its importance can be exaggerated and its rejection a symbol of the child's confronting the parent's expectations. Clearly, in the absence of an emphasis on food, the child's self-starvation does manipulate the parent's behaviour, giving the child a sense of control which, in the child's mind, may have been lacking.

The fact that anorexia is mostly confined to Western societies and is very infrequent in countries such as India would tend to indicate that anorexia is culture bound. It is often assumed that this is due to the great emphasis placed on the 'ideal female form' as very slim in Western advertising and other media.

This may indeed account for the vast increase in the disorder in the last 40 years; for example, there was a five-fold increase in hospitalised cases in Prague between 1974 and 1983. However, since anorexia has been diagnosed for about a century, it would be difficult to attribute all cases to dieting fads or fashionable body shapes in these societies. It is not commonly found among the poor. There are no answers to explain a very unfortunate problem in a relatively small fraction of today's young women.

Prevalence of anorexia is one in 250,000 (all will develop the disorder between the ages of 12 and 18) The mortality rate is estimated to be between 15 and 21 per cent; 95 per cent of anorexics are women. Anorexics typically refuse therapy, and frequently deny any illness.

Bulimia. In bulimia, the principal symptom is episodes of binge eating. These may be planned ahead of time, but are usually engaged in covertly, when the individual is alone. Bulimics gulp down their food as if emerging from a period of starvation. The binge-eating generates self-deprecating thoughts, guilt and even depression. Binges usually end with the individual in pain from a distended stomach, and are frequently followed by self-induced vomiting. Weight fluctuations are common because the individual alternates between binges and fasting. Despite binge-eating, or perhaps because of it, there is a continuing preoccupation with overweight.

Among those who have studied these eating problems, anorexia and bulimia are believed to stem from an identity crisis which can be traced back to early family relationships. Simply put, those who suffer from the disorder have either not answered the question 'Who am I?', or are dissatisfied with the answer.

Recurrent headaches

It is the rare person who has never experienced the unpleasantness of a headache. No one knows, with an exactitude, the number of people who suffer recurrent headaches during some period in their lives. One estimate, reported in *Newsweek* (1988) offers the statement, 'Forty-five million Americans suffer chronic or recurrent headaches that vary in intensity from dull to excruciating.' How exact that statement is is uncertain.

Headaches usually first appear during adolescence. A 1959 survey of college students found 52 per cent of them reporting headaches at least once or twice a week. Recurring headaches may be a lifetime pattern, or may disappear as a regular problem later in life. Their occurrence is almost always related to the presence of some stressor, major or minor.

Although one survey of headache research (1982) states that there is little support for believing that one type of headache can be distinguished from another, three types of headache are discussed in the literature: migraine, tension, and cluster headache.

Migraine headaches. Of the three types of headache, migraine has been studied most extensively. We have descriptions of migraine headaches going back to antiquity, but it was only in the 1940s that medical science was able to identify the physiological changes associated with migraine. Sudden dilation of certain cerebral and cranial arteries and the irritation of attached nerve endings causes the migraine pain. The actual dilation is preceded by a non-painful, reduced flow of blood to the affected parts of the brain. That event is experienced as an aura announcing the arrival of the migraine attack. Migraine is the most severe of all headaches, and attacks can last from a few hours to three or four days.

Migraine headaches are subdivided into two types, principally on the basis of the severity of the attack: classic and common.

Classic migraine. Characterised by pain that is described as excruciating, the classic migraine headache begins with a pulsating pain on one side of the head, coinciding with each heartbeat. Soon thereafter, the pain stabilises and becomes continuous. Classic migraine brings with it nausea and vomiting and such neurological symptoms as visual distortion, numbness, and speech and co-ordination problems.

Common migraine headaches. These headaches, although resulting from the same physiological pattern as classic migraine, differ from it in that they are less severe at each stage of the attack. The aura is less pronounced, the pain is less severe, and the neurological symptoms are likely to be absent.

Causative factors in migraine. Historically, migraine sufferers were stereotyped as rigidly moral, ambitious, perfectionistic, of better-than-average intelligence, and suffering from suppressed emotional expression. More recent research has not confirmed that description, nor have migraine victims been found to lead more stressful lives than do others. Contemporary thinking attributes migraine to genetic factors, possibly causing hypersensitivity in the cranial blood vessels. Some modern treatment approaches attempt to indirectly influence the constriction of the cranial blood vessels by exerting control over the extracranial vessels. That conclusion does not rule out a diathesis–stress interpretation of the illness.

Tension headaches. Despite the apparent prevalence of these headaches, which are much less severe than migraine and without neurological or gastric symptoms, no certain interpretation exists telling us why some people respond to tension with headaches and others do not. In Friedman's (1979) survey of 1,420 people with tension headaches, he reports that 77 per cent of them identified psychologically precipitating factors, which were wide-ranging in their nature. In the absence of a control group, it is difficult to draw any conclusions from that finding.

The problem of tension headaches only occasionally provokes a visit to the doctor.

Cluster headaches. These headaches occur less frequently than either migraine or tension headaches. The pain is extremely severe and often causes violent reactions in the affected individual, such as head-banging or wall-pounding. Psychological factors are thought to be involved, but no pattern has been established.

The possibility of psychological factors in cancer

Most people find it understandable that certain physical disorders can be caused by emotional strain. Among those disorders are those we have discussed. On the other hand, the possibility of such a relationship in cancer is most often greeted with scepticism. It is not the severity of the disorder that causes the scepticism – both cancer and coronary arterial disease have a high death rate. Perhaps the scepticism results form the appallingly imaginable physical nature of cancer's physical growth, increasing in size each day, or spreading in minute cells that travel throughout the body. Other diseases do not seem to be so vividly imaginable. Another factor in causing the scepticism may be the well-known emphasis medical science gives to biological treatment and its effectiveness in many cases. When we think of cancer, we think immediately of radiation, chemotherapy, or even surgery. However, Kiecolt-Glaser and colleagues reported in 1984 that part of the action of the body's immune reaction to cancer can be impaired by stress (in this case examination stress). Thus, given the high mortality rate and fear involved with cancer, any potential psychological influences should be considered seriously rather than ignored.

Emotional inhibition

One researcher (Caroline Bedell Thoms) had her own thoughts about that scepticism. She and other researchers, in the early 1940s, had noticed the coincidence of cancer and particular personality characteristics. In 1946, she administered a series of personality tests to a group of medical students who were conveniently available to her. Each year thereafter, with admirable persistence, she contacted them to inquire about their health. Since most of them were medical doctors, they were reasonably co-operative in replying. By 1977, 48 of her subjects had developed cancer. Comparing their personality profiles with those of her sample who had not developed cancer, she noted strong tendencies to repress strong emotions in the cancer patients. These individuals, she felt, might be described as emotionally inhibited personalities.

Other researchers have confirmed her original findings of relationships between cancer and psychological characteristics, but in a somewhat different way. Rogentine and others, for example, reported in 1979 that those cancer patients who freely expressed negative emotions about the illness were more likely to survive than those who were more emotionally restrained.

Hopelessness in cancer

Subsequent research has focused on hopelessness as a factor in the deveopment of cancer. One illustration of this is what might be called a serendipitous opportunity for research: 51 women who entered a clinic for a cancer test were interviewed after medical examinations had revealed suspicious cells in the cervix which had to be investigated further before a definite diagnosis of cancer could be made.

The interview revealed that 18 of the 51 had suffered significant losses in the preceding six months to which, the interview further revealed, they had responded with feelings of hopelessness and a resultant sence of helplessness. Of the 18, 11 had a cancer diagnosis. Among the other 33, with no such preceding life experiences reported, only eight had cancer. Although the difference seems small, statistical tests revealed those differences to be significant; that is, the likelihood was that they were more than chance happenings. Other research with different types of cancer (lung and breast cancer) has confirmed those earlier findings. One study reported that upon the news of a cancer diagnosis, a 'fighting' spirit was associated with a better rate of survival five years later. Those studies by no means designate hopelessness as a primary cause of cancer, they suggest rather that personality variables play a part, at least, in affecting survival rates once cancer is diagnosed.

Overview on causative factors in psychologically affected physical disorders

We have considered in this chapter eight of the principal so-called psychosomatic ailments. There are others: allergies, skin eruptions, chronic diarrhoea and ulcerative colitis, rheumatoid arthritis, diabetes, menstrual irregularities, and Raynaud's disease; and medical research is opening the door to the labelling of other physical disorders as psychosomatic.

With that number of psychosomatic ailments, and with so extensive a body of research on them, there is a place for each of the major perspectives on human behaviour to provide interpretations of their etiology.

The biogenic perspective

There are two principal emphases in the biogenic perspective on psychosomatic disorders. They are genetic influences and involvement of the body's immune system.

A genetic factor. Family studies, twin studies and animal research lend strong support to the presence of genetic factors in many disorders. Genetic factors may not only influence physiological systems but may also lead to differences in behaviour between individuals.

Extensive research of the development of ulcers supports the proposition that a vulnerability to ulcers is genetically based. Both family studies and twin studies indicate a genetic basis for hypertension.

Genetic hypothesising has suggested the somatic weakness theory. In that theory, it is speculated that genetic factors (but also prior illness or trauma) may create a vulnerability in some organ systems of the body, which makes them the weakest links in the body and thus especially sensitive to psychological tensions. A study (Rees 1964) of asthmatics reveals that 80 per cent of an asthmatic group had a history of earlier respiratory infections, but only 30 per cent of a non-asthmatic group did likewise. The suggestion is therefore present that the respiratory system is a genetically-weakened organ system.

There is also evidence that each of us has a unique physiological reaction to all types of stressful situations. That this pattern is an inherited one is implied by research indicating that the infant's distinctive autonomic responses persist throughout life. Given such a predisposition, it can be argued that any triggering emotional stress will produce a specific psychosomatic ailment.

The immune system. The body's immune system, as we have described earlier in this chapter, defends the body against disease-causing foreign agents. Much evidence from the animal laboratories demonstrates that in animals such psychological tensions as, for example, those created by a condition of helplessness, reduce the effectiveness of the immune system. In that way, the body's vulnerability to physical disease is increased.

A question that is now the target of a new and fast-growing branch of medicine, psychoneuroimmunology, is, are there other diseases not now considered psychosomatic which are triggered by emotional tension that consequently reduces the functioning of the immune system? A prime suspect is infectious disease. The role of that relationship in cancer is also the subject of study.

Current focus of the biogenic perspective is the diathesis–stress model as a way of thinking about the interaction between physical and psychological factors.

The psychodynamic perspective

The oldest, but not now the most vigorously researched, interpretation of psychosomatic illness is the psychodynamic perspective. Two elements of Freudian thinking provided the basis for early interpretations of psychosomatic ailments.

The first suggests that unresolved conflicts from early life create an excess of anxiety in adulthood. Secondly, the individual reacts to this with defensive behaviour. Early theory links psychosexual stage fixation to specific somatic symptoms, eg. 'oral conflict' for ulcers or 'anal conflict' for colitis. More recent psychodynamic approaches focus more on disturbances of the early parent–child relationship, treating the physical disorders in a similar manner to the anxiety-based disorders described earlier in this book.

Research has not provided support for this approach, although it may have value in helping to explain how any 'illness-prone' personality styles are formed, if indeed, such personalities are themselves acceptably supported.

The behavioural perspective

Until recently, the rationale for considering psychosomatic symptoms to be the result of conditioning, either classical or operant, was difficult to establish. For one thing, autonomic responses were considered to be beyond voluntary control. They therefore would not respond to operant conditioning. Secondly, to hypothesise classical conditioning as the cause of the illness would require frequent associations between a neutral stimulus to be conditioned and some unconditioned stimulus known to produce the response reflexively. In ordinary living, that eventuality would be a rare occurrence indeed.

In the 1960s, a principal block to a behavioural interpretation was removed when it was demonstrated that a variety of autonomic responses could be operantly conditioned in a very precise way; at least the theoretical possibility of a causal relationship between operant conditioning and a physical disorder was demonstrated. A powerful result of that research has been the development of a behavioural approach to the treatment of some forms of psychophysiological illness, which is known as biofeedback.

The cognitive perspective

One major early study (Grace and Graham, 1952) relates specific cognitions to specific psychophysiological disorders. For example, before a migraine attack, the individual may be thinking, 'I have a million things to do'. An asthma patient may be saying to himself or herself, 'I don't like what's going to happen. I can't face it.' Thus maladaptive thought patterns may exacerbate symptoms or precipitate an attack of these disorders and, as thinking processes can be altered, cognitive therapies have a definite role in psychosomatic disorders.

Treatment approaches to physical diseases affected by psychological factors

Psychophysiological illness almost always brings the individual first to a medical doctor; and biological measures, directed mostly to symptom control, are the principal treatments used in such illnesses. In extreme cases – for example, of a heart attack or a bleeding ulcer – hospitalisation, either on an emergency basis or for prolonged treatment, may be necessary.

In mild to moderate psychophysiological illness, with no life-threatening features, ameliorative medical measures are taken. These include tranquillisers to reduce the exacerbating effect of emotional tensions on the symptoms: antihypertensive medications, usually for a lifetime; or, for ulcer patients, suggested dietary changes.

Of the psychotherapeutic approaches, behavioural and cognitive therapies are more specifically prescribed than are psychodynamically-oriented therapies. Three of the most widely-used behaviour therapies are biofeedback, behaviour modification, and relaxation therapy.

Biofeedback

One study (Long *et al.* 1967), describing the use of biofeedback to control heart rate in a group of volunteers illustrates the main principle involved in that therapy. Subjects watched a visual display of their heart rate and were directed to limit the rate to a prescribed range. As anyone who has taken part in a biofeedback experiment will agree, the subjects could not explain how they did it; but in time, they had learned how to regulate their heart rate.

The technique has been used with limited success in several other psychophysiological disorders. They include hypertension, headaches and irregular heart beat. Immediately after treatment, patients control or moderate their symptoms. Control exerted over extracranial blood vessels using biofeedback has enabled patients to influence the constriction of cranial vessels in migraine headaches. For most of these disorders, a positive effect is noticeable in mild to moderate cases, although this is not always long-lasting. Biofeedback has been used to supplement psychotherapy in detecting physical responses during discussion, which may indicate a discussion topic that causes tension. However, as with the use of physiological responses in 'lie-detection', this is unreliable and limited by the effectiveness of the psychotherapy itself.

Behaviour modification

This technique is essentially the application of operant conditioning principles to efforts to reduce or change psychosomatic symptoms. That is, for example, following the symptom either with an aversive stimulus or with the absence of a reward. Such conditioning would, in time, extinguish the undesired symptom. In 1966 *Time* magazine reported the control of prolonged and energy-draining sneezing by following each sneeze with a painful, but not dangerous, electrical shock. A sixteen-month follow-up indicated that the sneezing had been controlled (Kusher 1968).

Relaxation therapy and systematic desensitisation

Joseph Wolpe, whose therapy approaches have been discussed in chapter 6, has used relaxation therapy, followed by systematic desensitisation, as a method of reducing emotional stress associated with headaches and ulcers. Once the stress was reduced, the psychosomatic symptoms either disappeared or were reduced substantially.

The therapy is a simple one. Under the guidance of the therapist, the individual has learned to relax. The therapist then encourages the patient to discuss stressful life situations which, it has been learned form a previous history-taking session, tended to trigger the psychosomatic attack. The therapy strategy builds on the incompatibility of tension and relaxation. Talking about situations that ordinarily produce tensions while an individual is deeply relaxed seems to disconnect the situation from tension. Wolpe would say that the individual is desensitised to the stressor.

This type of therapy forms the essence of stress management and can be combined with biofeedback techniques.

SUMMARY

Research establishing the existence of a causal relationship between certain physical diseases and psychological stress clearly suggests that the body and mind work as a unit. The key finding in that research is the demonstration made possible by modern technical developments, that various involuntary physiological reactions can be brought under voluntary control. With that finding, we may conclude that the body's functioning affects the way we feel and our psychological reactions affect the way in which the body functions.

A prime model for understanding the interaction between physical illness and psychological stress is the diathesis–stress format, which states that human disorders (physical and mental) result from the presence of a diathesis (a predisposition or vulnerability) which may be genetic, or the result of an early physical illness or injury. The vulnerability in this model is activated by some stressor in the environment, for example, a bereavement or loss of a job.

An external stessor activates the body's alarm reaction which, if maintained over a period of time, impairs the functioning of the body's immune system, comprising of the blood, thymus, bone marrow, spleen and lymph glands. With that impairment, there may be a reducion in the number of white blood cells in the bloodstream. These white blood cells function to destroy pathogens (hostile bodily invaders) such as bacteria, viruses, funguses and tumorous growths. As a result of that impairment, the body becomes especially susceptible to a number of physical ailments. Whether an illness will actually develop is influenced by the individual's life-style, 'explanatory style' (the way an individual tends to explain what happens to him or her), and various other personality traits.

A hazardous life-style includes bad eating habits, smoking, consuming alcohol, and such personality traits as impatience or a pressing drive to get things done. A hazardous 'explanatory style' is one that attributes bad happenings to fate or 'the way things are', explanations that dismiss any possibility of personal control of one's own destiny. The principal personality trait related to the development of psychologically caused physical disease is hopelessness.

The principal physical illnesses affected by those three aspects of the individual's personality are coronary disorder, peptic ulcer, essential hypertension, possibly asthma, anorexia and bulimia, and recurrent headaches, including migraine.

Among the psychological factors affecting coronary disease, the one most widely researched is Type A personality; that is aggressive, competitive, hostile, pressured, hypersensitive to being successful, and with a strong need to control others. Major large-scale studies have demonstrated a striking relationship between coronary disease and Type A personality. For example, in one study, Type A personalities had twice as many cardiac symptoms as Type B personalities (those that are more relaxed and complacent).

In peptic ulcers, although eating acidic foods, alcohol consumption, smoking and tension-inducing occupations all have been implicated in the development of ulcers, the diathesis–stress model is still very useful in explaining how psychological factors contribute to their development. Some researchers have suggested the controllability of stressful events as the main source of the stress component.

Essential hypertension is high blood pressure in the absence of an organic reason for it. The stress of overcrowding, especially in a busy occupational environment, and that of suppressed rage can contribute to hypertension as can most of the factors involved in coronary disease.

Asthma may be caused by a genetically-existing allergy, by an infection, or by such psychological factors (involved in more than one-third of asthmatic individuals) as anxiety, frustration, anger and depression. Psychological factors seem more to act as a trigger for an attack than as the primary cause of asthma.

Emotional distress and tension have at least an anecdotal place in explaining the occurrence of headaches. There is little research to support the anecdotes. Migraine headaches are thought to be based on a genetic vulnerability. Beyond that, research about psychological causation is inconclusive.

Beyond those psychosomatic illnesses, the personality traits of emotional inhibition and hopelessness have, in a small number of research studies, been related to the occurrence of cancer and its rate of remission.

Treatment of the mild and moderate psychosomatic illnesses is often ameliorative with the use of the minor tranquillisers (valium or zxanthan). Among the psychotherapeutic treatment techniques are biofeedback behaviour modification, use of operant conditioning, relaxation therapy and desensitisation (see chapter 7).

FURTHER READING

Fontana, D. 1989. *Managing Stress*. London: Routledge.

Gordon, R. 1990. *Anorexia and Bulimia*. Oxford: Basil Blackwell.

Kaptein, A. *et al.* 1990. *Behavioural Medicine: Psychological Treatment of Somatic Disorders*. Wiley.

Karasek, R. & Theorell, T. 1992. *Healthy Work*. London: HarperCollins.

Kessler, R. C. & J. D. McLean. 1985. Social Support and Mental Health in Community Samples. in S. Cohen and S. L. Syme (Eds.). *Social Support and Health*. New York: Academic Press.

Lewis, C., O'Sullivan, C. & Barraclough, J. 1994. *The Psychoimmunology of Cancer*. Oxford University Press.

Pitts, M. & Phillps, K. 1991. *The Psychology of Health: An Introduction*. London: Routledge.

Rees, L. 1964. The Importance of Psychological, Allergic and Infective Factors in Childhood Asthma. *Journal of Psychosomatic Research*, 7: 253–362.

Steptoe, A. & Appels, A. 1991. *Stress, Personal Control and Health*. Wiley.

Williams, S. 1993. *Chronic Respiratory Illness*. London: Routledge.

10 Personality Disorders

The psychiatric illness personality disorder includes an array of widely different types of maladaptive behaviour ranging from extreme passivity to violent antisocial behaviour. In between those extremes, an individual with a personality disorder may characteristically show any one of the following types of extreme behaviour: narcissistic, histrionic, eccentric, hypersensitive, reclusive, overdependent, or perfectionist or inflexible behaviour.

The common characteristic justifying the diagnosis of personality disorder among those widely differing groups of people is that they have developed, early in life, sometimes in childhood, personality traits (such as those described) that are persistent and maladaptive, and that cause either significant impairment in social and/or occupational adjustment or extreme personal distress. The behaviour pattern constituting the disorder can usually be recognised in adolescence. It persists through adulthood, though sometimes tapering off during the middle years. The behaviour of the personality-disordered individual is not episodic, nor is it notably related to stress. It is instead a characteristic way of behaving in all or most of the interpersonal relationships the individual enters.

Personality disorders differ in significant ways from the two other major categories of psychiatric illness: anxiety-related disorders (see chapters 7 and 8) and the psychoses (see chapter 12).

Anxiety-related disorders may appear at any time of life; the disorder manifests itself in specific fears, somatic symptoms, or memory loss. The core of the disorder is anxiety. Personality disorders are long-established traits of personality that characterise the individual's behaviour from adolescence or even childhood. The personality disorders involve the whole personality, permeating all of the individual's thoughts and behaviour. Although in certain types of personality disorder the individual often appears anxious or fearful, anxiety does not seem to be the central feature of the disorders as a group. In anxiety disorders, the victim acutely feels the pain of his or her disorder; personality disorders usually cause less pain to those with the disorder than to those with whom they are associated – fellow workers, friends and family.

The psychotic individual lives a seriously disordered life, is often disoriented as to time and place, and has seriously loosened contact with reality, which manifests itself in delusions and hallucinations; in contrast, given his or her ways of thinking about human relationships, individuals with a personality disorder lead highly patterned, often inflexible, lives; and, although likely to see the world principally through the very narrow perspective of their selfish interests, they usually maintain an adequate contact with reality.

This chapter describes the various types of personality disorders in DSM-IV and also provides a listing of those in ICD-10 which, although similar, show some differences. A major focus will be on antisocial personality disorder, about which there has been more research.

The classification of personality disorders in DSM-IV and ICD-10

The DSM-IV has ten personality disorders listed on axis II, which can be rated independently of axis I disorders. These can be found in table 10-1. In table 10-2 are ICD-10 personality disorder classifications, which will be referred to in the following descriptions where they are similar to the DSM category but carry a different name.

TABLE 10.1 DSM-IV Classification of personality disorders

Paranoid Personality Disorder
Schizoid Personality Disorder
Schizotypal Personality Disorder
Borderline Personality Disorder
Histrionic Personality Disorder
Narcissistic Personality Disorder
Avoidant Personality Disorder
Dependent Personality Disorder
Obsessive–Compulsive Personality Disorder
Antisocial Personality Disorder

TABLE 10.2 ICD-10 Classification of abnormalities of personality and behaviour

Paranoid Personality
Schizoid Personality
Dissocial Personality
Emotionally Unstable Personality
Histrionic Personality
Obsessional (also Anancastic) Personality
Dependent Personality
Also included in this section are:
Gender Identity Disorder
Factitious Disorder
(the original draft of ICD-10 included Avoidant Personality)

The types of personality disorders

While the earliest identification of one type of behaviour now classified as a personality disorder, the antisocial personality, goes back to the middle of the 19th century, when 'depraved', criminal or immoral behaviour was labelled 'moral insanity', the first systematic classification of the personality disorders appeared in the American Psychiatric Association DSM I, published in 1952. Since its first listing, various refinements have been made in it, and the process of refinement continues. The ten types of personality disorder are organised into three clusters, labelled here for convenience simply as A, B and C.

Cluster A personality disorders

Grouped into one cluster are three personality disorders – paranoid, schizoid and schizotypal – in all of which the characteristic established behaviour of the individual appears odd or eccentric, although indeed the behaviour may take varying forms. These disorders have been associated with psychotic behaviour, but this is inaccurate except perhaps in the case of schizotypal personality disorder. Although these disorders contain milder traces of schizophrenic behaviour, they have no actual psychotic symptoms and should not therefore be confused with symptoms of schizophrenia.

The degree of overlap between the personality disorders, changing criteria for each and the lack of a clear divide between them and 'normal' personality traits, mitigates against any accurate figures for this as well as many other personality disorders. The withdrawn characteristic of the schizoid personality has led professionals to speculate that a number of sufferers may be found among those living rough on the streets as well as individuals who work in occupations that allow them to work in conditions isolated from other people.

Paranoid personality disorder

Unreasonable, baseless and persistent suspiciousness is the hallmark of the paranoid personality. The trait shows itself in almost every aspect of the individual's behaviour.

Symptomatology. Ordinarily, being suspicious in some life situations can be a prudent response; the normal person gives up his or her suspicions when credible evidence to do so is presented. The paranoid individual ignores such evidence and may develop elaborate reasons to dismiss it or may become suspicious of the person presenting the evidence. The paranoid individual is hypervigilant, always looking for trickery or slipperiness in the behaviour of others. Such individuals trust no one's loyalty.

Each new situation they enter must be examined carefully for any possible pitfalls or entrapment. They will seize upon the slightest out-of-the-way occurrence to justify their suspicions. They delight in finding hidden meanings in what someone says or in catching anyone in a misstatement.

Other traits associated with their illness are argumentativeness and litigiousness; absence of sentimental or tender feeling; overseriousness and humourlessness. They are overly concerned with rank and class distinctions, are covertly envious of those in high positions and disdainful of those who seem to be weak or soft people. Although they frequently come close to difficulties with authority figures, an element of their behaviour that causes frequent job changes, their very suspiciousness causes them to back away from getting into real trouble. When it threatens, they are capable of covering up their symptoms.

Prevalence. Paranoid individuals rarely trust themselves to the close interpersonal contact of therapy. As a result, little is known about prevalence. The disorder is more frequently seen in males.

Schizoid personality disorder

The outstanding feature of the schizoid personality is an inability to form social relationships, a trait that makes them loners in any society.

Symptomatology. Schizoid persons show a lack of capacity to experience personal warmth or deep feeling; they are, as a result, unable to relate to others. They are insensitive to praise, criticism, or the feelings of others. Self-absorbed, they may appear to others to be absent-mined or in another world; they are nevertheless free of the eccentricities of behaviour, thought or speech characteristic of the schizotypal personality disorder (described next).

Associated with their illness are excessive daydreaming, vagueness about their goals, and indecision and hesitancy about their actions. They are, as one might expect, humourless, dull, cold and uninteresting as human beings. Nevertheless, given a job that allows them to function by themselves, they often make a good occupational adjustment.

There is little accurate information on prevalence.

Schizotypal personality disorder

The two separate categories of personality disorder, schizoid personality disorder and schizotypal personality disorder, were developed to distinguish more clearly between two types of schizoid behaviour and to separate both of them from schizophrenia. In schizoid personality disorder, the primary symptom is social withdrawal with few, if any, symptoms if eccentricity. The schizotypal personality disorder is characterised by oddities of perception, speech, thought and behaviour which are not extreme enough to meet the diagnostic criteria for schizophrenia. There is evidence of a familial pattern of schizophrenia among the relatives of the schizotypal individual. The schizoid personality is a less disturbed and more adequately functioning individual than the schizotypal personality.

Symptomatology. The oddities observed in the schizotypal person include rambling speech, although not the incoherence of the schizophrenic; borderline illusory experiences, reporting that he or she feels that something illusory was so (the schizophrenic would report it as actually happening); and magical thinking, in which the individual claims to be able to read the thoughts of others or tell the future.

Also present are ideas of reference, in which the individual reports (without foundation) that people are talking about him or her. Other symptoms include extreme superstitiousness, social isolation, suspiciousness bordering on the paranoid, and hypersensitivity to criticism which may be imagined. Under stress, there may be brief episodic psychotic behaviour.

The DSM-IV reports no information on prevalence.

Cluster B personality disorders

The four disorders gathered here present symptoms that are more dramatic, attention-seeking, impulsive and erratic than are the personality disorders in Cluster A. Three of the four personality disorders of Cluster B will be discussed here: histrionic personality disorder, narcissistic personality disorder, and borderline personality disorder. Antisocial personality disorder will be discussed later in the chapter.

Histrionic personality disorder

The central concern of the histrionic individual is to be 'on stage' at all times.

Symptomatology. Self-dramatisation, heightened emotionality, and the need to capture everyone's attention typify their life-style. Their behaviour is reactive and intensely expressed in dominating group discussions by dramatic recitals with elaborate exaggerations of events that others might mention in passing. Everything that happens to them is a major event which they seem to assume is of great interest to everyone else. On early acquaintance, they can be extremely charming, but that charm soon grows thin in the face of stormy explosions that often occur and the shallowness of emotions and selfishness of demands which are soon perceived by others.

The histrionic individual often is highly gullible in interpersonal relations, establishing unrealistic dependent relationships and expecting unreasonable favours from others. He or she may be seductive in the attention paid to others, but personal relations are superficial and sexual life is transitory.

Dramatically developed possible catastrophes, including threats of suicide, are manipulatively used by the individual to gain his or her ends. Impaired and stormy relationships follow the individual through life.

The disorder is a common one, more prevalent among women that men.

Narcissistic personality disorder

The dominating feature of this disorder is an all-consuming self-absorption with grandiose notions of the individual's own unique importance, talent, and right to special consideration.

Symptomatology. There is a total absence of any capacity to empathise with others or to consider their needs. Their self-fascination leads them to make exorbitant demands on others, to be exploitative with no pangs of conscience, and to respond with arrogance, disdain or dismissal when their demands are unfulfilled.

Yet with all of that felt self-importance, there is an underlying lowered sense of self-esteem, which reveals itself in a constant need for reassurance and admiration from others and a quick response of rage or disdain to any proffered criticism. The narcissist may dismiss failure with nonchalance, describing it as an unimportant experience. Some personality theorists consider narcissistic behaviour a compensatory and defensive response to deep feelings of inadequacy, perhaps stemming from early childhood experiences of disapproval and rejection. There is also the possibility that parents, through catering to the child and building unrealistic expectations about what he or she should expect from others, creates the narcissistic personality.

Histrionic and narcissistic persons may present themselves to society in highly dramatic ways, but only the histrionic person is aware of, or reactive to, the other person; narcissistic persons act as if those others did not exist or, at most, were unimportant.

Prevalence. The DSM-IV comments that the disorder seems to be more prevalent in today's society than in the past. It speculates that such increased notice of the disorder may only be due to the greater professional (particularly psychoanalytic) interest in the behaviour.

Borderline personality disorder

The ICD-10 classification of emotionally unstable personality is roughly equivalent to borderline personality disorder. As indicated by the ICD label, this disorder sometimes co-occurs with depression.

The distinguishing characteristic of the disorder is marked instability in interpersonal relations, mood, and even in image of self. Since the borderline personality from time to time shows symptoms of antisocial personality, schizotypal personality, narcissistic or histrionic personality, and occasionally the psychotic symptoms of the mood disorders (see chapter 12),the diagnosis of borderline personality disorder is a challenging problem.

Because of the instability of behaviour and the wide variations in the way the individual behaves, the diagnosis is in danger of becoming a 'kitchen sink' kind of evaluation in which any disorder not readily classified elsewhere is placed.

Symptomatology. In order to prevent this classification from becoming a catch-all term for ill-defined disorders, the DSM system requires five of nine symptomatic criteria to be met. The nine behaviours considered diagnostic are impulsive or unpredictable self-damaging emotional behaviour; physically self-damaging behaviour; instability and inappropriate or maladaptive intensity in interpersonal relationships; spells of intense and uncontrollable anger; self-identity disturbances; emotional instability involving marked and short-term shifts in mood; a high level of irritability or anxiety; intolerance of being alone; and unrelieved feelings of emptiness or boredom.

Prevalence. DSM sources report borderline personality disorder to be comparatively common and more frequently found in women.

Cluster C personality disorders

The third grouping of personality disorders brings together three disorders in which, unlike in those of the other clusters, the individuals may experience bouts of anxiety and apprehensiveness. The disorders are avoidant, dependent and obsessive–compulsive personality disorders.

Avoidant personality disorder

Although lonely and desirous of affection and acceptance, the avoidant personality avoids or withdraws from social contacts. Unlike the schizoid personality, who withdraws from social situations because he or she sees no value in them, the avoidant personality prizes social relationships, but self-esteem is so low and sensitivity so high that the person is afraid to reach out and make contact with others.

Symptomatology. The avoidant personality will choose to have lunch in a company cafeteria alone rather join a table of associates where there is a vacant place. He or she cannot gather together enough courage to make a telephone call, although the person may very much want the telephone to ring.

They can walk by even a small group of classmates and make no effort to join them. They often interpret even gentle kidding as a dreadful rebuff.

The individual soon finds himself or herself in a vicious cycle, demanding guarantees of acceptance and freedom from even hints of criticism, so that social life soon becomes extremely limited. The failure to make friends lowers self-esteem, which of course intensifies the anxiety at entering social situations. Left alone, the person worsens the problems by dwelling on shortcomings and magnifying social failings. The avoidant personality's behaviour is self-defeating; unwillingness to reach out results in the absence of the very relationships that are desired. As times goes by, any social skills are lost, and the isolation becomes more complete. Career opportunities are limited to those few positions where any social contact is momentary and unimportant.

Prevalence. A common disorder, especially among women.

Dependent personality disorder

Like the avoidant individual, the dependent personality's illness stems from a seriously low level of self-esteem. In dependency, however, the individual flees into turning over his or her life to other people, meekly carrying out decisions others are pressed to make for him or her.

Symptomatology. Because of a lack of self-confidence dependent personalities look to other people, such as parents, spouses, neighbours and friends, to make all their decisions: what career to pursue, whom to marry, where to live, how to dress. They tend to think they are too stupid to make their own decisions. Like the avoidant personality, the dependent personality is soon in a vicious cycle. The more passive the person becomes in accepting the decisions (orders) of other people, the more incompetent the individual feels, thus spiralling down into complete passivity, accepting whatever life brings. Dependent personalities are frequently self-effacing women whose passivity and dependence allows them to tolerate a spouse's drunkenness, infidelities and physical abuse for fear that if she objects, she will be abandoned.

A frequent complication of extreme dependency in an unhappy family situation is depression and loss of interest or pleasure in all usual activities.

Prevalence. Dependent personality is a common disorder, occurring more frequently in women.

Obsessive–compulsive personality disorder

Perfectionism, a dominating concern with the rightness of the way things are done, and a crippling preoccupation with detail, much of it trivia, is the all-consuming characteristic of the person handicapped by obsessive–compulsive personality disorder.

The disorder should be distinguished from the obsessive–compulsive anxiety disorder (described in chapter 8). In that disorder, the individual is distressed by the symptoms, sees they are irrational, and would be rid of them if only it were possible. In the obsessive–compulsive personality disorder, the individual takes pride in perfectionism and expects that others will see things as he or she does; the concern of the individual is with getting things right, not the possibility that he or she is sick. Obsessive–compulsive personality disorder lacks the clear obsessions and compulsions which are so dominant in obsessive–compulsive disorder.

Symptomatology. The obsessive–compulsive personality is so tied to the need to get everything right that he or she has no time to relax and no capacity to find pleasure in life. Life is filled with constant concern for detailed planning of every event, even vacations, to the extent that there is no opportunity to enjoy it by the individual or by others who share the experience; rigidity; over-conscientious-ness; overly-controlled behaviour of the individual. Although job success and hard work are of great significance, time-consuming checking of trivia usually makes success difficult or impossible. Although driven to be exacting and demanding of others, the individual is rarely open to the suggestions of others.

Prevalence. The personality disorder is more common, especially in men, than the anxiety disorder, which is relatively rare.

Overview of personality disorders

With the exception of the antisocial personality (to be described later in the chapter), relatively little empirical research has been undertaken on the person-ality disorders. They are relatively newly-classified clinical disorders which were made a part of the DSM classification of psychiatric disorders in 1952.

The student of abnormal psychology faces two problems in learning about these disorders. One problem is that not all psychologists agree on their existence as legitimate psychiatric syndromes. The disagreement hinges on the question of whether or not traits as consistent ways of responding across life situations really exist. For example, is an individual extrovert in all life situations? Behavioural psychologists, on the basis of their research, contend that the existence of cross-situational traits basic to the specific personality disorders is a false premise.

The second problem with the specific personality disorders is the unreliability of diagnosis. In the field trials of the psychiatric manual, the diagnoses of some of the individual personality disorders were considered too unreliable for practical usefulness. One reason for this is the dimensional quality of the characteristics of the disorders, which makes it difficult to decide at what points disorder really exists. The symptoms of personality disorders range from expressions commonly found in a normal population to severely pathological expressions. Many normal individuals are histrionic to a degree. Dependency of a mild sort is found in the interpersonal relationships of otherwise happily well-adjusted individuals. Further complicating the problem of diagnosis of the personality disorder is the overlapping of their symptoms with other psychiatric illness, especially other types of personality disorder.

Exemplifying the degree of uncertainty about the personality disorders is the decision, some years ago, of the American Psychiatric Association to postpone entering two other types of personality disorder in their diagnostic manual pending further studies. One delayed category is self-defeating personality disorder, originally labelled masochistic personality disorder. The objection to this disorder was that it could be used to blame the victim – for example, of rape or spousal abuse – for being victimised. The second category only tentatively put forward but not yet entered in the diagnostic manual is sadistic personality disorder, which is, in a sense, a balancing of the first disorder since it is the obverse of it.

Antisocial personality disorder

ICD-10 uses the label 'dissocial personality' for a disorder having the same char-acteristics as antisocial personality disorder.

Dissocial behaviour such as that now described as an antisocial personality was first identified and distinguished from other psychological disorders in 1837 by the British psychologist J. C. Prichard, who considered it to be 'moral insanity'. He described it in old-fashioned language that nevertheless captured the prin-cipal symptoms of the disease still recognised today. He wrote that while the intellectual abilities are unimpaired, 'the moral and active principles of the mind are strangely perverted and depraved; the power of self-government is lost or greatly impaired; and the individual is found to be incapable, not of talking or reasoning upon any subject proposed to him, for this he will often do with great shrewdness and volubility, but of conducting himself with decency and propriety in the business of life.'

History of the disorder

Clinicians of that day considered it a disorder of the will which made the person incapable of conforming to society's demands. In the late nineteenth century, the disorder came to be called psychopathic personality, and with the biogenic bias of the day, a hereditary basis for the disorder was assumed. This 'bad seed' interpretation held sway until the early part of the twentieth century when social influences were thought to be important causes of the illness and the disorder was named 'sociopathy'. Today the agreed-upon diagnosis is the neutral antisocial personality disorder, although both earlier terms frequently make their appearance. Modern thinking recognises inter-personal, biogenic and sociocultural factors as possible causative elements in the disorder.

Psychopathy and antisocial personality disorder

The terms psychopath and antisocial personality disorder tend to be used interchangeably. Although these disorders have many characteristics in common there are differences which need to be clarified. Both disorders indicate a lack of regard for the rights and feelings of others, antisocial and impulsive behaviour and dissatisfaction with the ordinary. Whereas antisocial personality disorder is behaviourally defined, psychoathy is defined by psychological characteristics as reported by Hervey Cleckley in 1976, psychopathy is a much rarer condition, and could be considered a more extreme case of antisocial personality disorder in which gross acts of insensitivity to others are more often found.

Examples of antisocial personality

Most examples of antisocial personality disorder tend to be extreme, and invariably could also be classed as psychopaths. Examples also inevitably involve extreme criminal acts, usually murder or rape. Two examples of these would be the British serial killer Dennis Neilsen and the American, Gary Gilmour.

Neilsen was approached by a police officer after parts of bodies had been found blocking the drains. He was asked about his part in two deaths, and he very calmly, without emotion, admitted to killing 15 or so people (he was unsure of the exact number) and dismembering the majority for disposal. He was found to have kept corpses around the house, sometimes as company, relating to them in social and sexual ways. Although Neilsen was clearly disturbed in other ways his acts and insensitivity to them were psychopathic.

Gilmour committed purposeless acts of extreme violence, again in the form of serial murder. In shooting his final victim he related that it was something he had to do and showed no remorse for the act or sympathy for the victim. On occasions Gilmour seemed proud of his 'achievements'.

Extreme examples such as these can be misleading, in that some psychopathic or antisocial individuals may escape criminal categorisation, as in the so called 'successful psychopath'. An example here would be the highly-successful businessman, who is ruthless in business but probably just as selfish and ruthless in relations with others. Whilst these characteristics are advantageous in business, their interpersonal consequences would be such things as marital infidelity, indifference to the well-being of relatives and the distrust and confusion caused by pathological lying.

Symptomatology. The symptoms to be described can be divided into the observable antisocial behaviours reaching into childhood, which form the criteria for antisocial personality disorder, and the underlying personality traits more associated with psychopathy. These characteristics usually co-occur, and would, in only extreme cases, satisfy the criteria for psychopathy.

Observable antisocial behaviour

The diagnostic manual, which rests its diagnosis on observable behaviour with no attribution of causality, indicates the following examples as characteristic of the personality disorder: truancy, suspension or expulsion from school; frequent job changes and long periods of unemployment; irresponsible parenting; failure to accept social norms; inability to maintain enduring attachments in heterosexual relationships; irritability and aggressiveness; irresponsibility in meeting financial obligations; impulsiveness and failure to plan ahead; disregard for the truth; reckless behaviour such as recurrent speeding or driving while intoxicated.

No one of these tendencies or a single instance of one or two, especially without an early life history of antisocial behaviour, justifies a diagnosis of personality disorder. Thus such a diagnosis requires that conduct disorder be present before the age of 15, and that at least three of the patterns of antisocial behaviour be present after this age.

Personality characteristics of the antisocial personality

Psychologists who have studied the antisocial personality go beyond the objective criteria of the diagnostic manual to identify personality characteristics of the disorder that seem to engender the described antisocial behaviour. Seven personality traits deeply ingrained in the antisocial personality have been identified by psychologists.

Emotional poverty. The antisocial personality seems never to have developed the capacity to feel strong or deep emotional attachments. There is no real capacity for deep love or loyalty to anyone else. The ordinary emotions of anger, grief and despair are absent. Antisocial personalities show no pity or sympathy for the victim of their crimes, not even much sadness about the sorry plight in which they ultimately find themselves as a result of their behaviour.

Absence of conscience. Along with a flat, affective life-style is a non-working conscience. Although intellectually able to know right from wrong and even ostentatiously mouthing the principles of ethical behaviour, they exhibit no remorse about unprincipled behaviour, no guilt about irresponsible, sometimes vicious behaviour. Nothing seems to affect them about their crimes except perhaps mild unhappiness about having been caught.

Facile charm, glibness and winning ways. A capacity to be charming and to use winning ways to manipulate or exploit others is characteristic of a person with antisocial behaviour disorder. An especially troublesome trait is their glibness and skill in talking others into victimisation. Many victims, even after having been exploited, maintain good feelings about the individual who victimised them. The antisocial personality is frequently able to escape arrest or punishment by their persuasiveness and deliberately-projected air of candour and sincerity.

They make friends easily, and just as easily give them up or take advantage of them. They easily persuade others of their good faith, and at times almost delude themselves into believing that what they say is all right.

Inadequately motivated behaviour. As much as we may deplore criminal behaviour, we can still make sense of what the normal criminal has attempted – to make money, to collect on an insurance policy, to make important connections. The antisocial behaviour of the disordered individual seems purposeless and spur of the moment: a crime committed, often a heinous one, because the individual felt like doing it. The individual is unable to say why he committed the crime. In place of the usual motives for the crime, there is impulsiveness and the need to seek thrills and excitement.

Inability to learn or profit from experience. Antisocial individuals go through life without ever seeming to learn from mistakes, to be more calculating in planning their behaviour the next time, or to make efforts to avoid detection. The ordinary punishments that most people would fear seem meaningless to them. Their needs are immediate, and memories of past punishments have little if any influence on what they will do today or tomorrow.

Shattered interpersonal relations. Initial friendships won by their glibness and exploitative charm are very quickly shattered by the antisocial individual's soon-to-be-discovered, cynical, ungrateful and unfeeling behaviour to the newly-acquired friends. Lifetime interpersonal relationships are nothing but a series of short contacts, callously looked upon by the antisocial personality as new opportunities for manipulation and exploitation.

Odd reactions to punishment. Certain punishments which normal people try diligently to avoid seem meaningless to antisocial personalities. They seem not to be influenced by physical punishment and care not a whit for social disapproval except as it might interfere with an immediate exploitative venture. But at least one experiment demonstrates a concern about loss of money. The proper conclusion to draw here is that the punishment is influential with such individuals only if it specifically interferes with an ongoing goal, and it is therefore especially noxious.

Prevalence

The DSM-IV, supported by other epidemiological studies, indicates the prevalence of antisocial personality to be between three and five per cent of males and less than one per cent of females. Onset for males is preadolescent: for females, during puberty.

Causative factors in antisocial personality disorder

Antisocial personality disorder, the first of the personality disorders to be identified, is the most widely researched and the best understood. Although there is some disagreement among psychologists about the other personality disorders, psychologists agree on the principal symptoms of the antisocial personality disorder, and the reliability of the diagnosis is high. There is also substantial evidence that the disorder develops out of some mix of four principal elements: early family relationships and parenting practices; defects in learning; biogenic factors, both genetic and physiological; and sociocultural factors.

Early family relationships and parenting practices

Four types of intrafamily experiences seem to be strongly associated with the development if antisocial personality disorder. They are as follows: loss of a parent, inconsistent parental behaviour, lack of emotional support from parents, and the modelling of sociopathic parents of the individual.

Loss of a parent.   Greer, in a 1964 study, reported that while 60 per cent of a group of psychopathic individuals had lost a parent, in two control groups in the study, the percentage was significantly less – 28 per cent of a control group of neurotic individuals and an almost equal number (27 per cent) of a control group of individuals classified as normal. There can be no doubt that loss of a parent is a catastrophic event in a child's growth, but since so many other children who have lost a parent, or even both parents, grow to maturity with no significant psychiatric illness, such a loss seems to fall short of being an adequate cause of psychopathy in itself. Other research suggests it is the loss of a parent in an already disturbed family situation that is a significant element.

Abnormal family relations.   A disrupted or hostile home environment can obviously lead to disturbance in the child, especially where this is sustained over a long period of time. Emotional poverty in relations with and between parents has been associated with antisocial behaviour in offspring. Disadvantaged parenting, for example single mothers or serious mental or physical disability in one or more parents can lead to a situation where the child's needs cannot be sufficiently coped with and disruptive behaviour is difficult to address. Similar outcomes can more readily result from marital distress, antisocial parents and child abuse. However, in this type of association, the possibility that the characteristics of the antisocial child may cause the parenting problem in the first place has to be considered.

Defective early learning experiences

Ethical values and principles are normally learned at home. When the models parents offer are inconsistent, children fail to develop any sense of discipline or ethical control.

Inconsistent discipline. When the reward/punishment practices at home are inconsistent, or when each parent takes a different approach – for example, a stern, disciplinarian father and a mother who compensates (perhaps out of hostility to her husband) by leniency, secretive rewards and giving in to any demands made by the child – the child grows up confused about values, may pick up hostility to all authority as representing a hated father, and learn manipulative and exploitative behaviour from the unwitting co-operation of his or her mother. Such skewed parental relations often transmit inconsistent values to the child, who may adopt these for itself.

Impulse control and goal-directed behaviour. Antisocial individuals are less able than others to suppress impulses to act or satisfy immediate needs which, it should be noted, is also a characteristic of young children. They are also poor at sustaining goal-directed behaviour, especially where the goal in question is not immediately obvious or readily attainable. Gorenstein (1991) drew these two aspects together in explaining each. In this Gorenstein assumes that the representations in the mind of events that are not immediately present are weak in these individuals. Thus long-term goals relying on such representations are easily lost or subverted by attention to those events in the immediate environment. Impulsive over-attention to the events or stimuli immediately present further increases this tendency, which can become a fixed pattern of dealing with immediate events and long-term goals.

Underarousal and defective avoidance learning. Several early studies of the antisocial personality indicate that they are underaroused by emotional or noxious stimuli which would strongly arouse normal individuals. There is physiological evidence to suggest that their autonomic nervous systems respond at a low level of variability, lowering the level of fear and anxiety they experience. (See discussion under Biogenic Factors.) A series of skilfully constructed and carefully controlled experiments seemed to demonstrate that their low level of arousal not only causes impulsive and stimulant-seeking behaviour, but also results in deficient avoidance learning.

To test the hypothesis that the sociopath's low level of arousal impairs ability to learn from negative experiences or punishment (avoidance learning), a group of sociopaths were compared with a group of healthy individuals in learning a mental maze. They were asked to learn which one of four levers turned on a green light. Two of the levers produced the wrong response of red. The fourth lever produced an electric shock. The task was one of considerable complexity. Sociopaths and nonsociopaths, as expected, made the same total number of errors; but while the normal subjects quickly learned to avoid the punishing electric shock, sociopaths took much longer to do so. Their capacity to avoid punishment seemed to be impaired, possibly because the electric shock was not as noxious, ie. punishing, for them as it was for normal subjects.

Biogenic factors

Possible biological factors causing antisocial behaviour fall into two categories – genetic and physiological – the latter of which may, however, be caused by the genetic anomalies.

Genetic factors. Much research has been devoted to the question of possible genetic causes of antisocial personality disorder. The safest conclusion to draw from those studies is that sociopathy is the result of a combination of hereditary and environmental influences. Two Danish studies illustrate the nature of the research conducted and the resultant findings.

Using official Copenhagen registration data and police files, the researcher isolated a group of sociopaths who had been adopted from infancy. He found that the biological relatives of the sociopaths were four to five times more likely than the adoptive relatives to meet the criteria for a diagnosis of antisocial personality. He nevertheless reported that the small differences justified only the conclusion that although there is a genetic factor operating, environmental influences must also be considered as significant.

In a second Danish study, the criminal records of adoptees were compared with the criminal records of the biological and adoptive parents. The incidence rate of crime, as might be expected, was lowest when neither biological nor adoptive fathers had been convicted of a crime. Differing only slightly from that comparison was the rate when the adoptive parent was a criminal but the biological father was not. On the contrary, when the biological father was a criminal, but not the adoptive father, the rate of criminal behaviour jumped significantly. However, the highest criminal rate was found among those adoptees both of whose fathers, biological and adoptive, had criminal records. Here is a finding that supports both hereditary and environmental influence on criminal behaviour.

While this study examined convicted criminals, not necessarily those that had been diagnosed as antisocial personalities, it is likely that a good number of the criminals were sociopaths. In any case, considering only this study, the evidence suggests a genetic factor, but one that interacts with environmental influences. To put it colloquially and loosely, it can be said that although a predisposition to antisocial behaviour has a genetic base, the mode of antisocial behaviour will be learned from the environment the individual experiences.

Physiological factors. Given possible genetic causative influence, the question remains, what is it that is inherited to cause the development of antisocial behaviour? One strongly supported interpretation suggests that the antisocial personality is born with a physiological deficiency that creates a cortical immaturity. A delayed development of the higher functions of the brain results. Two well-known characteristics of the sociopath give credence to this interpretation. Between 30 and 38 per cent of all antisocial personalities show abnormal brain wave patterns (electroencephalograph recordings). The most common feature of the abnormality is a slow brain wave activity characteristic of infants and children, but not of adults. Given time, the immature brain will, later on in life, finally mature. With the maturing of the brain, changes in behaviour can be expected. Such change does take place in many sociopaths as they grow older when much of their flagrant antisocial behaviour diminishes.

Since much of the abnormal slow brain wave activity comes from the temporal lobes and the limbic system of the brain (the second layer of the brain), areas of the brain that control both memory and emotional behaviour, it is thought that genetic influences operate by impairing those parts of the brain. Their impairment would seem to create a physiological basis for the low level of arousal characteristic of the antisocial personalities and their difficulties with avoidance learning.

Sociocultural causative factors

The diagnostic manual reports that the antisocial personality disorder is more common in lower socio-economic groups. In interpreting that statement, care must be taken not to identify poverty with psychiatric illness and not to conclude that poverty by itself is a cause of antisocial behaviour. At most, an impoverished home life can be only a contributory cause and only that when other social and biogenic causes are operative.

From an early age, children emulate the behaviour of parents. When that behaviour is irresponsible and antisocial, it is all too common that they follow the example set for them. The DSM manual relates this causative element to the socio-economic level of the child in these words: 'The disorder is more common in lower-class populations, partly because it is associated with impaired learning capacity, and partly because fathers of those with the disorder frequently have the disorder themselves and consequently their children grow up in impoverished homes'. One can add to this statement, 'with little opportunity to learn different ways of behaving'.

Treatment of antisocial personalities

Personality disorders are, by definition, not really treatable, being life-long propensities. Most professionals agree that antisocial personality disorder is virtually impossible to treat. The one ray of hope with such individuals is that their antisocial behaviour tends to subside or even remit as they pass the age of 40 or so. This means that those who have been imprisoned for their behaviour may eventually not return to prison as they grow older, perhaps a further sign of extended immaturity in this disorder. Other measures that can be taken lie in the detection of potentially disordered individuals before their behaviour results in harm to others. This can be carried out by using the symptomatic criteria as a kind of checklist, especially for those applying to children or adolescents.

Negative influences on response to therapy

Three elements work against successful therapy with the antisocial personality: the ingrained nature of their symptoms, their inability to relate to others, and the involuntary nature of the therapy that society frequently offers them.

Deeply ingrained personality traits. The underlying causes of the antisocial behaviour are personality traits that have developed in the individual from early childhood. Lifelong patterns of behaviour are resistant to change.

The nature of symptoms. The principal characteristics of the antisocial personality described previously make impossible any interpersonal relationship that is dependent upon mutual trust, and such trust is a requirement of all forms of psychotherapy.

Involuntary treatment. Antisocial personalities are more likely to wind up in the prison system than in the wards of the psychiatric hospital. The rehabilitation programmes provided are largely involuntary, and they have little impact on the antisocial personality. For them, the penal system seems to be a revolving door; in and out unchanged.

Caveats for attempts at therapy. Those clinicians attempting to establish therapies for antisocial or psychopathic individuals need to confront the limitations and false hopes arising from work with such a patient group. Manipulation and exploitation of the investigator and therapeutic situation is very likely, and a clinician wishing for success may be reluctant to recognise this. People with this disorder will also lie and fabricate material, usually to their advantage but sometimes just for fun or their own perverse entertainment. Any gains will usually be short term and must be realistically monitored over time to evaluate progress.

It is fair to state that the realisation that any therapeutic relationship with antisocial or psychopathic individuals can only be superficial and regarding these individuals for what they are, rather than assuming traits and sensitivites that are clearly absent, provides the best way forward in such research.

SUMMARY

The common characteristic of all personality disorders is the development early in life of personality traits that are persistent, maladaptive, and that cause either significant impairment in social or occupational adjustment or extreme personal distress.

The DSM-IV organises the ten types of personality disorder into three clusters.

Cluster A includes the paranoid, schizoid and schizotypal disorders. In all of these, the characteristic symptom is odd or eccentric (but not bizarre) behaviour.

Cluster B includes the histrionic personality disorder, narcissistic person-

ality disorder, antisocial personality disorder, and borderline personality disorder. Except for the last, in which wide-ranging instability of behaviour is characteristic, they are expressed in self-centred and inordinately selfish behaviour.

Cluster C includes avoidant, dependent and obsessive–compulsive personality disorders. These have in common the high degree of personal distress experienced by the victims of the disorder.

Of the personality disorders, more is known about antisocial personality disorder than any of the other personality disorders. With respect to the others, there is disagreement among clinicians as to whether or not they truly exist as separate clinical entities. The disagreement rests on controversy about the psychological existence of traits (persistent ways of reacting to the external world) in the expression of personality. Since each personality disorder, except antisocial personality, rests on the presence of an extreme personality trait, if traits as consistent ways of behaviour do not exist, neither do the personality disorders that rest on their existence.

The antisocial personality is characterised by emotional poverty, absense of conscience, often facile charm, inexplicable motivation, frequent bouts of violent or criminal behaviour, inability to profit from experience, shattered interpersonal relationships, and an indifferent reaction to punishment. Both organic and psychological factors are thought to operate in causing the disorder. Treatment is rarely undertaken voluntarily and is rarely successful.

FURTHER READING

Blackburn, R. 1988. On Moral Judgements and Personality Disorders. The Myth of Psychopathic Personality Revisited. *British Journal of Psychiatry,* 153: 505–512

Cleckley, H. 1976. *The Mask of Sanity*. St Louis: C. V. Mosby.

Derksen, J. 1955. *Personality Disorders: Clinical and Social Perspectives*. Wiley.

Prins, H.1995. *Offenders, Deviants or Patients?* (2nd ed). London: Routledge.

Ross, A. 1992. *Personality*. HarperCollins.

Siguardsson, S., C. R. Clonenger, M. Cohman, & A. L. von Knorring. 1982. Predisposition to Petty Criminality in Swedish Adoptees. III Sex Differences and Validation of the Male Typology. *Archives of General Psychiatry*, 39: 1248–1253.

Stafford-Clark, D., Bridges, P. & Black, D. 1989. *Psychiatry for Students* (7th ed). London: Routledge.

11 The Mood Disorders

Rare, indeed, if any, are those individuals who are never 'in a mood' – downcast, discouraged, even depressed; or, on the other hand, elated, optimistic and energetic beyond one's usual feelings. It is normal, occasionally, to be 'down in the dumps', a mood that may be triggered by a disturbing family argument. It is just as normal to go through a period of feeling that 'everything is rosy', when problems melt away, energy and optimism are high and much activity, sometimes bordering of the frenetic, goes on.

In the depressed mood, energy drains away, interest in old pleasures wanes, and little is accomplished. In a manic spell, much seems to get done, not always precisely as planned; new projects are begun, resolutions are made, old projects are finished, high hopes are preoccupying, only to fade away too soon when reality is confronted once again.

Among the normal populations, these moods have their beginning in some real-life situation and they are terminated by a real-life event. Depression disappears after a happy family day or upon receipt of an unexpected compliment. Elation disappears as the reality of life's problems captures our attention. They are both of relatively short duration, and they lead to no drastic or damaging actions.

Such moods are to be distinguished from the extreme moods or mood swings described later in this chapter. They are mentioned in order to reiterate a point that has been made before with other psychiatric disorders: that abnormal behaviour finds its place on a continuum of behaviour from the normal and well-adjusted to the extreme and severely maladaptive.

One other point needs mention here in this introductory statement. The array of diagnoses involving mood disturbances, especially for depression, may seem like hair splitting. But the distinctions made among mood disorders exist because, although on the surface they may seem similar, they represent different disorders that follow their own course, often respond to different therapies and, in extreme cases, lead to markedly different outcomes, including suicide or suicidal attempts.

This chapter first identifies the symptoms of depression and mania as mood disorders, then describes the classification of mood disturbances, and briefly indicates their prevalence. It continues with a discussion of possible causes of mood disorders, and then examines the principal therapies found helpful in their treatment. Finally, it examines the sad phenomenon of suicide, a possible outcome of a severe mood disorder.

Depression and mania

The two principal affective (emotional) states of the mood disorders are depression and mania. Although depression can appear alone as a diagnosis, mania is now classified as if accompanied by depression (ie. as bipolar disorder or cyclothemia).

Of the two states, depression is the much more frequent, occurring in 90 per cent of the mood disorders. A long-known form of the disorder is one that alternates between depression and mania. It was formerly labelled manic-depressive psychosis. Sadness, dejection and grieving dominate the life of the disordered individual during the depressed stage. Those feeling may be accompanied by feelings of worthlessness and a sense of the futility of life. There may be profuse weeping or periodic heavy sighing. The loss of a loved one may normally produce many of the same emotional feelings, but the normal individual gradually recovers and returns to normal pursuits. Prolonged grieving of the type described would suggest the presence of a mood disorder.

The individual's posture – stooping, head down, glum facial expression, flat voice – all signal the depression the individual is experiencing. Spontaneity and expressive movements disappear. Actions are slow and plodding in an overall psychomotor retardation. The person may remain all day in slippers and bathrobe; or, if depressed, clothing will be sloppy and stained, the hair uncombed. Women wear no make-up; men go about dishevelled. The behaviour of the individual says very clearly, 'I don't care anymore'.

If for no other reasons, the changed lifestyle of the individual will produce physiological changes. There may be loss of appetite and weight, or, on the contrary, the individual may overeat, not a full planned meal, but small servings, all day long. Constipation is a frequent symptom. Sleep patterns are disturbed; there may be difficulty in falling asleep or waking after an hour or two and being unable to sleep. Or, in contrast, there may be excessive sleeping or drowsing in bed all day long. Sexual interest wanes or disappears altogether.

Symptomatology of mania

As one would expect, in mania the behaviour is at the opposite extreme of that of the depressed individual. Characteristically, the manic individual is highly charged, and expends energy uselessly and steadily.

Elation, unrealistic optimism, expansiveness, planning, seemingly backed by endless energy, are the early symptoms. Blocked or criticised, the manic individual will turn irritable, which mood change can soon become belligerency, with abusive and profane language. The individual's strong and unleashed emotions lead to uninhibited behaviour, argumentative reactions to others and, occasionally, uninvited and unacceptable sexual advances.

The range of behaviour symptoms in the manic have been graded into three categories. Hypomania is the least disturbed. The individual seems supercharged in mood and overactive in behaviour. The push in their affective life leads to bad judgement, but not delusions. They are grandiose and dominating in conversation, and are unprepared to 'listen to reason'. Although this level of mania is indeed a mood disorder, it is often accepted by those who have grown used to it. They may, for example, simply describe the individual as boorish and unpleasant company, but basically harmless. Indeed, many very creative people, usually poets, have been diagnosed as hypomanic. They have harnessed the energy of the mania for creative purposes, but hypomanic people usually lead emotionally-tormented lives as a result of the other features of the disorder.

At the next level of mania, acute mania, all symptoms are more extreme. Maniacs become incoherent in speech. They are readily judged to be disordered. Irritability at rebuff, criticism or frustration may be frightening. The acute phase may be an outgrowth of hypomania, but also may spring up quite acutely and with no warning.

In the most extreme form of mania, delirious mania, the individual is completely out of control. The disorder at this stage is the stereotype of the 'wild maniac'. Hallucinations and delusions are present, and behaviour dangerous to the manic individual or to others is possible. Physical restraint or sedation in a hospital soon becomes necessary. The principal physiological change is sleeplessness, leading to exhaustion.

Classification of the mood disorders

In classifying the mood disorders, three major criteria are considered: the cyclical or non-cyclical nature of the illness – that is, whether or not there are alternating periods of depression and mania; the degree of the depression or mania – mild, moderate or severe. The difference between the mildest category of the disorder, whether manic or depressive, and the most extreme category, is considerable. The former border on the normal range of depressive or manic mood, and the latter usually justify the diagnosis, 'with psychotic features', and can require a period of hospitalisation. The third criterion, the duration of the illness, categorises the disorders as acute, chronic or intermittent.

The DSM-IV classification of mood disorders is presented below.

Depression: Depressive disorder (Unipolar disorder)
– Single episode
– Recurrent
Dysthemic disorder
Mood disorder with seasonal pattern (can also be bipolar)
Mood disorder with postpartum onset
Pre-menstrual dysphoric disorder

Bipolar: Bipolar disorder
                              Type I
                              Type II
                    Cyclothemia

The ICD-10 classification of mood disorders differs from this as below.

Depression: Depressive episode
                    Depressive episode with psychotic symptoms

Bipolar: Bipolar affective disorder
                    Cyclothemia
                    Manic episode

Normal Depression

Although there is no DSM-IV classification for normal depression, the condition is prevalent, and can be alleviated by help from a mental health specialist. Even though normal depression requires no outside help in most cases, when there is any doubt, it is better to err on the conservative side than to take chances.

Grief

Certain events in life bring on the emotion of grief and plunge the individual into the grieving process. The most common cause of grief is, of course, the death of a loved one. There are other grief-causing sorrows in life: the loss of a long-held job (even through promotion or transfer), thereby cutting the individual from a daily network of social experiences; the moving away of a lifelong friend; the sale of a home in which one has lived for years. Any of these experiences can bring on grieving. In psychological terms, they are called stressors, that is, any event or situation causing stress.

   As long as the grieving process does not go to extreme lengths or last longer than a month or two, it can be a quiet time of recovery from an emotionally affecting loss, and not at all abnormal. It is a frequent and probably useful device to break the grieving period by a treat of some sort: a short trip, a shopping spree, or a small family party.

Life situations causing normal depression

In some life situations, simple depression can follow very normal life experiences, such as the depression that sometimes follows the birth of a child. One study reports that almost 50 per cent of new mothers experience a 'down' mood. Students can also experience a kind of postpartum depression. Note that in the case of higher levels of depression in recent motherhood (within four weeks), DSM-IV now recognises this as a separate diagnosable disorder. Among doctoral candidates, depression might appear right after their final oral examinations; among undergraduates, a 'normal' depression often hits the day after graduation. Throughout the college years, students can be overwhelmed by dependency needs, by feelings of being ineffective or inadequate, with a resulting depressive spell, usually of short duration.

There is no sure antidote for depression caused by those unpleasant but normal and all-too-frequent life experiences. Reaching out to close and supportive friends or relatives, if the individual can mobilise the energy to do so, can be helpful. Also, the knowledge can be reassuring that in most cases (the percentage is difficult to estimate) the stimulation of the normal pleasures and demands of life soon terminate the depression.

Mild to moderate mood disorders

There are three mood disorders characterised as mild to moderate; one is cyclical, cylothymia; the second, dysthymia, is characterised only by depression. A further type of mood disorder, not included in DSM-IV, is essentially a depressive response to a recent stressor and has in the past been listed as an adjustment disorder. It has been considered useful to describe it here. Attention should be drawn also to the disorders listed further in the chapter as event specific mood disorders which may also be in a moderate form.

Cyclothymia

Cyclothymia was at one time considered a personality disorder because it seems to be a lifetime pattern of behaviour, in which the individual experiences moods alternating between hypomania (mild to moderate spells of heightened activity) and mild to moderate depressive periods. It is now listed as a mood disorder, not a personality disorder. There is research to suggest that it is a less severe form of bipolar mood disorder (discussed later).

Symptomatology. The DSM-IV lists as a diagnostic criterion for cyclothymic disorder a two-year period of numerous spells of alternating depressive and manic symptoms. The two phases may be separated by months-long periods of normal mood.

Among the prominent symptoms are the following: during the depressed phase, low energy level and chronic fatigue; insomnia or too much sleeping or drowsing; feelings of inadequacy; social isolation; reduced levels of functioning, complicated by concentration, memory and thinking problems.

During the hypomanic phase, there is a pattern of behaviour which is the very opposite of that which exists during the depressed phase, including more energy, less need for sleep; high self-esteem; talkativeness, with much laughter and bois-terousness; overoptimism; exaggerated efforts at productivity, including working at unusual hours; heightened social activity, with the possibility of hypersexu-ality, with little sense of responsibility; foolish activities, such as buying sprees, reckless driving, and baseless boasting.

None of the behaviour is extreme enough to justify a diagnosis of a major mood disorder. There are no hallucinations, delusions or loosened associations. Nevertheless, complications of this disorder may lead to major manic or depressive episodes. It is for that reason that cyclothymia is thought to be a mild form of a more serious bipolar disorder.

Prevalence. Now judged to be a common disorder, frequently accepted by the individual and family as an extreme way of behaving, without recognition of its disordered nature, cyclothymia begins early in life and has a chronic course. It is more common among women.

Dysthymia

The DSM-IV's diagnostic criterion for the disorder is a two-year period during which the individual suffers much of the time from symptoms of depression.

Symptomatology. Except for the absence of manic or hypomanic phases, the individual's symptoms are those of the depressed phase of cyclothymia. The depressed moods may be persistent, or interrupted by short periods of normal mood. There is an absence of psychotic features. Dysthymia may be a chronic condition in which a mild depressive mood is a characteristic way of responding to life.

Prevalence. A common mood disorder, dysthymia is more frequently found among women. Onset is usually early in life: and for this reason, in the past, this disorder was considered a personality disorder.

Adjustment disorder with depressed mood

Here the depressive symptoms of dysthymia are judged to be a response to a stressor known to have occurred within three months of its onset. The causative stressor can take a variety of forms, such as a single event, for example, a divorce after years of marriage, or a prolonged period of unhappiness caused by marital discord, business difficulties, or unpleasant living circumstances. The stressors may be a catastrophic experience or persecution resulting from racial or religious prejudice. Stressors may simply be times of difficult readjustment: starting school, having to move away from a long-time neighbourhood, marriage under certain circumstances, or occupational change.

It is assumed that the disorder will remit by itself when the pressure of the stressor wanes, or when a new level of adjustment is achieved, possibly with the help of short-term psychotherapy.

Symptomatology. In the adjustment disorder, there is the full range of depressive symptoms previously described for other mild to moderate depressive disorders. Vulnerability to depression, from whatever agents, may cause the disorder, even though the stressor would not normally affect others in the same way. On the other hand, extreme stressors may cause only mild depression or none at all in non-vulnerable individuals.

Prevalence. Adjustment disorders are common. The disorder may occur at any age. No sex differences are reported.

Moderate to severe disorders

The two categories of mood disorder discussed here are comparable to cyclothymia and dysthymia, because one, labelled bipolar, is cyclical; and the other, a unipolar disorder, usually labelled major depression, is not, since manic moods do not occur. The major difference between the two groups is that the latter grouping (bipolar and unipolar disorder) present a much more extreme set of symptoms, which may include psychotic features.

Bipolar disorder

This disorder of alternating patterns of depression and mania was labelled manic depressive psychosis by Kraepelin in 1899. That diagnosis was used for many years, and with it went Kraepelin's belief that there was a general favourable prognosis. His use of the label 'psychosis' suggests the severe nature of the disorder's symptoms in their most extreme form. The DSM-IV uses the term 'bipolar disorder', which is now divided into bipolar I disorders and bipolar II disorder. Bipolar II disorder refers to recurrent major depressive episodes with at least one episode of hypomania, but no episodes of mania. The subdivisions of bipolar I disorders are characterised by the form of the most recent episode, which could be: a single manic episode with no previous depression or mania; a hypomanic episode with previous mania; a manic episode with previous mood disorder; a mixed episode, ie. both mania and depression in this episode; an episode of depression with previous mania, and where the recent episode is unspecified. Thus there are six different divisions under bipolar I disorder and cyclothymia providing eight descriptive categories for the presentation of manic depressive symptoms.

Unipolar disorder

In the absence of manic features, a moderate to severe mood disorder is labelled 'unipolar disorder'. 'Major depression' is the more commonly used diagnosis. There are two subcategories of major depression: single episode, that is, without a prior history of depression; and recurrent, in which the individual has had one or more major depressions in the past.

Special features of moderate to severe mood disorders

There are two special features of these more serious mood disorders. They are the possible existence of a melancholic aspect to major depression and the presence of psychotic features in the more extreme mood disorders.

Melancholia

In major depression with melancholic aspects, in addition to the specific symptoms of the typical major depression, the individual shows a loss of pleasure in all activities, even those that were formerly pleasurable. The patient reports not feeling any better, even for the moment, when something good happens.

In addition, for a diagnosis of major depression, melancholic type, the DSM system requires that at least three of the following symptoms be present: a depression, regularly worse in the morning; early morning waking; notable psychomotor retardation or agitation; loss of appetite or weight loss; marked feelings of guilt.

The diagnosis, melancholic type, is considered of special significance for two reasons:

1 The psychiatric literature suggest that it is of endogenous causation, that is, it comes from within the individual and seems unrelated to external events (although the concept of 'endogenous depression' has been challenged in recent years).
2 It seems to respond to biologically-based therapy.

Mood disorders with psychotic features

Extreme types of mood disorder may include such symptoms of psychosis as marked impairment in reality testing, manifested in hallucinations or delusions; or the presence of a suppressive stupor, which is signalled when the individual becomes mute or is totally unresponsive.

The delusions or hallucinations may be 'mood congruent' – that is, consistent with such depressive themes as personal inadequacy, guilt, deserved punishment, disease, death or nihilism. Or they may be 'mood incongruent' – that is, where the content of the impaired reality testing is unrelated to depressive themes. Included here are persecutory themes and thought insertion or thought broadcasting, also characteristic of schizophrenia (see chapter 12).

Event-specific mood disorders

DSM-IV includes three categories of mood disorders which are associated with specific events: the seasons of the year, the weeks following childbirth and the pre-menstrual period for women.

Mood disorders with a seasonal pattern can be diagnosed if there is a regular relationship between the disorder and the time of the year, usually depression in winter and (with bipolar type) manic symptoms in spring/summer. Mood disorder with a postnatal onset is where a depressive episode occurs in a mother within four weeks of childbirth. This is usually associated with a pre-existing condition, pre-menstrual dysphoric disorder, where disturbed mood occurs during the last week of the luteal phase of the woman's cycle.

Overall prevalence of mood disorders

Although most surveys report that up to 16 per cent of men and 24 per cent of women report depressive symptoms, only four per cent of men and eight per cent of women (at the highest estimate) are actually diagnosed as having depressive illness. Mood disorders are very common amongst patient groups and with other patient groups and depression is often found with other psychiatric disorders.

In extreme forms, mood disorders are one of the most frequently diagnosed psychiatric conditions, leading to hospitalisation. Unipolar mood disorder (depression only) is the most frequently-occurring disorder: it has increased in the past 50 years. Bipolar or cyclical mood disorder, with a prevalence of 0.5 to one per cent, is also reported to have increased. Bipolar disorder is equally common among both sexes. The disorder is principally a disease of the adult years. However, one study reports a five per cent prevalence among primary school children.

Causative factors in mood disorders

Full explanations for the occurrence of mood disorders continue to challenge medical and psychological science. Two broad categories of possible causes have been established: biogenic factors and psychosocial factors. In neither does there exist an entirely adequate explanation for the aetiology of mood disorders.

Biogenic causative factors

There are three major factors that medical and psychological research have focused on: genetic, biochemical and neuroendocrine elements. There is research support of varying conclusiveness for the possible causative influence of each. Of the three, the most conclusive evidence is that which relates genetic factors to the development of a vulnerability to mood disorders.

Genetic predisposition

Three strands of evidence tend to establish faulty genes as influential, at least in predisposing the individual to a mood disorder. They are as follows:

1 Blood relatives of those with a mood disorder have a higher incidence of the disorder than is found in the general population.
2 The concordance rate for mood disorders is much higher for identical twins than for fraternal twins (those having different genes).

Neither of those approaches clearly disentangles environmental from hereditary influences. That job has been accomplished by the third type of study:

3 Studies of identical twins who have been reared apart assure that while genetic factors are identical, environmental influences are likely to be varied. High concordance rates for the presence of a mood disorder were found among the identical twins, even though the environments in which they grew up varied. In a variation of this study, mood disorders among the blood relatives of the mood-disordered population were eight times more common than among relatives of the normal population.

One of the distinctions between unipolar and bipolar disorders lies in their genetic risk factors. In this, the first degree relatives of an individual with unipolar disorder have a high risk of developing unipolar depression. However, the close relatives of an individual with bipolar disorder have a high risk of developing both unipolar and bipolar disorders.

Recent research has used 'linkage' to try to identify the location of the genetic component of mood disorders. This is where some genetic feature co-occurs with the disorder for which the location of the gene(s) is known. This gene is then assumed to be 'linked' to the disorder gene(s). Some success has been reported in achieving this in relation to bipolar disorder, although this study has not been replicated successfully. Despite the presence of a definite genetic component for mood disorders, there must be other influences on the actual incidence of the disorder that inheritance predisposes the individual to.

Biochemical factors

Research evidence, accumulating since the sixties, has brought under suspicion biochemical elements as a cause of mood disorders. Those elements seem to affect the neurotransmitters of the brain, which regulate the passage of nerve impulses across the synaptic gap between neurones in the brain.

Attention was drawn to this possibility by the observations that several biological therapies used with mood disorders – for example, electroconvulsive treatment, antidepressant drugs, and lithium – affect the concentration of biochemical substances at the synapses and determine whether particular pathways in the brain facilitate or slow down transmission of brain impulses. Thus there is clear evidence that synaptic transmission is altered during depression, but this could be a cause or a consequence of depression. If the neurochemical balance is causal, this in itself may be due to a genetically inherited defect. Still uncertain is whether or not that condition is brought about by genetic inheritance.

Neuroendocrine factors

The body's endocrine glands secrete fluids (hormones), and the effect of those hormonal influences is a focus of much research. One hormonal substance, cortisol, is particularly suspect as having an effect on the development of mood disorders. Hypothyroidism (underactivity of the thyroid gland) seems also to be related to depression.

An important outcome of research in the biological sciences is the suggestion that there is a variety of depressive reactions, traceable to different biological causes and reactive to different forms of biogenic therapy. Such findings tend to increase the role of medicine in the treatment of depression, a development that is in no way antithetical to the positive influences of psychotherapy on the reduction of depression.

Psychological factors

Although there is a firmly-established link between mood disorders and biological factors, there are a number of psychological factors which have been associated with these disorders. A final picture of the cause of mood disorder will almost certainly include the interaction of biological and psychological elements.

The possible effect of a large number of psychological factors has been the subject of psychological research, the principal of which are as follows: environmental stress; attitudes held by the individual towards life and the future; and learned helplessness.

Environmental stressors

It is well known that environmental stressors produce strong emotional responses that, in turn, affect the body's functioning in a variety of ways. When the stressors are operative over a period of time, or when they are catastrophic, the bodily changes they cause bring about biochemical/hormonal changes, especially in genetically predisposed individuals.

Beck, who has developed his own approach to the treatment of depression, identifies six types of stressors that are especially likely to trigger depression:

1 Those that lower the individual's self-esteem – for example, failure in an important endeavour or neglect from loved ones.
2 Frustration in achieving major life goals or facing unresolvable conflict.
3 Physical disease or illness that brings on thoughts of death.
4 Stressors of catastrophic dimension.
5 A series of stressful encounters that suggest a never-ending sequence.
6 Stressors, below the level of consciousness, that nevertheless sap the individual's energies and spirit .

Negative attitudes

Beck has also reported the prior existence among depressive individuals as a substratum of the individual's personality, of a set of negative attitudes: towards the self, the world, and the future. There is the suggestion in the psychological research that such bleak attitudes are frequently found in adults who, as children, have experienced the loss of a cherished parent. Beck's treatment of depressed individuals (described later) is directed at reversing those negative attitudes.

Pre-existent personality traits

Other research has sought, with mixed results, to identify pre-episodic personality traits among the mood disorders. Where such traits have been identified, as one might expect, the identified personality traits are different for manic-type and depressive-type individuals. The pre-episodic personality characteristics of manic-type individuals tend to be conventional and achievement-oriented.

Predepression traits tend toward self-deprecation, with some indications of repressed hostility. Despite the tentative research findings, it is inaccurate to assume that either set of traits predisposes an individual to mood disorders.

Learned helplessness

One of the most useful concepts to arise in the last 20 years or so, has been that of learned helplessness. This is based on the work of Martin Seligman in the area of learning theory but includes clear cognitive elements, and as such, has influenced the cognitive approaches of such therapists as Beck.

Seligman exposed dogs to a situation where they were unable to control electric shocks and found that the animals learned from this that they were unable to control significant events (in this case shock). This experience was generalised to future learning situations where the animals would adopt the behaviour (and appearance!) of clinically depressed humans in making no effort to control adverse events, simply accepting punishment passively.

In his book *Helplessness*, Seligman points to a similar series of events occurring in humans in various situations. In these situations the individuals were exposed to uncontrollable events, leaving them in a passive role. They suffered depression, biological depressive effects, increased mortality and physical illnesses. Learned helplessness has also been found to be an explanation of many of the depressive aspects of post-traumatic stress disorder and provides an explanation for the problem of suicide amongst young people who 'have everything'.

Although subsequent research by Seligman and his colleagues has limited the effects of learned helplessness to only some forms of depression, the principle is still a very useful one and one with strong support from the biological make-up of the endogenous reward system in the human brain, which 'rewards' successful behaviour neurochemically. In Seligman's theory, learning that one can be effective in controlling events can provide the antidote to learned helplessness. Clearly a sense of control seems to be an important concept in many psychological disorders.

Self-directed aggression

One psychosocial interpretation of depression, anger turned inward, is derived from the early psychoanalytical thinking of Sigmund Freud and Carl Abraham. Freud, in his classic paper, *Mourning and Melancholia*, traces the anger back to an early childhood rejection by a deeply-loved person, ordinarily the mother or father. Unable to express the anger because of guilt, the rejected individual identifies with or 'incorporates' the rejecting person into his or her own being and then directs the anger against himself or herself. It is, according to psychoanalytic theory, the self-anger that causes the lowered self-esteem. Open self-accusations and expressed need for punishment are characteristic of melancholic depression. In later life, any loss or rejection reactivates the anger (still self-directed) and engenders a depressive reaction.

This psychodynamic view is included for its historical value. Although some psychoanalysts still subscribe to this view, there is no empirical evidence to support the psychodynamic basis for it.

Treatment of mood disorders

Mood disorders respond to two major forms of treatment, biogenic and psychotherapeutic. There is abundant evidence to indicate that the best approach to the mood disorders is a well-planned combination of the two. For the severe disorders, in which there is likely to be some biological involvement, biogenic treatment, to begin with, is usually necessary. Psychotherapy should accompany it as soon as the patient seems open to it.

Medication, such as that found necessary for the severe mood disorders, has been found to also help with the mild to moderate mood disorders. Emphasis on psychotherapeutic approaches is considered appropriate, with cautious use of the antidepressant drugs.

Biogenic treatment

Two major types of drugs, the tricyclics and MAO inhibitors, are used in treatment of the moderate to severe mood disorders. In an increasing number of cases, electroconvulsive therapy may be used as an alternative to drugs where drug therapy may be dangerous, or has failed to be effective. Lithium carbonate is the treatment of choice in the bipolar mood disorders.

Tricyclic antidepressants

It is well established that a lack of availability of the neurotransmitter noradrenaline occurs in depression. Support for the hypothesis is provided by the successful use of the tricyclics in the treatment of depression, especially the endogenous or biologically based depression. The reasoning behind that statement is that an important effect of the tricyclics is an increase in the availability of noradrenaline, at the synapses (the gap between one neurone and another) which seems to reduce the depressive reaction.

Monoamine oxidase (MAO) inhibitors

MAO inhibitors are prescribed only for patients who have not responded to tricyclics. It is a secondary treatment because of possible serious side effects. It, too, increases the availability of noradrenaline between neurones.

There is a difference between the ways in which the tricyclics and the MAO inhibitors increase the availability of noradrenaline. The tricyclics block a process in which the sending neurones reabsorb the noradrenaline present at the synapse (the process is called re-uptake). The MAO inhibitors prevent the MAO enzyme from breaking down the noradrenaline at the synapse, which is that enzyme's work. Although the processes are different, the end result is the same: more noradrenaline is made available to reduce depression.

Side effects of antidepressant drugs

The two drugs are different in one other important way. Although the tricyclics have side effects, none of them are life-threatening. They are drowsiness, insomnia, agitation, tremors and blurred vision. Possible side effects of MAO inhibitors are quite serious and can be life-threatening. The MAO inhibitors prevent the MAO enzyme (monoamine oxidase) from carrying out its normal function, which is to break down tyramine, a substance found in cheese, beer, wine and chocolate. Failure to do so triggers what is known as the tyramine–cheese reaction, which causes increased blood pressure, vomiting, muscle twitching and can, if untreated, cause intracranial pressure and death. Patients on MAO inhibitors therefore must restrict their intake of these substances. Sometimes with seriously disturbed individuals, voluntary restriction of diet is a high risk to take. The drug is used only with patients who have not responded to the tricyclics. It is prescribed with strong precautions about proper diet.

Delayed effect of the antidepressant drugs
Aside from the unpleasant and possibly dangerous side effects of the antidepressant drugs, another potentially serious limitation is their delayed action on the depression. At least two weeks must go by before the patients will notice any relief from depression. That delay can be critical with suicidal patients or with restless and impatient individuals whose disappointment in the effect of the drug can cause them to fail to take the medication or to withdraw from treatment.

Electroconvulsive therapy (ECT)
Because of the difficulties of delay and side effects of antidepressant drugs and the persistent possibility of suicide in mood disorders, electroconvulsive therapy (ECT) is increasingly being used. Other benefits of the treatment are its efficiency (only a few weeks of therapy may be necessary), its pronounced therapeutic effect in producing a dramatic recovery in some patients, and avoidance of long-term drug use, which can be advantageous in the elderly.

Some of the greatest advocates of ECT are the patients it has helped. However, there are disadvantages to its use in some depressed patients who have complained of confusion and memory loss. Thus it should be restricted to those patients who are unlikely to recover without intervention and not on the basis of economy for less appropriate cases. The process by which ECT has its therapeutic effect is still a matter of speculation, although it does seem to elevate levels of noradrenaline, amongst other neurotransmitters. It is possible therefore, that its therapeutic value for the brains of some patients may in other cases create a more, rather than less pathological brain state.

Lithium treatment of bipolar mood disorders
In an Australian research study in 1949, lithium was discovered to create lethargy in guinea pigs. With that finding, it was then tried on humans to reduce mania. For more than 40 years now, lithium carbonate has been used in this country and around the world in treating both manic and depressive symptoms in bipolar disorder. Full or partial reduction of symptoms is reported for more that 70 per cent of manic depressives taking the medication. Lithium is not effective in the case of unipolar disorder, a further distinction between the two mood disorders. Its therapeutic mode of action is thought to involve the slowing of electrochemical transmission in neurones (brain cells), but this is not absolutely certain.

Lithium is considered a lifetime maintenance medication for bipolar mood disorder.

There is one serious problem with its use. For many patients needing the medication, the effective dosage is close to a toxic dose. If too much lithium is taken, the toxicity that results can cause convulsions and delirium. Fortunately, the onset of toxicity is accompanied by the unpleasant symptoms of nausea and vomiting, which warn the patient to discontinue the medication for a time. As a precaution against such toxic attacks, patients on maintenance dosages of lithium are sometimes advised to monitor the level of lithium in their system by having their blood tested regularly.

Psychotherapeutic approaches

Although not the only psychotherapeutic approach used in treating depression, a technique developed by Aaron T. Beck, a cognitive psychologist, has proven successful in treating depression, particularly depression in the mild to moderate range. It is a good example of a psychotherapeutic approach to depression. Beck uses a cognitive therapy similar to Ellis's rational emotive therapy.

Beck's therapy is based on his belief that a depressive triad of negative thoughts about the self, life experiences and prospects for the future dominate the patient's thinking. Added to this, Beck states, are five systematic logical errors that further cloud thinking and cause depression.

Systematic logical errors causing depression

1 Arbitrary inference: drawing a conclusion without supporting evidence. For example, the patient, without being able to point to any evidence, will nevertheless insist that his wife doesn't respect him.
2 Selective abstraction: the individual accents one relatively unimportant detail while ignoring significant aspects of a situation. For example, although a wife may be full of praise for her husband's talent and hard work, the client may brood over her comment that she doesn't like the ties he picks out for himself.
3 Overgeneralisation: here the patient draws broad conclusions, principally about self-worth, on the basis of a single, sometimes insignificant, failure; for example, brooding over a failure to fix a leaky tap. The average person would settle for calling a plumber and let it go at that.
4 Magnification and minimisation: here, small failures are magnified, and significant achievements are minimised. An example might be castigating oneself for the messiness of a computer room and ignoring the achievement of having created a new computer program.
5 Personalisation: incorrectly assuming personal responsibility for bad events that happen around an individual, for example, assuming responsibility for a neighbour's accident because the client never got around to suggesting that the neighbour have the car checked.

Beck believes that because the individual's cognitive life is dominated by the triad of negative thought and the systematic logical errors, he or she will express negative thoughts to themselves over and over again, even though fleetingly. It is those thoughts, Beck maintains, that support the depression.

Beck's procedures in therapy

Beck's therapy begins by his leading the patient to identify negative thoughts and faulty reasoning. His approach in doing so is soft, supportive and encouraging, yet persistent. Once the individual has verbalised a number of those negative thoughts and illogical cognitions, the therapist, in Socratic fashion, questions the individual to draw out the illogicality of the cognitions. When the client has recognised the faultiness of the cognitions, he or she is encouraged to re-evaluate real-life experiences from a more logical and less depressing perspective. As the therapy and the thinking progress, he or she directs the client's attention to problem-solving thoughts about difficult life circumstances.

An experimental test of biogenic and cognitive therapies

In a study reported in 1989, an interesting comparison was made of the differing effect on depression of tricyclic therapy, cognitive therapy, and both together. Sixty-four individuals with major depression were assigned randomly to one of the three treatment approaches:

The dependent variables (those contingent upon treatment used) were relief from depression, a change in explanatory style – that is, to what does an individual attribute failure or trouble – and relapse rate after a two-year period.

The findings and their significance

On variable 2, explanatory style, there was no relationship between treatment by tricyclics and an improved explanatory style. In the group receiving both treatments, improvement in style was strong. In the group receiving only cognitive therapy, improvement in explanatory style was very strong.

On variable 3, relapse after two years, evidence indicates that those who did not change their explanatory style showed a higher relapse rate than those who did change.

This does not suggest that drug therapy is inferior to cognitive therapy, indeed without it, the patient may have become suicidal and not have entered psychotherapy at all. However, the use of cognitive therapy with medication enables the patient to reverse the downward spiral of thought processes and make progress towards lasting improvement.

There is a flaw in this kind of study, in that the measures of improvement are those of cognition the same as the therapy, for the first finding. This tends to bias the result towards cognitive therapy, just as a physiological measure of improvement may have biased the evaluation towards drug therapy. The results reported suggest clearly, however, that if drug therapy alone is to be used, the only reason for doing so is resistance on the part of the patient to psychotherapy, or other reasons that make it impossible.

Suicide

A consideration in all depression is the possibility of a suicide attempt; and non-offensive, common sense protective measures should be taken to prevent it. All threats of suicide should be taken seriously: and suicidal talk should be considered as a warning. Yet it must be observed that a person determined to commit suicide is difficult, perhaps impossible, to stop.

The saddest fact about suicide is that, inexplicably to others, it often occurs during the recovery phase, at a point at which the patient seems to be coming out of the deepest gloom of the depression. One possible explanation is that it is only when enough energy has been recovered through an alleviation of the depression that the individual can plan and execute the suicide.

The danger of suicide is at a prevalence level of one per cent during the year of depression; it increases to 15 per cent during the lifetime of individuals with recurring depression.

The scope of the problem

Suicide and suicidal attempts are a significant problem which, in many countries, has been increasing steadily in recent years. The increase among women and the young is disproportionate to their numbers in the population. The greatest increase, a tripling since the mid-fifties, has occurred in the age group of 15 to 24 years of age. The increase is considerably beyond their increase in the population. Suicide is the third most common cause of death (after accidents) in that group.

A notable fact regarding suicide is that more females attempt suicide than males; however, more males successfully commit suicide than females. A sobering fact is that there is an increasing number of children as young as five attempting suicide each year, and many are succeeding.

Studies of suicide

Because of its significant consequences to the individual and those left behind, the problem has received a great deal of study. Yet neither the social sciences nor the medical sciences have provided us with any certain answer to the question, why do some people commit or attempt to commit suicide?

Various methods have been tried to find an understanding of the causes of suicide. Among them are examination of notes left behind, psychological autopsies, and biochemical analysis of the functioning of those considered to be at high risk of suicide.

Suicide notes

Although a number of investigators have studied notes left behind by suicides, other than identifying vital statistics typical of information about those who leave such notes (age, sex, marital status), little of significance for understanding motives for the suicide has been revealed. The major conclusion drawn from the study of notes is that the note writer seems more interested in communicating positive affect to surviving friends and relatives than to leaving behind fully explanatory statements of the reasons for his or her suicide.

The psychological autopsy

Patterned after a medical autopsy, the psychological autopsy is a post-suicidal study of the individual's life history, drawn from interviews with co-workers, relatives and friends, information gained from phone calls made by the individual, and public records. Although such studies can help in preventing suicides by others by identifying significant events and personal characteristics of the suicide – information that might serve as a warning of a potential suicide – they have revealed little about the urgent circumstances that lead to the desperation that provokes most suicides.

Possible aetiological factors in suicide

Factors that are considered to be at least contributory to a suicidal attempt include biochemical factors, social relationships, and adverse life circumstances. Among the complex psychosocial characteristics examined are internalised anger, depression and hopelessness. This section considers each briefly.

Biochemical factors

With the strong evidence that links biochemical elements to depression, it is no surprise that biochemical elements have been found in the brains of patients considered more likely than others to commit suicide. It is reported that patients in whom suspected biochemical elements have been found are more likely to choose violent methods of killing themselves and often have a history of impulsiveness, aggressiveness and violence. The finding has raised the possibility of a connection between suicide and aggression.

As with depression, the biochemical fault is attributed to abnormal enzyme activity in neurotransmitters. The chemical abnormality identified as a possible contributory cause of suicide is a low level of 5-hydroxyindoleacetic acid (5HIAA), an element produced when serotonin, a neurotransmitter that affects mood and emotions, is broken down.

Social relationships

Emile Durkheim, a French sociologist, in one of the earliest systematic studies of suicide, blames absence of cohesive relationships with others as a primary cause of suicide. In emphasising the importance of social forces in suicidal attempts, he identified and named three types of suicide resulting from different but troubled social relationships. They are egoistic suicide, which results when an individual has too few relationships with others; altruistic suicide, where the stimulus for suicide is the self-sacrificing wish to dramatise and thereby further an idealistically-conceived cause. In this type of suicide, one can suspect that the individual, through his or her suicide, hopes to gain a respected place in society that was not attainable in life. Finally, Durkheim recognised anomic suicide, which he felt resulted from unbalanced or damaged relationships in society, for example, being accused of a crime. Durkheim concluded from his studies that the most powerful deterrent to suicide is a sense of involvement and identification with other people.

Adverse life circumstances

In England and Wales there are around 4000–5000 suicides each year, accounting for one per cent of all deaths. During periods of economic depression, suicide rates in the population rise and are often found to be greater among disadvantaged minorities in society. Amongst those undergoing divorce or financial difficulty, especially unemployment, the rate is notably higher than that of the general population.

There is no question that adverse living circumstances, caused by financial problems, interpersonal unhappiness or severe health problems increase the likelihood of suicide; but by themselves, those adverse life circumstances do not provide an adequate explanation of suicide. Too many others face equal adversity without resorting to suicide as an escape; most of them, probably, without considering it.

Psychodynamic explanations

Early psychodynamic views were derived from the Freudian view that suicide was a consequence of rage against a loved but rejecting person with whom the suicidal individual identified. This anger thus becomes a self-destructive force within the individual, leading to suicide.

There is little support for this view amongst modern professionals dealing with suicidal individuals and little evidence for it from research.

Depression and hopelessness

The one condition most frequently found prior to suicide attempts is depression. Correlational studies conducted by various investigators among different populations uniformly report a high correlation between pre-existing depression and suicidal attempts. A sample of the findings: the suicide rate among a depressed population admitted to a psychiatric hospital was 36 times higher than for the general population; 80 per cent of another hospitalised population admitted for suicidal attempts were found, upon admission, to be depressed; even among children, depression is a frequent precursor to a suicide attempt.

Among a depressed population, hopelessness about the future (even beyond depression itself) seems to be the more determinative cause of a suicide attempt. A study by Beck provides persuasive evidence for that conclusion. His population was 207 hospitalised psychiatric patients who had expressed suicidal thoughts but who had no history of suicidal attempts. Within 72 hours of being admitted to the hospital, each of the patients was assessed on three psychological characteristics: degree of hopelessness, degree of depression, and extent of suicidal thinking. In a ten-year follow-up period, 14 of the patients had committed suicide. What differentiated that group of 14 from the other patients in the study was their high scores on hopelessness. Scores on level of depression and extent of suicidal thinking did not significantly vary between the suicidal group and the larger non-suicidal group. One study can never be definitive; but Beck's work, consistent with the thinking of other researchers in the field of depression, offers impressive evidence of the critical importance of feelings of hopelessness as a crucial factor causing suicide attempts. Clearly, there is a great similarity between hopelessness and the concept of helplessness put forward by Seligman. Taking Seligman's view, it would be useful to examine the potentially-suicidal individual's experience of significant events that were beyond their control. Efforts to prevent suicide surely must take account of these precursors to a suicidal attempt.

Overview of causal factors in a suicide

Suicide attempts have multiple causes. There is, first of all, the possibility of a vulnerability caused by biochemical factors which may be genetically produced. A great variety of life circumstances cause unhappiness which, when prolonged, will lead to depression. Depression itself is a multi-faceted psychological disorder, with an unpredictable course, including the possibility of suicide. There are influences of alcohol and drugs which, in lowering inhibitory controls, may help push the individual to the actual suicide attempt. Of lesser importance, but not to be neglected, are the immediate circumstances surrounding the individual during a depressed period; for example, a loaded gun in the house, or being alone in the house after watching a depressing television presentation. The one element that stands out as a crucial impelling force is a feeling of hopelessness in the individual's consciousness, even if circumstances do not justify such feelings.

Efforts at prevention

The success of any prevention programme depends upon our knowledge of signs of a suicidal effort and the speed with which that information can be communicated to a trained professional who will assume some level of responsibility for intervention. There are known danger signals: a state of extreme depression, mild depression with expressions of suicidal intent; bouts of depression with alcohol or drug abuse; and suicide in the family of a depressed individual. Any one of those conditions should trigger efforts to get professional help.

Individuals at risk

It is believed that most persons who attempt suicide do not want to die (often referred to as parasuicidal) and that early attempts warn of intention and try to draw the attention of others to their plight. This often goes unheeded by friends, relatives and professionals alike as the behaviour may be seen as purely attention seeking. Or the individual 'slips through the system' with no one picking up on the signs.

Suicide attempts are usually seen in a general medical casualty department, with the initial concern being over the medical consequences of the method of suicide, usually self-poisoning. Of secondary concern is the mental state of the individual and the potential for future suicide attempts. It is now a matter of policy that such individuals are seen by a psychiatrist prior to discharge and it is at this point that the risk assessment is crucial.

In their advice to professionals in this area, Goldberg and Creed (1994) consider certain areas of enquiry necessary when assessing suicidal risk:

1 The circumstances of any recent self-poisoning or injury. Focusing on whether the individual informed anyone or arranged to be found and the individual's insight into what they had done, their attitudes to surviving and view of the future.
2 The presence of illnesses associated with risk. This would include depression, alcoholism, schizophrenia, chronic or painful physical disease amongst others.
3 Demographic and other characteristics that point to higher risk. For example, being male, over 45, separated, socially isolated, unemployed, or having experienced a recent bereavement are all factors which would increase risk.

Access to services

The person who is attempting or contemplating suicide is clearly a psychiatric emergency and should have ready access to both supportive counselling help with the back-up of recourse to emergency psychiatric services. These are not always readily available. In the UK, the only available services of this sort are the general emergency services, which are not usually sought by suicidal individuals and the Samaritans. The Samaritans are a voluntary organisation who man telephones 24 hours a day, mostly to deal with this type of front-line counselling. Individuals working within this organisation receive limited training and have to abide by certain rules of practice. Most suicidal individuals who make attempts to contact someone, usually contact the Samaritans or a friend or relative.

Public policy can help to reduce the occurrence of successful suicide by simple measures such as control over the sale of guns, poisons, etc. Restrictions over media reports of suicides can reduce the effect that these may have in providing the catalyst which may be the start of suicidal ideation. The nationwide provision of a suicide crisis phone line, which could be linked to other services, would seem to be a useful step forward. However, in countries where this is in place, its use is limited and, of those that call it, 95 per cent of callers never call again and little is known of what happens to these people.

SUMMARY

Mood disorders are a significant psychiatric problem, affecting millions of people, and causing the hospitalisation of a large number of psychiatric patients. The most common form of mood disorder is depression. The disorder causes alternating spells of depression and mania.

In the more serious depressions, usually biological in aetiology, antidepressant drugs and, in some cases, electroconvulsive therapy, have proven successful in reducing depression. Psychotherapy is a necessary follow-up. In milder cases, psychotherapy alone may be all that is necessary.

Mounting evidence strongly indicates that a genetic factor causes vulnerability to depression. Biochemical elements, perhaps the result of faulty genes, also seem to be operative. Among the possible psychosocial causes of depression are overwhelming stressors in the environment; negative attitudes towards the self and the future, frequently based on illogical reasoning: pre-existing personality traits in the depressed individual, for example, a tendency to deprecate the self; unfortunate early learning patterns of helplessness which leave the individual with little hope of doing anything to reduce the adverse circumstances of his or her life.

Suicide is a major and growing problem in society, especially amongst its youth. It is often associated in that group with alcohol and other substance abuse. Depression, with feelings of helplessness, is very common in the pre-suicidal state.

Efforts at prevention include increased efforts to identify the early signs of suicidal risk, the provision of help lines such as the Samaritans, and emergency psychiatric services.

FURTHER READING

Cassano, G., Tundo, A. & Micheli, C. 1994. Bipolar and Psychotic Depressions. *Current Opinion in Psychiatry*, 1: 528.

Hawton, K. 1987. Assessment of Suicide Risk. *British Journal of Psychiatry,* 150:145–153.

Herbst, K. & Psykel, E. 1989. *Depression: An Integrative Approach.* Oxford: Heinemann Medical.

Roy, A. (Ed). 1986. *Suicide.* London: Williams & Wilkins.

Schatzberg, A. & Rothschild, A. 1992. Serotonin Activity in Psychotic (Delusional) Major Depression. *Journal of Clinical Psychiatry.* 53: 52–55.

Seligman, M. 1992. *Helplessness.* New York: Freeman.

Williams, J. M. 1992. *The Psychological Treatment of Depression* (2nd ed). London: Routledge.

Stroebe, M. S. & W. Stroebe. 1983. Who Suffers More? Sex Differences in Health Risks of the Widowed. *Psychological Bulletin*, 93(2): 279–301.

12 Schizophrenia and Other Psychotic Disorders

The most disabling of the psychological disorders are the psychoses; they bring with them disorientation, hallucinations, delusions, and social disorganisation. Among the most debilitating and complex of the psychoses is schizophrenia. That disorder is a complex illness, the nature of which is not yet fully understood; and the outcomes of its treatment are not as favourable as clinicians would like them to be.

In addition to a detailed examination of schizophrenia, this chapter will mention other psychotic conditions listed in DSM-IV: schizophreniform disorder, brief psychotic disorder, schizoaffective disorder, shared psychotic disorder and substance-induced psychotic disorder.

Although, as we shall see later, symptoms vary somewhat from culture to culture, schizophrenia exists worldwide. One per cent of the world's population is afflicted with the illness. Although the number has been falling, there are many thousands of people in the UK diagnosed as schizophrenic. Some of these people still occupy many of the long-stay beds in the health service and an increasing number can often be found amongst the homeless in our cities.

Kraepelin first identified the illness in 1896 when he distinguished it from the mood disorders. Kraepelin believed that all psychiatric disorders were caused by organic factors, and his experience suggested to him that the onset of the disease occurred early in the life of the individual. Hence, he called it dementia praecox, which means a premature deterioration of the brain.

In 1911, Eugene Bleuler, an eminent Swiss psychiatrist, disagreed with Kraepelin on both points. He had found that onset of the disease could occur in the later years, and he also reported that it was not always characterised by a progressive deterioration over the life of the individual, which he felt was suggested by the term 'dementia'. After an original severe deterioration, many schizophrenics stabilised and remained at the same point in their illness for years.

To avoid any misunderstanding of the nature of the illness that might be caused by what he considered a misnomer, and to give emphasis to its true nature, Bleuler invented the word 'schizophrenia', putting together two Greek words meaning 'split' and 'mind'. In that way, he emphasised the most basic feature of schizophrenia: a splitting of the mental functions, in particular, a splitting apart of the individual's affective and cognitive functioning.

Schizophrenia

Students will readily appreciate the complexity of schizophrenia when they consider the number of perspectives used to describe and classify the disorder. Psychologists first distinguish it from the anxiety-based disorders and the personality disorders. The lost contact with reality and the extreme deterioration make that distinction a relatively easy one. But they must also distinguish it from the mood disorders and the organic psychoses, a diagnostic process which is somewhat more difficult.

Because the disorder is now known to take several different forms, each of which may vary in onset, symptomatology, aetiology and responsiveness to treatment, clinicians must then describe the disorder and classify it from several other points of view.

The classification of schizophrenia and other psychotic disorders

The DSM-IV lists a number of subtypes of schizophrenia and related disorders under this heading. The ICD-10 system has fewer headings, but there is a high level of agreement between the two systems as to what characterises schizophrenia and its related disorders. The formal listings for both systems can be seen below.

The DSM-IV Classification of Schizophrenia and Other Psychotic Disorders

> Schizophrenia
>> Paranoid type
>> Disorganised type
>> Catatonic type
>> Undifferentiated type
>> Residual type
>
> Schizophreniform Disorder
> Brief Psychotic Disorder
> Schizoaffective Disorder
> Shared Psychotic Disorder
> Substance-Induced Psychotic Disorder
> Psychotic Disorder due to a General Medical Condition

The ICD-10 Classification of Schizophrenia and Delusional Disorders

> Schizophrenia
> Persistent Delusional Disorder
> Schizoaffective Disorder

Dimensions of schizophrenia

This has generally been achieved in four ways: by considering dimensions within the disorder, by variations in symptomatology, by considering differences in the course of the disorder and by forming subtypes of the disorder which are usually characterised by a particular symptom. These provide means by which a clinician may plan a more specific and appropriate treatment and make a more accurate prognosis. They can be presented as either/or propositions.

1 Is the disease the result of a long-term development? If so, it is called process schizophrenia. Or is it a relatively sudden reaction, apparently to some life crisis? Then it is called reactive or acute schizophrenia.
2 Is the illness manifest by the absence of normal human responses? For example, does the individual show flatness or blunting of affect? If so, the term used is negative symptomatology. Or are there such overt symptoms of disease as hallucinations or delusions? These are referred to as positive symptoms.
3 Is the illness characterised by paranoid symptomatology, or are paranoid symptoms absent or of minor importance?

Before going on to describe each of the dimensions more fully, it needs to be stated that the either/or descriptions of the dimensions describe extreme positions on a continuum. Many schizophrenics fall midpoint between the extremes. Since the identification of the disorder, clinicians have tried to find useful dimensions along which the disorder can be divided up. These have developed historically, although they are all still referred to by clinicians and all describe similar criteria for forming polar opposites in schizophrenia.

The process-reactive dimension
These dimensions have all been useful to clinicians in the past. Although the terminology from all three are still in use, most contemporary research tends to refer to the more recent positive–negative symptom dimension.

Process schizophrenia. Process schizophrenia, also referred to as poor premorbid schizophrenia, may take years to develop, with gradual insidious deterioration and only negative symptoms (absence of normal human response) and few, if any, florid symptoms until later on. Process schizophrenia does not seem to be related to any crisis or major life change.

The process schizophrenic's early history usually reveals a 'loner', rejected by family and peers. There is a lifetime pattern of shyness and social withdrawal. Kantor, Wallner and Winder (1953) report that victims of process schizophrenia typically did not belong to a group of friends in school, did not date regularly during the teen years, did not go beyond secondary school, never held a job for longer that two years, and never married. Their life, in other words, was an extremely maladjusted one which, in time, was followed by the development of the psychotic symptoms of the active schizophrenic. By the time that period of slow deterioration has led to the development of delusions, a sure sign of psychosis, other easily recognised symptoms of schizophrenia will also be present.

Reactive (acute) schizophrenia. The term 'reactive' has been replaced by 'acute' as the former term tended to infer that the disorder was *merely* a reaction to some event.

Its onset is usually sudden and seems to be a reaction to some life crisis.

Although florid symptoms of a psychosis are a principal early feature of the illness, they are reversible. In general, because the premorbid history is good, when the schizophrenia does manifest itself, it is still in an early phase of the illness. Whether for that reason, or because of a different etiological background, reactive schizophrenia is a more treatable form of schizophrenia than process or chronic schizophrenia.

Process type schizophrenia is associated with an especially poor prognosis with the illness developing in a slow and insidious way, in contrast to acute where the possibility of recovery is good.

Positive versus negative symptoms

By the positive dimension is meant the overt manifestation of psychotic symptoms such as bizarre behaviour, hallucinations and delusions. Negative symptoms refer to the absence of any adjustive behaviour in the important areas of life, a chronic maladaptiveness, flatness of affect, and absence of developed interpersonal relations.

In 1980, Timothy Crow identified two syndromes in schizophrenia, one characterised by predominantly negative symptoms (Type II) and the other by predominantly positive symptoms (Type I), roughly equivalent to process and reactive schizophrenia, respectively. However, a diagnosis of schizophrenia requires some positive symptoms to be definitely present and although negative syndrome schizophrenia has a preponderance of negative symptoms, positive symptoms must be present at the point of diagnosis for it to be classified as schizophrenia at all. Because positive symptoms are emphasised in diagnosis, negative symptoms have been of less clinical interest.

However, following the work of Crow and that of Nancy Andreason in America, the importance of negative symptoms has become a major area of schizophrenia research in the last 15 years.

Negative syndrome schizophrenia has been termed 'poor prognosis disorder' by Seymour Kety, as this syndrome has a close association with chronic schizophrenia. High levels of negative symptoms have been linked to poor response to medication, intellectual impairment and irreversible outcome, poor premorbid adjustment, neural cell loss and structural changes in the brain. Some research has equated high levels of negative symptoms with a more organic form of the disorder, and positive symptoms with an acute form in which biochemical imbalance is the underlying feature.

Paranoid versus non-paranoid symptoms

Schizophrenics can also be categorised on the basis of the presence or absence of paranoid symptomatology. There would seem to be a relationship between schizophrenia with paranoid thinking and acute schizophrenia. Buss (1966) reports that overtly paranoid and reactive schizophrenics 'are more intact intellectually, perform better on a variety of tasks, and have a higher level of maturity'. Research also indicates that patients suffering from a reactive schizophrenia with paranoid symptoms are hospitalised later than other schizophrenics, stay hospitalised for a shorter time, and have to be rehospitalised less often. Thus, the presence of paranoid symptoms early in the disorder seems to suggest a good prognosis in the same way as positive syndrome (Type I), or acute schizophrenia. Conversely, non-paranoid schizophrenics are associated with high levels of negative symptoms, slow process type onset and a poor prognosis.

Symptomatology

The specific symptom patterns defining schizophrenia have been debated since Kraepelin's early identification of the illness. DSM-IV imposes fairly strict criteria for making a definite diagnosis of schizophrenia.

With respect to timing of onset, duration and impact on functioning for a diagnosis of schizophrenia, the manual requires that:

1 Onset must occur before the age of 45.
2 Symptoms must last for a minimum period of six months.
3 There must be an observable deterioration from the individual's previous level of functioning. These criteria differ from those of the ICD-10 system with respect to schizophrenia; for example, a minimum duration of one month is required for a diagnosis.

Beyond these criteria, both systems specify that one or two psychotic symptoms should be present. These symptoms are evidence of a major impairment in the individual's contact with reality. Although there are other symptoms listed below that are found in schizophrenia, what Kurt Schneider in 1959 termed 'the first rank symptoms of schizophrenia' are of primary importance as they permit the diagnosis of the disorder.

The first rank symptoms of schizophrenia

Most diagnostic systems have listed the three first rank symptoms of schizophrenia as criteria for its diagnosis. ICD-10 requires one of these symptoms to be present for at least one month. DSM-IV requires two symptoms, but one of these may also include negative or motor symptoms, for a period of one month, although the patient must remain disturbed for at least six months. The first rank symptoms are generally termed delusions, thought disorder and hallucinations.

Delusions (content of thought)

Multiple delusions (bizarre and obviously false beliefs) are the principal disturbance in the content of the schizophrenic's thought processes. There are two categories into which the delusions usually fall: persecutory delusions, in which the schizophrenic believes that others are spying on, spreading false rumours about, or planning harm to the individual; and delusions of reference, in which the schizophrenic gives personal significance to totally unrelated events, objects or people. Those thoughts are usually self-deprecatory, for example, a newspaper or magazine may be accused of writing critical articles about the schizophrenic when there is no basis for the accusation. Delusions can also be grandiose, where the sufferer believes themselves to be omnipotent or some powerful or important person. One of the common such delusions, perhaps readily provided by religious imagery, is the patient's belief that they are Jesus Christ.

Common delusions are thought broadcasting, in which schizophrenics believe that their thoughts are being broadcast to the outside world; thought insertion, in which they may think that thoughts not their own are being inserted into their mind; and control by external forces.

Form of thought

To be distinguished from the content of thought is the way in which schizophrenics express their thoughts, a symptom that is labelled 'formal thought disorder'. Here, associations are loose, ideas shift from one subject to a completely unrelated one, statements meant to be connected are completely unrelated – the individual may shift frames of reference in conversation.

Sometimes there is 'poverty of content', meaning that the communication is so vague, overly abstract or concrete, repetitive or stereotyped as to be meaningless to the listener. Neologisms (the creation of new words), clanging (illogically stringing together words that rhyme or sound alike) and perseverative language may appear in writing or speech.

Hallucinations (distortions of perception)

Perceptions of the schizophrenic's world are distorted by hallucinations (a perception in the absence of any appropriate external stimulus). Hallucinations may occur in any sense mode, but they most frequently are auditory. The voices 'talking' to the patient may be of several people, of people familiar to the patient, or total strangers. Messages may take the form of commands from, for example, God or the Prime Minister, and they may be obeyed at high risk to others or to the patient.

Hallucinations may be tactile, as in the form of electric shock, tingling or burning sensations. Somatic hallucinations take the form of living things, such as snakes, crawling around inside the patient's body. Hallucinations in other sense modalities are rare.

Other symptoms of schizophrenia

Movement (motor symptoms)

Disorders of movement in schizophrenia range from effortful immobility as in the 'waxy flexibility' of catatonia, to extreme agitation and hyperactivity. Other peculiarities of movement behaviour include mannerisms, stereotypes (repeated movements), mutism and perseverance (movement continues when no longer required). Ataxia, a lack or slowing of movement, is a negative symptom of schizophrenia.

Affect

The principal and quite pronounced affective symptom is a blunting or flattening or inappropriateness in the individual's emotional responses. The symptoms display themselves in a monotonic voice and immobile face. An oddity is the extreme lack of concordance between what the individual is saying and the emotion displayed. An example of this would be laughing in a serious situation, such as an accident.

Volition
Significant ambivalence may paralyse the individual's will to take any action. The schizophrenic has difficulty in pursuing any interest or carrying out a planned course of action. Some negative symptoms are included here, eg. avolition-apathy, such as impersistence at work, and anhedonia, a lack of pleasure-seeking behaviour.

Sense of self
Normal people are aware of their own individuality and wholeness. The schizophrenic lacks this sense of self-identity. Victims feel no ego boundaries, have less awareness of the meaning of existence, and experience perplexity about who they are.

Relationship to the external world
Individuals with schizophrenia are often so preoccupied with their own disturbed thought that they are 'unavailable' to others, a symptom which has been referred to as 'autism' by Bleuler (not to be confused with the disorder autism). They live in a world of their own fantasies, egocentrisms and illogicalities. They take less notice of events around them or of major world events.

The course of schizophrenia
Many professionals consider schizophrenia to come in 'thirds'. There are the third of patients that get reasonably well without recurrence, a third who will recover but will relapse a number of times during their life, and a final third who never fully recover and are permanently, or chronically, disabled by the disorder. Whichever of these categories a particular case may fall into, the course of each episode can also be thought of as having three stages or phases: the prodromal phase, the active phase and the residual phase. In the patients with the best prognosis the prodromal and residual phases are milder and shorter but the active phase is pronounced. In those with a poor prognosis (the final third), the reverse is true with the residual phase never really ending.

Prodromal phase
The active or, as one might say, the florid phase, of the illness is usually preceded by a prodromal phase in which there is a notable but not yet acutely psychotic deterioration from the individual's prior level of adjustment, a change that is often commented upon by relatives and friends.

In a 1973 article describing early experiences in schizophrenic breakdown, Freedman and Chapman capture prodromal expressions and feelings of the schizophrenic. Patients are quoted as saying the following:

'I try to think and all of a sudden I can't say anything because it's like I turn off in my mind.'

'Maybe I'm not very sensitive . . . I keep thinking maybe I'm tired . . . the other night, in front of the television, I felt a sort of blurring like that.'

'My eyes seem to disappear when I look in the mirror.'

'Things sound more intense . . . sound louder. Interesting things sound louder that uninteresting things.'

'Say you're talking to another person, I don't understand a word they're saying . . . if there's more that one person talking, I don't follow them because it goes too quickly.'

As mentioned above, in schizophrenia with a good prognosis (acute or positive-Type I) the prodromal phase is of relatively short duration, whereas with a poor prognosis (negative-Type II) it can be years of slow deterioration.

In the short-term prodromal phase, the onset of illness is preceded by a heightened awareness, foreboding and urgency. Usually that reaction seems to be triggered by some relatively 'normal' crisis, such as an ordinary change in life circumstances. The patient may respond to this change with such comments, as, 'I had nowhere to turn,' or, 'There was no way out'.

As the individual comes closer to active schizophrenia, ideas of reference or of specialness begin to appear as the individual occasionally finds hidden meanings in ordinary events. Other, milder forms of later psychotic symptoms appear. Some of the more frequent are social withdrawal, impairment in role functioning, peculiar behaviour, carelessness in personal hygiene, vagueness or circumstantial communication, and occasional bizarre thoughts.

The active phase

Here the patient manifests the full array of symptoms associated with schizophrenia which distinguish it from other disorders. Those symptoms were described in the symptomatology section. In the active phase, the individual is frequently described as 'floridly psychotic'.

The residual phase

When the profound acutely psychotic symptoms remit, the patient is considered to be in the residual phase, which for those luckier patients may fade with time. Symptoms here are similar to the prodromal phase, perhaps masking the onset of a further episode in those patients with recurring episodes. Some professionals consider this as the 'burn-out' or residual state, which is only really appropriate for those unfortunate chronic patients who show many negative symptoms and side-effects of long-term medication later in life.

The three stages of schizophrenia are not always separated clearly one from another. The patient sometimes seems to fade in and out of different phases of the disorder.

Specific types of schizophrenia

Classical subtypes of schizophrenia were based on the predominance of one particular symptom. These subtypes were catatonic (motor symptoms), paranoid (delusions), hebephrenic (hallucinations and affective disturbance) and simple schizophrenia (negative symptoms, slow onset). In DSM-IV, some of these concepts remain but others have been altered by the DSM system in order to assist the clinician in making a more specific diagnosis reliably. The new subtypes are: catatonic, disorganised, paranoid and undifferentiated (reserved for those cases in which the individual cannot be classified as one of the other types).

Catatonic type

There are two polar opposites in the catatonic subtype of schizophrenia, both characterised by motor symptoms: agitated excitement and catatonic withdrawal.

Agitated excitement. This form of catatonic reaction is characterised by agitation and continuous movement. Often appearing aimless, the individual moves around unable to sit for any length of time, talking to themselves and sometimes shouting until they are exhausted. This behaviour is difficult to manage outside a hospital.

Even in exhaustion, catatonic individuals sleep only for short periods of time. During their agitation, they can become violent, attacking others or throwing things.

Withdrawn catatonics. Catatonics are often mute, and may adopt strange positions and hold them for long periods of time. At other times, they show a waxy flexibility, holding any position into which an outsider may 'arrange' them. This state has been termed catatonia or catatonic stupor.

Catatonics are, despite their withdrawal, highly suggestible. They will, for example, mimic sounds made by others (echolalia) or the actions of others (echopraxia). Despite exhibiting all the features of an individual totally withdrawn from the world, catatonics nevertheless show, in a variety of ways, that they are aware of what is going on around them.

Catatonics, especially in the withdrawal phase, will not eat or control their bowel or bladder functions. Some catatonic patients alternate between periods of extreme stupor and extreme excitement. In one study, Morrison (1973) reported that of 250 catatonic patients, almost 50 per cent were withdrawn, about 21 per cent were predominantly excited, and about 30 per cent were mixed.

The action of anti-schizophrenic drugs almost always reduces the catatonic symptoms, especially catatonic stupor. Thus patients in the catatonic state of 'waxy flexibility' are rarely seen nowadays, although they are often described in research literature.

Disorganised schizophrenia

Formerly called hebephrenic schizophrenia, and now one of the less common forms, this type of schizophrenia is the individual at his or her most disturbed. Much of the individual's behaviour is literally infantile. Cognitive processes are severely disorganised; speech is incoherent; there is much silly behaviour and giggling. While systematised delusions (or, for that matter, any systematised cognitions) are absent, bizarre behaviour, such as eating faeces or finger painting with it, may be expected. The disorganised schizophrenic may masturbate in public or fantasise publicly in a weird fashion. There is much grimacing, jumbling words together (word salad), and disconnected associations.

Onset is earlier than in other types of schizophrenia. Ordinarily, the more florid manifestations of the disorder are preceded by a history of oddness, scrupulosity about trivial misdeeds, and preoccupation with religious and philosophical themes distorted from their usual context.

Paranoid schizophrenia

The two most significant psychotic symptoms in the paranoid patient are as follows:

1 Persecutory delusions, in which patients weave bizarre plots about the hostile intentions and acts of relatives, friends or even people who pass them on the street. Being poisoned, watched, followed or influenced by outside forces are prominent in their delusions.
2 In addition, there frequently are delusions of grandiosity, in which the paranoid individual 'is', for example, a famed scholar, a millionaire, Christ or Napoleon.

Delusions may be accompanied by hallucinations which fit their persecutory delusions. For instance, God speaks to them, their enemies threaten them, or they hear confirmatory conversations.

The paranoid delusions of persecution and grandiosity are sometimes interpreted as mechanisms through which the individual provides a sense of identity and importance that reality does not match. Paranoid schizophrenics are notably different from other schizophrenics in that their coping mechanisms and cognitive skills are at a higher level.

Onset of paranoid schizophrenia is usually later than for disorganised schizophrenia. This has led some professionals to speculate that younger schizophrenic individuals are less mature and responsible becoming silly and disorganised (disorganised type), but older schizophrenic adults are frightened and concerned by what is happening to them and become paranoid. Although the paranoid subtype may be gradual in its onset, it rarely has the slow insidious quality of the Type II negative schizophrenia onset.

Undifferentiated schizophrenia

Clinicians use this diagnosis when the patient's symptoms clearly indicate schizophrenia but are so mixed or undifferentiated as to make classification into one of the above three types of schizophrenia impossible. Sometimes such an undifferentiated set of symptoms is the prelude to a more fully developed schizophrenia, conforming to one of the specific types of schizophrenia.

Residual schizophrenia

This diagnosis is to be used when individuals have been through at least one episode of schizophrenia (a six-month period of schizophrenic behaviour) but now present no extreme symptoms of the disorder. Minor delusions or hallucinations may be present, but they do not dominate the patient's behaviour. Negative symptoms are usually present such as emotional blunting or withdrawal, but positive symptoms are only present in mild forms, for example, eccentric, but not bizarre, behaviour.

Other psychotic disorders

Some schizophrenia-like states have been differentiated from schizophrenia where they have too much overlap with other disorders or can usefully be considered distinct. DSM-IV has identified six of these: schizophreniform disorder, brief psychotic disorder, schizoaffective disorder, shared psychotic disorder, substance-induced disorder and psychotic disorder due to a general medical condition. The ICD-10 does not make so many major distinctions, separating out only schizoaffective disorder, persistent delusional disorder and recognising acute schizophrenia-like disorder.

Schizophreniform disorder and brief psychotic disorder

Schizophrenic symptoms lasting less than six months but more than one month usually indicate a better prognosis than those for definite schizophrenia. For this reason they have been assigned the label schizophreniform disorder. This disorder is also characterised by a sudden onset and an absence of schizophrenia amongst the relatives of the sufferer.

In brief psychotic disorder, the disturbance is even briefer, having a duration of less than one month. In each case, the diagnoses are considered provisional until the illness duration is finally established. The ICD-10 system also regards symptoms lasting less than one month as not fulfilling the criteria for schizophrenia, terming this 'acute schizophrenia-like disorder' and suggesting substance abuse or stress as precipitating factors.

Schizoaffective disorder

The distinction between acute schizophrenia and mania has always been difficult for clinicians to establish. In some cases the mixture of psychotic and affective symptoms makes the establishment of a diagnosis of either mood disorder or schizophrenia dubious and the diagnosis of schizoaffective disorder has been provided in both DSM-IV and ICD-10. For this diagnosis the co-occurence of both types of symptoms is during the same episode, or within a few days of each other.

Shared psychotic disorder

Formerly known as induced psychotic disorder, this condition requires that a second person has a delusion, and that this person is in a close friendship with the primary case (the person being diagnosed). The primary case also has a delusion which is very similar in content to that of the second person, or the other people involved. Thus they share the same delusion and this is generally attributed to their living in close proximity in isolation from others. In the case of only two people being involved, it is sometimes referred to as 'folie a deux'.

Substance-induced, and psychotic disorder due to a general medical condition

Some psychoactive substances, such as amphetamine and some hallucinogens amongst others can produce schizophrenia-like symptoms. Likewise some medical conditions, for example temporal lobe epilepsy and Huntington's chorea, can also result in these symptoms. These conditions need to be eliminated before a diagnosis of definite schizophrenia can be made. In the case of drug-induced symptoms, these will disappear in time with abstinence (checked by urine analysis), which is around ten days for amphetamine-induced psychosis. Similarly, likely disease states should also be checked for and a thorough neurological analysis should always be carried out where organic damage or disease is suspected alongside schizophrenic symptoms.

Overall view of schizophrenia

It will be reassuring to the student of abnormal psychology to know that the nature of schizophrenia sometimes seems to clinicians and research psychologists to be as complex as it must seem to one approaching the study of psychological disorders for the first time. In summarising that complexity, we can nevertheless present five statements about schizophrenia with which psychologists generally agree:

1 There is no one symptom or type of behaviour that unequivocally points to the existence of a schizophrenic disorder.
2 The symptoms of one schizophrenic patient may be different from those of another.
3 Symptoms may change notably from one stage of the illness to another.
4 Schizophrenics slip in and out of periods of lucidity and contact with reality.
5 Schizophrenics vary in their treatability; but except for the schizophreniform type of schizophrenia, a complete recovery to earlier levels of functioning is rare. Most schizophrenics are left with a relatively stable residual form of the illness.

In giving emphasis to the complexity of the illness, the symptomatology of which we have just described, it is appropriate to recall Bleuler's very early way of writing about the illness. He described it as 'the group of schizophrenias'. Today, clinicians generally agree that what they are confronted with is a group of psychiatric patients who share a common diagnosis but who differ widely in the pattern of their symptoms, the etiological factors involved, and even in their treatability.

As attempts are being made to pinpoint the diagnostic signs of the illness (such as the changes in diagnostic criteria for schizophrenia as delineated in early editions of DSM and those provided more recently in DSM-IV) psychologists are expressing concern about the comparability of research using the earlier criteria and more recent research using the revised criteria. Over time studies have found that newer diagnostic criteria for schizophrenia result in fewer diagnoses of definite schizophrenia. This is sometimes dramatic, as in the study by Williams and colleagues in finding the number of definite diagnoses cut by half. This may seem like a case of shifting goalposts during a football match, and to some extent this criticism is true, but the poor reliability of earlier diagnoses was less acceptable than such moves.

It may take another decade of rigorous research before we can distinguish clearly the various illnesses now diagnosed as schizophrenia.

Causative factors in schizophrenia

Allowing for the disturbing diagnostic problems mentioned previously, we can still make certain statements about possible causality of the several diseases now called 'schizophrenia'. There is general agreement that those illnesses are the result of some interactive combination of biological and psychological factors. The weight given to one or another set of factors varies with the type of schizophrenia being considered. In general however, the current consensus gives greater weight to biological factors.

Biogenic factors

A number of biogenic factors have been proposed and studied as causes of schizophrenia. Four of these are described below: genetic factors, biochemical factors, neuroanatomical abnormalities and viral infections.

Genetic factors. This section summarises the research into the relationship between schizophrenia and genetic elements. It considers the variety of research designs used to test the hypothesis that genetics play a part in the development of schizophrenia and reports the findings of each type of research. There are three principal research designs: family studies, twin studies and adoptee studies.

Family studies. In a summary of published research on schizophrenia and genetics, Gottesman (1978) reports on the prevalence of schizophrenics among relatives of diagnosed schizophrenics. His analysis suggests that the closer the family relationship (and, therefore, the more genes in common), the higher the percentage of schizophrenic individuals. Typical of his results are that 12 to 13 per cent of the children of schizophrenics were also schizophrenic; in those cases in which both the schizophrenic and spouse were schizophrenic, the percentage of schizophrenic children jumped to 36–37 per cent. By comparison, schizophrenia appeared among nephews and cousins at the level of 2–3 per cent. Prevalence in the general population is one per cent. Thus there is a strong case for the role of genetics being partial, or predisposing towards schizophrenia.

The weakness in drawing a conclusion from this type of study is that it takes no account of the unfavourable environmental influences a child would experience living with one or both parents who are schizophrenic.

Comparison of monozygotic and dizygotic twins. Keep in mind that monozygotic twins have identical sets of genes; dizygotic twins are genetically no more alike than ordinary siblings. An argument in favour of a genetic influence in schizophrenia would be a high concordance rate (both twins having schizophrenia) in monozygotic twins and a significantly lower concordance rate among dizygotic twins. Cohen and colleagues (1972) report concordance among identical twins at the 23 per cent level and a concordance rate of 5.3 among fraternal twins. That is a statistically significant difference. Both figures, however, are much lower than other reports, no doubt because the sample was a highly selective group who had been screened for military service.

Gottesman and Shields (1972), with a more representative sample, report results more typical of those found in other studies. Their concordance rates for identical twins was 42 per cent, and for fraternal twins, nine per cent. Since the concordance rate between one schizophrenic twin and a co-twin is not 100 per cent, there is the suggestion that influences other than genetic operate in the aetiology of schizophrenia. Perhaps they are environmental, although it is hard to imagine extreme differences in the life experiences of identical twins who grow up in the same family. In fact, it is just because life experiences for identical twins may be assumed to be very much alike that the twin studies we have cited are criticised. They do not acknowledge common life experiences (even more so than for dizygotic twins) as a reason for the high concordance levels in identical twins.

Nevertheless, there is, in the studies cited, the very strong suggestion that genetics plays a part in the development of schizophrenia. Even though the genetic factors do not directly transmit the illness, they may create a vulnerability which, when activated by other factors, results in the illness.

Adoption studies. In Leonard Heston's study (1966) of children raised by foster parents or in adoptive homes, there is more certain evidence of the strong influence of genetic factors in creating a predisposition or vulnerability to schizophrenia. Heston controlled both genetic and environmental influences. Comparing 47 children of schizophrenic mothers who had been placed in foster or adoptive homes prior to one month of age, with 50 children in a control group who had been reared in the same homes as the children of the schizophrenic mothers, he found that 16.7 per cent of the 47 children of schizophrenic mothers had received a diagnosis of schizophrenia, but none of the 50 individuals in the control group had done so. In addition, suggesting that the apparent genetic deficiency influenced behaviour and pathology in other ways, the study found that 37 of the 47 children of schizophrenic mothers (a substantially larger number than in the control group) had received such diagnoses as mental retardation, neurosis and psychopathic personality. They also were involved more frequently in criminal activities and spent more time in prison than members of the control group.

In a differently designed study, Kety (1975) added more support to a genetic hypothesis in the etiology of schizophrenia. In his study of schizophrenics and normal adoptees, the critical finding was that there were almost twice as many schizophrenic or schizoid-like relatives in the families of the schizophrenic adoptees than in the families of normal adoptees. The significant point to be made is that though the schizophrenic adoptees had been reared apart from their families, the weakness they carried in their genes resulted in schizophrenia.

Overall view of genetic factors in schizophrenia. Psychologists generally consider that such studies as we have cited, especially in the adoptee studies, have provided conclusive proof of a genetic influence in the development of schizophrenia.

As the genetic influence detected by these studies was not absolute in predicting schizophrenia (ie. not 100 per cent of cases), then some additional factor must be precipitating the illness in those affected. This could be a further organic influence such as infection, or a psychological stressor following the diatheses-stress model for this disorder. Conversely, it may be that some factor is protecting those individuals who are genetically predisposed but do not develop the disorder.

Ongoing research is using the phenomenon of genetic linkage (two or more genetic traits which are 'linked' by being close together and tend to be inherited together) to find a genetic marker (the other trait) for schizophrenia. Such research may help to resolve some of the questions regarding the issue of how an individual inherits the disorder.

Biochemical factors. Among those researchers with strong convictions about the influence of biogenic elements in the development of schizophrenia, interest has focused recently on the dopamine hypothesis. That interest has replaced earlier interest in more simple hypotheses concerning biochemical influences on schizophrenia.

The possibility that there might be biochemical factors involved in the development of schizophrenia has long been the subject or research. Early efforts concentrated on analysis of chemicals in the blood and urine of schizophrenics for comparison with their content in non-schizophrenic individuals. The concept proved simplistic. What differences were found could more accurately be considered the result of dietary differences; for example, between hospitalised and non-hospitalised individuals, or influences other than essential differences directly related to the presence of schizophrenia.

The advent of what has come to be called the anti-psychotic medications – also called neuroleptics, or tranquillising agents, the most frequently prescribed of which are the phenothiazines – has revolutionised the treatment of schizophrenia. In addition, it has led scientists to a new way of considering possible biochemical influences in the etiology of schizophrenia. Phenomena associated with chlorpromazine (one of the neuroleptics) treatment of schizophrenics turned attention to the possibility of abnormalities in neurochemical functioning in that disorder, particularly in the effect of neutrotransmitters. That possibility has been expressed in the dopamine hypothesis.

The dopamine hypothesis. In treating schizophrenics with phenothiazines, it was soon observed that a course of treatment not only reduced schizophrenic symptoms but also caused side effects resembling Parkinson's disease. It is known that Parkinsonism results from low levels of the neurotransmitter dopamine, caused by a deterioration in a section of the limbic (or lower) area of the brain (specifically, the substantia nigra), which is involved in emotional behaviour. Biochemists hypothesised that excessive dopamine might be associated with the development of schizophrenia. Their reasoning, simply expressed, is as follows: phenothiazine reduces certain symptoms of schizophrenia, but it also induces Parkinsonian symptoms which, it is known, are the result of low levels of dopamine. It would seem that neuroleptic treatment reduces the effect of dopamine by blocking the receptors for the neurotransmitter. Thus higher use of dopamine by the brains of schizophrenic patients would seem to result in the florid symptoms (hallucinations, delusions and thought-disorders) of the disorder.

The action of transmitters in the brain is far more complex than the above reasoning may imply; for example, there are different receptors for dopamine with differing overall effects for the brain. Initial studies implicated the dopamine D2 receptors, although more recent evidence has tended to isolate the schizophrenic effects to that of the D4 receptors (see below). In considering the infinite complexity of the functioning of the brain where different substances and structures can have very different effects depending on the location of them, and subsequently further interact with each other in different combinations, then research in this area has to take a cautious and necessarily simplistic approach.

In examining dopamine activity as being highly related to psychotic symptoms, a great deal of research has been stimulated. Given the fact that dopamine disturbance could be a result of schizophrenia as well as a cause, evidence for its causal role has to be established cumulatively or clearly show that this disturbance leads to schizophrenia rather than vice versa. Thus research evidence needs to be examined carefully for these elements.

Evidence in support of the dopamine hypothesis.

1 There is the initial evidence that when dopamine levels are reduced (indicated by the development of Parkinson-type symptoms), schizophrenic symptoms are reduced. The powerful effect of clozapine (developed in the late eighties) in reducing the symptoms of schizophrenia – because its primary biochemical effect is to reduce levels of dopamine – adds strong support to the dopamine hypothesis. Although it can have its own serious side-effects, the clozapine works where neuroleptics fail to have an effect, does not work with amphetamine psychoses, and does not produce the side effects associated with neuroleptics. It is thought that the drug works on more specifically schizophrenia-related dopamine receptors (D3 or D4), which may be involved in symptoms less affected by D2 receptor blockage.

2 In large doses, the amphetamines are known to create a psychotic reaction indistinguishable from paranoid schizophrenia. That effect is known to be associated with the increased availability of dopamine caused by the amphetamines. Amphetamine psychosis is treated successfully with the same drug used to treat schizophrenics, the phenothiazines. As has been stated, the penothiazines block dopamine receptors, making less of it available. Thus the therapeutic effect in both types of psychoses may be a result of the same biochemical action. L-Dopa used to treat Parkinson's disease also raises levels

of dopamine and can, in excess, produce schizophrenic-like symptoms.
   It is thus argued that schizophrenia must result, in some way, from
excessive dopamine use.

3 Two lines of evidence made possible by PET (positron emission tomography)
   scans give direct support to the dopamine hypothesis.
      In PET scans of the brain of a normal individual and that of a schizophrenic
   individual of the same age, the latter's brain was shown to have a greater
   density of dopamine receptors, thus making more dopamine. This confirms
   earlier studies carried out by a post-mortem analysis of schizophrenic
   patients' brains also finding elevated numbers of dopamine receptors.
   However, the greater density of receptors could also have been the result of
   years of phenothiazine receptor-blocking activity (the brain can produce more
   to compensate for those blocked).

In 1986, Wong and colleagues used PET scans of living schizophrenic patients
and normal controls (*in vivo* analysis). The schizophrenic patients consisted of
two groups: those who had received medication and those who had been
neuroleptic medication-free. Significantly greater dopamine receptor density
was found in the medication free schizophrenic group than in the non-schizophrenic group, and greater than the medicated group. This suggests that the
increase in receptors is related to the disorder and not to the medication, in
support of the dopamine hypothesis.

Limitations of the dopamine hypothesis. There are points which seem to indicate that the dopamine hypothesis of schizophrenia is incomplete or limited in
its explanation.

1 Dopamine-blocking drugs, which are used so successfully with schizophrenics, are also effective in treating other psychiatric disorders, particularly,
   for example, some types of organic psychoses. The question asked is, how can
   excess dopamine be thought to cause schizophrenia when lowering levels of
   dopamine also has a positive effect on other psychiatric disorders unrelated to
   schizophrenia?
2 The effect of phenothiazines in reducing dopamine levels takes place quickly
   (in hours), but any change in the behaviour of the schizophrenic takes place
   gradually, over two or three weeks. If one causes the other, it might be assumed
   that the effect should be instantaneous.
3 Neuroleptic medication is only effective in treating some schizophrenic
   patients. There is a substantial group of patients, usually with high levels of
   negative symptoms, who are resistant to medication. Why are the phenothiazines not very effective with negative symptoms? Why should the effects of
   clozapine differ from the phenothiazines if the basic cause of the symptoms is
   excess dopamine?

Overview of the dopamine hypothesis. The evidence for dopamine being
involved in the symptoms of schizophrenia is indisputable. However, the
answers to the question as to whether this causes schizophrenia, and what the

exact mechanisms are in the dopamine link with schizophrenia, are far from resolved. The answer would seem to lie in further, more precise research.

The issue as to why only some schizophrenic patients benefit from neuroleptic medication would seem to lie along the distinction between positive (Type I) and negative symptoms of schizophrenia (Type II). As Crow (1980) pointed out, we can usefully consider there to be two syndromes in schizophrenia. Type I is associated with positive symptoms, genetic predisposition, rapid onset, dopamine involvement, response to medication and a good prognosis. Type II is associated with negative symptoms, neurological abnormalities (see next section), poor response to neuroleptic medication, slow onset and poor prognosis. From this it would seem that a genetic predisposition may be partly expressed by abnormalities in the dopamine system.

Further research into the dopamine hypothesis is revealing more types of dopamine receptors, which may provide the answer to the inconsistencies in the effects of different medications. With regard to the delayed effect of neuroleptic medication, the immediate receptor-blocking effect is not thought to directly lead to symptom relief. The therapeutic mechanism is thought to involve the compensatory change in the brain as a result of the blocked receptors.

Other research has complicated the dopamine hypothesis. Other neurotransmitters can influence the action of dopamine, perhaps suggesting that dopamine has a secondary role in the cause of schizophrenia and that transmitters such as gamma-aminobutyric acid (GABA) may have a primary role.

Neuroanatomical factors. A third connection between biological factors and the development of schizophrenia grows out of the discovery of structural anomalies in the brains of Type II schizophrenics. So far, four types of structural differences between the brains of nonschizophrenic individuals and Type II schizophrenics have been identified.

1 The ventricles of the schizophrenic brain have been observed to be larger and asymmetrical when compared with normal human brains. Ventricles are tissue-free, cavity-like chambers in the brain which are filled with fluid. Their anomalous enlargement is suggestive of deterioration or atrophy in the brain. The correlation of enlarged ventricles and schizophrenia is suggestive of, but not definitive proof of, a causal relationship between the two. It has also been noted that left-hemisphere ventricles of schizophrenic brains are much larger than those of the right hemisphere. What the effect of that is, or what its cause might be, has yet to be identified, but the temptation is to relate the difference to schizophrenia.

2 Cranium size, cerebrum size, and perhaps most significantly, frontal lobe size, are all smaller in schizophrenics; but again, primarily in the slow-developing Type II schizophrenia.

3 The highest level of brain function takes place in the cortex. Two 1986 studies report anomalies at that level in schizophrenic brains: neuronal deterioration and reduced blood flow.

4 Type II schizophrenia is also associated with a greater incidence of perinatal

neurological damage (brain injury at birth), for example, due to forceps delivery. This tends to account for the 'season of birth', in schizophrenia, where sufferers tend to be born in the late winter months, a time of greater perinatal complications.

All of these factors would seem to support Crow's distinction between Types I and II schizophrenia. Type II would seem to be more related to neurological abnormalities and damage than Type I. This could account for the slower, more insidious, onset of the disorder and a lesser association with dopamine excess and genetic factors. However, simply dividing schizophrenia into two distinct disorders would not suffice as the two types co-exist in a large number of individuals. Thus, although the syndromes would seem to have distinct features, they also seem to be related themselves.

Viral infection. As well as proposing the two syndromes in schizophrenia, Timothy Crow has also made frequent reference to the possibility of viral factors in the cause of schizophrenia. He does not accept the simple view put forward by others that schizophrenia relates directly to infection of the foetus by a viral disease such as influenza. However, viral damage would fit well as an environmental factor in non-genetic cases of schizophrenia, especially as this Type II form has a gradual onset. Evidence for this view is very limited and has been questioned by Crow himself.

Psychological factors in the development of schizophrenia

The biogenic factors associated with the development of schizophrenia, as we have just described, provide a reasonably solid basis for believing that there is a diathesis or vulnerability in the schizophrenic individual such that he or she can be thought of as schizophrenia-prone. That vulnerability does not always cause a schizophrenic breakdown. To understand why it does in some individuals and not in others, we need to know what psychologically stressful circumstances which, when imposed on a vulnerability to schizophrenia, could possibly push the individual into a schizophrenic breakdown.

A number of theories have been put forward to account for any psychological influence on schizophrenic episodes: the child's early relationships, family communication styles and family structure. Most of these are older theories drawing on psychoanalytic thought, having little evidence to support them and being of little value in treating patients. Others, such as the stress–diathesis model and the place of expressed emotion in schizophrenic relapse, have been more useful in terms of managing the disorder and generating future research.

Early relationship theories. Early psychodynamically-based theories placed the cause of the disorder with the closest relatives of the sufferer when they were developing, especially the mother. Frieda Fromm Reichmann used the term 'schizophrenogenic mother' and in doing so, did little to help the tormented relatives of schizophrenic offspring , if anything, worsening their problems by adding guilt. There is little to support these approaches and they have little to offer the sufferer, being based on retrospective speculation. Theories like these tend to ignore the fact that any deviant relationship could be a result of the schizophrenia in the offspring or genetically related disturbance in the rest of the family.

Family structure. Theodore Lidz and colleagues in 1957 examined the relationships of the parents of schizophrenic children, identifying two relationships – skew and schism – which he thought characteristic of schizophrenia. In skew, one parent is overly dominant (and disturbed), the other (often the father), correspondingly submissive and in schism – it is a cold marriage based on coercion and manipulation. In both cases, the child is seen as a pawn in these interactions. Although this theory seemed plausible, there is no evidence to substantiate it. The existentialist, R D Laing, also considered that a progressive maladaptive process takes place in families resulting in the schizophrenic family member being labelled as 'mad' in their efforts to cope with the situation. Again, there is little practical support for such an approach, with such family factors probably being a result rather than a cause of the disorder.

Communication theories. Bateson and colleagues (1956) identified a distorted communication in families, which he termed 'double blind'. In this, the parent (usually the mother) gives out conflicting messages to the potentially-schizophrenic offspring, normally verbal contradicted by non-verbal communications. In order to comply with this the child must either engage in self-deceit or risk rejection by questioning the ambiguity. Singer & Wynne also claimed that communication and relationships in the families of schizophrenics were distorted. However, a study by Liem tended to identify the schizophrenic child as the source of communication deviance, emphasising the need to consider the direction of causality in such approaches.

Stress. Although Bowers (1974) found little difference in life events (stressors) prior to a schizophrenic episode, Brown & Birley in 1968 found as much as a fourfold increase in such events in the weeks prior to the episode. Clearly, these events could have been a consequence of the prodromal state of the affected individual and there are many individuals who do not have schizophrenia who have undergone more stresses in such a period. However, this work has been followed up and fits very well into the stress–diathesis model, ie. a biological predisposition which is expressed as a result of a precipitating stressor. If we accept that stress can influence biochemical events within the brain, then the stress–diathesis model fits very well with the association of acute schizophrenic breakdown and abnormalities in the dopamine system.

Expressed emotion. Following the above work on the effects of stress, a style of interpersonal relations has been found to increase the risk of relapse in schizophrenic patients returning home.

The way in which the family (usually parents or spouse) of the schizophrenic individual express their feelings and concerns towards the sufferer has been examined in relation to the course of the disorder. In a pattern called *expressed emotion*, in schizophrenic families, research suggests, family members express their feelings openly and intensely in ways that negatively affect schizophrenia-prone individuals. Two elements of those emotional expressions are particularly crucial in causing a pathogenic effect: emotional over-involvement and excessive criticalness or hostility.

Based on the earlier work of Brown and his colleagues, Christine Vaughn and Julian Leff tested the relationship between expressed emotion and the probability of relapse in schizophrenic patients returning home from hospital. They rated the families on expressed emotion by means of a standardised interview, the Camberwell Family Inventory (CFI) and kept a record of other factors relating to the patient and their illness such as maintenance medication (a level of continuous medication intended to prevent relapse). Although the absence of maintenance medication predicted a higher relapse rate, the expressed emotion (EE) rating and amount of time spent with a high EE family also significantly increased relapse rate. These two factors also interacted in that a combination of high EE, mainly emotional over-involvement and critical comments, and a lack of maintenance medication produced the highest rates of relapse. Overall, patients returning to high EE environments were three to four times more likely to be rehospitalised than those returning to low EE families, depending on the amount of time spent in the family home.

Research has examined the potential for high levels of EE to precipitate a first episode of schizophrenia, ie. be causal in combination with a biological predisposition. Although Rodnick and colleagues examined this relationship, the difficulties involved in predicting potential schizophrenia breakdown can lead to the biased targeting of individuals who already show signs of schizophrenia.

EE research has led to a form of family intervention which has been useful in avoiding relapse in patients returning home. There are questions, however, surrounding the relationship between the patient's behaviour and levels of expressed emotion. Stirling and colleagues, amongst others, have highlighted the possibility that high levels of EE may be a consequence of the behaviour of the schizophrenic individual rather than a precipitating cause. Clearly, when examined, the day to day behaviour of a schizophrenic patient living at home can be very trying. Future research has begun to focus on whether the relatives attribute the less acceptable behaviour of the schizophrenic to the individual concerned or the disorder. It would seem that if the blame is on the individual, the tendency towards high EE is greater than if the relatives see the disorder as the source of the disruption of relationships.

Overview of psychological factors in schizophrenia. In the earlier section, four biological factors provide a clear predisposition for schizophrenia of all types. Psychological factors would seem to provide a limited, though still important, function of precipitating the disorder or relapse in a vulnerable individual.

Early theories have examined the effects of parenting and deviant family structures. These approaches tended to be highly theoretical with very little support from studies of actual patients and have not provided any useful therapies for schizophrenia.

Distorted communications in the families of schizophrenic offspring would seem to have some foundation. However, these distorted communications are again likely to be a consequence rather than a cause of the disorder, and studies of communication deviance have not been successfully replicated. However, another abnormality of communication, that of high levels of expressed emotion, has been shown to precipitate relapse in schizophrenics exposed to it.

Although cause and effect are often confounded when examining psychological effects on the cause of schizophrenia, the increased stress on the individual can only combine with any biological predisposition to increase the probability of breakdown. Stressful life events have also been linked to the onset of a schizophrenic episode.

Current research into the psychological factors involved in schizophrenia is tending to focus on areas where the course of the disorder can be influenced by intervention programmes.

Socioeconomic and cultural factors in the development of schizophrenia

Schizophrenia has been recorded throughout history and in all civilisations, regardless of culture, at an approximate rate of one per cent over the lifetime of the individual. However, this has been subject to some variation between cultures and socio-economic groups and has sometimes varied in history. For example, in Britain, there is currently a decline in the number of first-episode schizophrenic patients being admitted to hospitals.

Socioeconomic factors. Most studies (eg. Murphy, 1968) of social class level and schizophrenia show a relationship, in that schizophrenia is more common in the lower socio-economic classes. There are two self-evident explanations for his disparity, one being that lower social class level is associated with higher levels of stress. It has been argued that stress is equally associated with higher social classes. However, there are more sources of stress amongst the lower socio-economic groups. The other explanation for the disparity is that schizophrenic individuals tend to drift downwards towards lower socio-economic groups due to their prodromal or episodic schizophrenic symptoms. In times of economic depression, many schizophrenics will have found themselves at the bottom of the socio-economic ladder amongst the homeless living on the streets of cities.

Cultural factors. Significant differences in the rates of schizophrenia have been found between different cultures in the world. This can mostly be attributed to differences in the rates of diagnosis rather than in the rates of the actual illness itself. Thus, countries with a very narrow set of criteria for schizophrenia will have an apparently lower rate of the disorder compared with countries with a wider set of criteria. The diagnostic systems ie. DSM-IV and ICD-10, are intended to overcome such disparities by standardising the criteria for schizophrenia internationally.

Some studies have found cultural 'types' of schizophrenia. For example, schizophrenic individuals of Japanese origin have been described as withdrawn and passive and this has been attributed to elements of their culture combining with the symptoms of the disorder. Attempts to relate these to sub-types of schizophrenia have not met with much success. Some aspects of culture have been related to the pathology of disturbed individuals. For example, one under-graduate researcher has found a strong relationship between the degree of reli-gious belief and obsessive compulsive symptoms in some cultures but not others. In the case of schizophrenia, the relationship between the content of delusions and fervent cultural beliefs would seem to be of research interest.

Treatment of schizophrenia

The aims of treatment in schizophrenia are limited in that there is no known cure for the disorder. Therapeutic efforts are therefore aimed at ensuring the safety of the patient and people he or she may come into contact with, the amelioration of symptoms and the rehabilitation of patients who have been severely disturbed by the disorder.

Hospitalisation is still the first measure taken for severe schizophrenia, with drug therapy being the main form of treatment thereafter. The effective pharmaco-logical treatment for schizophrenia began in the 1950s with the discovery of the major tranquillisers. Prior to this, restraint and institutionalisation were all that could be offered to the patient and attempts at psychological treatment were largely unsuccessful.

Pre-1950 treatment of schizophrenia

Prior to the revolutionary changes in treatment of schizophrenics made possible by drug therapy, the future of the individual after a schizophrenic breakdown usually was quite bleak. Hospitalisation, which was usually required, brought the patient into a huge, highly-institutionalised setting, in which care was largely custodial, leaving the patient bored and hopeless. Low staff-to-patient ratios, very low mental health-care budgets, and a limited knowledge of effective treatment resulted in long periods of hospitalisation and brief visits home, followed by seemingly inevitable relapses and return to the hospital. The result was a slow but steady decline into extreme deterioration.

That period of hopelessness was occasionally interrupted by the efforts of clini-cians to attempt more active treatment. During the three decades prior to the devel-opment of antipsychotic medication, two radical organic treatment techniques were widely used: prefrontal lobotomy and insulin shock treatment. Although initial success was reported for both, they were soon stopped, and for good reason. Although a prefrontal lobotomy reduced the extreme agitation of the schizophrenic patient, it was soon discovered that it left him or her in a tragically passive and often vegetative state. Insulin shock, a high-risk therapy, was discovered to be more appropriate as treatment for depression than for schizophrenia. Electroconvulsive therapy (ECT) effectively replaced insulin shock for depression. In the last two decades, the use of ECT in schizophrenia has gradually increased, although its effectiveness in non-depressed schizophrenic patients is debatable.

At this time, psychoanalytic approaches to schizophrenia were tried but found ineffective. Early attempts at behavioural treatments for schizophrenia were limited to encouraging and discouraging simple behaviours.

Modern treatment for schizophrenics

The modern treatment of the schizophrenic patient takes a two-stage approach. In stage one, the goal is the reduction of the positive symptoms (hallucinations, delusions and agitation) of the patient, the initial stages of which take place immediately after hospitalisation. Successful control of those symptoms usually requires that the patient continue the antipsychotic medication for long periods even after discharge from the hospital. In stage two, the goal is to help the patient develop the ability to function socially. Pursuit of that goal begins before the patient's discharge into the community and should be continued in an aftercare programme tailored to the patient's needs. At his point, care also needs to be taken over the patient's maintenance medication to ensure that the dosage is correct and that the patient is faithfully taking this. This is often a problem in that when a patient feels well, they are very likely to assume that they can function without the medication. However, the effect of the medication at this point is prophylactic and discontinuation usually leads to relapse within a short time.

Symptom reduction and the antipsychotic medications. In using the newly synthesised antihistamines for the relief of asthma and other allergies, clinicians soon took note of their strong tranquillising effect on patients. Experimentally, at first, psychiatrists began to use the drug with disturbed psychiatric patients. It was soon discovered that the drug they were using, chlorpromazine, had a powerful tranquillising effect on schizophrenic patients with a dramatic reduction in their more florid symptoms. Below is a list of the current anti-schizophrenic medications commonly used.

Group Name	Specific Drug Name
Phenothiazines	Chlorpromazine
	Thioridazine
	Trifluorperazine
	Fluphenazine
	Prochlorperazine
Thioxanthenes	Chlorprothixene
	Thiothixene
Others	Clozapine
	Haloperidol
	Loxapine

The effect of drug therapy. The anti-schizophrenic drugs, also called neuroleptics, anti-psychotic or major tranquillisers have become standard treatment for the disorder.

In the late eighties, the new drug clozapine was experimentally tested and found to be highly effective in the treatment of schizophrenia. At the introduction of the drug for the regular treatment of schizophrenics, a number of psychiatrists reported that 'it worked wonders' in making it possible for schizophrenics to return to their families, even to find employment. Although without the usual negative side effects, the drug causes a fatal blood disorder in a small number of patients, requiring that all users be followed up with an expensive monitoring programme. The biochemical effect of the antipsychotic drugs is to lower levels of dopamine in the brain. Clinically, that change reduces fear, agitation, thought disorders, delusions and hallucinations, which are the most acutely disruptive of the patient's symptoms. Once these symptoms are brought under control and the patient's condition stabilised, discharge from the hospital will be considered by the consultant psychiatrist in charge of the case. This is often achieved in stages, for example initially going home at weekends only.

The effect of drug therapy on the number of people populating the large psychiatric institutions has been dramatic. In the 20 years following the discovery of the phenothiazines, this population has been reduced by three quarters. More recently, a further reduction in these numbers has been the dual result of more sophisticated long-term maintenance therapy (usually by depot injection – a long acting injected medication which removes the responsibility for taking medication from the client) and the general trend towards care in the community, for these patients. However, there are problems in the use of neuroleptic treatment, one of the major drawbacks being the long and short-term side effects of these drugs.

Negative effects of drug therapy. As stated, the primary problem of drug therapy for schizophrenia is the level of side effects, especially with long-term use. Other problems arise from the fact that patients stabilised on medication no longer need to stay within institutions. Although this is ostensibly a good thing, patients have problems in adjusting to the outside world, and it to them also.

Negative side effects. One set of troublesome side effects is the development of Parkinsonian-type symptoms: muscle rigidity, immobile facial expression, and tremors. These symptoms are unquestionably the result of lowered dopamine levels produced by the medication. In some patients, there may also develop itching in the muscles, which leads to a constant need to move around. To relieve that discomfort, patients resort to pacing about restlessly.

In time, use of the drugs leads to an exceedingly unpleasant disorder (tardive dyskinesia) in which patients continuously smack their lips and move their tongues in what have been described as flycatching movements. One quarter of those patients who have been on the drug for seven years or more, especially those with Type II symptoms, develop the reaction. The symptoms, which are, as can be imagined, extremely discomforting to the patient, grow worse as the patient ages. Some professionals have asserted that tardive dyskinesia is part of the disease process of schizophrenia and not a side effect of medication. This aside, such symptoms are also highly related to long-term medication and the patient is unfortunately not in a position to discontinue this treatment. Newer drugs such as clozapine do not have these side effects, although inevitably they carry their own side effects, at least for some individuals.

Other consequences of anti-schizophrenic medication. In the past, schizophrenic patients had to remain in hospital for very long periods, often until their deaths.

With the use of the antipsychotic medications, most patients can be discharged well before a year passes. But, as a consequence, re-admission rates have soared, leading to a phenomenon nicknamed 'the revolving door effect'. In 1986, Hogarty and associates reported that the re-admission rate within a two-year period was

79 per cent. One explanation for that increased re-admission rate is that in past years, many patients now discharged would never have been out of the hospital. Arguably, some patients who have been in hospital for many years are not suitable candidates for discharge into the community. They are often 'institutionalised', that is they have adjusted to life in the institution and lack the social and coping skills to survive in the outside world. For this group of patients, even the advent of newer drugs with fewer side effects, and the rehabilitation programmes available, will do little to overcome their incompatibility with outside life.

Trying to look on the bright side of things, we can say that at least 21 per cent of hospitalised schizophrenics now are able to stay out of the hospital for at least two years. For those who remain on medication and live in benign facilities at home or elsewhere, that period might be even longer. For others, perhaps most of the discharged patients, the period out of hospital may not have been a pleasant one. Unknown numbers of discharged patients become part of the urban homeless population; others, while not homeless, may spend their time out of the hospital with the same disruptive and fractious family that provided the setting for previous relapses. A high rate of relapse among such released patients is predictable.

In Britain, economic pressures on the health service have led to large numbers of schizophrenic patients being refused hospital beds, although they may be in an unstable state. Although this is ostensibly a feature of the 'care in the community' scheme, support services are severely lacking, and for a large number of these unfortunate patients there is neither care nor a community for them. The tragic case, witnessed on British television, of a patient being mauled by lions after climbing into their zoo enclosure, hopefully marked a turning point in a system that achieved economic targets but left patients to care for themselves, often without essential medication.

Post-hospital care and relapse rate. Studies of discharged schizophrenics have identified four conditions that influence the length of time before a relapse and return to the hospital occurs:

1 Whether or not the patient continued to take the antipsychotic medication.
2 The quality of family relations in the home to which the patient returns.
3 The availability of out-of-home activities for the patient.
4 The extent to which the patient has developed useful social skills and the availability of social support networks.

Maintenance drug therapy. Substantial research (Hogarty and Goldberg, 1973, for example) has related length of time before relapse and whether or not the patient has continued medication after hospital discharge. In their study, in a two-year period, 30 per cent of discharged patients who continued medication were back in the hospital, whereas 68 per cent of those who were given a placebo had relapsed. Although not the only factor involved, continued prophylactic medication is very important in maintaining the patient's independence in the community.

For the patient, the importance of maintenance medication is not always obvious. They are often influenced by periods of feeling well or fears about the side effects of their medication. In addition to the side effects mentioned above, patients are often annoyed by the tendancy to put on weight, and dryness of the mouth. Patients may thus decide to stop taking the drug, or may quite simply have forgotten to, or run out of their prescription. Conversely, some patients over-medicate or mix medication with alcohol, in which case the depot injections can help.

Family intervention programmes. A number of studies have examined the effects of training the families of schizophrenics in order to avoid relapse in patients returning to them. Leff and colleagues (1982) provided an early example of training family members to reduce levels of expressed emotion. In combination with drug therapy this reduced the relapse of patients to eight per cent, whereas with maintenance medication alone 50 per cent relapsed.

Intervention programmes such as these have been examined by Nick Tarier for ways of improving them. Although a reduction in expressed emotion clearly has a beneficial effect, other aspects of intervention are also useful. Educating family members as to the facts about the disorder can improve the way that relatives view the schizophrenic behaviour, attributing it to the disorder rather than the patient's intentions. Tackling the patient's practical needs and stressing the importance of support networks are also important.

There are limits to the extent to which a family can be expected to change to accommodate a schizophrenic relative. As one mother of a patient remarked, 'why should we change our normal behaviour, he's the one disrupting the family atmosphere.' Clearly this attitude would not help the patient, but the point should be born in mind by a clinician trying to alter family behaviour.

Importance of time away from the family. For some schizophrenics who are returning to difficult home situations, the opportunity to get away from the family, at least for some hours during the day, can reduce the likelihood of an early relapse. Arrangements for the patient to spend some time in a day-care unit or, when the patient is capable of it, in part-time employment, can be a helpful alternative to unalleviated time in a disruptive home setting.

Behaviour modification and social skills training. Ordinary social skills used in relating appropriately to others or in seeking their help – asking directions, for example – which are skills that most people use routinely with little difficulty, often have been completely lost during the schizophrenic illness; yet any successful attempt to resume a somewhat normal interpersonal life is dependent upon those skills. Once the individual's most disturbing symptoms have subsided, training can begin while the patient is still in the hospital and continue after discharge at an aftercare clinic.

The early work of Ayllon & Azrin (1965) showed the usefulness of operant conditioning techniques in modifying a patient's institutionalised or maladaptive behaviour. Using a 'token economy' in the hospital setting they successfully improved the behaviour of schizophrenic patients by selectively rewarding them with tokens for accomplishing tasks (eg. grooming themselves). The tokens could then be exchanged for things the patient may want. This principle of behaviour modification can be more selectively used in the patient's home environment, not just to encourage basic skills but to identify the consequences of the patient's unwanted behaviour, to see if altering the consequences extinguishes the behaviour.

Another approach to training was taken by Wallace and colleagues (1982). They attempted to gradually ease the patient into normal, outside-of-hospital social settings in stages.

The programme divided social skills into three phases:

1 Accurate perception of the social situation.
2 Planning choice of response options.
3 Implementing the chosen response.

Throughout this the patient was trained in each separate step, and then the patient integrated and practised the steps in role-playing situations – in the beginning, with the therapist, and later in group situations, with other patients.

For more lasting effect, the patient should have an opportunity to 'test' the new social skill in real life interpersonal situations, followed by a discussion with the therapist about any problems that may have developed.

Therapeutic communities. In the sixties and seventies a number of experimental full-time residential communities were set up to provide a stepping stone into independent living for patients leaving institutions. Although they tended to attract the more able patients (who were more likely to volunteer for the scheme), these were fairly successful and provided the model for later smaller self-help groups living in the community.

Care in the community. Although the implementation of this concept has had its limitations, as mentioned above, the original concept is sound, as demonstrated by the success of the therapeutic communities. The recently applied concept came from Italy where a programme of closing large institutions was implemented, replacing them with patient support systems within the community. This is a very expensive alternative, but allows the patient to avoid the consequences and limitations of institutionalisation. Unfortunately, as mentioned above, it has been looked upon as a cost-cutting exercise by some governments and the funding for the support in the community has not been provided.

The maintenance of schizophrenic patients in the community has been assisted by the provision of community psychiatric services, including community psychiatric nurses who travel to the patient, rather than vice versa. However, the public at large tend to resist having patients living in their neighbourhood, although they agree with the principle. These attitudes are beginning to change as the public begin to see the schizophrenic patient as part of their responsibility, rather than a nuisance to be hidden away from them.

Overview of outcomes in schizophrenia

The prospects for the schizophrenic patient nowadays have improved vastly from the prospects earlier this century. This change has been assisted greatly by the discovery of effective anti-schizophrenic medication in the 1950s. Optimistic views of prognosis in schizophrenia tend to examine the benefits these changes have made. However, more pessimistic views tend to be more testing of the meaning of the term 'recovery'.

On the optimistic side, we can say that since the introduction of drug therapy, almost 90 per cent of those individuals suffering a schizophrenic episode and entering a psychiatric hospital for the first time will improve and be discharged in a short time – for some, a few weeks, and for others, months – but for practically all of that 90 per cent group, in less than a year. To balance that optimism, it is necessary to report that many will have to be re-hospitalised within the subsequent two years.

A more pessimistic view acknowledges the fact that complete recovery, that is a return to pre-schizophrenic functioning, is very unlikely. There always seems to be some residual effect on the individual's emotional, social or other ways of functioning, and more frequently, residual symptoms of the disorder itself.

The concept of 'thirds' in schizophrenia recovery patterns referred to earlier, offered a rough guide to the roughly equal numbers of those who recover with little or no relapse; those who will relapse with recurrent episodes; and those who steadily decline with few periods of remission. More recent examinations of recovery rates tend to show a gradual improvement in these proportions, although the overall picture of the illness remains both bleak and an area for constant concern for the health services. In 1988 Carson and colleagues described the outcome for schizophrenic patients as follows.

They report that one-third of hospitalised schizophrenics 'recover', which they define as being symptom-free for five years. This is not quite the same as saying that they return to premorbid levels of functioning. At the other end of the scale are the ten per cent of the schizophrenic population who go into a steady decline towards deterioration and lifetime disability. The remaining 60 per cent of the schizophrenic population go through life in and out of hospitals after occasional recurrence of schizophrenic episodes and weakening of their personality.

SUMMARY

Schizophrenia, and to some extent the other psychotic disorders (schizophreniform disorder, brief psychotic disorder, schizoaffective disorder, shared psychotic disorder, and substance-induced and psychotic disorder due to a general medical condition) seriously disturb the thinking, behaviour and affective life of the individual. It is one of the most debilitating psychiatric disorders and affects approximately one per cent of the world's population at some point during their lifetime.

The heterogeneity of schizophrenia has been emphasised over the years. It has been studied by subdividing it along variously named dimensions, all of which are very similar in the distinctions they finally make. Three of these are:

1 The nature of the onset.
2 The presence of positive symptoms – for example, delusions or hallucinations, or negative symptoms, an absence of florid symptoms but serious deficiencies in normal functioning, for example, flatness of affective reaction.

3 *The presence or absence of paranoid elements in the symptomatology.*

The positive–negative dimension has been most popular in recent years and has led to schizophrenia being divided into these two broad classifications: positive symptom or Type I (acute) schizophrenia, characterised by acute, positive symptoms (eg. hallucinations and delusions) and a good prognosis; negative symptom or Type II (process) schizophrenia, with a slow onset, negative symptoms (eg. withdrawal and affective blunting), poor response to medication and a poor prognosis.

Maladaptive changes in the schizophrenic individual include bizarre thought content, anomalies in the form of the individual's thought processes, warped perceptions of the world, flattening or inappropriateness in emotional expression, paralysis of will, a loss of any sense of self-identity, and withdrawal from the outside world. There is no one symptom or type of behaviour that unequivocally identifies the schizophrenic.

In the development of schizophrenia, clinicians recognise three phases: the prodromal or early stage; the active stage, which brings on florid symptomatology; and the residual stage, which is what the schizophrenic is left with after a schizophrenic episode.

DSM-IV classifies five specific types of schizophrenia: catatonic, disorganised (formerly called hebephrenia), paranoid, residual and undifferentiated.

The causes of schizophrenia are a subject of on-going research, although there is some certainty about the involvement of biological factors. The evidence so far points to a biological basis in genetics or neurophysiological abnormality, which provides a vulnerability which is susceptible to stress from various sources.

Treatment usually involves hospitalisation and drug therapy. The drug treatment may have to be continued for some time and in some cases permanently in the form of maintenance medication. Rehabilitation is an important aim of therapy, and psychological factors are involved in this, and the prevention of relapse. Full recovery from schizophrenia is difficult, but many cases recover to a high degree.

FURTHER READING

Abraham, K. & Kulhara, P. 1987. The Efficacy of Electroconvulsive Therapy in the Treatment of Schizophrenia. *British Journal of Psychiatry*, 151: 152–155.

Birchwood, M. & Tarrier, N. 1994. *The Psychological Management of Schizophrenia*. London: Wiley.

Crow, T. 1989. A Current View of the Type II Syndrome. *British Journal of Psychiatry*, 155 (suppl. 7): 15–20.

Frith, C. 1993. *The Cognitive Neuropsychology of Schizophrenia*. London: Lawrence Earlbaum Associates Ltd.

Johnstone, E. 1994. *Searching for the Causes of Schizophrenia*. Oxford University Press.

Kavanagh, D. 1992. *Schizophrenia: An Overview and Practical Handbook*. London: Chapman & Hall.

Kirch, D. 1993. Infection and Autoimmunity as Aetiologicol Factors in Schizophrenia: A

Review and Reappraisal. *Schizophrenia Bulletin*, 19: 355–370.

McKenna, P. 1994. *Schizophrenia and Related Syndromes*. Oxford University Press.

Reynolds, G. 1989. Beyond the Dopamine Hypothesis: the Neurochemical Pathology of Schizophrenia. *British Journal of Psychiatry*, 155: 305–316.

13 Substance-Related Disorders

The three most medically dangerous substances of abuse, in order, are tobacco, alcohol and food. This fact is usually not apparent to the public who are very susceptible to scaremongering by the media and political pressure groups about 'drugs'. The public tend to refer to illicit substances as 'drugs' and are reluctant to admit that alcohol and tobacco are included, although these legal drugs lead to many times more deaths than all the illicit substances put together. The use of all drugs (including alcohol and tobacco) is rising worldwide, and health and criminal justice services lack agreement over a solution. For the public, who see media images of drug-dealers and crazed addicts, the solution is one of crime and punishment. However, for the many families of abusers and addicts, the solution is one of health care and psychological therapy, which is confounded by the involvement of the legal system.

The problems of drug addiction and drug abuse have led to the formation of a number of self-help groups and official organisations to help the sufferers. The consequences of substance-related disorders for the individual can be far-reaching, involving their familes and society at large. A large number of suicides, traffic accidents, murders and other crimes are alcohol-related, which is why this legal substance will be examined in more detail in this chapter. A growing number of crimes are also illicit-drug-related and the recent link between the use of contamintated intravenous needles and the spread of AIDS has fuelled further fears regarding these disorders.

Despite the negative effects of excessive use of alcohol and other psychoactive substances, they are, as the Diagnostic and Statistical Manual of Mental Disorders points out, frequently used to modify mood or behaviour, in a recreational way, under circumstances that are considered normal and appropriate. There exist subcultural groups who, in opposition to those practices, forbid, or at least strongly discourage, any use of alcohol, and by strong implication, all other psychoactive drugs.

Ill effects and all, the practice of using various substances to reduce pain and emotional tension, or to induce euphoria, is, as far as we can tell, an ancient practice. The virtues (if that is the right word) of wine were sung in the poetry of the Greeks and the Romans; the royalty of Persia and Egypt were subject to its influences. Persian history gives Cambysis, a sixth-century BC member of the royal family, the dubious distinction of being the first alcoholic in recorded history.

This chapter, although giving principal emphasis to alcohol, a substance negatively affecting many more individuals than all other drugs combined (bar tobacco) will describe the principal addictive substances, their effects, possible causes, and treatment programmes.

Classification of substance-related disorders

There are a large number of substance-related disorders recognised by both DSM-IV and ICD-10. Many of these relate to other psychological disorders which have been induced by the use of a wide variety of substances, such disorders as: psychoses, mood disorders, delirium and dementia, anxiety and sexual disorders. These disorders are similar in symptoms to the same conditions covered in the relevant chapters in this book, except their cause and treatment depend on the presence and absence of the substance in question, and as such will not be described here (see chapters 20 and 21 for a full listing).

A further distinction that is made in classifying substance-related disorders refers to substance dependence and substance abuse, with the former being seen as more serious.

Substance dependence

In classifying an individual as substance dependent, the individual is usually expected to show at least three of the following symptoms or patterns of behaviour.

1 When the substance is taken in larger quantities or over a longer period of time than the individual planned.
2 When despite a strong desire to reduce or control substance use, the individual fails to do so in several attempts.
3 When the individual spends inordinate time in trying to obtain the substance.
4 When obligations are not met, or when the individual fails to appear at school or for work because of intoxication or withdrawal symptoms.
5 When important social, occupational or recreational interests are given up or neglected.
6 When substance use is continued despite the knowledge of having a persistent social, psychological or physical problem that is caused or exacerbated by the use of the substance. Examples are as follows: exacerbation of an ulcer by continuing to drink alcohol; provoking a major family dispute because of drug abuse; or continuing use, even though it is followed by a severe depression.
7 When a marked tolerance of the substance causes the individual to increase use of the substance.
8 When there are significant withdrawal symptoms.
9 When the substance is taken to relieve or avoid withdrawal symptoms.

Substance abuse

A less severe reaction than substance dependence, substance abuse is diagnosed by DSM-IV, when there is a pattern of pathological use, accompanied by impaired social or occupational functioning, for at least a month's time.

Aetiological factors in substance-related disorders

More than any other psychological disorder, the development of substance-related disorders seems to be dependent upon the ready availability of the substance and its use by the individual's peers. Both biological and psychological factors have also been explored as possible causes of substance-abuse disorders. Alcohol use has been studied most extensively.

Essential conditions for the development of substance-related disorders

Not all individuals who have access to psychoactive substances or whose friends use one or more of them become victims of the substance. To those two conditions, there is usually added either a set of life circumstances that are so unhappy for the individual as to cause him or her to seek escape from them, or life circumstances so boring and unexciting as to provoke the need for artificial stimulation. Once individuals are tempted to try the substance, its immediate psychological effects draw them into regular use of the substance and hence into dependence.

To understand the aetiology of substance-related disorders, we begin by describing the way in which most psychoactive substances work.

Characteristics of the way in which psychoactive substances work

Richard Solomon (1977) describes three characteristics or phases of substance abuse that create a strong motive to continue using the substance. He has called his analysis the 'opponent-process' model of addiction. It is so named because of the opposition between two phases of substance abuse. Most approaches to the stages of addiction consider there to be three identifiable stages in becoming dependent on a substance and all require the continued availability of the substance in question. Not all substances are addictive in the same way: the physical effects of cannabis or LSD use do not make them physically addictive, leaving psychological addiction as the only basis for dependence. In either case, the move from the stage of pleasure, tolerance and withdrawal is similar if less serious in the case of non-physically addictive substances.

Pleasure phase

Psychoactive substances which can lead to dependence usually provide some pleasure or escape in the form of positive social, physical or emotional experiences. The nature of those experiences varies from one substance to another, but they are all, in one way or another, pleasing to the user. Alcohol releases inhibitions, overcomes shyness, and pushes current problems out of consciousness; heroin gives the user a 'rush', bathing the individual in a warm ecstasy; cocaine provides a 30-minute period of euphoria, well-being and tirelessness. Those pleasant experiences invite the individual to come back again. Sometimes the effect is paradoxical: individuals find the effects of a substance unpleasant, for example tobacco, but persist in its use for diverse reasons. In the case of LSD, those individuals who have a bad time (bad 'trip') often persist, tyring to have the kind of experience reported by others. As will be discussed later, it is often the case that unstable individuals tend to be attracted towards drug use.

Tolerance phase

Depending on the substance used, a tolerance for the substance may develop. This may be a physical tolerance in which the body changes slightly to accommodate the regular presence of the substance. With alcohol, one or two drinks may have initially caused euphoria (and a sizeable hangover), but with tolerance double or treble this amount would be needed to obtain the same effect. Alcoholics may consume two or three bottles of spirits or more a day just to get inebriated, a heroin addict will also use enough of the drug to kill a naive user just to 'stay normal'. Some drugs have a reverse tolerance. Cannabis gathers in the fatty tissues in parts of the body and so regular users actually require less of the drug to get 'high'. LSD cannot be used continuously, as it relies on endogenous substances, and loses its effect in a couple of days, even if larger doses are taken. This mechanism of tolerance is an important step in dependence.

   Tolerance may also be psychological. Individuals may become used to the boredom-relieving aspects of taking the drug and become used to managing the effects of the drug by compensating for it in their behaviour.

Withdrawal phase

Individuals, after a period of heavy substance abuse, may develop feelings of guilt about their habit; there may be pressure from a spouse, parents or employers. They may then decide to give up their habit. If, by that time, their body's physiological processes have become dependent upon use of the substance, they will develop withdrawal symptoms. These withdrawal symptoms vary greatly depending on the substance in question. For example, there are no notable physical withdrawal effects with cannabis use, only psychological ones. However with alcohol, heroin and barbiturates the effects of withdrawal are more serious and can include physical pain, panic, extreme irritability and even psychosis. The reaction is a very unpleasant one, and now drives the individual, not so much to seek pleasure, but to reduce the unpleasantness of the withdrawal symptoms. The more frequently relapses occur, the more drastic are the withdrawal symptoms, causing users to frantically seek 'a fix', sometimes at any cost.

They have moved from drug abuse to drug dependence, with dire effects upon their lives, including possible criminal acts to obtain money for purchasing the drugs upon which they have now become dependent.

Are there biogenic factors or personality characteristics that make the individual vulnerable to substance abuse? Most of the research on that question relates to alcohol use, and we will answer that question when we discuss alcoholism.

Types of psychoactive substances

This section describes five categories of psychoactive (that is, affecting cognitions, feelings or behaviour) substance: alcohol, narcotics (derived from opium), sedatives (principally the barbiturates), stimulants (principally cocaine and the amphetamines), and the hallucinogens (including marijuana). Some mention will also be made of tobacco, which is the most medically dangerous substance, and the 'designer drugs' which have more recently become popular substances for recreational use. The substances described in this chapter are not a complete listing as there are far too many to include here.

Alcohol

Consumption of alcohol is a major characteristic of the contemporary social scene. We discuss here prevalence, effects, causative factors, and treatment approaches.

Prevalence

According to a 1985 survey, 86 per cent of the population reported using alcohol in the recent past; 12 per cent reported using it at least 20 days each month. Its prevalence has been rising steadily, especially among females and the young. Frequencies of alcoholism are very difficult to estimate but vary at around five to ten per cent for men, though considerably lower for women.

The cost of damage done by alcohol is beyond estimation overall but a study of England and Wales in 1983 counted the cost to industry as £1,398 million and to the health service as £96 million. These costs have risen considerably and need to be added to by the cost of road and other accidents, and crime, amongst many other costs. A study in Finland found that 53 per cent of individuals reporting to a hospital out-patients department after suffering falls had been drinking. Such costs are the tip of a very large iceberg, in which the personal, relationship and social costs are hidden.

The effects of alcohol

There are both physiological and behavioural effects of drinking alcohol.

Physiological effects. Alcohol acts quickly. In a matter of minutes, alcohol is absorbed into the bloodstream through the walls of the stomach and the small intestine. It then goes to the liver, which has the capacity to metabolise (that is, to convert into energy) one ounce of 100-proof alcohol (per cent by volume) in one hour. In theory, if a person drank just one ounce of 100-proof alcohol every hour, there would be no alcohol available to the blood, and hence to the brain, to effect any behavioural changes. The alcohol that is not metabolised remains in the bloodstream for up to 24 hours.

Although many people think of alcohol as a stimulant, it is a central nervous system (CNS) depressant. Its 'stimulating' effect results from its depressant effect on the cortical control of emotion and behaviour. Thus, the cortex generally inhibits the activity of the emotional and instinctive brain areas and alcohol reduces this inhibtion. It turns an overly-inhibited individual into a relatively uninhibited one. With continued drinking, initial amiability may be converted into depression or aggression.

Behavioural effects. Even moderate doses of alcohol impair coordination and slow reaction time. It also interferes with speech, vision, and the higher mental processes, such as judgement and calculation. Alcoholics typically have trouble adding up the bill for the cost of a night's drinking.

Social effects. Two socially significant effects of alcohol are its impact on aggressive behaviour and sexual behaviour. The combination can be especially upsetting to those around the drinker. Small doses of alcohol cause aggression to be expressed in assertively arguing contrary political, ethical or religious views. With increased drinking, the individual may 'look for a fight', or, indeed, become assaultive. With respect to alcohol's effect on sexual behaviour, psychologists enjoy quoting Shakespeare, from *Macbeth:* 'Lechery, Sir, it provokes and it unprovokes; it provokes the desire, but it takes away the performance'.

The influence of expectations. There is research to indicate that much uninhibited behaviour, resulting from a drink or two, comes more from what the individual believes will be the effect of alcohol than from the alcohol itself. For example, in two separate studies, groups of males and females were given what they thought were alcoholic drinks. Their behavioural reactions were then observed. With respect to aggressive behaviour and to amorous behaviour, both males and females behaved in notably uninhibited ways.

The drinking cycle's influence on effects. There is also research to indicate that the effect of alcohol varies with the timing of the drinking cycle. Using tests of abstract problem-solving and memory, Jones and Parsons (1971) were able to show that with identical levels of alcohol in the blood, those moving towards intoxication were much more intellectually impaired than those on their way to sobriety, that is, on the downward cycle of the drinking episode. In either phase, performance was lower than performance without alcohol.

Long-term effects. The effects of alcohol discussed so far are those within a single drinking episode. With frequent drinking bouts over a prolonged period of time, there will be more damaging and long-term effects. Chronic alcoholism affects almost every tissue of the body. The most damaging long-term effects of chronic alcoholism are as follows:

1 Malnutrition. Although the calories of alcohol are devoid of nutritional value, the body will absorb alcohol in preference to food. In time, the body will break down as a result of the absence of nutrients essential for health, especially protein.

2 Severe psychiatric disorders develop. Korsakoff's syndrome (see chapter 16) is a direct result of the absence of B-complex vitamins that result from the diet of the chronic alcoholic.

3 Cirrhosis of the liver is a likely possibility. This serious illness, in which fat replaces healthy liver tissue, impairs the liver's functioning and causes inflammation. Cirrhosis of the liver is often fatal, ranking eighth among the principal causes of death.

One sad long-term effect of alcohol affects not only the woman alcoholic but, if she is pregnant, the foetus as well. In 1987, Ashton reported that 40 per cent of pregnant females who drank heavily, gave birth to babies who had suffered 'foetal alcohol syndrome'. This condition results in developmental defects of the foetus, especially in the central nervous system.

Special factors in the aetiology of alcoholism

Psychological research has focused on two possible causative factors in alcoholism: genetic and other biogenic causes, and personality characteristics. Certain psychosocial factors, such as ethnicity, occupation and social class, seem to be associated with alcoholism. They are not considered to be primary causes of the alcohol addiction.

Genetic causes of alcoholism. Although the genetic mechanism has not yet been described, there is clear evidence, from family and twin studies, that genetic factors play a part in causing alcoholism. The parent or sibling of an alcoholic is two and a half times as likely to be alcoholic as a member of the general population. The fact that sons of alcoholics who leave home are just as likely to follow in their father's drinking as those who stay, would suggest that such effects cannot be attributed entirely to the environment, as bad as that environment may be. The mechanism by which a genetic influence has its effect has been attributed to dopamine receptors (D2), lowered levels of serotonin (raising the level of serotonin can reduce the craving for alcohol) and the idea of a genetically determined 'addictive personality'. 'Addictive personalities' are associated with an under-sensitive punishment mechansim within the brain and tend not to respond to danger signals in the environment.

Evidence for genetic factors in alcoholism comes from studies of both animals and humans. Rats have been bred to show a preference for alcohol over other beverages, which is strong evidence of the heritability of the condition.

In humans, Cloninger and colleagues (1986) report the following figures from the family histories of alcoholics. In a population of males with one alcoholic parent, the rate of alcoholism in family members was 29.5 per cent, compared to 11.4 per cent in the general population; with two alcoholic parents, that percentage jumps to 41.2 per cent. Comparable rates in females were 9.5 to 5.0 per cent with one alcoholic parent, and 25 per cent with two alcoholic parents. The weakness of this evidence is the fact that common heredity is not the only variable operating. Relatives, including children of alcoholics, may have been surrounded by an alcohol-drinking environment.

Stronger evidence is provided in a study by Godwin and others (1973). That study reported that when children of alcoholic parents were raised apart from their parents by adoptive parents, the rate of alcoholism at the age of 20 among the adopted children was almost twice as high as among a matched control group. Comparing children of alcoholic parents raised by their own parents with those raised by adoptive parents, Godwin's group, in a second study, found statistically insignificant differences between the two groups; that is, 25 per cent and 17 per cent. Those figures can only suggest some small influence from the home environment. But what is most significant in causing alcoholism is the parents to whom you were born, and not the parents who raised you.

On the other hand, there is one study that reports no significant differences between children of alcoholics and a matched control group (Schulsinger *et al.* 1986). However, it is possible that this sample contained a high proportion of non-genetic forms of alcoholism.

Types of alcohol dependence and aetiological factors.

Cloninger also identified the characteristics of individuals who tended towards two types of alcoholism.

1 The steady drinker. The first type of dependency involves individuals who regulated their frequent intake, beginning before the age of 25. They are disorderly and distractible and often show hyperactivity as a child. This hyperactivity, and to a greater extent antisocial behaviour, are good predictors of this form of alcoholism. They tend not to show fear or avoidance of dangerous or socially unacceptable situations and thus may be the type that have a weakened punishment mechanism in the brain. They are easily bored and seek novelty and excitement, often ending in violence.

2 The binge drinker. The binge drinker has some of the opposite tendencies to the steady drinker. They can go without a drink for long periods but cannot stop once they begin a bout, or 'binge' of drinking, a behaviour that begins after the age of about 25. They tend to be rigid, sensitive perfectionists, giving great attention to detail. They are also anxious and emotionally dependent, being cautious, apprehensive and sensitive to social cues. They have difficulty in relaxing and report that alcohol helps them overcome this.

Biological and personality factors. The two types of drinker above have differing personality types which may have a basis in biology. The steady drinker would seem to have underactive reward and punishment mechanisms in the brain.

The brain has endogenous reward systems which assist behavioural learning. After achieving something, especially physical achievement, we feel good and are often immune to the pain and exhaustion involved. This is due to the endogenous opiate system, in which endorphins and other similar substances are released providing pleasure (reward) and pain reduction. In a reverse situation, fear of threat and guilt over misbehaviour or lack of achievement can produce a reverse effect leading to the avoidance of dangerous or guilt-producing behaviour. These systems appear to be crucial in understanding the process of addiction to a number of drugs including alcohol.

Thus the steady drinker seeks the artificial pleasure of alcohol. However, binge drinkers are normally too guilt-ridden to drink but once started, the effect of the alcohol in suppressing the punishment mechanism makes it unlikely they will stop. Thus alcohol, amongst a number of drugs, corrupts the basic endogenous learning mechanism. Prolonged exposure to alcohol seems to worsen these pre-existing traits.

Psychosocial factors.   There are ethnic, occupational and socioeconomic correlates of alcoholism. Such factors cannot be causative in any real sense; they are likely to be environmental conditions that make it easy to drink alcohol, and social conditions in which peers drink alcohol.

In France, the national consumption of alcohol for each person aged 15 or older is the highest in the world. The French also apparently have the highest rate of alcohol abuse in the world. About 15 per cent of the French population have alcohol problems. As a major wine-producing country, France's high rate of alcoholism is perhaps understandable.

From an occupational perspective, prevalence of alcohol abuse is highest in such occupations as railroad workers, sailors, bartenders, waiters, and liquor salesmen. Here, too, availability and peer group practices provide the environmental impetus for drinking.

Not so easily explained is the high prevalence of alcoholism in the middle socioeconomic class when compared with the lower class. Perhaps it is too simplistic to say that lower socioeconomic classes do not have the money necessary to pay for alcohol. In the worst cases of alcoholism, a drop from middle-class to lower-class family income can be the result.

Treatment for alcohol abuse and alcohol dependence

The principal hurdle for all treatment programmes is the prevention of a relapse. Professional treatment for alcoholism usually takes place in three stages. An important adjunct to professional treatment is the help of such groups as Alcoholics Anonymous.

Stage one of treatment.   Hospitalisation for a minimum of a month begins the process. That period is sometimes called a drying-out time. In any case, the time in the hospital should be long enough to give the individual a significant period of time without using alcohol. The discovery that he or she has done without alcohol, even though in a protected environment, can give the individual a sense of accomplishment.

Stage two of treatment.   At the end of that initial period, the individual must be confronted with his or her alcohol problem, which may, up to this point, have been denied. The alcoholics are led to admit that they have been alcoholics and that they may have a vulnerability to the problem. That possible vulnerability requires an 'on guard' defensive stance for the rest of their lives.

Stage three of treatment. At this point, a period of psychotherapy is initiated, often in a group setting. A principal emphasis here is identification of the types of situation that usually lead to heavy drinking. In therapy, many approaches focus on the development of cognitive strategies to handle situations that put the alcoholic at risk. These strategies may range from how to graciously refuse an offered drink (that is, if the goal is abstinence, which it may not be) to dealing with tension-provoking situations at home or at work.

Cognitive-oriented therapy. In one widely-used cognitive therapeutic approach, the individual is first weaned away from any tendency to believe that his or her alcoholism results from a craving for alcohol which the individual may blame on some poorly-understood physiological condition. Instead, individuals are encouraged to believe that their weakness is a matter of self-indulgence. The longer individuals are able to maintain control, the greater the sense of self-mastery and confidence. With those feelings strong, the more likely it is that they will triumph over their excessive drinking.

Unanticipated consequences after therapy. Once a short-term programme is concluded, two possible developments may take place that tend to destabilise the individual.

1 Therapists report that the danger is not that there will be a sudden major alcoholic episode, but that through a series of seemingly harmless 'minor' decisions, alcoholics will gradually head toward a relapse. Sometimes a spouse will unwittingly elicit such a decision. For example, the simple statement, 'Helen and Joe are coming over for dinner tonight'; in the interest of being a hospitable host, such a comment may lead the husband to bring home a bottle of Scotch, saying to himself, 'I know Joe likes Scotch'. With that act, temptation is brought home. Warning about such mini-decisions can help alcoholics see their danger and avoid making such decisions.
2 A second problem occurs if, in therapy, the goal of absolute abstinence has been set. Alcoholics may accidentally, in the course of a social evening, or by deliberate choice, take a single drink. Stopping after a single drink is a victory; but if the goal was abstinence, alcoholics may not perceive their accomplishment, but assign such significance to that one violation that their confidence is destroyed and they lose their past determination to avoid heavy drinking. This is another important area in which advance warning about such possibilities can be helpful.

Aversive substances in treatment. In the course of the treatment programme, the therapist may use the help of an aversive deterrent to drinking, antabuse. This is a chemical that disrupts the metabolic processing of alcohol for two days after it is taken. If the individual is in a total abstinence programme, and he or she drinks alcohol during the two-day period, the consequences are very unpleasant: flushing, increased heartbeat, and severe nausea, an event likely to deter the desire to take another drink during the two crucial days following a dose of antabuse. This treatment is a form of behaviour therapy based on classical conditioning, in which the alcohol is associated with the feeling ill. The rationale behind the use of antabuse is that it stops impulsive, unplanned drinking. If the alcoholic decides to resume drinking, he or she has to plan two days ahead to do so. In that time, therapists believe, there is a good chance that the determination not to drink will have become re-established. The problem with such aversive therapy is that unless underlying problems motivating the drinking are solved, the alcoholic will simply decide to give up antabuse once out of the hospital.

Self-help groups. The most widely known, and for some 20 per cent of those who seek its help, the most effective self-help programme, is that offered by Alcoholics Anonymous. With no professional staff, AA offers alcoholics the opportunity to meet in groups with other problem drinkers and also with those who have completely and securely reformed. In the course of the meetings, those who have reformed (often well-known personalities) describe the indignities and unwholesomeness of their lives while drinking as an example to avoid and as an example of the possibility of overcoming a drinking problem.

Alcoholics Anonymous uses the 'buddy' system, which enables an alcoholic who feels the urge to drink to call his or her 'sponsor' for help. Ordinarily, in quick order, a healthy member will arrive and stay with the individual until his or her desire to drink disappears. It is a part of the AA philosophy that in this practice, both individuals are helped; the buddy is reinforced in maintaining an alcohol-free life, and the newcomer survives a crisis.

Established in 1935 by two former alcoholics, the programme has developed its own philosophy of treatment based on three propositions:

1 Once an alcoholic, always an alcoholic. The weakness is always there.
2 No one can stop drinking without help.
3 A spiritual but nonsectarian approach to life is helpful to everyone, and is especially needed by alcoholics.

When the programme works, cured individuals are generous in their praise of it. Unfortunately, a dropout rate of 80 per cent limits its usefulness to the 20 per cent who persist. In Britain the health service has a number of Alcohol Treatment Units (ATU) dealing with both inpatients and outpatients. These are usually located in psychiatric units. They often deal with more difficult cases than those who volunteer themselves to Alcoholics Anonymous, but often adopt some of the same principles of peer support in addition to other treatment approaches.

Overall view of alcohol treatment programmes. Treatment programmes for those who use excessive amounts of alcohol get mixed reviews, and how one interprets the research findings depend upon one's expectations of what should happen.

The most extensive research on the effects of treatment is that reported by Polich and colleagues in a 1981 report. They reported the negative side of the picture as follows. Only seven per cent of a group of 922 males studied had not used alcohol in the four years following treatment; 54 per cent of the group continued to have alcohol-related problems during that time.

When the statistics (drawn accurately from the study) are presented differently, one can feel more encouraged about the possibility of treating alcoholics. Of the 922 men in the study, more than 90 per cent had serious drinking problems to start with; only 54 per cent continued to have problems with alcohol. That is a substantial reduction.

Conditions for effective treatment. Carson *et al.* (1988), describe conditions that improve the likelihood of favourable treatment outcomes. They are early recognition of the problem, acceptance by the individual that he or she has a problem and needs help, the availability of adequate treatment facilities, and the use of a criterion of reduced alcohol consumption, not abstinence.

Other types of psychoactive and addictive substances

Here we consider three major groups of psychoactive drugs: the depressants, the stimulants, and the hallucinogens. Varieties of these drugs may be taken orally, by sniffing, smoking or 'snorting', or intravenously. We examine the nature of the various substances, their effects, aetiological factors, and possible therapies.

The depressants

In addition to alcohol, the depressants are categorised as narcotics, sedatives, and tranquillisers. All have similar characteristics: the user grows tolerant of them and requires increased dosages to produce the desired relaxing effects; withdrawal symptoms develop when the substance is unavailable; and overdoses of the substances depress the functioning of various bodily systems; for example, blood pressure and rate of respiration.

Extreme overdoses of any of the depressants can cause death by reducing vital activities to the point where they can no longer support life.

Opium

A principal source of substance abuse, it has been around at least since the Sumerian civilisation in 7,000 BC. Opium is derived from the poppy plant. The principal forms of its modern use are morphine and heroin, which are chemically refined forms of raw opium with heroin being the more refined derivative.

Morphine. Morphine is a powerful sedative and pain reliever. Prior to knowledge of its addictive powers, it was used widely in patent medicines and as a means of reducing pain. It is still used occasionally, under strict medical supervision, when intractable and unbearable pain is present.

Heroin. This opium derivative was developed as a means of controlling the use of morphine, but soon discovered to have stronger addictive power than morphine, and other negative physiological and behavioural effects, as well. Although many times less common, heroin, like alcohol, is one of the major drugs of addiction and carries a legal penalty (it is a class A drug) for non-authorised possession.

Although it has always had a number of users over the last 50 years, it has shown trends in times when it has been viewed as more or less favourable. In the 1960s it was considered unfashionable in the face of the widespread use of the less harmful hallucinogens. However, its use continued, especially amongst the wealthy and famous who could afford it and the necessary privacy. In the late 1980s and 1990s the increased use amongst the young and unemployed in Britain has accelerated and with it the levels of petty crime to pay for these habits. In some other countries the use has fallen.

Effects of morphine and heroin. Both drugs produce euphoria, reverie and drowsiness. In addition, heroin causes a 'rush' effect from intravenous injections, in which the individual is suffused with feelings of warmth and ecstasy. For four to six hours, the individual can be in a stupor and seems 'out of things'.

Heroin fits well into the pleasure, tolerance and withdrawal pattern of addiction. In that model (as discussed earlier), the first appeal is pleasure; when later withdrawal symptoms develop, heroin is then sought to escape the extreme discomfort of withdrawal. Withdrawal symptoms result when neither the drug nor the body's natural processes are at work to produce a sense of well-being. Many heroin-dependent individuals take enough of the drug to remain 'normal' and avoid withdrawal. Such individuals often hold down responsible jobs and are not suspected of being addicts, unless something disturbs their pattern of taking the drug.

Prevalence. There are thought to be around 15,000 opiate addicts in Britain. Although the number of registered heroin addicts is small compared with the number of alcohol-dependent individuals, there are a large number of users who do not register or are otherwise excluded from the figures.

Sedatives

The principal sedatives are the barbiturates (phenobarbitone, secobarbital and amobarbital). There are two types of barbiturates, a long-acting type for prolonged periods of sedation, and the short-acting type, which has an immediate effect, causing short-term sedation or sleep.

Prescriptive use of sedatives. As prescribed medically, barbiturates relax muscles and provide a sense of well-being. The barbiturates have been often prescribed for the elderly, but are very addictive and easily overdosed on. As a result of this, their use has been discouraged by the British Medical Association and other bodies. When used excessively, they cause loss of motor coordination, slurring of speech, and concentration and cognitive difficulties. As the effect of the drug continues, there is a loss of emotional control and periods of verbal hostility and aggressive behaviour.

Types of users. The problem of excessive use of barbiturates affects two quite different populations:

1 Young antisocial poly-drug users.

2 So-called respectable middle-aged and middle-class men and women, who originally take the drug on a doctor's prescription. Their gradually developed tolerance for small doses causes them to increase dosages to an abusive level, with the strong possibility of withdrawal effects. At that point, they have become addicted to the substance.

3 Doctors and medical workers who begin by taking advantage of the ready availability of the drug, only soon find that they cannot do without it.

Stimulants

Amphetamine and cocaine are the two stimulants in common use, although newer 'designer' drugs (synthetically manufactured to imitate the action of illegal substances) include those with stimulant properties. The drugs methylene-dioxymethamphetamine (MDMA) and methylenedioxyamphetamine (MDA) which trade under the street name of 'ecstasy', now very popular in British youth dance culture, are early synthetics which have both stimulant and hallucinogenic properties. They are notably different in the types of users they attract. The amphetamines were available initially as a non-prescription inhalant for clogged nasal passages. The stimulating properites of the easily synthesised drugs were soon realised and exploited by a variety of abusers. When this was realised in the 1960s, the prescription of the drug for weight reduction or its antidepressant effects was restricted and such prescriptions were more or less ended in the 1970s. However it is widely available on the black market and its use has increased dramatically in recent years.

Amphetamine users. Because of its stimulating effect – a user seems to be more alert, have more energy, and feel stronger – its use by soldiers in World War II was encouraged by both sides. For the same reasons, it now appeals to long-distance truck drivers and night-shift workers. Among the 18–25 age group, it is frequently taken as a 'shot in the arm' by college students cramming for exams and by athletes, including professionals. With amphetamine not being available on prescription, the black market has started to supply individuals wishing to lose weight rapidly. This is a physically dangerous practice if unsupervised, given its potential to hasten anorexia. Some youth groups, such as the British 'mods' of the 1960s, take larger doses going beyond the stimulating effects to a stage where the effects can be physically felt and thinking is disrupted or 'blocked'. Excessive use of amphetamines will have serious deleterious effects on one's health, including the possibility of death.

Amphetamines have been obtained in three different prescription formulations: Benzedrine, Dexedrine, and the more potent and therefore more dangerous Methedrine. They all cause both physical and psychological changes.

Effects of amphetamines. The drug is addictive whether taken orally or intravenously. Exceeding the small dosages usually prescribed medically causes increased heart rate, a jump in blood pressure (sometimes to levels high enough to cause death), impaired intestinal functioning, and constriction of the blood vessels on the surface of the body and in bodily membranes. Heavy doses cause such psychological states as nervousness, agitation, heart palpitations, dizziness and sleeplessness. Beyond those changes, the individual under the influence of the substance may become suicidal or hostile and dangerously assaultive. Such prolonged or heavy use often brings about 'amphetamine psychosis' where an individual demonstrates the delusions and hallucinations of paranoid psychosis. The action of the drug in increasing dopamine turnover means this psychotic state can be mistaken for acute schizophrenia.

Cocaine.   Like opium and marijuana (to be described later), cocaine is a plant product; it is extracted from the leaves of the cocoa plant, which is grown extensively in some South American countries.

Prevalence.   Earlier in his career, Freud advocated the use of cocaine which was freely available at the time and was an essential element in the original ingredients of the famous soft drink until 1906. Once its addictive and long-term effects were established, its use was restricted and then made illegal. It has since become a highly fashionable illicit substance, especially among middle and upper-income groups, partly due to its higher cost (hence an 'elite' status). Its use has increased rapidly in the last 20 years, as has its availability, with estimates of the number of users in Britain today rising towards half a million. Cocaine use is more common in the United States where over 20 million Americans admit to having used it.

Effects of cocaine.   The drug acts rapidly on the cortex of the brain, sharpening sensory awareness and suffusing the individual in a haze of euphoria. It accentuates sexual desire, feelings of well-being, and tirelessness. Taking an overdose results in psychotic-like hallucinations and paranoid thinking and other such physical changes as nausea, chills, and sleeplessness. Inveterate cocaine users soon isolate themselves from former friends by their irritability and paranoid thinking. Heavy users frequently find themselves in a Casualty Department with a heart attack resulting from a myocardial infarct (see chapter 16).

Varieties of cocaine use.   Because of the tolerance effect following regular use, cocaine addicts seek to intensify its effect. One way of doing so is to heat the cocaine with the highly inflammatory ether (a highly dangerous practice), which purifies the cocaine as it produces what is known as a 'free base', sometimes labelled 'white tornado' or 'snow'. The practice is a frequent one among long-time users of the drug.

A recent and rapidly growing addition to the various ways of using cocaine, introduced initially around 1985, is crack. Crack is a free-base form of cocaine, readily available in small doses at relatively low cost. That diabolically clever marketing scheme has made it an increasingly used form of drug addiction. Professional groups concerned with drug abuse consider crack to be the most dangerously and addictive drug now in use.

Hallucinogens

Here we discuss the two most widely used hallucinogens: LSD (lysergic acid diethylamide) and marijuana. There are others: mescaline, psilocybin, and PCP (or angel dust). Since the effects of LSD are similar (but not identical) to psilocybin and mescaline, it is only necessary to describe one of these, LSD. Phencyclidine (PCP) is very different in its effects. PCP produces a dose dependent psychotic-like state with the individual being highly sensitive to sensory stimulation. In stark contrast with LSD, PCP users are uncommunicative and frequently become extremely violent, requiring several people to restrain them, and the medical effects can result in death.

Psychedelic drugs. LSD and related drugs are frequently labelled 'psychedelic' drugs. They were first studied during the 1950s because they were believed to produce psychotic reactions, and it was thought that their study might shed light on certain psychotic disorders. The importance of LSD and its attractiveness to a small, highly specialised fraction of the drug-using population grew out of a research decision made by Timothy Leary and Richard Alpert at Harvard in the USA (1957). They became interested in the possibility that one of the hallucinogens might have a positive effect on antisocial behaviour. Their early, very tentative studies on a population of prisoners suggested that an experience with psilocybin reduced the number of post-prison arrests in the same sample population.

Seemingly attracted by what they thought were the mind-expanding effects of the drug, Leary and Alpert began to use it themselves and encouraged a small group of others to do so. The activity soon attracted the interest of law enforcement authorities. The two left Harvard and set up their own organisation to study the so-called mind-expanding properties of LSD and its associated hallucinogens. Following the publicity given to Leary and the promise of mind expansion, a number of well-known artists, writers and composers took to using the hallucinogenic substances, and an LSD movement developed.

It became clear that the artistic role of LSD was to inspire rather than create. Many artists and musicians tried desperately to re-create the exquisite (and sometimes frightening) sounds and visions they experienced under the drug. Although they almost always failed in this, some of their attempts have been successfully received by a public not party to the original experience. The use of LSD tends to be self-regulating as it cannot be taken very regularly, possibly due to its reliance on endogenous processes which cease to act after a few days. Regular users (once a week or fortnight) comprise less than one per cent of the population but this number has been increasing in Britain during the last ten years.

Effects of the psychedelic drugs. The effects of LSD can be produced by minute dosages; larger dosages are required for mescaline and psilocybin. The amount of LSD needed being so small, the usual form of ingestion has taken a variety of shapes. Currently the liquid is absorbed into multi-coloured 'blotters', or scraps of blotting paper. One carefully manufactured form, common in the 1970s, was the 'microdot' tablet, which was almost impossible to detect during a police search due to its size. The drug does not take immediate effect and it can be over an hour before the effects begin, which can then last for over eight hours (longer for mescaline and shorter for psilocybin).

As with alcohol, the psychological effects that follow use of the psychedelic drugs depend to a considerable extent upon what the user expects to happen. There is a very real danger of a 'bad trip'. Panic and profuse anxiety occur; for a small group of users, the result can be a psychotic episode. LSD tends to precipitate pre-existing psychological disorders and problems, which probably accounts for such reactions, and individuals with such conditions, although attracted to such drugs, should really avoid them.

A typical trip, about eight hours long, brings on kaleidoscopic sensory experiences, shifting emotional experiences, and feelings of detachment and depersonalisation. There is little or none of the euphoria of other drugs. The individual experiences heightened sensory awareness in which distortions of the senses may occur. In their first experience, they may not be prepared for the changes that occur and if their expectation is that of being drunk, they usually become very apprehensive at the profound increase (rather than decrease with alcohol) in awareness that takes place, becoming highly suggestible. Having largely the opposite effect to alcohol, the appeal is restricted to those who can cope with the subjective effects of LSD. The outward appearance and manner of the individual is quite normal (pupils are overly dilated and they seem 'well behaved' or restrained in behaviour) and sometimes it is difficult to equate this with the profound changes in subjective experience.

Flashbacks. One unusual and unpleasant effect of the psychedelic drugs is the occasional occurrence of 'flashbacks'. Soon after a trip, without further use of the substance, there is a short-term but dramatic recurrence of the original psychedelic experience. Flashbacks may occur repeatedly for one or two months after use of the substance. Fifteen to 30 per cent of psychedelic users have flashback experiences. They are not accompanied by physiological changes that might explain their occurrence. For most individuals who experience them, they are an upsetting, perhaps even frightening, event. Again, the drug may be interacting with a pre-existing psychological disturbance in the majority of these cases and expectation may also play a part.

The expectation factor as an influence on what will actually happen would suggest that the psychedelic user is extremely suggestible. If so and if flashbacks are expected, they may simply be triggered by ordinary changes in consciousness such as we all experience; but psychedelic users give them a more dramatic interpretation.

Marijuana or cannabis. This hallucinogen is smoked as a cigarette, usually referred to as a 'joint'. As with other hallucinogens, its effect is influenced by what individuals expect. The effects are again the opposite of those of alcohol, and as such, are not always recognised by first time users who may become dizzy or confused because they fail to recognise the more subtle effects and take too much. The user is euphoric and experiences a pleasant sense of being relaxed and drifting or floating. Marijuana stands apart from some other substances discussed here in that there has been a strong movement to legalise its use.

The issue of legalising marijuana. There are a number of issues in this debate. It is thought that legalisation would sever the link between marijuana use and that of other 'harder drugs'. In the past, dealers in marijuana tended to deal only in this, but the risks are higher (it is bulky and strongly scented) with equal, if not greater, legal pressure than for 'harder drugs' such as heroin or cocaine. The market for marijuana is steady, but without the addictive qualities of the opiates, it is far less profitable and with the greater risks less scrupulous dealers have moved to hard drugs and encouraged their customers to follow suit. Thus legalisation would remove the marijuana user from this pressure and contact. There is no evidence that marijuana users move to 'hard drugs' for any other reason.

The experience and effects of marijuana are thought to be more socially acceptable than those of, say, alcohol. Whereas alcohol is associated with violence, accidents and 'loutish' behaviour, marijuana tends to be associated with intellectual, artistic and nonagressive activity. This could be partly a result of the type of person attracted to the different substances and the cultural setting, but to some degree reflects the actual effects of the drugs on the individual.

It is the area of long-term physical and mental effects where the debate becomes obscured by seemingly contradictory evidence and suspiciousness over propaganda. There are individuals in commerce and politics with a vested interest in keeping marijuana illegal, which inevitably leads to research funds being available for this end. However, the basic argument for the legalisation of marijuana is that the current legal recreational drug, alcohol, is many times more physically harmful and dangerous in its use than marijuana. This basic fact is true. The fatal dose of marijuana represents around ten years supply of the drug taken at once, whereas that for alcohol is as little as a bottle of spirits, and the damage to the body and society are in similar proportions. This is confounded by research based on marijuana always being smoked and taken in excessive quantities. High levels of marijuana use have been associated with memory impairment, lowering of testosterone levels and other effects for which there are conflicting results. These effects are almost always reversible and far less evident in moderate use. When smoked, the user is exposed to all the health risks of smoking (which are considerable), with the additional risks from the extra carcinogens in the marijuana smoke, especially if smoked without a filter. Thus it is only a safe alternative if eaten or perhaps dissolved in coffee.

Thus legalisation or decriminalisation of marijuana, perhaps encouraging a non-smoking form, would seem reasonable, especially if it led to a reduction in alcohol consumption. However, the authorities concerned may have differing priorities in making such a decision.

Tobacco and nicotine

Although not commonly thought of as a drug of addiction, but more of a habitual behaviour, tobacco is the most addictive and medically dangerous substance of abuse. It results in more deaths and illness than its nearest rival, alcohol. The space given to the problem here does not do justice to the damage caused by smoking, nor does it represent the prevalence of the problem which does not need statistics to convey its extent as smoking is self-evidently very common.

The treatment of nicotine addiction has taken many forms, including 'nicotine patches' which supply the nicotine whilst the smoking habit is broken, bearing some resemblance to methadone treatment in heroin addition. A combination of public information and education, and the establishment of no-smoking areas in public have done much to reduce smoking. However, it is on the increase amongst women and the young.

Treatment for drug abuse and dependence

There are two principal therapies for drug addiction. One is substitution therapy, in which the addict is given a harmless drug capable of relieving withdrawal symptoms. This can be assisted by reducing the addict's responses to the expectation of the drug. The second mode of treatment is the residential treatment centre.

Substitution therapy

An essential first step in treating addicts is detoxification; that is, completely withdrawing the addict from drug use. The major challenge here is limiting the pain of withdrawal symptoms. The most successful substitution programme is the use of methadone for heroin addiction.

Methadone treatment. Methadone is a synthetic narcotic developed by Dole and Nyswander in 1966 at Rockefeller University. It is related to heroin and is addictive, but does not have heroin's negative psychological effects.

Advantages of using methadone. Most heroin users who stay in the methadone programme find that while taking methadone, they can do without heroin and yet not experience the withdrawal effects of giving it up. Since reducing the withdrawal effects is the strong second-stage reason for taking a drug, that effect of methadone has significant value.

There are secondary advantages to the methadone programme. Its pharmacological effect, that is, its helpful effect in preventing withdrawal symptoms, lasts for more than 24 hours, in contrast to a four-hour effect produced by heroin. The advantage of that is to give the former heroin user a longer period of time when he or she has no reason to visit old haunts in pursuit of heroin. During that 24-hour period during which, in the past, the individual sought contacts from whom to obtain heroin, the repeated pairings of environmental cues, followed by the reinforcement of taking heroin, are eliminated. Thus, in conditioning terms, their motivational value for triggering a heroin trip should be extinguished, or at least reduced significantly. A useful behavioural approach has been based on this principle termed response extinction. The user prepares for their usual injection or smoking of the drug in a slow, methodical manner whilst their body and mind go through the changes resulting from anticipation. At the point of putting the drug into the body the process halts and the user relaxes. Repetition of this process eventually extinguishes the anticipatory response making physical and psychological withdrawal easier.

Another advantage of methadone is that with high doses of methadone, over a period of time, intravenous heroin no longer produces the sought-after high. Thus, should the individual have a relapse, the heroin would not provide a satisfactory experience.

Disadvantages of methadone. Methadone substitution does have some serious limitations. For one thing, it keeps the individual drug-dependent and requires that he or she visit a hospital or clinic daily to be given the methadone, which is usually taken orally and always supervised by a staff member. And it does have some negative physical effects, such as insomnia, constipation, and diminished sexual performance.

The negative physical effects and probably the absence of a high following methadone cause a high drop-out rate in most methadone programmes.

Many methadone programmes are accompanied by psychotherapy. Contrary to what one might expect, methadone users not in psychotherapy seem to do as well, socially and psychologically, as do those users who received psychotherapy (Rounsaville 1986). There are no substitution programmes for drugs other than heroin, although benzodiazepines have in the past been substituted for alcohol.

Residential treatment centres: therapeutic communities
Drug-abusers are sometimes treated individually on a private basis by psychiatrists, psychologists and social workers. Treatment offered is similar to what would be offered to individuals with any other psychiatric disorder. Little is known about how extensive or effective such treatment is.

A well-publicised approach to the treatment of drug addiction is that of the therapeutic communities. These are spoken of highly by the users themselves and their use of peer support resembles that of the treatment of alcoholism in a residential setting. Narcotics Anonymous also provides peer support for those wishing to give up the drug. Such programmes have as their goal the restructuring of the individual's life perspective so that drugs of any sort no longer have a place in his or her life. The use of methadone is usually discouraged.

Characteristics of successful residential treatment
Davison and Neale (1990) describe five features of such therapeutic communities that seem to promote success. Therapeutic programmes are successful when:

1 They surround individuals with a drug-free environment in which former drug addicts are supported psychologically as they seek to establish a drug-free existence.

2 Former addicts who are successfully living free of drugs serve as models and

describe their past problems and how they solved them. This is one of the successful techniques also used by Alcoholics Anonymous.

3 Confrontational encounters occur in which former drug users are challenged to accept responsibility for their problems and are pressed to take charge of their lives.

4 Each resident is respected as a fully independent and worthwhile human being and is not stigmatised or criticised for past failures.

5 The residential nature of the treatment centre separates the individual from former friends and old haunts and, in that way, breaks up the person's old drug-dominated social network.

Effectiveness of therapeutic centres

Residential therapeutic centres pride themselves on the success of their former patients. Nevertheless, it must be recognised that they are relating to a very select segment of the drug-user population. All participants volunteer to join the community, which means that they come in with high motivation. Even so, the drop-out rate is exceptionally high, an occurrence which leaves an even more select group who eventually rehabilitate successfully. One of the few research reports (Jaffe 1985) on therapeutic communities concludes that for those who spend a year or more in the centre, the experience helps 'a large number' of them.

SUMMARY

Drug abuse is a major concern throughout most countries in the world. The DSM-IV distinguishes between: substance dependence, which is diagnosed when the individual manifests three of nine symptoms, all of which clearly indicate that the individual's loss of control of substance use has seriously disrupted life; and substance abuse, a less severe pattern than dependence, which interferes with social or occupational functioning for at least a month.

Four causative elements operate in the development of substance-use disorder. They are ready availability of the substance and use of the substance by peers. When to these two conditions are added unhappy life circumstances or a life that is unexciting or boring, a substance disorder frequently develops.

The 'opponent-process' model describes the motivations for the development of a substance disorder. At first the relaxing or euphoric effect (in either case, a pleasant one) of the drug attracts the individual and continues to motivate substance use. In time, growing tolerance of the substance causes the individual to take larger doses. Guilt feelings or external pressures from family or friends cause the individual to withdraw from substance use. Withdrawal symptoms cause the individual to return to drug use. Initially, the individual seeks pleasure; later on, he or she seeks to avoid pain. These are antagonistic or opponent processes.

There are five generic types of psychoactive substances. They are alcohol, narcotics (derived from opium), sedatives (principally barbiturates), stimulants (principally cocaine and the amphetamines) and the hallucinogens, which include marijuana.

Around ten per cent of the male population are dependent on alcohol; this is over twice the figure for females, although the latter is growing more rapidly. The general use of alcohol is increasing also, involving over three quarters of the general population. Alcohol produces both physiological effects, principally affecting the liver and the brain, and psychological effects, mainly a dampening effect on the individual's inhibitions. Long-term use of alcohol causes malnutrition and severe psychiatric disorders, including Korsakoff's syndrome. Alcohol use by pregnant women is a principal cause of birth defects.

Alcoholism may be caused by genetic factors and personality traits such as low self-esteem, and seems to be related to such psychosocial factors as ethnicity, occupation, and social class level. Middle-income groups seem to be especially vulnerable.

Treatment is best undertaken in a residential centre. There are three stages of such treatment. They are a drying-out period, a confrontational period, during which the individual is helped to recognise the problem, and a prolonged period of psychotherapy, in which the goal is to restructure the individual's personality. Self-help groups, such as Alcoholics Anonymous, play a prominent and helpful part in treating alcoholism.

The principal depressants are opium, morphine and heroin. Although once falling, the use of narcotic depressants has increased in recent years. Particularly affected by the sedatives are members of the middle socioeconomic class, for whom a barbiturate is initially prescribed, and doctors and medical workers, to whom the drug is readily available.

The principal stimulants are amphetamines and cocaine. Users are principally those who, for whatever reason, seek to find new sources of energy. Heavy doses cause major and dangerous physiological changes and psychological tension. Overdoses can cause suicide or assaultive behaviour. Estimates of cocaine use are difficult but there may be as many as half a million users in Britain today, showing a large increase in the last 20 years.

Two well-known hallucinogens are LSD and marijuana. Other psychedelic drugs are mescaline and psilocybin. All of these have no potential for physical addiction. PCP is included here but has very different effects from the others, including violence, and is physically damaging. These drugs cause varied and unusual sensory experiences and feelings of detachment and depersonalisation.

Marijuana should be considered separately from the other hallucinogens. Its harmful effects are dramatically less evident than those of alcohol. It has some harmful effects when it is smoked with tobacco or taken very frequently. Arguments pro and con for legalisation of marijuana have been advanced for several years without resulting in legalisation of its use. Tobacco and its nicotine content are recognised in DSM-IV. It is the most medically harmful substance of abuse.

There are two principal therapies for drug use. They are substitution therapy, principally the use of methadone for heroin use, and residential treatment centres.

FURTHER READING

Critchlow, B. 1986. The Powers of John Barleycorn: Beliefs About the Effects of Alcohol on Social Behaviour. *American Psychologist*, 41: 746–751.

Davidson, R., Rollnick, S. & MacEwan, I. 1991. *Counselling Problem Drinkers*. London: Routledge.

DeLeon, G. & Schwartz, S. 1984. Therapeutic Communities: What are the Retention Rates? *American Journal of Drug Abuse*, 10: 267–284.

Drummond, D.C., Tiffany, S., Glautier, S. & Remington, F. 1995. *Addictive Behaviour: Cue Exposure Theory and Practice*. London: Wiley.

Edwards, G., Strang, J. & Jaffe, J. 1993. *Drugs Alcohol and Tobacco: Making the Science and Policy Connections*. Oxford University Press.

Jarvis, T., Tebbut, J. & Mattick, R. 1995. *Treatment Approaches for Alcohol and Drug Dependence: An Introductory Guide*. Wiley.

Lader, M., Edwards, G. & Drummond, D.C. 1992. *The Nature of Alcohol and Drug Related Problems*. Oxford University Press.

Orleans, C. T. & Slade, J. 1994. *Nicotine Addiction: Principles and Managment*. Oxford University Press.

Royal College of Psychiatrists. 1987. *Alcohol: Our Favourite Drug*. London: Tavistock.

Schlaadt, R. & Shannon, P. 1994. *Drugs* (4th ed). Prentice-Hall.

Shener, M. A., Kumor, K.M., Cone, E. J. & Jaffe, S. 1988. Suspiciousness Induced by Four-Hour Intravenous Infusions of Cocaine: Preliminary Findings. *Archives of General Psychiatry*, 45: 673–677.

Steel, C. M., Southwick, L. & Pagano, R. 1986. Drinking Your Troubles Away: The Role of Activity in Mediating Reduction of Psychological Stress. *Journal of Abnormal Psychology*, 95: 173–180.

Strang, J. & Gossop, M. 1994. *Heroin Addiction and Drug Policy: The British System*. Oxford University Press.

14 Sexual Disorders

The prevalence of sexual disorders is difficult to ascertain. All available information would indicate that collectively they are possibly one of the commonest of disorders, along with substance abuse. One of the difficulties in making such estimates is that people do not readily come forward to present these disorders. This is possibly as a result of embarrassment, shame or guilt over the type of problem they have, or simply that they do not recognise they have a problem and the complainant may then be their partner. Education on these issues has always been hampered by the nature of the subject, and ignorance has often prevented individuals with problems from recognising that they actually have a treatable disorder.

Society's understanding of normal sexual behaviour and deviations from it have been changing gradually, partially in response to two pioneering and courageous studies: one, the 'Kinsey Report' on frequency of various forms of sexual behaviour; the other, the Masters and Johnson studies of sexual disorders. Attitudes towards normal sexual behaviour have broadened, and different ways of expressing sexual needs are given more understanding. Today, individuals troubled by sexual problems are increasingly seeking treatment for those problems.

The DSM-IV categorises sexual disorders into three groupings: psychosexual dysfunctions, in which inhibitions prevent or reduce the individual's enjoyment of normal sex and prevent or reduce the usual physiological changes brought on by sexual arousal; the paraphilias, in which the individual associates sexual release with objects or situations not part of normal sexual arousal behaviour; and gender identity disorders in which the individual is unhappy with their designated sex typing and may strongly desire to change this. This differs from a state of homosexuality (no longer listed as a disorder) where there may be no strong desire to change sex.

After a brief description of normal sexual activity, this chapter describes the symptomatology of each subtype of the sexual disorders. Possible causes and therapies are described separately for each disorder. The chapter adds rape and incest to the disorders listed in DSM- IV, and will also explore some perspectives on homosexuality, which is no longer mentioned in DSM-IV.

Aspects of normal sexual activity

In its most rudimentary aspects, sexual activity can satisfy two important and related (but not congruent) human needs: the procreation of children and the experiencing of a unique, sensory, physical and emotional pleasure. As practised by almost all human beings, the primary motivation for sexual activity is the pleasure it provides; only occasionally in the sexual lifetime of the individual is procreation the primary purpose of sexual activity. Both functions are important, one because of the unique pleasure one receives and is able to give a partner, the other because it fulfils a much-desired goal of family life and, in a less personal but more instinctive sense, because it continues the life of the species and maintains membership in particular social groups.

Within cultures and between individuals a great deal of variation in sexual practice can occur, both of type and frequency. However, most cultures, whilst often remaining liberal in their tolerance of variation, will tend to impose a very similar norm on their population, that of penile/vaginal coitus for the purpose of procreation. Thus, the interests of the society as a whole are imposed on individuals who may, or may not, be willing or able to comply with them.

We know from the Kinsey Report of 1948 that substantial fractions of a normal population engage in sexual activities other than penile/vaginal intercourse, some of which lead to orgasm. The ICD and DSM diagnostic systems have not listed homosexuality as a disorder, although individuals who are distressed or unhappy with their orientation may seek therapy. This can be taken to indicate that a modern view of sexual disorders only considers activities (or the lack of them) causing distress to the individual concerned or others to be a treatable disorder.

Classification of sexual disorders

The ICD-10 diagnostic system lists seven sexual disorders: lack of sexual desire, lack of sexual enjoyment, failure of genital response, orgasmic dysfunction, premature ejaculation, vaginismus and dyspareunia, under the heading of physiological dysfunction associated with mental factors. However, this system also lists gender identity disorder under abnormalities of adult personality and behaviour, with the other personality disorders of ICD-10.

DSM-IV lists three principal categories of sexual disorder. The first of these is sexual dysfunction, ie. the inability to participate fully and enjoy sexual activity including coitus. The second is paraphilia where the DSM system lists eight variations in which sexual arousal is stimulated by inappropriate objects, situations or behaviour. The third is gender identity disorder. In this chapter, the issues involved in rape, incest and contemporary views of homosexuality have been added.

Sexual dysfunctions

Sexual dysfunctions can be grouped in different ways, for example, by gender. Below is a list of major dysfunctions in relation to one another (See Table 14.1).

TABLE 14.1

Sexual Phase	In Males	In Females
Desire phase	Sexual desire disorder	Sexual desire disorder
Arousal phase	Erectile dysfunction	Sexual arousal disorder
Orgasm phase	Premature ejaculation	Orgasm disorder
	Retarded ejaculation	
Other	Dyspareunia (Sexual pain disorder)	Dyspareunia
		Sexual phobia
	Sexual phobia	Vaginismus

Grouping sexual dysfunctions approximately into the phase of the sexual cycle of activity in which they occur can be a useful way of both ordering and describing them. Thus in the following description sexual phobia would occur at the desire phase.

Disorders of the desire phase

There are two levels of this disorder: hypoactive desire and aversion to sex.

Hypoactive desire

Here, the dysfunction is a lack of interest in sex. In its milder form, the diagnostic term 'hypoactive desire' is used. Since desire for sexual intercourse is so variable a characteristic, problems sometimes develop between spouses who differ in their desire for sex. It would not be accurate to dismiss a mate as having a sexual disorder simply because he or she desired sex three times a week and not seven.

The sexual disorder hypoactive desire refers to a complete or almost complete lack of interest in sex, resulting, for example, in routine or uninvolved participation in sexual intercourse simply because it is a marital duty. Here, too, a too-quick diagnosis may be out of order, since the fault might lie in the technique of the individual's sexual partner.

Aversion to sex

Hypoactive sex desire must be differentiated from aversion to sex, in which sexual approaches or imposed sexual activity cause repulsion and apprehension. Such aversion to sex or sexual phobia can be associated with sexual pain disorder (or dyspareunia), although the possibility of early aversive learning due to abuse as a child or rape should be considered as a factor.

Disorders of the arousal phase

Sexual desire normally leads to specific physiological changes preparing the individual for sexual intercourse. In the male, the penis fills with blood and becomes enlarged and erect. In the female, an increased flow of blood causes the woman's genitals to swell; in addition, the walls of the vagina secrete a lubricating fluid. If these physiological responses fail to occur or are not adequate for sexual activity to proceed, erectile dysfunction in males and sexual arousal disorder in females are the usual presenting complaints.

Disorders of the orgasm phase

The peak of sexual activity towards which normal sexual behavior leads is orgasm. At this point, rhythmic contractions of the muscles in the genital region occur, accompanied by heightened sexual excitement. In males, an ejaculatory problem, usually premature ejaculation (although retarded ejaculation, the inability of the male to reach orgasm and ejaculate, can also occur) can cause great distress to both partners. With regard to premature ejaculation, this is considered a problem if it occurs on or before penetration and beyond this it is a matter for the couple to decide. Despite wild claims on the subject, most studies find the average time between penetration and ejaculation to be about two minutes. Women commonly suffer from difficulty with, or complete absence of, orgasm. Around 15 per cent of women never achieve an orgasm.

Sexual pain disorders

There are two disorders which can result in pain for one or other partner, the main sexual pain disorder being dyspareunia. It is predominantly a female complaint, although it occasionally occurs in men. The second, vaginismus, is exclusively a female disorder. The symptoms are involuntary spasmodic muscle contractions at the entrance to the vagina when an attempt is made to insert the penis into it. Ordinarily, the result is an inability to proceed with intercourse. If the attempt is made to persist with intercourse, a painful sexual experience results.

Special factors in understanding sexual dysfunction

The diagnosis of sexual dysfunction is made only when the disability persists. Such dysfunctions can occur occasionally in all sexual relationships. Fatigue, worry, sickness or alcohol or drugs may interfere in any phase of the sexual relationship. Inexperience in sexual relations may cause anxieties and concern about performing well, with a resulting failure in performance or desire. An embarrassing failure in sex may cause a lingering effect on subsequent sexual attempts.

Distinctions are made in the diagnosis of sexual dysfunction. One is to establish whether the disorder has always existed (primary dysfunction) or has only recently been acquired (secondary dysfunction), which may suggest differing aetiologies. Another distinction is whether the individual is dysfunctional in only some situations (partial) or in all situations (complete). Examples of the latter are these: a man may successfully masturbate to ejaculation but not be able to ejaculate in sexual intercourse; or one partner in a marriage may experience orgasm only in an extramarital affair.

Sexual dysfunction is often diagnosed in both members of a marriage; particularly frequent in marriages are premature ejaculation by the husband and orgasmic dysfunction in the wife. Often such conditions as these can clearly exacerbate one another and both can be made worse by the two individuals being too busy to spend sufficient time physically relating to improve the problem.

Causative factors in sexual dysfunction

Sexual desire and sexual functioning may be influenced by both psychosocial and physical factors.

Psychosocial influences on sexual dysfunction

A variety of psychosocial influences can cause sexual dysfunction: faulty learning, negative emotional feelings related to sex, faulty interpersonal relationships between partners, early-life sexually traumatic experiences and egotistically-oriented attitudes toward sexual relations by one of the partners.

Faulty learning. Behavioural theorists, in particular (but most other clinicians join them), focus on the importance of early classical conditioning, in which sexual events are associated with negative emotional experiences of shame, fearfulness, feelings of inadequacy or expectations of failure. Those feelings cause the individual to approach sex tentatively, uncertain about performance. Masters and Johnson state that these feelings cause the individual to adopt a 'spectator role' in sexual relations. The individual, on guard, instead of relaxing and enjoying the sexual experience, is more concerned about whether or not performance is adequate. That very concern interferes with the adequacy and enjoyment of the performance.

Negative emotions producing that effect may have been picked up from parents, from other misguided elders, or from punishments administered following early childhood sexual play. Concern about sexual performance may also result from lack of knowledge or experience. Here, especially, the individual is likely to assume the spectator role. An early failure because of that behaviour may increase the concern and make it impossible later to enjoy sex fully. One of the most powerful factors sustaining a sexual dysfunction is the self-fulfilling prophesy of the expectation of failure leading to failure itself.

Relationship problems. Absence of love, closeness, respect, of feelings of admiration for the physical being of the other person in a marital or other relationship, can cause any one of the sexual dysfunctions, at least in that relationship. Dysfunction can develop in a relationship that has previously been satisfying when strong disagreement about other issues becomes heated. Couples may fight over financial matters, ways of raising children, jealousy or the existence of an extramarital affair on the part of one of the couple. The result can be a sexual dysfunction in one or both partners. To this end, the sexual relationship can be seen as a barometer for the marital relationship.

The negative feelings toward the other person in other areas of life soon overshadow the desirability of sex and impair sexual performance. Once such failures occur, their very existence threatens future sexual relationships, and the dysfunctional behaviour sets in and becomes a long-term pattern.

Psychodynamic aspects. Consideration has been given to factors in the child's psychosexual development as seen from a psychodynamic point of view by such researchers as Kaplan (1974). These views have not been of much practical value in helping dysfunctional individuals. However, Kaplan also considered other 'immediate' causes (as opposed to 'remote' psychodynamic ones) such as: performance anxiety, overconcern with pleasing the partner, poor technique, lack of communication about sex and marital conflict. These were more useful in guiding the therapy of her clients.

Physical causes of sexual dysfunction

There are a large number of physical or biological causes of sexual dysfunction and these must always be eliminated *before* other causes are considered. The sexual dysfunction may be the first sign of an underlying organic disorder, which if ignored could endanger more than the client's sex life. Other physical causes may be more transitory in their effect, such as substance abuse.

Substance use. Alcohol use, especially if heavy, has long been known to impair sexual activity and, in the case of prolonged use, sexual dysfunction can take some time to re-establish itself following abstinence. There are a number of prescribed medications which also adversely affect both performance and sexual desire, for example propranolol. Sometimes the treatment for a disorder can adversely affect performance and this can be further exacerbated by fears associated with the disorder. For example, the sexually inhibiting effect of the treatment for hypertension following a heart attack can be amplified by the fear that sexual exertion could put the individual at risk of a further attack. Other drugs that suppress levels of testosterone, such as barbiturates and narcotics, usually lead to a lack of sexual desire.

Hormonal influences. Abnormal hormonal states in both males and females may both create sexual dysfunctions and create a vulnerability to such dysfunction in combination with other factors. Most male problems have been associated with reduced levels of testosterone, for example a study by Schiavi and colleagues in 1988 found this led to lowered sexual desire. In females, both testosterone and oestrogen are thought to be involved, although testosterone would seem to have the more causal role. The relationship between lowered oestrogen levels and lowered sexual desire at the menopause is unclear, as other factors may be acting at this point in addition to simple levels of hormones.

Physical and psychological disorders. The comorbidity of sexual and psychological disorders has long been recorded. One example of this would be depression, where lowered sexual desire is just one symptom of this disorder.

There are a number of diseases, injuries and physical abnormalities that can lead to sexual dysfunction. Clearly, physical damage to sexual organs can have a direct effect on either sex, with a fear of further injury being an added complication. In some males, diabetes mellitus reduces erectile responses due to damage following chronic high blood glucose levels. Again, this condition is exacerbated by the adverse psychological consequences of the diabetes. Some disorders can have effects on sexual functioning which are indirect and sometimes difficult to identify. This is often where there is hidden damage to the vascular system or nervous system. One example here would be the consequences of cerebrovascular accidents (strokes), which could directly affect sexual performance and, depending upon location, desire and response.

Treatment of sexual dysfunction

Masters and Johnson have been leaders in developing treatment techniques reported to show a high degree of success, at the 80 to 90 per cent level in some reports. Also significant about sex therapy is the fact that so many more of those who suffer from the disorder are now seeking treatment. Due to the number of possible causal routes to sexual dysfunction, virtually every possible treatment approach has been found useful for these disorders. Researchers are still finding new methods, sometimes adapted from those of other disorders, that can usefully be added to this large battery of therapies.

The Masters and Johnson programme

Following a comprehensive study of sexual dysfunctions, Masters and Johnson developed their programme of direct sex therapy. It differs in three principal ways from earlier efforts at treating the problem. In the first place, Masters and Johnson avoided the somewhat unproductive approach of psychoanalytically-oriented therapists and others who concentrated on exploring hidden background factors. Approaches which assume a 'deeper underlying cause' for sexual dysfunctions have not only proved less useful, but have on occasion been very destructive in uncovering traumatic situations which had until then been coped with well, even if suppressed. In the worst scenario, actual incidents of the recently reported 'false memory syndrome' would seem to be examples of creating a serious problem where none had previously existed.

Masters and Johnson offered a simpler explanation: the individual has, for example, inhibitions of sexual arousal, which should be treated by eliminating the reasons for the inhibitions.

Second, Masters and Johnson treated couples, not individuals, on the premise that sex is a co-operative and interactive process. They felt there existed the possibility that either individual could enable sexual fulfilment or block it.

Third, they believe that couples should be encouraged to practise sex in ways that remove anxiety and apprehension. In this, Masters and Johnson used variations of systematic desensitisation which is firmly based in classical conditioning, as described in an earlier chapter. Graded exercises were recommended to lead the couple from simple touching and caressing, with no expectation of intercourse or orgasm, eventually to the culmination of a mutually satisfying sexual experience. The pace of advancement in the exercises is set by the couple's progress in finding enjoyment in what they are doing. Enjoyment at an early level of sexual enjoyment leads to taking each next step. Anxiety is kept to a minimum because actual intercourse is not expected, therefore the 'fear of failure' is avoided. Eventually (it is hoped), the couple will break the rule of not having actual coitus, partly as a consequence of the attraction of something which is 'forbidden'. In treating premature ejaculation, for example, the woman is encouraged to stimulate the penis but to stop just before the moment of ejaculation. The female is taught the 'squeeze technique' (firmly gripping the base of the penis) of preventing ejaculation at this point to assist this process. In this way, through desensitisation to sexual stimulation, the male will learn to delay ejaculation to accommodate the pace of his partner.

A major postulate of the Masters and Johnson therapeutic approach is that anxiety blocks sexual excitement and performance by interfering with the preliminary physiological changes that normally precede sexual enjoyment. These are, in the female, vaginal enlargement and lubrication and, in the male, penile erection. Without those changes, coitus is neither possible nor enjoyable. Clients are encouraged to avoid being spectators of their own sexual activity and to focus on the sensual pleasures of the graded sexual exercises in which they are engaged. In the spectator role there is a tendency to focus primarily on the dysfunction in a very mechanical way, ignoring the more pleasurable sensations. To illustrate the futility of spectatoring, it is worth considering that it is impossible to produce an erection by willpower, an erection is a consequence of pleasurable sensation.

Sensate focus in treatment

Clients are taught that there are three stages in what therapists call 'sensate focus': giving pleasure, achieved principally through stroking and caressing the body; tender, genital stimulation; and finally, nondemanding intercourse, that is, intercourse that is enjoyed with no other demands from one's partner.

Taking each treatment exercise one step at a time desensitises the individual and gradually lifts the oppressive anxiety, making pleasure in coitus possible.

The technique was reported to be highly successful by Masters and Johnson and is still in use today in a more or less unchanged form. Subsequently, success rates have been found to vary and some of the original assumptions challenged but the sound behavioural basis of their techniques has endured.

The paraphilias

In earlier editions of the DSM-IV the label 'sexual deviations' was used to describe what are now called the paraphilias. The authors of the manual now prefer to use the Greek roots, *para,* meaning beyond or to the side of, and *philia,* meaning preferred, as more descriptive of the disorder and less pejorative. The DSM-IV describes the paraphilias as sexual disorders in which inappropriate unusual or bizarre objects or acts are required for sexual excitement. It sorts the paraphilias into three types of behaviour:

1 Those in which there exists a preference for nonhuman objects for sexual arousal; for example, shoes.
2 Repetitive sexual activity with human beings involving real or simulated suffering and humiliation.
3 Repetitive sexual activity with non-consenting partners. (See chapter 20 for a listing.) This section describes symptomatology, cause and treatment of all the paraphilias.

Types of paraphilias

The paraphilias include a group of psychological disorders that range widely in their impact on other people. The spectrum extends from those that affect only the suffering individual, or that individual and his or her partner, to those that threaten the well-being of other unrelated individuals. In all, DSM-IV recognises eight paraphilias, which can be grouped into three broad categories, as described below.

Sexual arousal and preferences for non-human objects

There are two: fetishism and transvestism.

Fetishism. A fetish exists when a person is aroused by a non-living object. Fetishes may be manifest in one of two ways, one more seriously disordered than the other. One form of fetish is associating coitus with some object, most frequently women's panties or other undergarments. Here the individual, usually a male, seeks to intensify sexual urges by preceding coitus by talking about or holding and fondling the object, for example, a pair of silk panties. It is relatively harmless if the action is taken playfully and is acceptable to his partner. If, on the other hand, the man persists even when the sexual partner objects to or resents the use of the object as a substitute for herself, the fetish must be considered a disorder and harmful, at least in its effect on the individual's partner.

Focusing on the parts of the female body (hair, toes or ears, for example), except as part of the pleasurable foreplay, can become fetishistic in its hold on the individual.

A more extreme form of fetishism is one in which an inanimate object completely substitutes for a human partner. The most common articles used in such fetishes are female underwear, boots and shoes, and such textured objects as rubber, silk or velvet. Rubber is such a common fetish that in Britain there is a 'Mackintosh society' with a large membership. Here, ejaculation is achieved when the individual is alone, fondling the cherished article. Fetishism can cause trouble with the law when it leads to shoplifting special articles, which it occasionally does. Such activity – that is, the shoplifting – seems to cause sexual excitement in the individual. Similarly, articles, especially clothing, can be stolen from individuals, again involving the law. One individual was found to have thousands of pairs of children's shoes and whilst no harm had been intended to the children concerned, this may not have been entirely clear to the officers of the law at the time.

Fetishes can be quite bizarre by normal standards. For example, King (1990) reported a man who was sexually aroused by and attracted to sneezing and had broken off a relationship through jealousy over the perceived attractiveness of his partner's sneeze.

Transvestism. This paraphilia exists when sexual excitement is achieved by cross-dressing, for example, a male dressing as a female. Two quite different purposes seem to be served in different individuals by transvestism. In one, the individual seeks to intensify sexual excitement in coitus with a partner by partially dressing as a woman. In the other form of transvestism, in which the male, for example, moves about in the full regalia of a woman, the disorder suggests some type of gender identity problem but not necessarily homosexuality. Transvestites usually report less frequent homosexual urges than do average American males. For many transvestites, the main goal of their activity is to be mistaken in public for a member of the opposite sex, usually without any urge to change their actual sexual identity.

The transvestite describes his problem as one in which he is both a 'he' person and a 'she' person, with the she person gaining expression only through cross-dressing. Transvestism is ordinarily kept secret from others, so there is little known about its prevalence. Estimates suggest that it occurs in one per cent of the male population. It is extremely rare among females.

Causal factors in fetishes. Much has yet to be learned about the causes of fetishism and transvestism. Aetiological factors in fetishism probably operate at two levels. Primarily existing is a set of early life experiences leading to maladjustment, lowered self-esteem and feelings of inadequacy, especially in sexual roles. A fetishistic direction is usually given to expressions of that psychic disturbance by some triggering experience. That is often a conditioning event in which orgasm has been stimulated, sometimes accidentally, by strong emotional reactions to some inanimate object. More often, the fetish is traceable to the use of some object, such as female underwear, to increase sexual intensity in early masturbatory activities. Since much masturbation is performed with some stimulating object – a sex picture, a garment, perhaps a perfume bottle – and relatively few males seem to develop a fetish from that activity, the suggestion is present that some underlying psychopathology might exist in the background of individuals who develop such fetishes.

Causal factors in transvestism. Causative factors in transvestism are quite different from those described above for fetishes. Extensive studies indicate that transvestites are frequently married men who have children. Psychological testing of transvestites indicates that they show no more evidence of psychiatric disorder than would be found in the general population. An additional problem for such married individuals is obviously the friction within the marriage directly resulting from the transvestite's activities.

Transvestites do frequently have an early history of being dressed up like a girl in early boyhood by unwise mothers, and perhaps by emotionally over-involved female relatives. Such happenings suggest either the absence of a father with whom the boy can identify or, if a father is present, that he must be either very weak or not very interested in his son's upbringing. Childhood cross-dressing that meets the approval of a mother or other well-regarded relative brings operant conditioning into the picture, that is, rewarding and thereby reinforcing the wearing of female dress. Given certain patterns of reinforcement, such behaviour would be difficult to overcome.

Sexual arousal and preferences for situations causing suffering

There are two such disorders: sadism and masochism. They are complementary in nature: what the sadist needs to inflict, the masochist needs to receive. They are best discussed together.

Sadism and masochism: symptomatology. Although sexual activity fundamentally is, or should be, a loving and tender activity, there appears to be an element of aggressiveness in much sexual activity among normal individuals. Some who are neither sadist nor masochist have sexual fantasies about suffering or humiliation in sex. Kinsey found that about 20 per cent of his male sample and 12 per cent of his female sample reported sexual arousal on hearing stories about rape, bondage, chains, whips and imposed hardships.

Two points need to be raised here: first, Kinsey's sample was a group of individuals who volunteered to be interviewed about their sex lives. It may be assumed that their attitude toward sex would be freer than those individuals who would not volunteer; and second, of more significance is the apparent absence of any need, prior to sexual arousal, for such fantasies. The sadist or masochist finds essential to his or her sexual arousal either inflicting suffering or receiving pain or humiliation.

The terms *sadist* and *masochist* apply correctly only to suffering associated with sexual arousal. The terms are often used much more loosely to describe socially punitive individuals or long-suffering martyrs. The behaviour of neither type of individual comes at all close to that of the disorders. The terms, as psychological disorders, refer to the repeated and intentional infliction on another person of suffering (sometimes a non-consenting person) in association with sexual arousal; or, for masochism, it requires that an individual ask for the infliction of pain or humiliation in order to be aroused sexually.

The terms are derived from the reported sexual exploits of the Marquis de Sade (1740–1814) and the writing of Leopold von Sacher-Masoch (c.1831), whose male characters sought out women who would beat them.

Sadists may seek relationships promiscuously with obliging women who have masochistic needs; masochists often relate to prostitutes who encourage or accept a masochistic clientele. But stable coupling of sadists and masochists also takes place in heterosexual and homosexual life. In certain areas of this country, where such demand exists, shops provide suitable equipment, and there are publications that run classified ads that openly suggest invitations for sadomasochistic activities.

Among sadists, there exists the possibility that, over time, the individual will need to inflict increasingly more pain and suffering, occasionally the final result of which is torture, rape and murder. Masochists may also need to increase their suffering, with the possibility that their relationship will lead to their own injury or murder. The course of the disorder is chronic and may continue to exist throughout the sexual lifetime of the individual, either promiscuously or in a stable relationship. Although treatment for these conditions is possible, studies have estimated that only about 15 per cent of sado-masochists seek therapy.

In recent years, there have been a number of reports in the press of individuals who have died during auto-erotic activities, which involve both masochistic and fetishistic elements often focusing on self-strangulation (usually hanging) or suffocation. This is a particularly dangerous activity as often excitement is contingent upon the threat of death and as the activity is a solitary one, there is no-one to intervene should things go too far.

Causative factors in sadomasochism. Sadism and masochism will be considered separately here.

Sadism. The causes of sadism are similar in pattern to the causes of fetishes. Strong emotions of any sort can trigger involuntary feelings of sexual arousal. When there is early association of such emotional feelings in response to someone inflicting pain or even torturing an animal, and when the experience is a vivid, even a haunting one, the result may be a relatively stable linking of inflicting pain with sexual arousal.

Sadism may also be caused in a prudish, narrowly restricted personality with negative attitudes toward sex, perhaps developed on a religious basis. Here the sadism may be seen as a warped, perhaps even bizarre, attempt to punish the woman who is permitting or even enjoying sex. One can speculate that the occasional individual who makes the headlines for murdering a number of prostitutes is manifesting that kind of motivation.

Masochism. Masochism would seem to be triggered by an early life experience of extreme pain (with strong emotion) which, in some, perhaps accidental way, is associated with a satisfying sexual event. The literature, for example, reports the history of a masochistic individual, as follows: a boy having a bone painfully set without an anaesthetic becomes aware of a nurse in attendance caressing him and holding him close to her breast in a consoling way. For the boy, the experience produced a sexual reaction immediately following severe pain. The case report suggests that the experience also later provoked a sadistic response. In such cases as this where apparently single trial learning has taken place, ie. the initial experience was a single event, there may be other pathological factors perpetuating the growth of the sadomasochistic activity.

Sexual arousal and preference for non-consenting partners

This grouping of paraphilias includes exhibitionism, frotteurism, voyeurism and paedophilia. All four are considered crimes in most countries. However, frotteurism is not thought of as a crime under that name and prosecutions would probably be brought as a form of indecent assault.

These are usually thought of as male activities, although females are occasionally prosecuted for such activities.

Exhibitionism. Indecent exposure is the most common sexual offence leading to arrest. It accounts for one-third of all sexual crimes. Oddly and inexplicably, it appears mainly in Western society and is totally absent in such countries as Japan, Burma and India. Generally due to the ease of capture and identification, exhibitionists have more frequent involvement with the law than any other sexual activity. In most countries, exhibitionism is seen as a male crime with females who exhibit themselves being seen as victims of voyeurs. This is a peculiarity of the way women are seen by the criminal justice systems across the world, rather than a denial of the fact that women can be exhibitionists.

As a crime, exhibitionism is exposure of one's genital organs in a public place. From a psychological point of view, it should be noted that there is a pattern, almost standardised way, in which males exhibit themselves. There are three characteristic features of the exhibition:

1 It is always performed for unknown women or a young girl (or girls).
2 It always takes place where sexual intercourse is impossible; for example, in a crowded shopping centre.
3 It seems designed to surprise and shock the woman. There are reports that when a woman shows no reaction, the act lacks the power to produce sexual arousal in the individual.

Favoured settings for exhibitionistic activities are outside of churches and schools, in shopping centres, in the dark of a movie theatre, in the middle of the relative seclusion of a park, or any place where the individual can find victims likely to be shocked and where there are no supervising police officers. The exhibitionist usually exhibits an erect penis, but that does not seem to be an essential for the activity. Ejaculation may occur at the moment of exposure or develop later with masturbatory stimulation.

Exhibitionists are not usually assaultive and are considered to be more of a nuisance than a danger.

Frotteurism. In frotteurism, sexual pleasure is gained by rubbing against an individual close by, usually with the genitalia, and usually against the buttocks of the 'victim' or the touching of female breasts. Images of the office pest squeezing past a secretary or other female member of staff, as the perpetrator is usually male, breaching acceptable codes of behaviour, does not represent a true picture of frotteurism. A key characteristic of this activity is anonymity, thus this usually takes place on crowded buses, trains or in lifts, where accidental contact with strangers would not seem unusual. Acts of frottage usually occur in late adolescence and early adulthood and then decline in frequency with age.

The criteria for frotteurism state that the 'victim' is non-consenting. However, reports indicate that this activity is not always repelled and indeed transient relationships have been observed, which have very definite rules. The main rule is that of anonymity, which must be maintained throughout, even to the point of avoiding eye contact during sexual encounters in crowded public places, which may be quite involved.

DSM-IV criteria state that such behaviour should recur for at least six months and that the fantasies, urges or these behaviours should cause significant distress in the individual concerned.

Voyeurism. A relatively common, apparently normal activity, is that of looking at sexually arousing pictures or situations. Today's off-mainstream marketplace is full of opportunities to do so. One television channel in America features erotic films, and 'adult' videotapes are readily available. Bars with 'erotic' dancing are not far from many neighbourhoods, and there are magazines featuring naked and erotically posed women and men.

The difference between those activities and voyeurism lies in the function served by the viewing. In normal watching, the viewing is ordinarily a prelude to more usual sexual activities. Some married couples view erotic films both to learn and to increase the intensity of their sexual activities. For the voyeur, the 'Peeping Tom' experience replaces normal sexual activity. Nevertheless, voyeurism may exist in a person who also engages in normal heterosexual activity. One report states that 30 to 50 per cent of voyeurs are married, with no more marital conflict or more frequent divorces than exist in the general population.

For whatever reason, voyeurs are more likely to have a juvenile history of minor offences. 'Peeping Tom' behaviour requires somewhat the same kind of covert climbing as does burglary; and although it may be stretching a point, looking through a window into a home is a kind of vicarious 'breaking and entering' for sexual robbery. This is not to trivialise the behaviour which can, albeit very rarely, progress from voyeurism to assault.

Paedophilia. This paraphilia, because of its damaging impact on the non-consenting partner, a child, is radically different from exhibitionism, frotteurism and voyeurism, and the strongly condemnatory attitude of the public reflects their concern about the hurtful effects on the child.

Paedophilia is the act of fondling a child sexually or attempting intercourse with one. Contrary to a common view, paedophiles do not skulk about waiting to pounce on an unaccompanied and helpless child, nor is assaultive behaviour an important part of the problem. Violence occurs in no more than three per cent of paedophilic activities; some coercion or force is nevertheless used in more than 15 per cent of the cases.

Ordinarily, the paedophile, usually in his thirties, is someone who has ready access to the child; he may be a close male relative, a teacher, a recreational leader, occasionally a clergyman. The child or parent would have no reason to suspect the possibility of a paedophilic orientation.

The paedophilic activity itself may begin with the individual exposing himself to the child or alternatively taking the child on his lap. Occasionally it involves picture-taking of naked or posing children. Several children at a time may be involved. Some plausible explanation may be given to the child, who may be unsuspecting or very frightened. Sexual aspects include fondling the child's private parts or having the child fondle the man's penis. Coercive aspects come into play when they are used to pledge the child or children to secrecy. As the events are often covered up at the time in this way, the trauma for the child may be double edged. They have to face the acts themselves and then, possibly after a time when they may have been allowed to forget, they could have to re-live the trauma from the perspective of an adult.

Causative aspects of paraphilia with non-consenting partners. A common psychological characteristic shared by personalities who become exhibitionists, voyeurs or paedophiles is social isolation, low self-esteem and, particularly, feelings of sexual inadequacy. Not psychologically at ease in usual heterosexual relationships, or not willing to risk the rejection of their attempts to create more mature relationships, paraphiliacs resort to abnormal sexual activity. The tendency to place such individuals, especially paedophiles, in prison without treatment will tend to increase their feelings of inadequacy and reduce their social skills, making a return to such behaviour more likely.

Theoretical perspectives on the paraphilias

The theoretical perspective on paraphilias is usually a behavioural one, although psychodynamic interpretations are still popular in the USA.

Behavioural interpretations

The basic behavioural interpretation is that sexual arousal has been linked with some unusual object or some activity such as watching (for voyeurs) or exposure (in exhibitionism) through either a Pavlovian-type conditioning process or operant conditioning. Pavlovian conditioning seems to fit the fetishist better. A stimulus (for example, a shoe) is associated with the strongly emotional response of sexual arousal.

But for paraphilias that cause the individual to carry out some extreme action to arouse sexual feelings (exhibitionism, for example), the formula may be that of operant conditioning; a response – for example, exhibiting oneself – is reinforced by the pleasure of the resultant sexual activity. When those conditioning events occur in the early life of an individual who, for other reasons, is dominated by feelings of inadequacy and low self-esteem, which limit social life and tend to isolate the individual, a paraphilia readily develops. Thus it would seem that classical conditioning provides the initial learning for the paraphilia, whilst operant conditioning provides an explanation as to why this behaviour is sustained or increased.

Psychodynamic interpretations

Psychodynamic interpretations assume disruption of the normal psychosexual development taken from Freudian theory and that, as an individual becomes fixated, strong feelings develop in attachments and relationships with objects.

In contrast with the behavioural view, there is very little evidence supporting such an interpretation of the growth of paraphilias.

Treatment of the paraphilias

There are many reports of successful behavioural treatment of these disorders. Although the paraphilias are rather stubborn behaviours to remove, modern behavioural techniques can usually succeed where the client is willing to be treated.

The traditional approach is to use a form of aversion therapy, ie. the pairing of a paraphilic object or activity with an aversive stimulus, usually a nausea-producing agent. This can be done by covert means where the client imagines a paraphilic scenario followed by embarrassing or aversive consequences. More modern approaches should usually include the encouragement or conditioning of normal responses to normal sexual activity. This combination usually provides the best outcome for the client.

Psychodynamic treatments have not produced objectively verifiable successes with these disorders.

Sexual identity disorder

A sexual identity disorder exists when individuals, male or female, experience confusion, vagueness or conflict in their feelings about their own sexual identity. There is a sharp struggle between the individual's anatomical sex gender and subjective feelings about choosing a masculine or feminine style of living.

Elements in sexual identity

In understanding this disorder, it is helpful to distinguish among the terms *gender identity, gender role,* and *sexual partner choice.*

Gender identity

Awareness of being male or female, of knowing 'I am a girl (or woman, or boy, or man)', is called gender identity by psychologists. Children can distinguish maleness and femaleness by the age of two. Between their second and third birthdays, they will, when asked, readily identify themselves as girl or boy.

Sexual role

Reminiscent of Shakespeare's, 'All the world's a stage . . .' role is the public living of a part. Between their third and fourth birthdays, children can identify a variety of gender differences and have learned that boys and girls behave in somewhat different ways. They begin to assume a male or female sexual role.

Sexual object choice

This aspect of gender relates to what will arouse sexual feeling in the individual: the types of people, the part of the body, and the specifics to which the individual will respond sexually. It is not usually until a child completes the pubescent process at age 15 or so that sexual-object choice becomes definite.

Influences affecting gender identity

Both psychosocial and biological factors affect gender identity.

Psychosocial influences

Aetiological answers are by no means certain; some psychologists call them speculative. Nevertheless, psychologists tend to believe that for most individuals with gender identity problems, two elements of growing up are influential in shaping gender identity, sexual role, and sexual-object choice:

1 How parents relate to the child; that is, do they treat the child as a girl or as a boy?
2 The emotional relationship between the child and the same-sex parent.

Parental behaviour. With a young boy, for example, if parents allow his hair to remain long with a feminine coiffure, frequently dress him in girl's clothing, or allow him to wear such clothing long after infancy, that behaviour will cause confusion in the child's feelings about his proper sexual role. Studies have shown that children are treated differently from birth depending on whether they are believed to be male or female and have their behaviour shaped to a fair extent by the process of operant conditioning. Often collateral members of the family take a leading role in inducing such reactions. A favoured aunt, often unmarried, may spend special time with the little boy, applying cosmetics and dressing him up in mother's dresses and high-heeled shoes. The problem here is not necessarily that the boy will become homosexual, but that he will develop effeminate mannerisms in assuming his sexual role and become uncertain as to whether he is really, at heart, a girl. With girls, fathers can encourage tomboy behaviour and skill in principally male activities, leaving the girl with mixed feelings about sexual identity and masculine ways of behaving.

Same-sex relationships. The boy's relationship with his father (or the girl's relationship with her mother) could have some significance in the formation of sexual identity. If the father is domineering or hostile to the boy, or remote and indifferent, the boy moves away from male identification. In the process, he moves closer to his mother and often takes on her feminine mannerisms. More usually the child identifies with the same sex parent, adopting many of their characteristics including attitudes.

Same sex relationships in adolescence and later can lead to gender identity problems, especially where homosexual acts or cross sexual mannerisms are common. However, most individuals who succumb to such peer pressure, for example in prisons, revert to their normal patterns of behaviour on leaving the situation.

Biological influences on gender disorder

Biologically speaking, humans are by default female. At the earliest stages of pregnancy, although they differ in their genetic makeup, males and females are physically the same. The genetic influence brings about the changes in the male foetus at the seventh or eighth week of gestation via hormonal influences, influences which continue to govern some of their sexual characteristics throughout life.

Biological factors operating during the foetal stage can also cause the malformation of genital organs so that, in appearance and function, they are neither fully male nor fully female. The result is an individual who has been scientifically labelled as a pseudohermaphrodite. The condition principally affects females.

During the foetal stages, the mother's body surrounds the embryo with a fluid of mixed hormones. Those hormones promote development and differentiation of parts of the embryo's body. When the fluid is overly rich in androgens, the male hormone, it makes an hermaphroditic child of a female embryo. Girls born to women who had taken synthetic progestins to avoid bleeding in pregnancy were found to behave in a 'tomboyish way', and in rare cases have male features of the genitalia. Thus precursors to androgens, the progestins, can be linked to a level of hermaphroditism.

This situation is best illustrated by looking at what happens when it goes drastically wrong. If the process of masculinisation of the foetus fails in the case of an individual with a male genotype (ie genetically male), the result can be very bizarre. One such case illustrates the point well. A family doctor was approached by a happily married, attractive woman in her twenties, who was having problems conceiving a child. Although outwardly difficult to believe, the doctor found her problem was that 'she' was in fact a man and lacked the internal reproductive organs to conceive or carry a child. Given the circumstances, the doctor wisely decided to withhold this information leaving the 'man' to lead a relatively happy, if infertile, life as a woman.

Variations in gender disorders

Before focusing on the more extreme forms of gender identity disorder, transsexualism, two milder manifestations of the disorder need be mentioned.

Transitory cross-sex behaviour in young children. There are children who, before the age of four, will show cross-sexual behaviour, for example, boys who exhibit softness in emotion, gentleness in play, enjoyment of dolls as toys. Most often, with no other efforts at change, psychosocial pressures, especially those with playmates outside the home, will cause that type of behaviour to taper off, with no carryover into later life.

Gender identification problems in adults. Research has found a positive relationship between strong gender identification in men and women and their successful and effective functioning in life. It could be assumed that such individuals are more self-assured, readily acceptable to others and less distracted by concerns over their sexuality. This situation is thought to be changing as sex-specific behaviour is not as highly regarded as it was a number of years ago.

Transsexualism

In this most extreme form of gender identity disorder, the individual, if a male, feels he is a woman trapped in a male body and wishes to change his genitals, become a woman, and behave like a woman. If the individual is a woman, she likewise feels trapped and unreal as a woman and would like to develop a penis and become a man. Their anatomical gender at birth has fitted them with a set of genitals that disgusts them. Those feelings are accompanied by depression and suicidal thoughts. Transsexualism is a totally disheartening illness, bringing the individual close to desperation.

Nevertheless, many such troubled people settle for deceptively living life as a member of the opposite sex. Until the 1950s, for the most part, they had little other choice.

Although the first sex-reassignment surgery was performed in 1930, the operation performed in 1952 in Copenhagen on George (later Christine) Jorgensen attracted so much publicity that within 20 years thousands of such operations were performed on transsexual individuals. In the male operation, hormonal injections stimulate breast development and inhibit beard growth. Surgery removes the penis and testicles and constructs a partial vagina.

In the female, hormones affect vocal changes and stimulate beard growth. A non-functioning penis is constructed from other parts of the body.

There are many transsexuals who eagerly push for and anticipate sex-reassignment surgery, and in the somewhat painful period following the operation find the achievement a cause for celebration. In a number of cases the outcome remains positive, providing the individual has realistic expectations of the change and can readjust to it well. Abramovitz (1986) found this more the case with female to male surgery. However, many individuals have expectations that could never be fulfilled by the operation and the ensuing disappointment combined with the trauma of the procedure can lead to frustration, depression and occasionally suicide. These negative outcomes and the more numerous cases of post-operative maladjustment have led some clinics to cease providing the service. Thus, transsexuals wishing to change are rigorously tested for their true motivations beforehand, usually requiring them to live in the other sex role for at least a year.

Homosexuality

This section contains a limited discussion of homosexuality, not as a disorder, but as a common form of sexuality which can create difficulties of adjustment in society. The DSM-IV does not make any mention of homosexuality.

Social attitudes and public policy

Social attitudes toward homosexuality vary widely across time, and place or culture. Homosexuality has been practised from time immemorial. The Old Testament suggests its early existence by condemning it in Sodom and Gomorrah. On the other hand, Greek, Roman, Moslem and Persian civilisations all condoned it if practised in discreet fashion; that is, not between two members of the upper classes. A number of eminent historical figures have been homosexual or lesbian, including Alexander the Great, Sappho, Michaelangelo, Oscar Wilde (who was imprisoned for it), Gertrude Stein and Virginia Wolfe.

Public attitudes to homosexuality in the modern world are constantly changing and there is a long-term movement towards acceptance. However, as with racial intolerance, this varies greatly from area to area both between and within countries. Suffice to say that intolerance is greatest where it is least challenged as a cultural norm.

The public's fear of AIDS in the 1980s had a two-way effect on the status of male homosexuals. Initially this was very negative but had the positive effect of testing the legal status of the homosexual in society. The secondary effect was to increase public sympathy for the many sufferers of the disorder (many famous individuals included) and respect for the way the homosexual communities conducted themselves in limiting the disorder.

Types of homosexuality

Homosexuality may be divided into two broad categories: male homosexuality and lesbianism. It is inaccurate to consider the two alike in either the form of the relationship or in the needs which the behaviour fulfils. Lesbians place much more emphasis on emotional support and similarity of values. The consequence is that they put less emphasis on overt sexual activities than do male homosexuals.

Within these groupings, a further division has more importance for psychologists. Ego syntonic homosexuality refers to those individuals who are content with their sexual orientation and gender, and may only be troubled by adjusting to the attitudes of relatives and others. Ego dystonic homosexuals, although content with their gender, are distressed by their sexual orientation and express a desire to change it. It is this latter group who may make a request for help in sexual re-orientation, although in practice this occurs very rarely. The DSM-IV allows for such a complaint in the residual category of 'sexual disorders not otherwise specified', although this does not specify whether the orientation is homosexual or heterosexual.

Prevalence

Prevalence estimates suggest that male homosexuality is much more common than lesbianism. In terms of known lesbian relationships, larger numbers are now being reported than previously. This may simply be an effect of a change in social attitudes toward self-sex orientation, with more lesbians admitting to that sexual orientation.

Those males who engage in homosexual activities cannot all be grouped together. They vary widely in the nature of their sexual activities. Kinsey's 1948 study was the first extensive report on the range of homosexual activities. The figures are for males. His study indicates that only four per cent of his male population were exclusively homosexual as adults; 18 per cent were bisexual; and 37 per cent had at least one homosexual experience as adults. What is important about these figures is not the percentages, but the range of the differences among those who engage in any form of homosexuality. No comparable figures are available for women.

Homosexual life-style

Most studies of homosexual life-styles have reinforced the similarities between these and heterosexual life-styles. Thus, in this and other investigations, greater factual information has helped to modify old-fashioned views of homosexuality as being abnormal.

Relationships with sexual mates

In a 1978 study, Bell and Weinberg identified five styles of homosexual living among both homosexuals and lesbians. An attitude that seems to lie at the basis of their classification system is that the closer the individual comes to a stable, two-person relationship, the closer to normality is the relationship. The distribution of the five life-styles is as follows: 28 per cent of lesbians and ten per cent of male homosexuals lived in 'closed-couple' relationships and were content with that homosexual adjustment; 18 per cent of males and 17 per cent of females, 'open coupled', lived with a primary mate but participated in outside sexual relationships.

So-called 'functionals' remained single with no commitment. Their attachment seemed to be to the gay world and the cause of homosexuality. The sexual breakdown for this group was 15 per cent for men and ten per cent for women. The possibility of contracting AIDS has significantly complicated sex life and choice for that group.

The researchers reported that 12 per cent of males and five per cent of females reported a dystonic aspect to their homosexuality. They had no settled relationships, regretted their homosexuality, and described other adjustment problems. However, an oddity of the study was that it could not categorise 29 per cent of the research population.

Homosexuals and lesbians cannot be known by their physical appearance. They look like other men and women; some are strong and muscular, and others are not; lesbians do not characteristically look masculine. Among both males and females, some are striking in appearance and others very average.

The change in attitudes and public policy now makes it easier for homosexuals, to use a colloquialism, 'to come out of the closet'. But the decision to reveal their sexual preference is fraught with problems. There are parents to tell, not all of whom are understanding; lifelong friends who 'never knew'; employers who may change their attitudes and hesitate about promotions. There is even the possibility of loss of employment opportunities, despite laws that seek to prevent discrimination.

Forms of homosexual sexual activities

There is no mystery about how homosexuals relate sexually to each other. In many ways, with one or two exceptions, their practices are similar to a large fraction of the non-homosexual population.

For those with stable relationships, there is love, commitment and tenderness. For males, orgasm results frequently from fellatio (oral sex). Manual stimulation of the penis is an alternative. Anal intercourse is a third possibility. The fear of AIDS has introduced the use of condoms in homosexual intercourse. For lesbians, there are also deep feelings of love and tenderness and commitment in stable relationships. Sexual activity to orgasm involves oral-genital sex, manual stimulation, and possibly, in imitation of heterosexual intercourse, there is the rubbing of genitals of each partner against the other to arouse clitoral orgasm. There is no research on the subject, but homosexuals probably experience the same levels of sexual dysfunction as do heterosexuals. Yet, the fact that they are more familiar with what is sexually arousing in their mates may make homosexuals and lesbians more successful sexually than are average heterosexuals.

The causes of homosexual orientation

There is no explanation of homosexual behaviour that is universally accepted by psychologists. 'Speculative' best categorises the status of aetiological factors in homosexuality.

What is certain is that, although variable, homosexuality is both geographically and historically universal in mankind. With this fact in mind, it would seem likely that any factors leading to homosexuality would have to be principally biological. However, learning and social factors may be more important in individuals less predisposed to homosexuality, who may adopt this orientation later in life. There are professionals and others who would challenge the need to look for a cause for homosexuality, given it no longer has the status of a disorder.

Psychodynamic factors

Freud speculated on the causes of homosexuality and psychodynamic views still basically reflect his focus on the failure to resolve the Oedipal and Electra conflicts, although they focus more on the specifics of these early relationship conflicts. These views have tended to be viewed as somewhat dated and their emphasis on the parents as causal factors has exposed them to further criticism on the grounds that they add to the burden of the parents, who are having to adjust to the consequences, let alone accepting the blame.

Behavioural approaches

From a behavioral perspective, homosexuality may be learned either from reinforced early same-sex sexual activities or from negative or aversive conditioning associated with heterosexual activity.

Positive reinforcement. Several studies of both homosexual males and females report early satisfying same-sex sexual activities that are then frequently reinforced. Those studies report such findings as these: two thirds of a group of lesbians had willingly experienced a satisfying homosexual relationship before the age of 20; four per cent of the group had proceeded to orgasm. Other studies have reported differing groups of male and female homosexuals having early homosexual experienced which they found reinforcing of that behaviour, that is the satisfaction they experienced would lead them to repeat the activity. In one study, these early experiences were found to be *the* common factor amongst male homosexuals.

It could be said that the homosexual tendency pre-dated these experiences, producing a 'chicken or egg' situation regarding causality. However, as can be seen from studies such as Rachman (1966), in which a fetish was produced in a previously normal male, and many similar studies, abnormal behaviour can be produced from learning alone and then becomes self-sustaining. Thus sexual orientation can also be a result of operant conditioning.

Negative conditioning. When early heterosexual experiences are found unsatisfying because of failure, or because they were ridiculed, rebuffed or even punished, the individual may turn to homosexual behaviour to avoid the aversive outcomes of heterosexual behaviour. Examples of such aversive experiences are parental punishment when a little boy is found playing at sex with a little girl, or a heterosexual venture in which the partner rejects an amateurish first-time sexual effort. Among lesbians, paternal rape may turn the individual to homosexuality, or disenchantment with a faithless lover may cause the woman to seek more loyalty in a lesbian relationship.

Biogenic causative factors

The principal biogenic variable considered as a possible biogenic cause or contributory agent in homosexuality is some combination of genetic, hormonal and neurological elements that interferes with the full masculinisation of the male foetus. The most widely-accepted explanation of that effect is a 1989 study of Ellis and Ames. Their findings apply only to male homosexuals and therefore hardly seem an adequate explanation for all homosexual behaviour.

Ellis and Ames report the possibility that some time between the second and fourth months of pregnancy, a disruption of neurochemical elements in the mother produces a weakness in development of fully masculine characteristics. When later in the life of the individual pubertal changes effect other hormonal activities, the inadequate masculine elements express themselves in homosexual behaviour.

Causes listed as initiating the process are as follows:

1 A genetic hormonal defect in which receptors for androgen, the male sex hormone, are inadequate.
2 An oversupply of progesterone drugs (those that increase femininity) taken by the mother during pregnancy.
3 Maternal stress, such as bereavement or divorce, at an early stage of the pregnancy.

The Ellis and Ames hypothesis has been partially supported by other research but needs fuller substantiation. In any case, it would explain only a fraction of male homosexuality and none of female homosexuality.

In August 1991, Simon Levay reported in *Science* a study suggesting that there is a significant structural difference between the brains of homosexual men and heterosexual men. Levay states that in homosexual men, one segment of the hypothalamus, a key neural structure at the base of the brain which affects both emotion and motivation, is only a quarter to a half the size of the same region in heterosexual men. The special significance of this finding in understanding the aetiology of homosexuality is that prior research on animals has found that injury to this portion of the brain causes male animals to lose interest in females while continuing to express sexual interest in masturbation. The conclusion Levay suggests is that his finding would mean that there is a possible biological influence – even if only in creating a predisposition – in the development of homosexuality.

Needless to say, this finding promoted a great deal of controversy and criticism. However clear the finding was, the sample used was small and exclusively male, and would need replication.

Treatment of ego-dystonic homosexuality

The concept of treating homosexuality is controversial. Even in the case of ego-dystonic homosexuality, the individual's reason for complaint may not be viewed as the homosexuality as such, but rather their maladjustment to it.

When the desire to change sexual orientation is strong, as in ego-dystonic homosexuality, two small-scale studies report success with aversive conditioning in 60 per cent of the cases. In the therapies used, homosexual fantasies are followed by either actual aversive consequences, such as electric shock, or such consequences as can be imagined vividly by the individual. Masters and Johnson report success by using sensate focus exercises with a heterosexual partner. The reaction of some psychologists to that reported success is that the treated individuals were not fully homosexual but actually bisexual.

Rape and incest

Although both of these forms of sexual activity are ignored in the most recent revision of the official diagnostic manual, most textbook authors consider them in their discussions of sexual disorders.

Sexual activity imposed on an unwilling partner, either by actual force or threat, is labelled rape. From a legal point of view, two types of rape are distinguished: forcible rape, which is defined as an attempt to penetrate an opening of the body by a penis or other object; and statutory rape, which is sexual involvement with a minor, whether or not that minor has participated willingly.

Here we consider the motivations for rape, characteristics of the rapist, legal and social issues, and prevalence.

Motivations, characteristics, and issues of rape

Power and anger in rape

In 1977, Groth, Burgess, and Holmstrom completed a systematic study of rapists. They divided motivation for rape into four categories:

1 Power-assertive rape, in which the attack is motivated by a desire for conquest, which is sought by sexual penetration. Forty-four per cent of the rapes studied fell into this category.
2 Power-reassurance rape, in which the conquering of the female is sought to provide reassurance to an individual who has weak feelings of his own masculinity. Twenty-one per cent of the group exemplified that motivational basis for rape.
3 Anger-retaliation rape, the most dangerous form of rape, which often results in the murder of the victim when the rape has been completed, grows out of a generalised hatred of women. That hatred of women, the source of which can only be surmised, and not a desire for sexual release, was the motivation of 30 per cent of the rapes studied.
4 Anger-excitation rape can be seen as an extreme form of sadistic behaviour in which sexual arousal comes from the violence, not the intercourse, which may or may not take place. Five per cent of the rapes were of this type.

Other types of causation in rape

Two other types of rape need to be discussed: gang rape and date rape.

Gang rape. This form of rape is especially traumatic for the victim. Unfortunately, the media tend to look upon such incidences as highly newsworthy. Although the victim's name is usually withheld, the publicity of the details of such rapes which may involve large numbers of males and are usually accompanied by descriptions of additional acts of violence, can only add to the victim's suffering.

Such incidences are very common, as is individual rape, during wars or invasions of countries by armed forces. For propaganda purposes, these incidences are usually suppressed or simply never reported, but show the clear link between aggressive dominance and rape. Peer pressure is usually also a factor in gang rape.

Date rape. Research on date rape describes these rapists, frequently college undergraduates, as 'sexually very active, successful and aspiring'. In the study, the motivations the date-rapist verbalised were that the rapist was given 'the come-on' by a sexual tease or notoriously promiscuous woman, and he was not to be 'put on' in that way. Once sexually aroused, he was not to be frustrated. Perhaps previous experience of finding dates who were willing to 'have sex' poorly prepared the rapist for refusal.

Such males are astonished and enraged by such a refusal, and they resort to force. Added to this explanation could be the frequent association in the media of sex and violence, a phenomenon that, it would seem, can only weaken any sense of responsibility and control an individual might have been brought up to exercise.

Date rape probably accounts for the large majority of rapes. The incidence of these is impossible to determine as the majority probably go unreported. Victims in the case of date rape have great difficulty in bringing the perpetrators to court as the claims of mitigation by the rapist look more plausible when the two individuals are on a date. In such cases, the victims often undergo intensive questioning in court, which can deter less resolute individuals from pursuing the case.

Other characteristics of rapists

Police reports of arrested rapists (by no means all rapists) indicate that they are most often under 25 years of age. Thirty per cent of arrested rapists were in the age bracket 18 to 21. In this available (because arrested) sample of rapists, 50 per cent were married and living with their spouses. The group studied was predominantly of low intelligence, had low occupational skills, and earned low-level salaries. Those statistics say more in answer to the question, Who gets arrested for rape? than to the question, Who are the rapists?

Legal and social issues

Legal issues relate to the incidence of arrest for rape and the weight to be given to the rapist's mental condition in determining punishment. There is a relatively low conviction rate, principally because of the difficulty in identifying the rapist. This is becoming far easier as a result of improved methods of 'genetic fingerprinting' (ie. characterising the perpetrator's genetic make-up from fragments of tissue or body fluids left at the scene of the crime) and its acceptance as evidence in court. It is accurate to state that more rapists are free in the community than are behind bars. Yet rapists are ordinarily repeat offenders. Perhaps we should be asking, is rape today being judged seriously enough?

A principal destructive effect of rape is the serious damage it causes in the victim's later adjustment. A 1983 study reports that raped women are seven times more likely to experience depression than other women. Almost always there is a disruption in their normal sexual life, and they often live unbearably apprehensive lives.

Beyond those disturbing consequences, there is the humiliation the victim may experience at the rapist's trial. It is fair enough that an accused rapist be considered innocent until proven guilty, but some laws and some judicial behaviour suggest that the woman herself is on trial. In an effort to prevent a vengeful woman from falsely charging rape, the law has perhaps gone too far in the opposite direction and made it too difficult to prove guilt. For example, the prosecution has in the past enquired into the victim's normal sexual activity and history, or even now may question the provocativeness of her attire at the time. To avoid such humiliation, many women fail to report attempts at rape.

In Britain, a number of notorious decisions by judges have been reported in the media. These sometimes involve the judge's conduct in court including the judge's manner of questioning of the victim. The public have sometimes been outraged when upon conviction (which of course is very difficult to achieve), the sentence given is so light as to ridicule both the police and victim's efforts.

Prevalence of rapes

As stated previously, the prevalence of rape is virtually impossible to determine, as the majority of cases are never reported and of those that are, only those that are successfully prosecuted can be recorded. Figures for complaints to the police regarding rape may possibly give a more realistic picture, but even this may only be the tip of the iceberg.

Incest

Legally and narrowly defined, incest is coitus between parent and child or brother and sister. Almost universally across time and cultures, incest has been forbidden. There are sound reasons for this taboo. This section briefly examines three reasons, considers causative factors, and comments on the prevalence of incest.

Reasons for the universal taboo on incest

There are three negative effects of incestuous sexual relations: biological, familial and psychological.

Biological reasons. Coitus (leading to pregnancy) between blood relatives increases the likelihood that defective recessive genes will be present in both sexual partners and will be matched. The result of that matching will be the likely appearance of defects in the offspring. Evidence of that fact is reported in a 1967 study of 18 children of either father/daughter or brother/sister pregnancies matched against a carefully constructed control group.

Among 18 offspring of an incestuous pregnancy, the following outcomes were reported: in six months, five children born of such a pregnancy died; two were severely mentally retarded; three were of borderline intelligence; and one was born with a cleft palate. Seven of the infants were normal, suggesting the absence of defective recessive genes. Among the children of normal (non-incestuous) pregnancies, two children had defects, one physical, the other intellectual.

Familial reasons. Incestuous sexual activity, whether between parent and child or between siblings, introduces highly emotional and divisive strains into family life. Wife and husband can hardly be comfortable with each other when father and daughter are sharing sexual relations. Among siblings, tensions and rivalries divide the family. The taboo against incest is necessary to keep families intact and a positive force in the functioning of society.

Psychological. Women who have experienced an incestuous relationship, especially with their fathers, are prone, in later life, to distressing emotional reactions: depression, guilt, anxiety, and lowered self-esteem. Their capacity to develop warm interpersonal relationships is lost or badly damaged, and they often carry with them hostile and vengeful feelings toward the opposite sex. When incestuous relations have been frequent or with several relatives, the individual often drifts into prostitution, a form of sex without feelings.

Causative factors in incest

Seductive behaviour by a daughter occasionally provokes incest, but only rarely, and, of course, only when, for whatever reasons, the father is receptive to the seduction. Discovering what those reasons might be requires that we examine the characteristics of the paternal participant.

One might jump to the conclusion that such fathers would have to be amoral and indiscriminate in their sexual behaviour. What research has been conducted on the problem suggests a contrary conclusion. An early study (1965), for example, indicates that such fathers are frequently moralistic with fundamentalist religious beliefs. There is invariably a troubled marriage that serves as a precipitating cause. A number of clinicians report father/daughter sex growing out of a long, loving and tender relationship between father and adult daughter in a situation in which the mother has died or is absent from the home. It is, nevertheless, a reasonable conclusion to draw that some fraction of incestuous activities occur in severely pathological families or are attempted by irresponsible or sexually promiscuous fathers.

Prevalence

Estimates of prevalence vary widely in this infrequently researched area of the sexual disorders. Data from the Kinsey Report, now more than 40 years old, indicate a figure of three per cent. Two other more recent studies suggest much higher levels. The one study in which interviews were conducted in a representative sample of the general population reports a prevalence figure of 16 per cent. Other details of that study are that 40 per cent of the incidents were carried to abusive lengths; much of it was at the level of child molestation, in which uncles were most frequently involved. Although many of the occurrences were single events, more than half were multiple; and in a small number of cases, several relatives attempted incest.

SUMMARY

The DSM-IV divides sexual disorders into three major categories. First, is sexual dysfunction in which inhibitions prevent or reduce the individual's enjoyment of normal sex and/or the physiological changes normally brought on by sexual arousal. The dysfunction may be manifest at any of the three stages of sexual activity: the desire stage, the arousal stage, or the orgasm stage.

Disorders of the desire stage are hypoactive desire, a lack of interest in sex, or the more extreme form of the disorder, aversion to sex. Disorders of the arousal stage manifest themselves in an absence or weakness of the specific physiological changes that prepare the individual for intercourse. In the orgasm stage, the male disorder is premature ejaculation; in the female, it is an inhibited orgasm. There are two sexual pain disorders: they are dyspareunia, which is pain during intercourse, predominantly a female disorder, and vaginismus, exclusively a female disorder, which produces contractions at the entrance to the vagina and prevents penile entry.

There are both psychosocial and physical factors that may cause sexual dysfunction. Among the psychosocial causes are faulty learning, negative attitudes toward sex learned in early traumatic sexual experiences, or friction or hostility between the two sexual partners. The physical causes of sexual dysfunction include the effect of ingested external substances such as alcohol. The principal internal factor is hormonal imbalance.

Treatment of sexual dysfunctions is much more frequently sought today than in earlier decades. Illustrative of treatment approaches are those suggested by Masters and Johnson, who prescribe graded sexual exercises and encourage partners to focus on the sexual pleasures (sensate focus) rather than on whether or not they are 'performing' satisfactorily. High levels of success are reported for such treatment approaches.

The second major category of sexual disorders are the eight paraphilias, which can be grouped into three broad clusters.

Cluster 1 includes fetishes and transvestic disorders, in which there is a sexual preference for nonhuman objects. A fetish is an attachment to such objects as shoes, female clothes or textured material, either as a supplement to coitus or as a substitute for it. Transvestism is finding sexual excitement by cross-sex dressing.

Fetishes occur in those persons with lowered self-esteem and feelings of sexual inadequacy. The fetish is usually triggered by an early conditioning experience in which the fetishistic object stimulated, often accidentally, an orgasm. When followed by planned use of the object, the fetish soon becomes established. Transvestites often have early experiences in which a boy is dressed as a girl or a girl as a boy.

A second grouping of paraphilias is those disorders in which there is a preference either for causing suffering as an aspect of sex (sadism) or desiring to have pain inflicted (masochism). Both are developed out of early life experiences which relate pain (given or received) to an orgasm, very much in the same way that fetishes are developed.

Another major grouping of the paraphilias is that of sexual preference and arousal with non-consenting partners. These paraphilias take the form of paedophilia (child molesting), frotteurism (the deliberate rubbing against strangers in public) and exhibitionism or voyeurism (secret viewing of sexual scenes). All of them involve the participation of non-consenting individuals in some aspect of a sexual activity. The basis for these paraphiliac activities is profound feelings of sexual inadequacy and fear of being embarrassed or rebuffed in normal heterosexual activities. The paraphilias do not respond easily to treatment.

The third major sexual disorder, gender identity disorder, exists when individuals, male or female, express confusion, vagueness or conflict in their feelings about their sexual identity. These disturbing feelings may relate to gender identity, gender roles, or choice of sexual partner. Here, as with transvestism, early prolonged experiences in being treated as a child of the opposite sex can have drastic later effects on the individual's sense of gender identity.

Biological influences can cause malformation of the sex organs and both predispose to and precipitate later gender identity problems via later hormonal influences.

Transsexualism is the most extreme form of gender identity disorder. In that disorder, the individual, either male or female, feels trapped in a body of a non-preferred sex. Since 1953, almost 3,000 persons suffering from transsexualism have sought sex-change operations. Research reports that most sex-changed transsexuals continue to live unfulfilled social and sexual lives.

Historically, social attitudes towards homosexuality have varied widely across time and culture. The DSM-IV makes no mention of homosexuality. However, individuals who are unhappy with their sexual orientation, whether homosexual or heterosexual, can still be categorised under sexual disorders not otherwise specified. Such individuals may often seek and receive therapy for this, which usually involves some attempt at sexual re-orientation.

Individuals with same-sex sexual preferences differ widely in appearances, life-style and reasons for their sexual orientation.

There is no universally accepted explanation for homosexuality. Both psychosocial factors, including parent/child relationships and early conditioning, and biogenic factors, such as genetic, hormonal and neurological causes are considered as possible causes.

Although rape and incest are not listed as disorders in the DSM-IV, most textbook authorities consider them in their discussion of the sexual disorders. Strong feelings of need for power and anger against the female are considered primary motivations for rape.

Official reports of the numbers of rapes seriously underestimate its true prevalence. The reluctance of many women to report rape attacks largely accounts for this hidden figure.

Incest is coitus between parent and child or brother and sister. Kinsey's figures suggest a prevalency rate of three per cent; more recent studies cite a high rate.

There are good reasons for the universal taboo against incest – biological, familial and psychological. An example of these is the greatly increased incidence of genetic disorders amongst the offspring of such relationships. Women who have experienced incestuous relations early in life suffer greatly in adulthood.

FURTHER READING

Bancroft, J. 1989. *Human sexuality and its problems*. Edinburgh: Churchill Livingstone.

Cole, M. 1985. Sex therapy: a critical appraisal. *British Journal of Psychiatry*, 147: 337–351.

Cole, M. & Dryden, W. 1988. *Sex therapy in Britain*. Open University Press.

Cole, M. & Dryden, W. 1991. *Clinical Problems: a cognitive-behavioural approach*. London: Routledge.

Eskapa, R. 1987. *Bizarre sex*. Grafton Books: Collins Publishing Group.

Masters, W., Johnson, V. & Kolodny, R. 1986. *Masters and Johnson on sex and human loving*. Macmillan.

Money, J. 1987. Sin, Sickness or Status? Homosexual Gender Identity and Psychoneuroendocrinology. *American Psychologist*, 42:384–399.

Spence, S. 1991. *Psychosexual Therapy: A Cognitive-Behavioural Approach*. London: Chapman & Hall.

Wilson, G. 1987. *Variant sexuality research and theory*. Croom Helm.

Zilbergeld, M. 1980. *The inadequacy of Masters & Johnson. Psychology Today*, August, 29–43.

15 Organic Mental Disorders

All human behaviour, normal and abnormal, has its basis in the activities of the nervous system. The organising, executive, and most crucial part of the nervous system is the brain. To reflect the two different ways in which the brain affects the development of abnormal behaviour, mental disorders are grouped into two broad categories:

1 Organic disorders, those mental disorders known to be caused directly and primarily by pathology in the brain itself.
2 Functional disorders, which result from abnormal life experiences imposed on a normal brain. This division is not considered fixed as some functional disorders are renamed organic as more is known of their causes. Organic disorders account for 25 per cent of all first admissions to mental hospitals.

The inclusion of specifically organic disorders in the old versions of the classificatory system has in itself been controversial. Some professionals claim that this implies that all other disorders are not organic, whereas a better description would be 'disorders where an organic basis has yet to be found'. Thus disorders which have been referred to as functional but have a definite organic component, eg. schizophrenia, can confuse the student who is looking for certainty. For this reason the DSM-IV does not use the heading 'organic disorders'. However, a realistic view of this dimension of pathology would be to accept that there are purely organic disorders, such as those in this chapter, other disorders which are purely a product of non- organic influences, and a larger group of disorders where organic and functional causes both operate in unknown proportions.

Organic and functional factors also interact. A disorder of function may lead to brain changes which, in turn, may influence the further course of that disorder. It is also the case that environmental influences may alter the course of an organic disorder, and that both factors may combine to precipitate some disorders (as in the diathesis–stress model).

Functional disorders are generally considered the province of psychologists and psychiatrists; neurologists diagnose and treat the organic disorders. Depending upon the needs of the patient, a team of all three may work together to help the individual.

This chapter considers the following: the various parts of the brain and their functions; characteristic symptoms of organic disorders; the problems of distinguishing between organic and functional disorders; causes of organic disorders; the principal organic disorders; and neurological approaches to treatment.

The DSM-IV classification of organic disorders is of more value to medical students than to students of abnormal behaviour. For that reason, it is not outlined in this presentation.

The human brain

Human advantage over animals rests principally on the development of the human brain. The human brain is the best-protected organ in the body. The bony structure of the skull and three enveloping layers of tissue afford protection from many, but not all, of life's accidents or illnesses.

The brain is described by neurologists as the most complex biological structure in existence. They also say we know more about the brain than we know about any other organ of the body, perhaps because there is so much more to know about so complex an organ; but they say further that there is so much more that we don't yet know. For that reason, learning all about how the brain functions is one of the most challenging goals of both medicine and psychology.

Here we consider the following: the neurone, the basic functioning unit of the brain; localisation of function; spatial organisation of the brain; and the effects of brain damage.

The neurone

There are said to be billions of these hard-working units of the brain. The neurone consists of

1 A cell body, which provides the life support functions of the neurone.
2 Dendrites, a system of fine branches that receive electrochemical impulses (messages) from other neurones.
3 Terminal endings that transmit messages to other neurones.

The small gap between one neurone and another is the synapse. Messages are enabled to cross that gap by the neurone's release of neurotransmitter substances into the synapse. The transmitters, as enabling agents, either activate or inhibit the functioning of other neurones.

The complex events that take place within and around the synaptic gap are very important for brain function and ultimately behaviour. The process of production and release of neurotransmitter substances of various types and their targeting and activation of receptors at the dendrite side of the gap, is where the communication between two neurones is most vulnerable. This is the normal site of action for psychoactive drugs, which may mimic neurotransmitters, block receptors or interrupt the process of neurotransmitter re-uptake in the synapse amongst other functions. Drug action at the synapse is a broad and complex topic, which can often provide evidence of what specific functions fail in many disorders.

The importance of the transmitter enzymes is exemplified in Parkinson's disease, a debilitating disease affecting older people. The disease is caused by a degeneration of brain cells (neurones), which degeneration limits the supply of the transmitter agent dopamine. In the absence of dopamine, the message telling certain groups of muscles to flex or to expand is not transmitted across the relevant synapses, and movement control is impossible or severely limited. The symptoms of Parkinsonism can be reduced by the administration of a synthetic form of dopamine.

Localisation of function

Bundles of neurones controlling similar functions are located in the different regions of the brain; thus, there is correlation between behavioural symptoms produced by brain damage and location of the damage.

Collections of neurones serving similar functions are located in one or another of the lobes of the cerebral cortex (the surface layer of the cerebrum, which is the main part of the brain). The four lobes are named frontal, parietal, occipital and temporal. The entire cerebrum is separated into two symmetrical hemispheres.

The cell bodies of neurones of the brain are concentrated in what is called the 'grey matter' of the brain. That grey matter makes possible the higher mental functioning of the human being. The axons, wirelike structures called the 'white matter' because of their white myelin sheath, are bundled into tracts that connect areas of the grey matter.

A convenient way of thinking about the structure of the brain is to consider the grey matter as a group of modules, each with a specialised job to do. The white matter, or bundles of axons, serves to connect the various modules. Some modules, for example, those in the frontal lobes, control wide-ranging functions, such as processing of information. Others are limited, for example, to receiving sensations from the various sense receptors.

Spatial organisation and brain function

There are three axes or ways of thinking spatially about the brain: front/back, left/right, and up/down. Those axes relate to various human functions.

Front/back organisation of the brain

Motor functions are generally located in the front of this axis and sensory functions at the back. Various aspects of both activities will also be located on the up/down axis in the front and back of the brain.

Illustrative of this localisation of function in the cerebral cortex is a description of two higher functions of the brain provided by the Russian neuropsychologist Alexander Luria. He named one of those functions the information-processing activity, and he located the place where it was controlled in the back portion of the cerebral cortex. Damage to that part of the brain will cause loss of sensation; damage at other levels of the back portion of the brain will cause such symptoms as poor representation of space or even inability to identify common objects. The condition is known as *agnosia*.

Luria named the other function planning-verification, and located that function in the front of the brain. The area controls the actions the individual takes in his environment. One result of damage to this area is perseverative behaviour, in which the individual repetitively makes the same response instead of taking the next step in the normal way of responding.

Left/right organisation of the brain

This axis separates the cerebrum into two symmetrical hemispheres. The left hemisphere receives sensory input from, and controls actions of, the right side of the body. The right hemisphere serves the left side of the body in a similar way. Damage to either hemisphere will affect the opposite side of the body.

Aside from that basic localisation of function, there is a qualitative difference in the way each hemisphere functions. The left hemisphere contributes an analysing ability and organises the perceptual world; it sorts things out. The right hemisphere is better at synthesising; that is, reassembling discrete information into units. Damage to either hemisphere will affect its normal functioning; the particular malfunction will depend upon the up/down location of the damage.

Up/down organisation of the brain

The vertical organisation of the brain affects functioning in a hierarchical way. The upper levels of the brain have to do with cognitive and voluntary behaviour. That level builds on and moderates functions of lower levels. There is evidence that in such general disease of the brain as that of the degeneration caused by aging, there is greater vulnerability to dysfunction of the upper levels of the brain. In senility, for example, the first functions to be affected are the higher cognitive functions, such as memory, adjusting to new situations, or keeping things in sequence. Only later are more basic biological functions disrupted. A sad example is the individual in a coma who goes on living vegetatively.

Major symptoms of organic disorders

There are three clusters of symptoms that suggest the presence of organic disease: defects in basic mental activities, impairment in higher intellectual functioning, and certain types of affective symptoms.

Defects in basic mental activities

Memory loss is a significant indicator of brain dysfunction, although it may also be a symptom of a functional disorder. It is one of the earliest signs of cerebral deterioration associated with senility. A prime example is the impairment of memory that is a primary symptom of Alzheimer's disease. The memory impairment in functional disorders manifests itself in markedly different ways from that produced by cerebral degeneration (see chapter 9).

An even more severe indication of brain damage, and one on which initial diagnosis can more confidently be based (although psychosis would also have to be considered), is loss of orientation, in which the individual cannot locate himself or herself in space, has no awareness of the date or even the season, and may not be able to report self-identity.

Impairment in higher mental functioning

Persons with brain disorders have trouble in making decisions. They make them only after much hesitation and uncertainty, or make foolish decisions about everyday activities. They also make gross errors in financial matters. There can be slowness and inaccuracy in calculating. Their fund of general information is reduced, and knowledge of common items, such as who is the prime minister, can be lost.

Affective symptoms

There may be lability of affect in which the individual shifts suddenly and inappropriately from one emotion to its opposite; for instance, from unpleasantness to hostility, or from laughing to weeping. Included in this type of symptom is a loss of resilience. When fatigued or emotionally upset or puzzled, the necessity of making a decision, or solving even a simple problem is just too much for the individual.

All of the symptoms described above can be suggestive of possible organic involvement; a number of them also are present in functional disorders. A diagnosis of organic damage can be made only after careful neurological and psychological study.

In the DSM-IV, these are listed as cognitive disorders under which the symptom groupings are given the headings Deleria, Dementia and Amnestic. These terms correspond only approximately to those above, amnestic referring to memory disruption, dementia to loss of higher order and some basic functioning, and deleria to clouding of consciousness. The DSM-IV has deliberately omitted 'organic disorders' as a separate section to avoid implying that other disorders do not have an organic basis as mentioned above.

Diagnosing organic mental disorders

With the possible overlap in symptoms of functional and organic disorders, diagnosis can be a problem. Mistaking one for the other will, of course, block effective treatment. In organic disorders of some types, delayed treatment can result in death.

Correct diagnostic practice requires that even for apparently minor symptoms that cannot be explained, a thorough physical examination be undertaken before a diagnosis is made. A good dictum to follow is to exclude physical causes before consideration of psychological causation.

Sometimes doing that is easy; for example, a long-time specific phobia, with no other symptoms, is less likely to have an organic cause. On the other hand, even a brief loss of consciousness is quite another matter. Such an event could be caused by physical exhaustion, high temperature, or the early sign of a brain tumour.

Fortunately, recent advances in medical technology, especially advances in brain imaging techniques (such as computer-assisted tomography, CAT scan or the more recently-developed magnetic resonance imaging, MRI) make diagnosing brain damage an easier process than in the past. Accurate diagnosis in pinpointing specific performance defects is now also possible with the help of specially developed psychological tests; for example, the Halsted–Reitan Neuropsychological Battery. The performance profiles of those tests can help locate the region of the brain damage and also the extent of the damage remarkably accurately.

Aetiological aspects

There are broad categories of agents that cause brain damage. They are, as we will discuss them, a degenerative process in the brain, brain tumours, brain trauma or insult, vascular accidents, nutritional deficiency, and endocrine disorders.

A separate category of organic disorders is epilepsy. For each of the disorders, the extent of behavioural disruption, and the specific nature of the symptoms depends upon the amount of brain damage and the location of the damage.

Before discussing the specific causes of organic disorders, we consider broadly the types of effect the causes can produce, factors that affect the vulnerability of certain parts of the brain to damage, and the availability of redundant systems that can take over lost functions.

The range of effects of brain damage

The agents of brain damage may cause acute symptoms, some lasting only a few months (for example, some strokes), or chronic symptoms, which may handicap and disrupt the individual's functioning for the rest of his or her life, or indeed cause death; for example, neurosyphilis. The symptoms of brain damage may be localised and affect only specific functions, such as speech and/or mobility, as in many strokes; or they may, when extensive areas of the brain are affected, as in the degenerative disorders, cause generalised debility and disorganisation of functioning. Symptoms may come on suddenly, as, for example, the early signs of brain tumour or appear gradually with increasing severity, as with senile dementia.

Most damage to the brain causes negative effects; that is, there is an impairment in the functioning of the affected area. In particular instances, the damage may also increase the activity of the adjoining area. For example, the increased irritation caused by the damage may have the 'positive' effect of exciting and activating the nearby area. The effect may nevertheless be disruptive. The convulsive seizures of epilepsy (periods of heightened activity) are explained in this way.

Vulnerable parts of the brain

Since an adequate supply of blood is essential to the proper functioning of a neurone, positioning of a neurone cluster that limits access to a supply of blood or that makes it exceptionally susceptible to stroke increases the likelihood of brain damage in the area. The area controlling speech is one such area, and speech impairment is a frequent symptom of brain damage.

Even the axial length of the neurone may make it more vulnerable than a neurone of shorter length, since the greater length requires more than average nourishment for its full functioning. A vitamin deficiency, for example, would have stronger impact on the functioning of an axially long neurone than it would have on a shorter neurone. Parts of the brain involved in memory are particularly vulnerable for such reasons. As a result, memory is frequently affected by concussion of the brain.

Redundancy

Redundancy in the brain is the presence of multiple cerebral pathways performing the same function. Redundancy is common in the human body. The two kidneys are an example; one is all that is needed. Cellular redundancy makes it possible for a partial liver to function adequately.

Three possible redundancies in the human brain make it possible for damaged functions to be maintained or shifted elsewhere. They are as follows:

1 A surplus of neurones for a particular function. If only some are damaged, the remaining undamaged neurones can maintain the function.
2 Alternative pathways are available for some functions. For example, left-hemisphere damage can be mitigated by a neural passage going between hemispheres. Some functions (for example, basic biological activities) can be carried on from either hemisphere.
3 Finally, the individual can design behavioural strategies to compensate for disabilities caused by brain damage. Such adjustment would be comparable to the blind person learning to depend more heavily on hearing in order to avoid obstacles.

Causative agents in brain damage

Here we identify seven principal agents of brain damage and illustrate the types of symptoms that result from each.

Brain degeneration

The wear and tear of living is hard on the organs of the body. Biologists report that the wearing out of the body begins virtually at birth. When one is young, the worn-out cells of the body are replaced regularly by new growth. As the individual grows older the replacement process slows down; a generalised degeneration of the body's tissues gradually takes place. The brain is as affected as are other parts of the body. The rate of biological aging varies among individuals and seems to be related to the individual's genetic heritage. Science has not yet learned to understand the full nature of aging.

When this degeneration process produces changes in the brain, certain alterations in intellectual functioning gradually appear. For most people, these changes initially affect daily life only in minor ways; for example, occasional memory lapses, the inability to recall a name, or failing to remember what the individual set out to do just a moment ago. As the individual grows older, in a normal and to-be-expected way, the disabilities increase. Examples are a slower way of walking, lessened capacity to handle complex information, and decreased efficiency of memory and in the learning of new tasks.

Aside from this normal aging of the mental and motor processes, in four per cent of the population over age 65, a condition called dementia develops, which brings on a progressive loss of a variety of the higher mental processes. The percentage increases with age, so that beyond 80 years of age, 20 per cent of the population show varying degrees of senile dementia. There are two types of senile dementia: Alzheimer's disease and multi-infarct disease.

Dementia of Alzheimer's type

There are two symptom patterns to expect in dementia of Alzheimer's type, or Alzheimer's disease.

In half of the group, the illness follows the pattern of simple deterioration. In others, a system of paranoid thinking may develop.

Simple deterioration. Here, various mental capacities begin to fail. Memory loss is usually first. Loss of memory is followed by periods of disorientation, poor judgment, indifference to personal hygiene, and ultimately a complete loss of contact with reality.

The behavioural expressions of the disease may vary. None of them make caring for the individual any easier. Some typical examples of Alzheimer behaviour are repetitive asking of the same question, walking out of the house and getting lost, or forgetting to turn off running bath water or appliances around the house.

There may be genial amiability (but also irritability) and a busyness about useless but harmless activities, for instance, saving string or ritualising household activities to a painful extreme.

Paranoid reactions to Alzheimer's disease. Much more difficult to deal with is the Alzheimer patient who develops paranoid thinking. Although this is a less frequent reaction pattern than simple dementia, when it occurs it is the symptom about which most caretakers complain and the one which they find the most difficult to manage. The individual is suspicious and busy concocting plots of the nefarious activities engaged in by the very people who are providing care. Strangely, with this symptom pattern, deficiencies in cognitive functioning seem to be less noticeable. The individual becomes more observant about the behaviour of others and uses those observations to justify suspicions. Although rare, paranoid thinking can lead to assaultive behaviour. Most often, however, the feebleness of the individual prevents much harm being done.

Causes of Alzheimer's disease. The exact cause or causes of this disorder are still relatively unknown. However, a genetic component, at least to some cases of the disorder, are reasonably certain. The neural plaques and tangles found in the brains of Alzheimer's patients can also result from aluminium, which has been found in excess in these patients.

Other possible causes, such as the presence of a novel antigen in the brains of these patients or the association of dementia symptoms with infections of the brain, should also be borne in mind when trying to identify a single cause for dementia of Alzheimer's type.

Increased aluminium. A notable number of studies of the disease report high levels of aluminium in the patient's blood, especially in those areas of the brain known to be involved with the disease. Since such heavy metals as aluminium are known to accumulate at sites of neural damage, the question of cause and effect has been raised. However, though animal research has found such damage to be caused by the aluminium, whether this is the case in Alzheimer's disease is a matter for further research.

Genetic factors. A dominant gene would seem to be responsible for at least some cases of Alzheimer's disease. The inheritance pattern of the disorder seems to lend support to this assumption. In addition, Tanzi and colleagues 1987 have used genetic linkage to speculate as to the possible location of such a gene.

Inconsistencies in the results of genetic studies of the disorder indicate that forms of the disorder which begin early in life are distinct from those starting later in life, in terms of their aetiologies.

Prevalence. With an increasing aging population, Alzheimer's disease has become a major health problem with troublesome resultant social problems. As stated previously 10–20 per cent of the population over 65 suffer the disorder, and this figure appears to be rising rapidly. Since there is no known cure for it and proper management of the illness at later stages is difficult, nursing homes carry much of the burden. Estimates report that 30 to 40 per cent of all nursing home residents currently suffer from the disease.

Multi-infarct dementia

Symptoms similar to those described for Alzheimer's disease can also result from multi-infarct disease. That disease is not as specifically age-related as is Alzheimer's disease. It is a vascular (blood vessel) disease which may occur earlier in life than is likely with Alzheimer's disease. Brain degeneration in multi-infarct disease results from the cumulative damage of multiple small strokes, which are caused by a blockage in the supply of blood to a specific area of the brain. The cause of the blockage is usually a blood clot. The impacted area is called an infarct, which loses its ability to function and soon begins to degenerate. As those small strokes grow more frequent and the neural damage spreads, dementia ultimately results.

The condition is associated with hardening of the arteries. In that condition, calcified fatty substances accumulate on the interior arterial walls, narrowing them and slowing the flow of blood through them. Eventually, a blood clot forms, and the resulting blockage ruptures the blood vessel, allowing blood to haemorrhage into the brain. A single stroke of that type may result in a variety of psychological and physical symptoms. As they occur more frequently, dementia follows.

A sudden onset of symptoms occurs in 50 per cent of the cases, presumably as a result of a major stroke involving extensive areas of the brain.

Other degenerative disorders

There are two other degenerative disorders, Huntington's chorea and Parkinson's disease. Both involve specific but unrelated areas of the brain at subcortical levels.

Huntington's Chorea. This organic disease is transmitted genetically by a dominant gene of either parent. Its presence can first be observed only when the individual is in his or her thirties. The brain area affected is the basal ganglia, which are bundles of neurones deep within the cerebrum. The characteristic symptom, for which the illness is named, is a spasmodic jerking of the limbs. The disease is a serious one, causing bizarre behaviour and loss of bodily functions, resulting in death, usually some 14 years after the onset of the symptoms.

Parkinson's disease. The disorder results from a degeneration of the neurones in the substantia nigra, a part of the basal ganglia. The absence of the neurotransmitter dopamine makes conduction of impulses across the synapses impossible in the affected area. Characteristically developing in later life, in the sixties, it appears occasionally as early as the forties. Symptoms include muscular rigidity, tremors, and a masklike fixedness of facial expression. In severe cases, in the latter phases of the disease, dementia may be present.

Although the disease cannot be cured, symptoms can be greatly moderated by regular doses of a synthesised substitute for the missing dopamine. The problem with that drug is that the body gradually accommodates to it, therefore requiring that the dosage be increased gradually, with the danger that its effect may be lost altogether.

A radical treatment in degenerative conditions where there is brain cell loss, is the theoretical implantation of foetal brain tissue. After successful, but controversial, animal experiments, this research has been halted on the grounds of ethical concerns regarding the concept of 'brain transplants'.

Brain tumours

A tumour is an abnormal growth of body tissues. Some tumours are benign, affecting the individual only because of the pressure they exert. Upon removal of the tumour, symptoms usually disappear. Others are malignant, and unless removed in time, will cause the individual's death. Tumours may appear in many parts of the body, including the brain.

Types of brain tumours

Brain tumours are of two types: primary tumours, which originate in the brain itself and may be malignant; and secondary tumours, usually cancerous, originating in other parts of the body and carried to the brain through the vascular system. As the brain tumours grow in the cerebrum of the brain, they increase intracranial pressure and cause a variety of serious physical and behavioural symptoms; and unless removed or reduced, eventually cause death. The secondary tumours are just as dangerous as primary tumours; they simply arise from a place outside the brain, metastasise (that is, break up), and travel to the brain through the blood vessels.

Symptomatology

Intracranial tumors show their presence initially in relatively minor symptoms – headache, visual problems, a brief loss of consciousness. As the tumour continues to grow and affects other parts of the brain, symptoms increase and more seriously affect the health and mental functioning of the individual. Higher mental functions deteriorate, abnormal reflexes develop, emotional expression is blunted, memory and concentration are affected, and disorientation as to time and place results. When brain tumours cannot be removed because of their location or size, they eventually cause unbearable pain and extreme personality changes. The patient ultimately becomes floridly psychotic, sinks into a coma, and dies.

Many brain tumours can be removed by surgery or reduced by radiation therapy.

Brain trauma

There are three types of brain trauma: concussion, contusion and laceration. They most frequently result from falls, automobile or motorcycle accidents, blows to the head, or penetration of the brain by a foreign object such as a bullet. The critical elements in each type of injury are the extent of the injury and its location in the brain. The most frequent victims of brain trauma are young males. With speed and violence on the increase in society, it is remarkable that brain trauma occurs no more frequently than it does, which is 200 per 100,000 of the population in any one year.

Concussion

In concussion, the brain is momentarily jarred and shifted from its position. The result is usually nothing more than a brief loss of consciousness, lasting only seconds, or perhaps a minute or two. The longer the period of unconsciousness, the more severe and longer-lasting will the symptoms be. When the individual regains consciousness, he or she may not be able to recall events immediately preceding the accident. Post-traumatic symptoms may continue for several weeks. Those symptoms – their nature, length and severity – reflect pre-trauma personality characteristics, hypersensitivity to pain, or preoccupation with bodily symptoms. The range of such symptoms includes headache and dizziness (most frequent symptoms), memory and concentration difficulties, irritability and insomnia. Doctors usually recommend a period of quiet for the individual and close observation of behaviour. The extent of the brain damage may not be immediately observable.

Damage to the brain from a number of concussions, such as those experienced in prize-fighting, have a cumulative effect, eventually matching the symptoms caused by a more serious brain injury.

Contusion

Contusion is a more serious jarring of the brain, forcing it out of position and pressing it against the skull. Brain tissue on the cerebral cortex (exterior surface of the brain) may be damaged. The result will be more serious symptoms than those that occur from concussion.

Contusion will cause a longer period of unconsciousness, sometimes days. The individual may experience convulsions and speech impairment when coming out of the coma. Confusion and some disorientation may also be present. Repeated concussions or contusions may result in permanent brain damage.

Lacerations

When a foreign object passes through the skull and enters the brain itself, the injury is a laceration. It is the most serious of brain traumas. The severity of the injury depends upon its location and the extent of the collateral damage the object causes as it passes through the brain. The effect of laceration varies widely, from death to intellectual, sensory or motor impairment. In rare cases, there will be only minor residual impairment.

Cerebral vascular accidents

There are two distinguishable cerebral vascular accidents: cerebral occlusion and cerebral haemorrhage.

Cerebral occlusion

A blood vessel of the brain may clog from an embolus, that is, a ball-like clump of clotted blood, or fat may move through a blood vessel until the vessel becomes too narrow for its passage. When the blood from that blocked vessel no longer provides adequate support for an area of the brain, the brain cells in that area degenerate and can no longer function. The same result can be caused by a thrombus, which is a build-up of fatty material on the inner surface of the vessel. As the build-up continues, it gradually reduces blood supplied to that area of the brain. When a cerebral vascular accident produces a sudden and dramatic set of symptoms, such as paralysis or inability to talk, an embolus, producing an instant clogging of the vessel, is likely to be the cause. A thrombus grows slowly at the same spot in the vessel, gradually reducing the supply of blood and progressively causing the development of symptoms. Cerebral vascular accidents cause a variety of symptoms, from death to such handicaps as aphasia, agnosia, apraxia (see glossary in Appendix) and a right- or left-sided paralysis.

Cerebral haemorrhage

Here, a blood vessel ruptures, and blood pours out onto brain tissue, limiting the capacity of the brain to function. It is that kind of accident about which the individual with high blood pressure should be concerned. The rupture is usually caused by an aneurysm, which is a bulging in the blood vessel. Cerebral haemorrhaging is a serious condition that may cause the death of the victim immediately or in a matter of days. In less extensive haemorrhaging, the symptoms can nevertheless be quite disabling. They may include memory loss, impaired judgement, speech impairment and/or paralysis. As always with brain damage, its expression in symptoms depends upon its location and the extent of the damage.

Brain insult

As mentioned in relation to Alzheimer's disease, aluminium has been found to cause lesions in the brains of animals. Such metals entering the brain are often associated with damage. Lead is another example which can cause dementia, delirium and psychosis in addition to lesser symptoms. Children are especially prone to absorb lead. Many other substances can result in damage to the brain, such as solvents or pesticides. The damaging of the brain by neurotoxic substances is commonly referred to as brain insult. Some substances of abuse, if taken in large quantities or regularly over a period of time, can result in irreversible change to brain structure or function and hence insult. In the case of alcohol however, part of this process is indirect as described in the following section.

Nutritional deficiency

In this type of brain damage, the cause is the lack of certain vitamins necessary for brain function. The principal disorders resulting from vitamin deficiency are Korsakoff's syndrome, pellagra, and beriberi. The latter two are practically nonexistent in Western societies.

Korsakoff's syndrome

This disease is a direct result of the inadequate diet that accompanies chronic alcoholism. In particular, a deficiency of vitamin B1 and thiamine causes the disease. It causes foolish thinking and talking and, in time, generalised weakness and gross intellectual impairment. Damage caused by the disease is irreversible.

Pellagra

An organic disease that has all but disappeared in most countries, pellagra results from a diet deficient in niacin, a B vitamin. In this century, the diets of some communities were deficient in this vitamin, for example heavily corn-based diets, and the disorder was a major cause of psychiatric admissions in these areas.

Early symptoms are rash and diarrhoea. If the diet deficiency is uncorrected, more serious psychological symptoms may develop, ranging from depression and anxiety to psychosis. When detected early enough, massive doses of the needed vitamin can correct the disorder.

Beriberi

The disorder is most prevalent in Far Eastern countries, where vitamin deficient polished rice is a major part of the diet. The critical missing ingredient is thiamine. Symptoms are lassitude, irritability, and concentration and sleep disorders.

Endocrine disorders

The endocrine glands secrete hormones that are critical for such important bodily functions as growth, energy level and sexual activity. Oversecretions or undersecretions of some hormones can produce serious physical and mental disorders. The two glands in which that problem occurs most frequently are the thyroid and adrenal glands.

Problems of the thyroid gland

In the thyroid gland, either oversecretion or undersecretion can cause problems. Hyperthyroidism, that is, too much secretion, causes Graves' disease. The increase in thyroxin creates bodily changes that ordinarily accompany anxiety: sweating, apprehensiveness and hyperactivity. In extreme cases, hallucinations may develop.

Hypothyroidism, a deficiency of thyroxin, may cause myxedema, which, as might be expected, causes symptoms the opposite of those produced by hyperthyroidism. Its principal symptoms are sluggishness and depression.

In both disorders, patterning of symptoms will be influenced by the individual's personality before onset of the disorders; for example, a worrying type of person will show more of it with the hyperthyroidism, while a depressed and gloomy person will become more so in hypothyroidism.

Brain damage from infection

A number of infectious diseases can produce brain damage. They are encephalitis, meningitis and neurosyphilis.

Encephalitis

The term is a generic one meaning inflammation of brain tissue. The source of the infection can be any of a number of living and nonliving agents. The principal culprits are mosquitoes and ticks. The disease can also be caused by infections that travel from other organs of the body to the brain, principally from the ears and sinuses.

A particular epidemic of encephalitis, encephalitis lethargica, occurred in Europe during the period of World War I. The most prominent symptom, that which gave it its name, sleeping sickness, was an extreme lethargy, causing the infected individual to sleep for days, even weeks. The disease is not seen often now.

Encephalitis causes a number of physical symptoms, including vomiting, stiffness of neck and back, fever and tremors. In its acute phase, with high fever, delirium and disorientation will also occur. Most victims recover completely, although some may be left with paralysis of an arm or leg, severe tremors, and sensory and speech disorders. In infants, the disease may cause mental retardation.

Meningitis

Bacterial infection may inflame the three layers, or coats, that envelope and protect the brain. Such inflammation of the meninges causes symptoms similar to those of encephalitis. The principal epidemic form of the disease results from a meningococcal infection, which is worldwide in its occurrence, tending to reappear in an eight- or twelve-year cycle.

Neurosyphilis

This disorder, the most devastating of the infectious disorders, results from a long-term and untreated infection caused by the syphilis spirochete. Since the development of the Wassermann test, which makes possible the early and reliable diagnosis of syphilis, neurosyphilis has largely been brought under control.

The syphilis infection is contracted by either coitus or oral–genital sex. It may also be transmitted from mother to foetus. The early symptom is a small sore at the site of the infection, which develops during the first three weeks after the event causing the infection. That early indication is followed by a darkish rash covering much of the body. Accompanying the rash will be fever, headache and fatigue, sore throat, and open sores in the mucous membranes of the mouth and genitals.

The insidious and dangerous aspect of untreated syphilis follows as the disease seems to abate or even disappear. Bitter disappointment is in store for the individual who believes so. The spirochetes are busy invading other organs of the body, including the heart and the cerebral tissues. About 30 per cent of those infected in this way develop neurological impairment. In this paretic phase of the illness, the individual becomes paralysed, inarticulate and convulsive, and gradually declines into a horrible death.

Treatment of organic disorders

As might be expected, the treatment of organic disorders is different from the treatment of functional disorders. It is principally a medically administered problem and makes use of skilled and delicate surgery, pharmaceutical drugs, such as the antibiotics, and medical procedures for maintaining the individual's general health. Counselling can be an important addition to the physical treatments, especially where the patient may have to adjust to dramatic change or a very poor prognosis. Other treatments may also be used in this such as physiotherapy, behaviour therapy and other forms of psychotherapy.

We consider here basic characteristics of neural tissue and neural damage that affect treatment, and then the principal approaches to treatment of the organic disorders.

Characteristics of neural tissue and neural damage that affect treatment

Neurologists attempting treatment of organic disorders take account of three characteristics of the nervous system:

1 The impossibility of creating new neural tissue.
2 The recoverability of damaged neurones.
3 The existence of redundant areas.

An example of taking account of those characteristics in neurological treatment is consideration of the fact that when neural tissue in an area of the brain has been completely destroyed, only if there are redundant areas matching the function of the destroyed area is there hope of recovering the lost function.

Another example illustrates a different consideration. When arteriosclerosis or pressure on the brain reduces the supply of oxygen or other nutrients, the affected neural tissue is damaged. In such cases, the appropriate intervention, such as surgical removal of the pressure-causing tumour, can resume the supply of nutrients, after which the neurologist's focus will be to strengthen the general health of the individual in the hope that doing so will enable the damaged neural tissue to recover.

Neurological treatment approaches

There are three possibilities:

1 The most urgent is to remove or contain the condition causing the damage. Examples are surgical removal of a brain tumour; treatment of an infection with antibiotics; or drainage of fluid that is causing intracranial pressure. The possibility of attempting such procedures depends upon the extent of the neural damage and its accessibility.
2 A second approach is to treat the symptoms so that they interfere less with normal living. The treatment of Parkinson's disease by controlled doses of synthesised dopamine, which ameliorates the symptoms, is an example.
3 A third approach is to modify the patient's mode of carrying out everyday activities. The help of family members here is usually necessary. Strong motivation is a vital ingredient in order for such an approach to succeed.

When considering prognosis, three factors will be uppermost: extent of the damage; its location; and such secondary factors as the general health of the individual, energy level, personality and living circumstances.

Epilepsy

Epilepsy is best considered apart from the other organic mental disorders. In most victims, it manifests itself during childhood, sometimes before the age of four. Occurring in 0.5 per cent of the population, no cause for the illness can be identified in more than three-quarters of the affected group.

Epilepsy is known principally by its most prominent symptom, the epileptic seizure, but an assortment of the other organic disorders also cause convulsions or seizures. In most cases, such seizures are distinguishable from the typical epileptic seizure. Seizures from known pathology other than epilepsy are sometimes loosely referred to as acquired epilepsy; they are the result of very different causes, and should more properly be diagnosed for what they are, ie, brain tumour, encephalitis, etc. Apart from such convulsion-causing organic conditions, there is what might be called a true epilepsy, which is diagnosed as idiopathic epilepsy. The cause of that condition has not yet been identified.

Four types of epileptoid seizure have been identified: grand mal (or major sickness), petit mal (or small sickness), psychomotor epilepsy, and Jacksonian epilepsy.

Grand mal epilepsy

The grand mal epileptic attack is preceded by a visual or auditory aura, signalling the impending occurrence of the attack. The aura is a generally distinctive pattern of changing lights or sounds. The patient will then cry out and lose consciousness.

There are four distinguishable phases to the grand mal attack:

1 The aura stage.
2 The tonic phase; the individual becomes rigid, with arms tightly flexed and legs outstretched. Muscular contractions continue for a minute or so, and breathing is interrupted briefly.
3 The clonic phase; jerking motions take the place of the tonic, or rigid, phase. A danger during this phase of the seizure is that the strong jerking movements will cause bodily injury.
4 Soon after, the individual falls into a coma.

Coming out of this coma, the individual is confused and responds weakly. There is no recollection of events preceding the attack.

Petit mal epilepsy

In one sense, petit mal has been well-named. Compared to the grand mal attack, it is indeed a small illness. For some seconds, ten to thirty, without warning, the individual is 'absent', sitting or falling, staring, unaware of what is going on, and usually immobile. The attack is so fleeting, with so brief a period of unconsciousness and so few external symptoms, that those around the patient may be unaware of the attack. The individual may also give no sign of being aware of it, picking up the uncompleted activity begun before the attack.

The critical element of the small attack, like the proverbial dripping of water, is the wearing effect of repetitive seizures. Some patients may have literally a hundred petit mal 'absences' in a day. That frequency of seizure ultimately can have profound consequences.

Psychomotor epilepsy

This combination of motor and psychic disturbance is the most unusual of epileptic seizures. Following the advance warning of an aura, the attack consists of a loss of consciousness, during which there will be repetitive, seemingly automatic activities. Despite the reduced consciousness, the individual is frequently aware enough to resist attempts to control his or her activities. A grand mal attack may follow a psychomotor seizure.

An unusual feature of the psychomotor attack is the assortment of confused, sometimes psychotic-like, mental content that may accompany the episode. These include perceptual changes, in which ordinary objects take on different shapes and sizes; changes in self- awareness, causing the individual to experience depersonalisation; and extreme cognitive and affective reactions. Schizophrenic-like experiences, such as hallucinations or delusions and irrational behaviour, are occasionally part of a severe psychomotor seizure. Assaultive behaviour, although possible, is rare, and most often takes the form of resistance to efforts to control the bizarre behaviour of the patient.

Jacksonian epilepsy

Named after Hughlings Jackson, who first reported it, this type of epilepsy is more limited in behavioural and mental change than either grand mal or psychomotor epilepsy. Its symptoms principally are tingling and twitching of hands or feet, which may then spread to other parts of the body. Its cause has been localised in a small area of the brain, which may be excised to control the disorder.

SUMMARY

Most psychiatric disorders can be roughly grouped into three broad categories. There are purely organic disorders, which are caused directly and primarily by specific pathology in the brain. There are those disorders which seem to be disorders of function, ie, have no known organic component, such as post-traumatic stress disorder. Finally, there is a large group of disorders in which the organic basis is uncertain or unknown where the aetiology is clearly a product of both organic and functional factors. Organic disorders account for 25 per cent of all first admissions to mental hospitals.

The functioning unit of the brain is the neurone. It consists of:

1 A cell body, providing the neurone's life support.
2 The dendrites, a system of fine branches that receives impulses from other neurones.

3 Terminal endings that transmit messages to other neurones. The gap between one neurone and another is the synapse. Impulses are transmitted across synapses by neurotransmitters.

Localisation of function. Various human activities are controlled by highly specific areas of the brain. In localising function, we may consider its three axes. They are front/back, left/right, and up/down.

In the front part of the brain is located the planning-verification functions; the information-processing unit is located in the back part of the brain. The left side of the brain (the left hemisphere) receives sensory input from the right side of the body and controls motor behaviour of the right side of the body, and vice-versa. The left hemisphere sorts things out; the right hemisphere synthesises. The higher levels of the brain have to do with cognitive and voluntary behaviour.

There are three major symptom clusters in organic disorders. They are defects in basic mental activities, such as memory; impairment in higher mental functioning; and affective symptoms.

The principal causes of organic disorders are brain degeneration – that is, deadening of brain cells (neurones) – brain tumours, vascular accidents, brain insult, nutritional deficiency, endocrine disorders, and infection.

The effects of brain damage range from short-term memory loss to death. Vulnerability of the brain to behavioural impairment depends upon the presence of multiple cerebral pathways (redundancy).

Four organic mental disorders result from brain deterioration. They are:

1 *Alzheimer's disease, initially manifesting itself in severe memory loss.*
2 *Multi-infarct disease, resulting from blockage in the blood vessels of the brain, the primary result of which is a stroke, producing partial to extensive paralysis, with later signs of dementia.*
3 *Huntington's Chorea, which is transmitted by a dominant gene. Its symptoms are spasmodic jerking of arms and legs, bizarre behaviour and loss of bodily function. It is a terminal illness.*
4 *Parkinson's disease, which causes limited mobility, rigidity of facial and body muscles and, in later stages, dementia.*

Brain tumours, which may develop within the brain or move from other parts of the body, may be benign or cancerous. A full array of psychiatric symptoms and death results if the tumour cannot be excised.

Brain trauma includes: a concussion, or slight jarring of the brain; contusion, or jarring which produces a displacement of the brain; and laceration, or penetration of the brain. Impairment depends upon location and extent of the damage.

Clogging of a cerebral blood vessel, either from clotted blood or fat moving into a narrow blood vessel or accumulation of fatty material on the interior of the blood vessel, is called cerebral occlusion and causes the paralysis and associated symptoms of a stroke. A ruptured cerebral blood vessel causes the same symptoms. Either can be fatal.

The principal organic mental disorders resulting from nutritional deficiency are:

1 Korsakoff's syndrome, which is caused by a deficiency of vitamin B1 and thiamine, brought about by bad dietary habits of alcoholics.

2 Pellagra, which results from diets deficiency in niacin, a B vitamin.

Overactivity of the thyroid gland can cause such psychological symptoms as anxiety, sweating and hyperactivity. The condition is known as Graves' disease. Undersecretion of the thyroid gland causes lassitude and depression.

The principal infectious diseases resulting in organically-caused psychological disorders are encephalitis, meningitis and neurosyphilis. The primary treatments of organic disorders are physical/medical, often involving surgery, antibiotics and drug therapy. However, these may be supplemented with counselling, physiotherapy, behavioural therapy or other psychotherapies, which may all be very useful in enabling the patient and their relatives face up to drastic change in the patient's functioning or life expectations.

Epilepsy is known principally by the epileptic seizure. There are four types of epileptic seizure. They are grand mal (or major sickness); petit mal (or small sickness); psychomotor epilepsy, causing automatic repetitive motor activities; and Jacksonian epilepsy, the symptoms of which are severe tingling and twitching of hands and feet. The causes of idiopathic (or true) epilepsy are unknown.

FURTHER READING

Davison, K. 1989. Acute Organic Brain Syndromes. *British Journal of Hospital Medicine*, 41: 89–92.

Ellis, A. & Young, A. 1988. *Human Cognitive Neuropsychology*. London: Lawrence Earlbaum Associates.

Lezak, M. 1995. *Neurological Assessment* (3rd ed). Oxford University Press.

Lishman, W. 1987. *Organic Psychiatry: Psychological Consequences of Cerebral Disorder* (2nd ed). Oxford: Blackwell Scientific Publications.

Miller, E. & Morris, R. 1993. *The Psychology of Dementia*. London: Wiley.

Parks, R., Zec, R. & Wilson, R. 1994. *Neuropsychology of Alzheimer's Disease and Other Dementias*. Oxford University Press.

Pearce, J. 1992. *Parkinson's Disease and its Management*. Oxford University Press.

Sacks, O. 1986. *The Man Who Mistook His Wife for a Hat*. Picador (Pan Books).

16 Mental Retardation

Known in earlier years as feeblemindedness and mental deficiency, mental retardation is said to exist when an individual fails to develop the various skills requisite for independently and adequately solving the problems of ordinary living. If such impairment develops after the age of 18, it is an entirely different disorder, which is categorised as dementia.

The amended British Mental Health Act 1983 provides a definition of mental retardation as 'a state of arrested or incomplete development of the mind including significant impairment of intelligence and social functioning'. Such definitions are often couched in absolute terms whereas development in these individuals can only be partially arrested. The criteria in practice usually rely on intelligence quotient levels where a threshold of less than an IQ of 70 would indicate handicap but not necessarily to the degree that the individual would require special care or need help to lead an independent life. IQs below this level occur in about 2.5 per cent of the general population and are more common in males.

In the UK the term 'learning disability' has replaced the use of 'mental retardation'. Although a preferable term, to avoid confusion it has not been used here as international literature (including the DSM-IV) still refers to mental retardation.

Types of mental retardation

There are two distinguishable types of mental retardation:

1 Cultural/familial retardation, which is caused by some combination or interaction between normal genetic variation and an impoverished and unstimulating environment.
2 Organic retardation, the result of some physical condition that limits the development of the brain.

Cultural familial retardation

The condition usually results in a mild retardation (in the upper range of those classed as mentally retarded). Cultural/familial retardation accounts for the majority of those with a mild degree of retardation. Individuals with this form of mental retardation have reasonably good, normal physical growth, are normal in appearance, and fall within the normal range in physical abilities. Most of them learn to function in a marginally independent fashion if they are provided with suitable living accommodation. This type of mental retardation appears more prevalently in families at the lower end of the socioeconomic scale.

Organic retardation

This form of mental retardation affects about 25 per cent of the mentally retarded population. It results from a physiological or anatomical anomaly affecting brain development. Individuals with this form of mental retardation typically are different in appearance and behaviour from others, characteristics that result from the underlying organic malfunction. They are often more seriously retarded, but this evaluation may be the result of the physical and behavioural anomalies that may mask intellectual functioning.

Misconceptions about mental retardation

Despite the prevalence of the disorder and possibly due to the institutionalisation of the mentally retarded in earlier years, the general public still tend to hold misconceptions about individuals so affected.

A common misjudgement is to equate communication with comprehension. Some mentally retarded individuals have a mild intellectual handicap but have greater difficulties in language production, and this can lead to the illusion that their intellectual functioning is far lower if the interactant is not observant, or prone to making stereotyped judgements. A further misconception is that these individuals are not aware of their handicap or the limitations it imposes. They are usually painfully aware of their exact limitations and, apart from their making attempts to overcome them, welcome the nonjudgemental help of others, providing it is asked for.

The mentally retarded are no more dangerous than nonhandicapped people of the same mental age, and are as varied in their personalities and other such characteristics.

Subclassifications of retardation

The ICD-10 and DSM-IV systems both recognise four levels of retardation. These distinctions are based on Intelligence Quotient (IQ) scores. As these can only be approximate and the descriptions can label the individual in a negative way, the boundaries should not be looked upon as absolute, certainly not from a single testing of IQ. The four levels are:

- **Mild mental retardation**. This is taken to be between IQ scores of 50 and 70.

This affects about two per cent of the general population and 75 per cent of all people with this disability.

- **Moderate mental retardation**. This is between IQ scores of 35 and 49 and affects about 0.4 per cent of the general population.
- **Severe mental retardation**. This is between IQ scores of 20 and 34 and affects less than 0.2 per cent of the general population.
- **Profound mental retardation**. This indicates an IQ of below 20 and affects less than 0.1 per cent of the general population and only accounts for around five per cent of all people with learning disabilities. It is worth noting that IQ measurement at this level is not very reliable.

Mild mental retardation

This level of retardation may not be diagnosed certainly until the child is three or four years old. In many cases, it is first officially diagnosed soon after the child begins school. For purposes of educational planning, this group is diagnosed as 'educable', which means that they can benefit from academic schooling. Even before the time of school attendance, with a caring home environment (which, unfortunately, is often lacking for these children), the mildly retarded can develop simple social and communication skills. Their vocabulary will be notably limited and their enunciation poor. There is no notable impairment in sensorimotor areas, although learning to walk and talk will be delayed. They make progress very slowly, and in their late teens they can learn academic skills up to second year senior level. As adults, given the motivation, they will usually develop sufficient social and occupational skills to provide some portion of their own support. They will continue, however, to require guidance and social support throughout their lifetime.

The mildly mentally retarded comprise 75 per cent of the total mentally retarded population.

Moderate mental retardation

From the point of view of expected achievement level, this group is distinguished from the mildly mentally retarded as 'trainable' (rather than educable). The term means that with care at home, they can be trained in simple communication skills but will respond poorly to schooling in academic subjects and are usually unable to progress beyond the year three primary level. The schooling experience, under the best circumstances, can provide occupational and social skills that enable them, as adults, to work under supervision in sheltered workshops. Here they work at unskilled or semiskilled jobs and are able to earn some money for their own maintenance. Placement in the sheltered workshop not only provides some income, but provides, as well, supervision during the daytime hours. Twelve per cent of the mentally retarded population fall into the category of moderate mental retardation.

Severe mental retardation

In every criterion of performance, this group falls behind the less severely retarded. Their retardation is manifest at an earlier age; there is poor motor coordination and meaningless speech. Later in childhood, they acquire simple speech skills, sometimes only monosyllables, and can be taught rudimentary habits of hygiene. Never developing vocational skills, they can find employment, if at all, only in highly protective environments, where they may be taught simple, useful tasks, for example, putting items into containers.

Profound mental retardation

During the preschool years, these children develop little sensorimotor capacity; for example, coordinating what they see with hand movements. As time goes on, they will show further motor development and rudimentary self-care behaviour. As adults, they continue to require constant aid and supervision, ultimately learning some useful self-care habits. This five per cent of the mentally retarded population will continue, throughout their lifetimes, to be almost totally dependent upon hour-to-hour aid and constant supervision. Whether that care can ever be provided at home is questionable, but only the parents of a handicapped child can make that decision, and they usually need professional support and guidance to do so.

Special symptomatology (other than intellectual deficit) of the mentally retarded

Such symptoms vary with the severity of the disorder.

Mild to moderate retardation

Here the symptoms are likely to be such personality traits as dependency, passivity, low tolerance for frustration, depression, and self-injurious behaviour.

Severe or profound retardation

Here the special symptoms may be speech disorders, vision and hearing problems, coupled with cerebral palsy or other neurological disorders.

Course of mental retardation

In planning for the mentally retarded, not only should the level of the retardation be considered, but also the long-term course of the disorder. The course followed by mental retardation varies with the two types of the disorder: cultural/familial retardation and organic retardation.

Course of cultural/familial retardation

Given a stimulating environment along the way, mentally retarded individuals, especially those with the two lesser degrees of impairment, will justify their own preferred name for themselves, ie., 'I am slow at learning things'. By adulthood, they may show a notable improvement in adaptive behaviour. Their problem is that it takes them longer to reach that point and requires a more caring environment. Sometimes that spurt in adaptive behaviour appears when they are freed from the more restrictive demands of school attendance. That possibility should not cause parents to remove a child hastily from a good (tolerant) school setting. There will be enough time for that.

Course of organic retardation

When the cause of the retardation is a specific biological abnormality, the expected course is bleaker. In these types of retardation, the disorder is likely to be chronic and without remission and with little hope from treatment. Symptoms may become more severe.

Mental disorders associated with mental deficiency

The mental retardation of the individual may be made even more complex when it is accompanied by other mental disorders. The DSM-IV lists three such mental disorders that appear three or four times more frequently in the mentally retarded group than in the general population. They are stereotyped movement disorder, infantile autism, and attention deficit with hyperactivity. They are described briefly here and more fully in chapter 18.

Stereotyped movement disorder

This developmental disorder is characterised by abnormal gross motor activity, tics (which are involuntary twitches) and repetitive movements or vocalisations.

Infantile autism

This developmental disorder manifests itself during the first year-and-a-half of life, in which there is a lack of responsiveness to others, extremely limited communication skills and abnormal behaviour.

Attention deficit disorder with hyperactivity

The principal feature of this developmental disorder is inappropriate attention deficits accompanied by hyperactivity.

Causative factors in mental retardation

The pattern of aetiological factors and the effects of those causal factors are notably different for the two major types of mental retardation, cultural/familial and organic.

Cultural/familial retardation

Both severe environmental impoverishment and hereditary influences must be considered here.

Impoverished environment

It may seem strange that, in modern times, levels of mild retardation can still result from environmental deprivation. Such deprivation exists not only in materially deprived societies, but also in highly materialistic societies where deprivation often co-exists side by side with great wealth. Although the degree of retardation is far less than that resulting from genetic abnormality and disease, the prevalence of these lesser levels of retardation is often greater than one would like to think. Studies of impoverished environments have examined the different factors influencing mild retardation.

There are four especially significant adverse conditions that block intellectual developments in impoverished homes. They are as follows:

1 Inadequate diet that leads to malnutrition can produce low levels of energy and weak motivation. There is, in addition, an absence of medical care which, for example, by leaving sensory deficits in vision and hearing unattended, can seriously handicap an individual's development.
2 Parents who are so beset and distracted by the struggle to make ends meet may have little time available for their children. The resulting emotional impoverishment and the absence of a rich communication and social exchange among family members provide no stimulus for intellectual growth. Verbal ability, so much a part of intellectual functioning, is stunted.
3 Impoverished parents have low expectations for their children and offer them little stimulation for problem solving activities, curiosity, reading or even social conversation.
4 Children growing up in impoverished homes soon develop the lowered self-esteem of their parents, which discourages them from making any effort to advance.

Entering school with those handicaps and performing poorly, they soon fall further and further behind, causing their teachers to develop low expectations of any progress from them. In many countries such as Britain, there are safeguards in place to prevent children from slipping through the system, such as the work of educational psychologists and the legal requirements for school attendance. However, the disruption caused by lower achieving children in schools and the financial and competitive pressures on the education system mean that safeguards are less able to prevent such children reaching a life on the streets, where their limited skills leave them open to exploitation and crime.

Hereditary influence

The mental retardation we are discussing here is not randomly distributed among families living in poverty; it seems to be concentrated in certain families. One study reports that 80 per cent of the children with IQs below 80 had mothers with IQs below 80. The report further indicates that the lower the mother's IQ, the greater the probability that her children will have low IQs.

It should be noted that such a correlational finding does not necessarily indicate causation. It does not, by itself, establish a hereditary factor. The mother's low intelligence may only worsen the conditions which impoverishment imposes. However, hereditary factors alone can undoubtedly lead to levels of mental retardation as well as other psychiatric conditions. This can be greatly accelerated by levels of interbreeding, which can be found in isolated communities of many countries. These effects usually result from the greatly increased matching of detrimental recessive genes.

Organically caused mental retardation

The 25 per cent of the mentally retarded whose retardation is organically caused have more severe levels of retardation than those who fall into the category of cultural/familial, and they also show more associated physical anomalies. Their retardation may be caused by genetic abnormalities, metabolic abnormalities or by such environmental factors as brain trauma, severe malnutrition, infection or premature birth.

Genetic factors

There are two types of genetic influence on the development of mental retardation: chromosomal anomalies and detrimental recessive genes which, when matched from both parents, produce the disorder. In 1991, two studies, one conducted in England and one in the USA identified gene mutations on chromosomes 19 and 21 as contributory to the development of mental retardation.

Chromosomal anomalies. In humans there are 21 pairs of differentiating chromosomes (called autosomal chromosomes), and one pair of sex chromosomes. Mental retardation may result from aberrations in either type.

Autosomal aberrations. Here the normal splitting and matching of each parent's chromosomes (meiosis), the mother's in the egg and the father's in the sperm, does not occur normally; for example, the failure of one parent's number 21 chromosome to split. When fertilisation takes place, there are then three number 21 chromosomes, giving the foetus one more chromosome than the normal 46. The aberrant process is known as trisomy-21. The result is a type of mental retardation known as Down's syndrome. The chances of a mother conceiving a child with Down's syndrome is age-related. One study reports that the chance of a woman under the age of 29 conceiving a Down's syndrome child is one in every

1,500 births; by the age of 45, those chances become one in 30.

A medical procedure called amniocentesis can now identify the presence of this anomaly in the growing foetus. That medical possibility confronts the mother with the choice of preventing the birth of a Down's syndrome child with an abortion.

The Down's child is born with three types of handicap:

1 Shortened life expectancy. Because of vulnerability to cardiac and respiratory illness, these children are at high risk during the first six months of life. Advances in medicine have increased the survival rate during those months, and many Down's children now live to adulthood. At age one, having survived the early risks, their life expectancy is 22 years, although many now live a lot longer.

2 Physical appearance. There are well-known physical characteristics that mark the child as a Down's child. They include unusual almond-shaped eyes (which in past years led to these children being called 'Mongoloid'), a flattened nose and broadened face, enlarged tongue with deep grooves, and stubby fingers. Cosmetic surgery reduces the abnormalities, particularly that of the tongue. Such an operation considerably improves eating habits and speech and makes interaction with other children more normal. Growth remains stunted.

Most, but not all, Down's children have IQs below 50 and are therefore moderately mentally retarded. About ten per cent of the moderately to severely retarded suffer this syndrome.

Sex chromosome anomalies. There are three types of sex chromosome anomalies: one occurring only in females, another occurring only in males, and a third affecting both sexes. The twenty-third chromosome, which is responsible for the determination of the embryo's sex, normally has two X chromosomes in the female, and an XY pair in the male. Aberrations in this pattern can occur in both sexes. In the female, a condition known as Turner's syndrome results when there is only one X chromosome. Such physical characteristics as retarded growth and absence of secondary sexual characteristics result. Only 20 per cent of this population are mentally retarded; others may show a variety of perceptual deficiencies.

In the male, a comparable anomaly results when there are more than two X chromosomes. Known as Klinefelter's syndrome, the disorder causes mental retardation in 25 per cent of the children affected.

The third sex chromosome anomaly results from what is known as the fragile X syndrome. Here a malformation of the X chromosome produces the disorder, which is estimated to cause ten per cent of all mental retardation. There are anomalous physical characteristics such as elongated face and prominent jaw and forehead. Of more significance is its seeming relationship to childhood autism. Ten to 15 per cent of autistic children also have a fragile X chromosome. Because females have two X chromosomes (XX), the stronger one seems to compensate for the fragile X chromosome, and, as a result, females are less frequently mentally retarded.

Recessive genes. A recessive gene is one whose effect on the physical being of the child can only appear when it is matched with another identical recessive gene from the other parent. This is more likely to occur in the children of married relatives. Detrimental recessive genes have been identified as responsible for three types of mental retardation: phenylketonuria (PKU), Tay–Sachs disease, and congenital hypothyroidism. In all of these conditions, the recessive genes produce a malfunction in the metabolic processes.

Phenylketonuria (PKU). In this genetic disorder, the matched recessive genes leave the child with an excess of phenylalanine. The end result is serious damage to the developing central nervous system, in turn causing mental retardation, seizures, hyperactivity and erratic behaviour.

Early diagnosis, which is now possible and likely because tests for the condition are routinely performed soon after birth, will initiate a regimen of feeding begun during the first months of life and continued until the child is six years old. The diet keeps from the child all foods high in phenylalanine. Because of the possibility of eliminating necessary nutrients in the diet of the child, such a diet must be supervised by a competent physician.

When PKU goes untreated, the condition produces severe to profound mental retardation, with the IQ typically below 40, and such other problems as to require institutionalisation. On the other hand, when the condition has been treated successfully and an appropriate diet maintained, if a treated woman should become pregnant, there is a high likelihood that her children would be born healthy and with normal intelligence. In any case, where the possibility of PKU exists, genetic counselling should be sought prior to pregnancy.

Tay–Sachs disease. Another genetic disorder transmitted by matched recessive genes and impacting on the body's metabolic processes is Tay–Sachs disease. The disorder damages metabolism as a result of the absence of the enzyme hexosaminidase A in the cerebral tissues. Although not manifest at birth, it is usually detected between the eighth and twenty-fourth month, when the infant shows progressive muscle weakness, expressed in inability to roll over, to raise the head or torso, or to initiate movement. There is a lack of appetite and loss of sight and hearing. Death usually occurs between the second and fourth years.

Congenital hypothyroidism. In this one of the enzymes involved in thyroid hormone production is lacking. This leads to general retardation of development and a 'puffy' appearance. Treatment with thyroxin on a lifetime basis can reduce the symptoms. Other non-genetic causes can lead to this condition, such as iodine deficiency, infectious diseases or perinatal injury (birth injury).

Environmental causes
Environmental causes of mental retardation fall into three categories: those that operate in the prenatal environment, those resulting from injuries at birth, and postnatal causes.

Prenatal causes.   There are two principal prenatal causes of mental retardation:

1 Viral or bacterial infections of the mother during pregnancy which are transmitted to the foetus through the placenta (protective membrane lining the uterus). Such infections create inflammation of the brain and degeneration of brain tissue. Rubella, or German measles, when contracted by pregnant women, although only a mild illness in the mother, with low temperature and a rash, can cause mental retardation when transmitted to the child. The danger to the foetus is greatest during the first three months of pregnancy. During that period, 50 per cent of infected mothers transmit the disease to the foetus. The result, depending upon the severity and location of the resulting brain damage, can be mental retardation, sensory defects and congenital heart disease.
2 Foetal alcoholic syndrome (FAS). This preventable condition results from heavy use of alcohol during pregnancy. (Any consumption of alcohol during pregnancy is unwise.) Alcohol present in the mother's body acts directly on the child, causing brain damage and the possibility of various physical and mental defects. One of the effects can be microcephaly (development of a small brain). Microcephaly causes mental retardation, mild to moderate. Apart from mental retardation, which is not always present in FAS, other symptoms are likely, including attention and academic problems, hyperactivity and behavioural problems.

Incidence estimates of FAS in children of alcoholic mothers range from 26 to 76 per cent, depending on the strictness of the diagnosis. It is now estimated that one case of FAS occurs in every 750 live births. That statistic indicates use of alcohol by pregnant women as one of the most common causes of organically determined mental retardation.

Birth injuries. A variety of conditions existing during the birth of a child can damage the brain and cause mental retardation. They include prolonged birth, which can deny the foetal brain necessary oxygen and inflict pressure on the head, and physical trauma. Birth injuries account for a relatively small fraction of organically-based mental retardation. Among premature infants, approximately 20 per cent show some signs of neurological problems. They range from later difficulty in learning to mental retardation. Markedly low birth weight shows a correlation with lower-than-average intelligence.

A worrying cause of brain damage after birth, seemingly on the increase, is child abuse. Statistics are lacking, but one authority suggests that child abuse should be considered a major cause of organic brain damage in children, which condition becomes mental retardation in many cases, especially among infants.

Caring for the mentally retarded

Since almost 90 per cent of the mentally retarded fall only marginally below the IQ requirement for classification within the normal range of intelligence (an IQ of 68 or above), and since an even larger percentage of them, despite below-normal

IQs, are able to adapt and to manage in simple environments, the goal of caring for the mentally retarded should be to bring them as close to normal living as their capacity (latent as well as manifest) makes possible.

Considerations for doing that can be examined under three principal headings: the role of parents; society and the mentally retarded; prevention and treatment.

The role of parents

Issues here are initial response of parents to the birth of a retarded child; problems of rearing; and dealing with emotional problems.

Initial response

Disappointment and hurt in the hearts and minds of parents are the frequent, perhaps universal, greeting that meets children born mentally retarded. For the organically and severely retarded, with notable physical signs, that disappointment, undoubtedly accompanied by anguish for the child's illness, may appear early in the life of the child. For the mildly mentally retarded with no physical stigmata, the disappointment may come gradually as the child fails to meet benchmarks of normal development. The disappointment may be expressed in the way in which parents hold the child or talk to him or her.

Those initial responses are a natural, human response. What matters for the future of the child is what feelings follow that initial disappointment. Later responses are dependent upon characteristics of the parents themselves – their own feelings of self-esteem and adequacy, the state of their marriage, their socio-economic status, the place of intellectual development in their value system, and, indeed, their own intellectual level.

Studies of parental reactions report certain responses to be common.

1 Parents may persistently deny that their child could be mentally retarded. That denial can cause individuals to go from one doctor or psychologist to another, seeking a different opinion.
2 Parents may covertly feel guilt and/or anger. All sorts of past actions will be dredged up; in some cases, used to feed guilt; or in others, to fuel anger at a spouse.
3 Parents may feel that the retardation of their child is punishment for past misdeeds or sins.

The best resource parents can have is the comfort they can give each other; that, with the help of a professional counsellor, clergyperson or physician, can draw the parents back to their child and the love and care the child will need. Such issues have been dealt with by the television serial *Brookside*, where the mixed emotions of the new parents of a Down's syndrome child have been sensitively explored.

Caring for the child

Professionals familiar with the needs of the retarded and their special problems will point out to parents that the needs of their child are the same as the needs of the normal child: physical care and proper nutrition, love, and a relationship that builds the child's self-esteem and provides opportunity for social life as they grow. A need that may be more pressing for the retarded is the satisfaction of discovering what they can do for themselves. Achievements, although they may be at a lower level than those of siblings or normal children, are nevertheless rewarding to the retarded; and a significant part of that reward is the pleasure parents find in their child and the special ways that are created to give recognition to such children for their special accomplishments.

Parents face a problem in the achievement area; the achievements of retarded children should be measured by a standard that is all their own. Achievement is an advance over previous behaviour, simple things such as feeding themselves, learning to walk independently, and first efforts at communication. For the mildly retarded, as they approach school age, there will be learning to recognise the meaning in a picture, the interpretation of symbols, and then simple words. A big accomplishment will be in writing their own name.

The care parents must take is to encourage their child to stretch toward his or her potential, always on guard not to show disappointment at slowness and faltering steps the retarded child will take toward more advanced behaviour. There should not be pressure, but 'soft' challenge, admiration and pleasure, even when the child takes only half a step in the right direction.

When siblings are present, they, too, must be taught the proper standards for judging the performance of a handicapped brother or sister. Yet the siblings' own efforts at growth and accomplishment must also be recognised. It is indeed a happy family when the retarded child and his or her normal brothers and sisters take pleasure in each other's different accomplishments.

Choosing a school and knowing what to expect is an anguishing problem. Parents need preparation for this decision, as does the child. Schools in different communities and in different parts of the country vary widely in accommodating the retarded. Parents will profit not only from talking to experts in the field, but also from speaking with other parents of retarded children, especially if their children are similar in adaptability and if parents have the reputation of doing a good job.

Education

Children with retardation usually have special educational needs. Current opinion is that, as far as possible, the child should be catered for in mainstream education, although this is not always possible. The aim here is to keep the child's socialisation and other educational needs as normal as possible in the hope that their richer educational environment may lead them to better achievement.

More severely retarded children will require the services of special schools which are currently provided under the education system. Adult Training Centres can provide more training after school age is exceeded. Many parents attempt to cater for a retarded child in the home environment. The resulting social and financial problems can place extra pressures on already stressed parents. In these situations, it must be borne in mind that these efforts are intended to provide the child with a rich educational environment. People with these disabilities can suffer high rates of some illnesses, although probably as a result of their decreased ability to communicate problems, they often receive less medical treatment than the general population. Thus, higher levels of screening for medical problems should be available whether the child is in the home, special or mainstream school.

Although mildly retarded individuals are quite capable of living independently in adulthood, severe cases may need permanent care. Improved skill and intellectual functioning can be sustained in adulthood by the continued use of behavioural programmes initiated in childhood and partially independent living in sheltered community homes and hostels provided by the local authority.

Emotional problems

The life of a retarded child, even in a home with caring parents, is a more emotionally trying life than that which most children normally experience. It is no surprise, then, that the mentally retarded suffer emotional disorders, from anxiety-based disorders to schizophrenia, more frequently than do normal children. Parents of mentally retarded children can expect 'down' periods that can approach depression, feelings of inadequacy, and apprehension about venturing into new environments. More serious disorders – schizophrenia, alcoholism or severe behaviour disorders occur in the retarded at a level of 15 per cent.

Parents who have come to accept the retardation of their child may find the additional burden of emotional problems that develop as the child grows older a heavy burden, indeed. There is help to be found. Increasingly, professionals who specialise in the field of mental retardation are coming to recognise that it is in the mental health area particularly where they can be especially helpful to parents. Specialist units for mental retardation and allied disorders are being established where funding is available. These units not only offer specialist advice and therapy but many are in teaching hospitals and conduct research into the disorder.

As the mentally retarded individual approaches adolescence, emotional problems become more acute, for the child and for the parents. Now the need for increased independence and peer contact, male and female, becomes more important; physical changes bring on sexual urges. It will be easier for the parent to deal with such problems if he or she has learned how to deal with the intellectual problems. The same common sense, prudence, and supervision that parents of normal children must use are also useful in responding to the retarded adolescent. With such children, it all requires a lot more time and greater attention.

Social attitudes and public policy

For much of the first half of the twentieth century, neglect and denial dominated society's attitudes toward the mentally retarded, and there were few laws protecting their rights. Although many minority groups have secured active legislation to prevent discrimination in employment and other areas of life, this has not been the case with the physically and mentally handicapped in Britain. This does not mean that the rights of the mentally handicapped have not been advanced; they benefit from the same provisions in the Mental Health Acts as other psychiatrically disordered individuals. However, their rights beyond this are only reinforced by policy recommendations not legally enforceable standards. In the USA, pressure groups, such as the National Association for Retarded Citizens (NARC), have been slightly more successful in advancing the civil rights of the mentally retarded beyond the issues of accommodation and education.

In Britain there is a conflict of policies. On the one hand there is a movement towards 'care in the community', which for mentally retarded individuals means a push towards independent living and sheltered occupation for the moderate to severely handicapped and normal living and occupations for the mildly handicapped. On the other hand if employment and other rights are not in place, then the move to independence may be a move towards exploitation or failure to secure a reasonable standard of living, which are both progressively detrimental to the individual's self-esteem and life skill development. Independence in the community is intended to reinforce the social and occupational rehabilitation of psychiatric patients, countering the negative effects of institutionalisation. In the case of the mentally retarded, the process is one of habilitation not rehabilitation, where active learning is a necessary part. Failure in the support and monitoring systems provision leaves these individuals exposed to unfair market forces and vulnerable to abuse in many ways, without the additional protection of legislation backed by effective penalties. The need for such legislation to be in place is urgent. A 1989 white paper (HMSO, 1989) section 10.24 cites a study in which it was recommended that 90 per cent of people with a mental handicap currently in institutions would be capable of living in the community.

Adjustment as adults

Independent living

Beginning in the sixties, the establishment of small residential centres for groups of mentally retarded adults now provides one of the most helpful resources for the parents of the mentally retarded. Here, in locations close to the homes of the residents, it is possible to offer them a family atmosphere and some sense of independence with whatever level of supervision is necessary. The centres, at their best, offer three levels of care: supported living arrangements, in which residents work during the day in sheltered workshops and return to the centre in the evening; centres that provide community living facilities and 24-hour supervision; and for the severely retarded; small-scale nursing home type care.

Employment

Employment of mentally retarded adults is a controversial area. As mentioned above, without the legislation to prevent discrimination, the type of employment is restricted to low-grade jobs and the individuals may be open to exploitation. For the more severely handicapped this is less of an issue, as their forms of occupation are almost always sheltered and usually take place within a centre for the disorder. Although independence is encouraged in this setting, guidelines and monitoring schedules are more strictly adhered to compared with the circumstances of the more able, and therefore more independent, handicapped individual.

Marriage

In the past, stable relationships between male and female retarded adults were discouraged, marriage was forbidden, and involuntary sterilisation was practised. A more tolerant attitude now exists, with recognition given to the rights of retarded individuals to set up relationships consistent with their ability and sense of responsibility.

SUMMARY

Mental retardation affects one in every 100 live births. Some live only a few years after birth, and others die early in adulthood. The DSM-IV recognised four levels of retardation: mild, with IQs ranging from 50 to 70; moderate, with IQs of 35 to 49; severe, with IQs of 20 to 34; and profound, with IQs below 20.

There are two major types of mental retardation, separated on the basis of etiological factors. They are as follows:

1 Cultural/familial retardation, in which causation is judged to be a result of cultural deprivation during early upbringing, and the possibility of hereditary influences.

2 Organically related mental retardation. The cultural/familial type of retardation accounts for many of those with mild retardation. Organic factors are operative in 25 per cent of the mentally retarded population.

Organically caused mental retardation may result from genetic abnormalities, metabolic abnormalities, or environmental influences, such as birth injuries or brain injuries. The principal types of organic retardation are Down's syndrome, Klinefelter's syndrome, Turner's syndrome, phenylketonuria (PKU), Tay–Sachs disease, and congenital hypothyroidism. Foetal alcohol syndrome, related to alcohol consumption during pregnancy, causes the development of a small brain (microcephaly). Children of such pregnancies are often at least mildly retarded.

Although the rights of mentally retarded individuals have improved along with those of other psychiatrically disordered individuals, specific legislation protecting their employment rights in Britain and other countries has been limited to recommendations and guidelines and thus not enforceable. With a move towards care in the community for such individuals, the exposure to exploitation and abuse is a real possibility. Thus, although independence of lifestyle for the less severely handicapped is a desirable aim, a number of provisions need to be made before this is fully implemented.

FURTHER READING

Clements, J. 1987. *Severe Learning Disability and Psychological Handicap.* Wiley.

Dockrell, J. & McShane, J. 1992. *Children's Learning Difficulties.* Oxford: Blackwell.

Linsey, M. 1989. *Dictionary of Mental Handicap.* London: Routledge.

Remington, R. 1991. *The Challenge of Severe Mental Handicap.* Wiley.

Rourke, B. & Del Dotto, J. 1994. *Learning Disabilities: A Neuropsychological Perspective.* London: Sage.

Russell, O. 1985. *Current Reviews in Psychiatry: Mental Handicap.* Edinburgh: Churchill Livingstone.

17 Disorders Beginning in Infancy, Childhood or Adolescence

Sensitivity to the differences between childhood psychological disorders and adult psychological disorders is a fairly recent development. Early theories tended to view children as small adults and did not recognise the cognitive and emotional differences between the two age groups. The developmental processes of childhood and adolescence had not been studied closely; and it was therefore difficult to achieve an accurate understanding of what constituted normal and abnormal behaviour for children.

More recently, theorists have acknowledged these processes, and substantial progress has been made in the study of childhood disorders. This increased understanding has led to improved treatment facilities for children and to a more meaningful classification system for maladaptive behaviours. This is reflected in the difference between the DSM-I, published in 1952, and the DSM-IV, published in 1993, which is more comprehensive. The ICD-10 has separate sections for 'developmental disorders' and 'behavioural and emotional disorders of childhood and adolescence' whereas the DSM-IV has a single section for 'Disorders usually first diagnosed in infancy, childhood, or adolescence', which contains a wide selection of disorders including mental retardation (see chapter 16). In this chapter a selection of the main disorders covered in these sections from the manuals are described. The prevalence of these disorders helps to emphasise their growing importance for psychopathology. Around 22 per cent of pre-school children have significant behavioural difficulties and in adolescence there are still about 20 per cent of individuals needing psychological help.

Specific difficulties in studying childhood disorders

Three possible difficulties are considered here: the influence of adults, developmental considerations, and defining 'abnormal'.

The influence of adults

It is impossible to understand a child's behaviour without understanding the role of the important adult figures in the child's life. Children rarely seek help for their psychological problems on their own, so it is up to adults to act on behalf of the child. Parents, other relatives and school personnel are the obvious key people. Parents can be reluctant to seek help for their child because they may feel that any problems reflect upon their ability as parents. They often view the difficulty as a 'phase' though which the child is going, with the expectation that the child will soon 'outgrow' this stage. This is particularly true of the less impairing disorders such as fears, simple phobias, and social anxiety.

Sometimes, however, too much parental intervention can be a problem. By focusing undue or excessive attention on a difficulty, parents can exacerbate a problem that might be only transitory.

The start of school is frequently the time when a child's psychological problems are first recognised. One reason for this may be that behaviour that has been allowed at home cannot be tolerated in a school setting. An attention deficit hyperactivity disorder (to be discussed later) is an example of this type of problem.

Furthermore, teachers and other educational personnel are exposed to a broad range of children and can use this exposure, in addition to their training and experience, to assess abnormal behaviour.

Developmental considerations

The behaviour of children must be evaluated within the developmental context in which the behaviour occurs. Normal development involves the interaction of three areas of individual functioning: the cognitive–intellectual; interpersonal and emotional; and physical–motor areas. Some theorists consider the child to pass through stages of development. Although the concept of stages is debatable, there are certainly milestones of development that the child must both achieve and adapt to, in order to progress to the next and on to adulthood. It is therefore important to recognise and treat any developmental abnormalities as early as possible.

A complicating factor in this process is that children often develop at varying rates, and it is often difficult to differentiate between what is just slow development and what is disruptive or abnormal behaviour.

What is 'abnormal'?

In most cases, the differences between normal and abnormal behaviour are not as clearly defined in children as they are in adults. All children, at times, display maladaptive behaviour, such as bedwetting or temper tantrums. Such behaviour may be a result of specific stress and be a normal response to that stress for a child at a certain developmental stage. Most theorists in this area state that any behaviour should be viewed as a problem if it occurs repeatedly and interferes seriously with the child's, or another person's, functioning.

Classifying children's disorders

Until very recently, diagnosis and classification of the psychological disorders of children have been a woefully neglected and confused area of abnormal psychology. For example, the first *Diagnostic and Statistical Manual*, issued in 1952, listed only two categories of children's disorders: childhood schizophrenia and a catch-all type of category which was labelled 'adjustment reaction of childhood'.

Eighteen years later, with the publication of the DSM III, most clinicians still found the proposed system unreliable and inappropriate. Not until the 1987 revision, DSM IIIR, was a generally accepted classification system provided for children's disorders.

The DSM-IIIR classification of childhood disorders has been further revised for the DSM-IV. A major difference here is the moving of many of these disorders from axis II to axis I of the system, leaving only personality disorders on axis II. The DSM-IV lists ten sub-sections, one more than DSM-IIIR. In this chapter we will examine a selection of childhood disorders under five headings:

- **Attention deficit and disruption disorders**. This is the same heading and selection of disorders as appears in DSM-IV.
- **Attachment and separation anxiety disorders**. The main disorders to be described under this heading appear in DSM-IV under the rather uninformative heading of 'other disorders of infancy, childhood and adolescence'. To these has been added school phobia, which is not in the DSM section but is often referred to by parents seeking advice.
- **Elimination disorders**. As in the DSM-IV, these include enuresis and encopresis, which are common events in childhood but can be termed disorders if they persist, especially in an older child.
- **Communication disorders**. Here the examples taken from DSM-IV are stuttering and phonological disorder.
- **Pervasive developmental disorders**. Autism is the example given here, although reference is also made to Asperger's disorder (or syndrome) which has been listed for the first time in the fourth revision of the DSM.

In making the above selection, some disorders have not been covered including: learning, motor skills, feeding, and tic disorders. The inclusion of all of these would be beyond the scope of a book of this size; however, provision will be made in the suggested reading for further information on these disorders.

Attention-deficit and disruptive behaviour disorders

Under this heading DSM-IV has five subtypes of these disorders. Attention-deficit hyperactivity disorder, or ADHD for brevity, is listed as having a number of subtypes and also in the not otherwise specified form (NOS). Two other subtypes are described briefly in this chapter; these are conduct disorder and oppositional defiant disorder. The last subtype is disruptive disorder NOS, which with the many default categories of NOS behaviour in DSM-IV, has not been examined in this book. Each of these disorders have in common the child's disregard of the rights of others and can be indicators of future anti-social behaviour.

Attention deficit hyperactivity disorder (ADHD)

Behaviour of the ADHD child is troublesome to parents and teachers; because of its disruptive effect in the classroom, it is a frequently used diagnosis.

Symptomatology

The behaviour of children diagnosed as having attention-deficit hyperactivity disorder is characterised by impulsiveness, inattention, and physical hyperactivity that is inappropriate for the child's age. These highly distractible children have difficulty remaining still and will race from one activity to another. Nothing seems to hold their attention for very long. They frequently act with little thought of the consequences of their actions and are disruptive when engaged in social activities. In the classroom, they do not attend to directions, are frequently out of their seats, and will call out at inappropriate times. While these children often have average or above average intelligence, they are underachievers in school and often exhibit specific learning disabilities. Because of their poor scholastic achievement and social difficulties, ADHD children often display low self-esteem. In addition, their relationship with their parents is frequently strained by their inability to follow rules and their high level of motor activity.

ADHD is a frequent childhood problem to be referred to psychologists, which is probably a product of the extreme annoyance experienced by a parent coping with the disorder. Taylor in 1986 estimated the prevalence of the disorder among those attending clinics in the UK to be as low as 0.06 per cent, whereas in the USA it has been estimated at 1.2 per cent. Although there may be diagnostic variation, this cannot account for this large difference. As with most childhood disorders, the number of boys diagnosed as ADHD greatly exceeds the number of girls receiving this diagnosis.

Prognosis

An important issue in studying this disorder is whether or not it persists into adolescence and adulthood. The answer is far from conclusive. In one study (Hechtman and Weiss 1983), adolescent boys with ADHD and adolescent boys without ADHD were compared. The results suggested that the ADHD boys had a substantially higher rate of delinquent behaviour. The study also revealed, however, that most of the ADHD adolescents did not become habitual offenders as adults. Milder symptoms, such as impoverished interpersonal relationships and poor self-concept, did persist into adulthood.

Many researchers believe that when evaluating long-term prognosis, it is important to differentiate between subjects who exhibit pure ADHD symptoms and those who also display aggressive symptoms. A study by Satterfield (1982) initially demonstrated that hyperactive boys were 20 times more likely to be in trouble with the law than was a sample of 'normal' boys. He then divided the hyperactive group into two subgroups, one with aggressive symptoms and one without, and determined that the non-aggressive group had no more legal problems than did the normal population.

It can be generalised from these and other studies that while many ADHD children exhibit improvement in their behaviour as they enter late adolescence, the subgroup with aggressive behaviour in addition to ADHD symptoms will continue to have significant problems as teenagers and adults.

Causes of attention-deficit hyperactivity disorder

No one definitive cause of ADHD has been discovered. A recent study (Greenhill 1990), however, has provided evidence for a biological basis for ADHD. The study determined that ADHD subjects utilised 12 per cent less glucose, a source of fuel for the brain, than did normal subjects. The brain area most deprived of glucose was an area associated with attention and motor control, which are the central problems of ADHD children. The study does not clarify whether ADHD is caused by the glucose imbalance or whether other brain chemicals are also involved. However, animal studies have revealed abnormal dopamine metabolism when hyperactivity has been induced.

Other researchers have focused on the central nervous system as a factor in the development of this disorder. Zentall and Zentall (1983) have posited that ADHD children are underaroused, and without adequate motivation, they find it hard to focus attention. Coleman and Lewis (1988) have hypothesised that a genetic predisposition, along with environmental stress, may lead to ADHD.

Feingold (1977) ties attention-deficit hyperactivity disorder to the child's diet. He focuses particularly on food additives such as food colouring. Tartrazine is one additive which has been implicated, and additive-free diets have been used widely for targeting a number of such substances. Sugar has been a popular target for similar accusations, although this is difficult to assess or control in the diet of a child, given the availability and pressure on children to consume sugar-rich products.

Low levels of lead entering the body has been linked to hyperactivity. The evidence for this link is not certain. However, lowered IQ ratings in children have been associated with proximity to busy roads, which may be mediated by lead. Such a link may be tested by the uptake of lead-free petrol for cars.

Another possible factor is a genetic, or hereditary, basis. A study by Rie and Rie (1980) reported that the relatives of ADHD children have a higher rate of personality disorders than does the normal population. On this basis, they hypothesised a possible genetic basis for the disorder.

Other theories suggest that difficulties during pregnancy and delivery of these children may contribute to the development of ADHD.

Treatment

There are three main treatment approaches for ADHD. These are pharmacological, cognitive–behavioural, and dietary.

The use of medication. The use of drugs to treat the symptoms of ADHD is probably the most common form of treatment. The drugs most frequently used are central nervous stimulants such as Ritalin. These stimulants have the paradoxical effect of reducing motor activity and thereby improving a child's ability to focus and maintain attention. Studies (Ottenbacher and Cooper 1983) indicate that these drugs achieve their results without impairing the child's cognitive abilities. School performance is often improved. Not all ADHD children respond to medication; about 35 per cent of this population receive no benefits. Some researchers believe that those ADHD children who also exhibit symptoms of conduct disorder are also those who are least likely to benefit from medication.

There are many critics of the use of drug therapy. Gadow (1986) questions the long-term benefits of medication, especially when the underlying causes of the disorder are neglected. In most instances, when the medication is discontinued, the symptoms reappear. A troublesome result of medication is the physical side effects they produce, such as insomnia, slowed growth and impaired appetite, which are particularly attributed to the use of Ritalin and other stimulants. Furthermore, the long-range physical effects upon children of these medications have not been studied fully.

Behavioural and cognitive–behavioural therapies. The use of behaviour modification techniques has proven effective in the treatment of ADHD. These include token economy systems, which involve providing a clear explanation of expected behaviour to the child and then a tangible reward system for satisfactory performance. These systems have achieved positive results (Kazdin 1977) in the classroom, such as increasing concentration and decreasing disruptive behaviour. A problem with token economies, however, is that they do not adapt easily to other situations.

Cognitive–behavioural approaches also attempt to teach ADHD children the use of verbal self-instructions to increase attention span and decrease impulsive actions. The children are taught to stop before acting impulsively and to use learned self-instruction to monitor and modify their behaviour (Meichenbaum 1977); for example, saying to themselves before taking action, 'Wait; let me think about this for a minute'.

Many researchers report that the use of drug therapy, in conjunction with cognitive–behavioural techniques, is most effective in treating ADHD (Gittelman-Klein *et al.* 1980).

Dietary modifications. This type of treatment focuses on removing food additives and sugar from the child's diet. While anecdotal findings suggest some positive benefits from this type of diet, research studies have provided little support for a dietary method of treating ADHD (Milich 1986).

Conduct disorder

This diagnosis may be considered a more extreme type of disruptive disorder than ADHD and includes antisocial and occasionally delinquent behaviour. It must, however, be considered a separate disorder with its own aetiology.

Symptomatology

In defining conduct disorder the DSM-IV uses the description, 'a repetitive and persistent pattern of behaviour in which the basic rights of others, or major age-appropriate societal norms or rules are violated'. The characteristics include problems at home and in school, poor frustration tolerance, and the destruction or theft of the property of others. These children are often involved in physical fights and are at increased risk for developing early substance abuse and precocious sexual activity. It is not unusual for a conduct-disordered child to suffer from emotional problems, particularly depression.

It is estimated that about 3.5 per cent of children can be diagnosed as having conduct disorders. This figure rises to about nine per cent for adolescents (Gittelman *et al.* 1985). Again, males are much more likely to be diagnosed as having conduct disorders. The DSM-IV reports prevalence rate for males as being three times as high as those for females.

Prognosis

Conduct disorder before the age of 15 is a requirement for an adult diagnosis of antisocial personality disorder. In the absence of the latter diagnosis, conduct disorder can be diagnosed in adults. Unfortunately, it is often the case that conduct disorder in adolescence strongly predicts similar behaviour in adulthood. One study (Kazdin 1987) reports that children with conduct disorders, later on as adults, in many cases continue the pattern in criminal activities. As adults they have difficulty maintaining employment and frequently experience marital problems.

Another study reports that a child diagnosed as conduct-disordered is significantly more likely to become an alcoholic or to become an antisocial personality as he or she grows older than are children with other emotional problems (Rutter and Garmezz 1983).

Many theorists believe that the diagnosis of conduct disorder more accurately predicts impaired adult functioning than does any other factor or diagnosis, except for childhood psychosis.

Causes of conduct disorders

The family environment is viewed as an important factor in the development of conduct disorders. These families are often disrupted by marital problems, emotional instability, and inconsistent displays of affection and support. Discipline is often inappropriate and is characterised by particularly harsh or extremely lenient methods. Patterson (1986) addressed the matter of disciplining techniques in a study with conduct-disordered children. His results indicated that the parents of these children are inconsistent in punishing misbehaviour and fail to teach skills necessary for social and academic success.

There is some support for the role of genetic factors in the development of conduct disorders. Mednick (1986), in a comprehensive study of more than fourteen thousand adopted children, concluded that adopted children are more likely to have engaged in criminal behaviour if their biological parents were criminals, even if they had never lived with their biological parents.

Treatment

Since family influences are important in the development of this disorder, many treatment methods focus on treating the family unit. These include teaching effective parenting techniques and family therapy to reduce discord in the home. Given the problems and stresses in many of these families, this approach has had limited success.

Educating the conduct-disordered child in the use of cognitive–behavioural skills is another treatment approach. These skills include the identification of problems, the use of self-statements to modify behaviour, and the development of more appropriate behaviour. This method appears to be most effective with pre-adolescent children.

It often becomes necessary to remove the conduct-disordered child from the home and place him or her in a residential treatment setting. This is most common with adolescents. Many of these settings use behaviour management techniques and control the child's complete environment. The child must comply with rules and demonstrate appropriate behaviour in order to achieve specific privileges and rewards. It is also important, through the use of various methods such as role playing, to teach new ways of behaving and important social and academic skills.

Oppositional defiant disorder

This diagnosis is used for children who show negative, argumentative or hostile behaviour. Such children lose their tempers frequently, object to doing chores, and ignore rules. The behaviour is most frequently expressed in family settings, but may also be carried over to school or other settings involving authority figures. Occasionally, the child will be relatively subdued at home and act out his or her disruptive behaviour only elsewhere, usually in the classroom. One can surmise that such behaviour is a displacement of anger felt about a home problem that cannot be expressed there.

The diagnosis is a relatively new entry into the classification system for children's disorders and has met with some resistance from some clinicians who feel that giving a child a psychiatric diagnosis for such behaviour is an example of overkill which may handicap a child in later years.

Many parents of teenagers or pre-teens will recognise the behaviour described as a phase their children have 'gone through'. How long such a phase lasts depends principally upon how parents handle it and how rich a social and recreational life is available to the child. In the average stable family, it usually does not involve the more serious antisocial behaviour of the conduct-disordered child. Many clinicians consider it an unattractive and upsetting phase that is experienced by many children on their way to a normal maturity.

Attachment and separation anxiety disorders

The DSM-IV section 'other disorders of infancy, childhood and adolescence' includes separation anxiety disorder and reactive attachment disorder. These disorders are described in this section, and in addition, the common complaint of school phobia has been included. These disorders are less likely to have the serious prognostic implications for adult life than those of the previous section.

Separation anxiety disorder

Some degree of emotional pain at being separated from parents is shown by many children, especially in close-knit families in which the child has developed an emotionally dependent relationship with his or her parents (particularly the mother). However, when excessive anxiety, to the point of panic, is shown by the child, he or she is said to be suffering from a separation anxiety disorder. Extreme manifestations of the illness are shadowing the parent around the house, refusing to stay alone in a room at home, extreme difficulty in falling asleep without a parent being in the same room, and the appearance of physical symptoms when threat of separation from parents exists. Physical symptoms may range from stomach disorders to heart palpitations and dizziness. The DSM-IV estimates prevalence of the disorder as being around four per cent of children and young adolescents. Anderson and colleagues (1987) provide a more specific prevalency estimate of 3.5 per cent among pre-adolescent children. They also report it as much more common in girls than in boys.

Although the symptoms of separation anxiety can be controlled by drugs, they should rarely be used because of harmful side effects. Such behavioural therapies as modelling and systematic desensitisation are considered helpful psychotherapeutic approaches (see chapter 7).

School phobia

Although not separately classified as a childhood psychological disorder by the DSM-IV school phobias are a frequent symptom, early or late in the school years. Such phobic children refuse to go to school, develop illness to avoid going, hide instead of going to school, and even, at older ages, play truant and walk the streets until the hour arrives for going home.

School phobias may develop in children at three points in their development:

1 For the first one or two years after starting school, when the phobic reaction is likely to be an expression of separation anxiety.
2 Later on in school, in the fifth or sixth grade, when school achievement is increasingly emphasised. The phobia paradoxically occurs more frequently among children earning good grades, whose concern about maintaining those grades makes school an unpleasant place. But children who are earning failing grades may also become school phobic to avoid being in school situations where the embarrassment of failing or 'not knowing the answer' to teachers'

questions may be overwhelming for the child.

3 Soon after transfer to an upper school, when children are 13 or 14, are emotionally insecure, uncertain about fitting into new social groups or made fearful by the sterner demands of upper school teachers, a child may also become school phobic.

In the last case, the truancy must be distinguished and treated differently from the truancy of antisocial children.

The maxim suggesting that a thrown rider get right back on the horse is the best one to follow with school phobias. It is important to get school-phobic children back in regular attendance at almost any cost. It is frequently necessary for a parent, ignoring all complaints of physical ailments, to walk or drive the child to school and see him or her through the classroom door. A word or two, after hours, to a sympathetic teacher, can sometimes do wonders. Along the way, a parent can find a means of explaining to the child why going back to school is the 'only way'.

Reactive attachment disorder

This disorder is characterised by disturbed and developmentally inappropriate social relatedness to others beginning before the age of five. The DSM-IV relates this behaviour to 'grossly pathological' care which can take the form of a persistent disregard of the child's emotional needs, such as comfort, stimulation or affection, by the parent or carer. However, such pathological care does not necessarily lead to the disorder.

The disorder can take two forms:

- **The inhibited type**. In this, the child makes excessively inhibited, hypervigilant or ambivalent responses, and their behaviour to social interactions are inappropriate for their stage of development. The ambivalence may be expressed in resisting comfort or exhibiting approach avoidance behaviour.
- **Disinhibited type**. In the disinhibited type of reactive attachment disorder, the child is indiscriminate in their choice of attachment figures and social relatedness.

Reactive attachment disorder is stated as being uncommon in the DSM-IV, and must be distinguished from pervasive developmental disorders and mental retardation. When the precipitating factors are severe and long lasting, the disorder tends to continue after its initial onset before the age of five. An appropriately supportive environment can lead to improvement in the child's behaviour, or even recovery from the disorder.

Causes of attachment and separation anxiety disorders

Studies have looked at the effects of inappropriate early learning or conditioning in the production of these disorders. Last and colleagues (1987) have suggested that the parents of these children frequently suffer from similar symptoms or disorders themselves and could therefore act as poor role models for their children. In addition the child will sense fears in the parent which may come to be associated with specific events such as separation. Genetic influences cannot be ruled out of the process of fears being transmitted between generations.

Some parents may communicate to their children a belief that above-average achievement is necessary in order to be loved and accepted by them. Such children may react by being intensely self-critical and excessively anxious about their performance.

John Bowlby's work on attachment is of obvious relevance here. The child's difficulties in establishing a secure attachment to a parent or carer in the first two years of life and having this bond disrupted before the age of six or so can produce difficulties in relating to others, according to Bowlby, for life.

There is also some support for the theory that a child is born with characteristics that predispose him or her to develop certain behaviour. Such a predisposition interacts with familial and environmental factors to create such specific disorders.

Treatment of attachment and separation anxiety disorders

The general prognosis in these disorders is good and many of the difficulties improve with time and the normal demands of life, providing the child is neither abandoned to, nor overprotected from, these demands. In other cases treatment will be necessary in order to make progress possible. Drug therapy can alleviate many of the symptoms of these disorders, permitting change to be brought about in the child's behaviour by conditioning techniques. Sometimes a period of drug therapy can provide a platform for the less disturbed child to regain their securities, although the reliance on pharmacotherapy in such young individuals for extended periods cannot be recommended, and side-effects have also to be considered.

As indicated, the major treatment approaches tend to be behavioural, although family intervention should always be considered where possible and appropriate. Modelling, assertiveness training, relaxation and desensitisation techniques have all been useful in this context. Behavioural analysis of the parent–child interactions can be of great value in establishing how changes in behaviour may be encouraged by modifying responses and contingencies.

Elimination disorders

Elimination disorders are disorders where anxieties or other problems lead to the development of a specific symptom, although elimination disorder may also be part of a pattern of anxiety symptoms. The two forms of elimination disorders are enuresis, involuntary urinating (eg bedwetting), and encopresis, which is bowel movement in an inappropriate context (eg soiling the bed). Both disorders are embarrassing to the individual concerned.

Enuresis

Involuntary voiding of urine may occur in the daytime or at night. Occasional involuntary daytime voiding, often referred to in the family as 'an accident', is common soon after the child has been toilet trained, most often when the child is absorbed in a pleasant activity which the child chooses not to leave or during a time of emotional or otherwise exciting play.

Usually the term enuresis is taken to mean nocturnal (night-time) bedwetting. However, there are three subtypes of the disorder:

- **Nocturnal only**. The common type of the disorder usually involves voiding during the first third of the night, sometimes during dreaming.
- **Diurnal only**. The inappropriate passage of urine during waking hours affects females more often than males and often takes place in the early afternoon or at school, where the child may be preoccupied with activity or anxious about using the shared toilet.
- **Nocturnal and diurnal**. A combination of the above types. The DSM-IV specifies that for diagnosis of enuresis the child should be of an age where continence would be expected, usually five or six, and that voiding must occur at least twice a week for a period of three months or more.

Enuresis is more prevalent among boys (seven per cent), double that of girls at early ages (five or six years of age). It remains higher, at a diminishing rate, through young adulthood.

Causes of enuresis. A variety of psychological factors have been associated with enuresis. None is given special prominence. Among possible causes of enuresis are:

1 Regression on the birth of another child.
2 Emotional immaturity that causes a child to retain babyish habits.
3 Frequent emotional upheavals in the child's home life.
  However, one of the most common causes of nocturnal enuresis is
4 Fear and anxiety in the child, sometimes referred to as 'night-time terrors', which both precipitates voiding and prevents the child getting up in the night to use the toilet.

Treatment approaches to enuresis. Two notably successful treatment programmes are available to the parents of the enuretic child.

The first and simpler method, developed by Mowrer in 1938, requires a special bed pad which, when moistened by the child's urine, sets off a loud signal, waking the child and sending him or her off to the toilet.

The second method uses a form of aversive therapy and requires only a very short training period, usually less than a week. Azrin and colleagues (1974), who developed the programme, prefer an outside trainer rather than the parents to accomplish the programme. Before any training, the 'dry bed' programme is explained to the child and parents. In phase one, the child drinks a preferred beverage and lies down in his or her bed, and counts to 50; then, in an unhurried fashion, walks to the toilet and tries to urinate. After several such trials, in phase two, the child is given more to drink and told that he or she will be awakened hourly to urinate. Accidents result in the child being required to change the sheets and to begin training all over again. In the Azrin report on outcome, the group reports that all trained children were continent for at least six months after four nights of training.

In both behaviourally oriented therapies, a success rate of 90 per cent has been regularly reported.

Encopresis

A habit disorder that is much less common than enuresis, encopresis is said to exist if a child older than four years passes faeces in inappropriate places, including his or her clothing, at least once a month. The problem occurs in one per cent of five-year-olds, more frequently in boys than in girls.

When involuntary rather than deliberate (a determination not always easy to make), the cause may be constipation or a tendency to retain faecal matter. When it is deliberate, there is the possibility of oppositional or antisocial tendencies or even more severe pathology. Whether involuntary or deliberate, a physical examination is in order to identify any organic problem that may be present.

Inconsistent or overly rigid toilet training may contribute to development of this problem. Although there is a paucity of research on encopresis, Levine and Bakow (1975) do report a better than 50 per cent success rate when they combined medical and behavioural therapy. The DSM-IV states that the disorder rarely becomes chronic, although it may persist for a number of years.

Communication disorders

As a child leaves infancy, speech becomes increasingly important for social development. When this is impaired, limitations are placed on the child's social life and if this persists into the school years, their academic abilities may be affected. There are two principal speech disorders listed here, stuttering and phonological disorder.

Stuttering

Also occasionally referred to as stammering, stuttering is the most disturbing psychologically caused speech disorder. It is a marked disturbance in speech rhythm, resulting in frequent repetitions, prolongations or hesitations in producing sounds, syllables or words that occasionally may have special emotional connotations for the child. It may be less the word than the tension of the situation for the child.

Symptomatology. A characteristic blockage in stuttering is repetition of an initial consonant, which the child repeats perhaps five to ten times before being able to complete the word. Explosive sounds cause particular difficulty.

Many children three or four years of age experience transitory periods of stammering. In four or five per cent of children, the problem may persist for as long as six months. Usually, if parents and others scrupulously avoid calling the problem to the child's attention in any way, the speech dysrhythmia simply disappears as the child moves along in his or her development. About one per cent of all children continue to stutter into adolescence. The problem occurs four times more frequently in boys than in girls and seems to run in families.

Social and educational consequences of stuttering. When marked stuttering persists to school age, it can have substantial impact on the child's interactions with peers and interfere seriously with classroom performance. Other children respond quickly to another child's stuttering, often making fun of the child or mimicking the stutterer in ridicule, or sometimes simply avoiding the child because of his or her problem. Teachers sometimes respond to stutterers protectively by not calling on them in class. Either type of response, in play or in the classroom, intensifies the child's anxiety about speaking. Stuttering tends to feed upon the response it creates in others.

Causation in stuttering. There was a time when much was made of changing a child's handedness as a cause of stuttering and more sophisticated theorising about mixed cerebral dominance. However, there is little evidence for the involvement of cerebral dominance. The disorder runs in families in a manner which would suggest a polygenic inheritance pattern. Although no particular style of child rearing has been associated with stuttering, it may be that parents and others lead the child to associate speech hesitation with anxiety in a behavioural learning sense. Parents sometimes unwittingly show their alarm about transitory hesitations in the child's speaking and transmit their anxiety to the child. The child may sometimes be made anxious by demands for better enunciation or in other ways be made to feel insecure about speaking. Precise psychological causes of stuttering have not been identified, but most psychologists agree that anxiety that has been focused by the child on speaking is a possible component of the aetiology of stuttering. Once the problem begins, there are environmental stimuli to increase the child's awareness of a speech problem. It is that awareness of a speech problem that maintains and aggravates stuttering.

Phonological disorder

Phonological disorder, or dyslalia as it is also known, is a fairly common disorder, in which the child fails to develop appropriate speech sounds and is usually first recognised at the age of three or four, when speech becomes more exact. The disorder may be expressed in sound production, use, representation or organisation and has sometimes been referred to as 'baby-talk'. The usual form of the problem is the substitution of incorrect sounds for certain consonants.

The three that seem most troublesome are K, L and R, but other consonants may also be affected. When the child has trouble with S, he or she is said to lisp.

Phonological disorder can be seen as a cognitive problem in processing language, which would suggest a neurodevelopmental problem. The disorder is associated with neurological conditions such as cerebral palsy and mental retardation, as well as hearing difficulties. In less severe forms, and in the absence of any brain pathology, it is often found to be the result of laziness on the part of the child reinforced by the parents' lack of discrimination in responding to the child. In this, the child may not have had to correct their speech as the parent responds as readily to the incorrect form, inadvertently encouraging immaturity.

The problem is troublesome when the child begins to spend more time with other children, who will have difficulty understanding the child's speech (which difficulty may force the child to work harder at enunciation and thus cure the problem). However, such a reaction from other children may also have the effect of embarrassing the child and lead to shyness or retreat from normal play activities.

Parents can help by gently insisting on more clearly articulated speech; but the help of an outside speech therapist is usually a better way of dealing with the problem.

Pervasive developmental disorders

Pervasive developmental disorders include autism, Rett's disorder, childhood disintegrative disorder, Asperger's syndrome, and in the absence of one of these specific diagnoses, pervasive developmental disorder NOS.

In this section the disorder of autism will be described and reference will be made to a separate disorder, Asperger's syndrome, which has some similarities to autism.

Autistic disorder

First described by Leo Kanner in 1943 as Kanner's syndrome and later given the name infantile autism, from the term 'autism' used by Bleuler to describe the withdrawn aspects of schizophrenia. Over the years, reference to autism as 'childhood psychosis' has led to its confusion with childhood schizophrenia, from which it is quite distinct. This confusion was not helped when Hans Asperger (1944) described a similar, but less severe set of disabilities, which he termed 'autistic psychopathy', later to be known as Asperger's syndrome.

Depending on the strictness of diagnostic criteria, autism is a rare disorder affecting about four in ten thousand children, although this figure has risen rapidly in recent years, probably as a result of greater awareness of the disorder. It is characterised by onset before 30 months, difficulties in the development of language and other communication skills, social and interpersonal withdrawal, and inflexible thinking. The disorder commonly occurs with mental retardation, although there are many children in whom 'pure' autistic symptoms can be seen in the absence of other handicap. In contrast, Asperger's children tend to be intelligent, develop language early but use it oddly, and show the social withdrawal, poor non-verbal abilities and lack of empathy found in autism. Asperger's disorder is less common than autism and many professionals consider these individuals to be the more able children with autism.

A diagnosis of autism is particularly damning for parents as there is no cure and treatment success is very limited, especially with the most handicapped children. At least three quarters of the children with autism have further handicaps indicating a poor prognosis. However, there is a great deal of research interest in the disorder and advances have been made in the intensive behavioural treatment of autism. The cause, or causes, are as yet unspecified, although genetic and neurological factors are almost certainly paramount. As adults, autistic individuals tend to be of less research interest, the disabilities remain and they are usually socially isolated, living in hostels, specialist units or with relatives.

Leo Kanner (1971), who specialised in the treatment of autism, offers this plaintive portrait of an autistic child as he appeared in the doctor's office: '. . . he wandered aimlessly about for a few moments, then sat down, uttering unintelligible sounds, and abruptly lay down, smiling. Questions and requests, if reacted to at all, were repeated in echolalic fashion. Objects absorbed him, and he showed good attention in handling them. He seemed to regard people as unwelcome intruders. When a hand was held out before him so that he could not possibly ignore it, he played with it as if it were a detached object. He promptly noticed the wooden form boards and worked at them spontaneously, interestedly and skilfully.'

This section considers the symptomatology of autism, the present status of our understanding of its aetiology, and therapies used with the autistic child.

Symptomatology

Among autistic children, 70 per cent are mentally retarded, 40 per cent severely so, with IQs below 50. The DSM-IV lists a number of detailed diagnostic criteria for autism. Broadly speaking, before the age of three, the child must show deficits in one or more of the following:

1 Social interaction.
2 Language in social communication.
3 Symbolic or imaginative play.

There are a number of such features which help to distinguish autism and some of these are further described as follows.

Disturbance in relating to others. Autistic children avoid interaction with other children and adults. This is not simple shyness, but an attempt at total exclusion of people from the child's world. The preference of autistic children is for inanimate things, which seem to preoccupy them. One father describes his child's behaviour in this sentence: 'When Robert turned to you, he looked through you as if you were transparent.' (Kaufman, 1976).

A particularly disconcerting aspect of their behaviour is their unwillingness (perhaps inability) to maintain eye contact. Clinical speculation (Hutt and Ounstead, 1966) suggests that since eye contact is the essence of interaction with others, that is the one response that the autistic child must avoid at all costs.

The DSM-IV reports that some of the least handicapped children later on develop a sham and deceptive sociability; for example, they may run along with a group of other children, but they nevertheless remain socially apart from them.

Delayed language development. About 50 per cent of autistic children remain mute or use only three or four necessary phrases, which may later disappear. Of the remaining 50 per cent, very few use language normally, and many who have been taught language by painstaking behavioural reinforcement show little interest in using it, especially in its social use.

The use of speech oddities. Autistic children confuse pronouns, for example, using 'you' for 'I', which is rarely used. Parents must learn that repeating the parental question, 'Do you want your dinner?' means 'Yes, I do'. Autistics will use parts of an object or event for the whole, referring to dinner, for example, as milk. When they do use words or react to them, they will be very literal in their usage; for example, correcting the expression, 'Please put your coat on the chair,' to 'Lay your coat on the chair.' Their language may be metaphorical, such as the use of a prohibiting command learned from parents; for example, 'Don't crayon the walls,' as a universal expression for 'No' or 'Don't do that'. Emphasis in speech is inappropriate and other aspects of non-verbal behaviour are abnormal or infrequent.

Their thinking is inflexible and they find imaginative play difficult. As a result of this, they tend to take everything literally and are at a disadvantage with jokes involving double meanings. Along with stereotyped behaviour, mannerisms, poor speech and non-verbal behaviour, this inflexibility in seeing other points of view and therefore an inability to empathise with others isolates them and leaves them with little social skill or social awareness. As a consequence, older autistic individuals, who may then express an interest in friendship, lack the social skills or appropriate interests and behaviour to sustain friendships.

Idiosyncratic or odd responses to the environment. Autistic children develop peculiar attachments to inanimate objects, for example, carrying around a toy mechanised truck as a normal child might carry around a cuddly teddy bear, or exhaustively fingering a light switch.

Absence of delusions, hallucinations or loosened associations. Autism is distinguished from childhood schizophrenia, which it resembles in some of its surface characteristics, by the absence of such schizophrenic symptoms as delusions, hallucinations or incoherent associations.

Obsessive–compulsive behaviour. In addition to their inflexibility of thinking they are obsessed with maintaining sameness in the environment.

With surprising perceptual acuity and spatial memory, autistic children will order and reorder their world to maintain things as they were, frequently going into temper tantrums when changes caused by others are first noticed. The need for sameness may carry over to the food they choose to eat, the toys with which they play, and the arrangement of their room or bed. This obsessive behaviour can lead to tyranny over the parents, who may allow the child to progressively order their lives to avoid the violent tantrums that can accompany a change in routine. Cases have been found where parents have been house-bound for years, eating the same meals at the same time of day, instead of confronting the child at the outset. The child's fear of unpredictability also extends to chaotic environments (eg. a supermarket), sudden noise and other people.

Autistic individuals engage in mannerisms and stereotyped movements far more frequently than normal children. Included are tiptoeing around the room, sudden starts and stops, flapping of their arms, body rocking or whirling, head rolling, and playing with their fingers pulled up close to their eyes. Objects may be endlessly twirled or fingered in detail. Autistic children may play with pieces of a game but actually play no game.

Causative factors in autism

Although a great deal of research has been carried out into the cause or causes of autism, no specific aetiological factor has been implicated. However, the influences of genetic and organic factors are strongly implicated.

Early causal theories of autism

Kanner thought of autism as a biologically-based disorder, but commented on the cool intellectual way in which the parents he observed related to their children. This observation was picked up on by psychodynamically-oriented writers such as Bruno Bettelheim as evidence of the parents having a causal role in not responding to the child. Such theories have since been refuted by studies of the parents such as McAdoo and DeMeyer (1978). It is quite likely that such parental behaviour is a result, rather than a cause, of an unemotional child who avoids contact. Professionals such as Lorna Wing have commented on the fact that these early approaches merely added to the burden of very stressed parents, who had quite enough to cope with without being blamed for the condition.

Ferster (1961) sought to explain autistic behaviour in terms of maladaptive reinforcement of abnormal behaviour. Although this may account for some of the extremes of parental disruption, it is difficult to accept that such precise learning patterns could be replicated in such a coherent group of individuals.

Biological factors in the aetiology of autism

There is strong evidence that genetic and biological factors are involved in causing autism, although specific neurological sites or genes have proven elusive. Recent theories have combined biological and cognitive explanations.

Biological differences. Rosenhan and Seligman (1989) state that 30 per cent of autistic children late in life develop epileptic seizures. Such seizures are known to be biologically caused.

Autistic children show a higher rate of abnormal brain waves than do normal children; but not all autistic children do so. Campbell and colleagues (1975) indicate that almost one-third of autistics have abnormal serotonin levels. Serotonin is a neurotransmitter related to perception and memory. Both of these functions may be affected in autism.

Perinatal complications are more common in the histories of autistic children. This would indicate that any neurological damage resulting from birth injuries could produce autistic symptoms. There is a strong association between autism and established diseases, such as PKU and tuberous sclerosis, which would indicate again that damage to the central nervous system as a result of these disorders may precipitate autistic symptoms. Much of the evidence from neurological studies of autistic individuals indicates differing sites for neurological abnormalities. Taken as a whole, this evidence would tend to support the views of Wing (1981) that autism is not a single disorder but occurs in combination with many other developmental and organic disorders.

Genetic factors. Folstein and Rutter (1978) provide strong evidence for the existence of a genetic factor in autism. In a study of 21 pairs of twins, among whom at least one of the twins was autistic, 11 of the twin pairs were identical (with identical genes). Of those 11, four co-twins were also autistic; in addition, five co-twins showed abnormalities in speech and language usage (a problem in the autistic child). Among the non-identical twin pairs, none of the co-twins was autistic. The researchers report that autistic twins also experienced much more difficult births than the non-autistic twins. Folstein and Rutter concluded that in the development, genetic factors play an influential part.

Recent explanations of autism

Simon Baron-Cohen, Uta Frith and Alan Leslie have developed a cognitive–neurodevelopmental explanation of autistic deficits. This is based on a lack of, or retarded development of, a 'theory of mind'. This means that the autistic individual lacks 'a theory' of what another person is thinking and thus has difficulty in empathising and understanding pretence, and probably regards others as unpredictable entities to be avoided. These researchers use this basic deficit to explain many of the symptoms of autism. This has been challenged by Hobson (1990) who suggests emotional deficits to be central to the disorder. Frith and colleagues have suggested that a neurological abnormality leads to the deficit in thinking they describe as a failure of 'theory of mind'. They do not identify this abnormality with any precision but do give a coherent account of its influence on autistic behaviour.

Treatment of autism

Clearly, there is no cure for autism. The general picture is very bleak for the severely handicapped and, despite somewhat ambitious claims, the treatment of moderately handicapped autistic individuals is also limited. The overall prognosis is strongly influenced by certain factors. Response to treatment is correlated directly with the autistic child's measured IQ and with the presence of intelligible language before the age of five. Both those factors are, of course, related, and both indicate a less severe form of autism. What the relationship between those two factors and response to therapy means is that children with mild to moderate autism may respond to treatment. But even for those treatable autistic children, the course of treatment is prolonged (two to three years) and intense (in some programmes, as many as 40 hours a week). The cost of such programmes is out of the reach of many, perhaps most, families with autistic children. Such programmes are often experimental and supported by research grants rather than being part of health care. The success of such programmes may mean their wider implementation.

Specific treatments that have been tried in the case of autism are varied. The higher levels of serotonin have been reduced by the use of inhibiting drugs, and this has produced some behavioural improvement. Other drug treatments have been tried, such as neuroleptics, again with limited success. Megavitamin treatment has been reported to produce minimal improvement in behaviour.

Martha Walsh has pioneered what she calls 'holding therapy' in which the parent(s) of the child physically holds the child against their will, enforcing eye contact. This traumatic procedure, she claims, overcomes the social and emotional isolation of the autistic child and within this, she claims to be able to talk in terms of cure as opposed to treatment. Re-examining this procedure would seem to reveal it as the behavioural procedure of flooding; both procedures reach 'resolution' phases in which (in this case) the autistic child ceases to struggle and accepts human contact. This form of treatment does not appear in much of the literature, perhaps due to it having the same 'parent as the cause' theoretical approach. However, although there are no empirical studies of its effectiveness, the procedure as a form of behavioural therapy should be worthy of empirical research.

The most successful approach to autism is the behavioural approach. This treatment approach makes few causal assumptions and simply identifies abnormal behaviours and alters them by reinforcement. For the very handicapped, only basic behaviours can be encouraged and destructive or 'challenging' behaviours reduced. In cases suitable for the procedure, Lovaas (1987) reports on highly intensive behavioural treatments over long periods of time, which have resulted in quite impressive numbers of autistic children being able to enter mainstream education. As referred to above, these courses are strenuous and costly, but offer definite hope where little previously existed.

As with most disorders, effective treatment usually relies on establishing a clear cause and until a clear aetiology for autism is known, treatment as such will always be limited.

SUMMARY

Recognition of the presence of mental disorders among children and adolescents and research on those disorders has lagged behind the efforts at understanding adult mental disorder. The fourth edition of the DSM has provided a further expansion of the number of disorders beginning in childhood and now features them on axis I of the system. Three special difficulties exist in trying to understand the mental disorders of the young:

1 Attitudes of adults in the home who so significantly shape their children's behaviour and often deny the existence of problems.

2 Developmental considerations, which would cause behaviour considered normal at one age but which would be considered abnormal at a later age.

3 The great difficulty in delineating between the normal and the abnormal in children.

The DSM-IV now lists ten categories of children's disorders. This chapter has discussed the major categories under five headings.

ATTENTION DEFICIT AND DISRUPTIVE BEHAVIOUR DISORDERS. There are three such disruptive mental disorders. They are attention-deficit personality disorder (ADHD), which is characterised by impulsiveness, inattention and hyperactivity inappropriate for the age of the child; conduct disorders, which are like a more extreme form of ADHD and include antisocial and delinquent behaviour; and oppositional–defiant disorder, which is manifest in negative, argumentative or hostile behaviour.

ATTACHMENT AND SEPARATION ANXIETY DISORDERS. Three disorders are described here which are classified in DSM-IV as 'other disorders of infancy, childhood or adolescence'. They are: separation anxiety disorder, in which the child shows high levels of anxiety when separated from home and family; school phobia, which is not listed in the DSM-IV, where the child seeks out ways to avoid going to school for a number of reasons; and reactive attachment disorder where a child has an abnormal way of relating to others, which can be inhibited or disinhibited.

ELIMINATION DISORDERS. There are two forms of elimination disorder: enuresis is where there is involuntary voiding of the bladder; and encopresis where defecation takes place inappropriately. Both forms usually indicate anxiety in the child, but may occasionally be acts of defiance.

COMMUNICATION DISORDERS. Two examples are given here: stuttering and the consequent pressure put on individuals who suffer such hesitancy in speech; and phonological disorder where often childish speech patterns are carried on by the child as they develop beyond the age when these are acceptable.

PERVASIVE DEVELOPMENTAL DISORDERS. Two examples are described here. The major disorder of this category is autism, which begins early in life with a child who rejects human interaction, is obsessive, has poor communication abilities, abnormal behaviour and is prone to other disorders such as retardation. The similar, though less severe, disorder of Asperger's syndrome is also mentioned in the context of autism.

Aetiological factors mainly involve genetic and biological factors for the latter disorders. However, these initial disturbances are often combined with maladaptive learning experiences, which provide the main causes of some of the former disorders described.

FURTHER READING

Aarons, M. & Gittens, T. 1991. *The Handbook of Autism: A Guide for Parents & Professionals*. Routledge.

Baron-Cohen, S., Tager-Flusberg, H. & Cohen, D. 1994. *Understanding Other Minds: Perspectives from Autism*. Oxford University Press.

Frith, U. (ed). 1991. *Autism and Asperger Syndrome*. Cambridge University Press.

Graham, P. 1991. *Child Psychiatry* (2nd ed). Oxford University Press.

Harris, P. 1989. *Children and Emotion*. Oxford: Blackwell Publishers.

Herbert, M. 1991. *Clinical Child Psychology*. London: Wiley.

Howlin, P., Rutter, M. *et al.* 1987. *Treatment of Autistic Children*. London: Wiley.

Murray Parkes, C. & Stevenson-Hinde, J. 1993. *Attachment Across the Life Cycle*. Routledge.

Tantam, D. 1992. Characterising the Fundamental Social Handicap in Autism. *Acta Paedopsychiatrica*, 55: 83–91.

Webster-Stratton, C. & Herbert, M. 1994. *Troubled Families–Problem Children*. London: Wiley.

18 Legal Issues and Social Policy

Throughout this book, our focus has been the individual: the nature of his or her illness, possible causes of the illness, and treatment approaches. Other people, when they were considered at all, were those who were directly affected by the abnormal behaviour, particularly spouses and children. Here we shift our focus and consider larger societal issues: legal issues posed by abnormal behaviour and social policy questions related to it, what might be considered the conscience issues that the problems of mental illness create for all of us.

Those issues fall into three categories:

1 Legal issues – those concerning the questions, broadly put, what are the rights of patients, and how can they be protected, and, at the same time, how can we protect the entitlement of the general public to a safe and secure society in which to live?
2 The issue of prevention: what is society doing now to prevent mental illness, and what more must it do?
3 What organised efforts on behalf of the mentally ill exist? What is the current state of community care, and how can the public be drawn into these efforts?

In examining legal aspects of abnormal psychology, there are difficulties in accounting for the differences between the laws of different countries. Although there are basic similarities between countries with regard to what is seen as criminal, laws and legal procedures vary considerably. For example, even within mainland Britain the laws of England and Scotland vary somewhat.

Legal issues

Abnormal behaviour, as we have seen, occasionally causes an individual to violate society's norms, sometimes in ways that are criminal. When a mentally ill person commits a crime, especially a serious one, several questions have to be answered. Is the mental condition a defence against being punished? If the crime is unrelated to the illness, can the illness be used in mitigation? Is the individual competent to stand trial? When the threat of criminal or dangerous behaviour is present, how can an involuntary commitment be achieved in ways that are fair to all? How can treatment be provided to an unwilling mentally ill person?

Some of these questions have been considered by the courts of many countries, and by governments, their various committees and specially-commissioned bodies. The decisions handed down have not always pointed the way to practical and universally-accepted answers to the questions raised. Psychologists and psychiatrists are often drawn into attempts to find answers to these questions; their testimony in court is often required. In addition, they may be requested to join the specially commissioned bodies to report on the matters, or often to appear in court as 'expert witnesses' (forensic psychologists/psychiatrists).

The insanity plea

Placing an individual on trial for criminal behaviour is based on the belief that he or she chose to commit a crime knowingly and was therefore responsible for it and should be punished. Punishment for criminal behaviour has as its rationale the effect of deterring others who might be contemplating a crime; the hoped-for deterrent against the individual's future bad behaviour; and, when punishment involves incarceration, the guarantee that at least for the term of imprisonment, the individual will not commit a similar crime. Although in Britain the official first consideration is to the rehabilitation of offenders, the function of imprisonment is primarily one of protecting the public.

Criminal responsibility

There are criteria which must be fulfilled for a conviction in an English court. The English justice system insists on the offender having 'mens rea', committing the offence with guilty intent and of their own free will. A second criterion is that of 'actus reus'; there must be proof that the defendant actually carried out the illegal act. There are occasions when these criteria are not met.

There are a number of exemptions from criminal responsibility which can be accepted, these being: if the act was carried out by mistake or was an accident; if it was done under duress or of necessity; the perpetrator being incapable of intent due to drink, drugs or by virtue of being too young to understand (usually less than ten years old). The final exemptions are 'automatism', a confused state which can follow an epileptic seizure, and a plea of insanity. This final exemption is important to professionals in psychology and psychiatry, who may be involved in giving evidence to verify, often retrospectively, that the defendant did not know what they did was wrong.

There are a number of issues involved here, two of which are the practical considerations of the courts in allowing the plea of insanity. One is how such a plea can be supported and made acceptable. The other is how to deal with the defendant if such a plea is accepted.

Establishing a diagnosis of 'insanity'

The idea that a person should have committed a crime as a result of an irresistible impulse, due to insanity, is a concept recognised in a number of countries early in the nineteenth century. The example of an individual acting on a 'command from

God' compelling them to act as a result of insanity, providing this was verified by an expert, may then have been acceptable as a defence in a court.

The law recognising a defence plea of insanity was first established during the trial of McNaghten in England in 1843, introducing the idea that, by virtue of their mental state, the individual did not know what they were doing at the time of the act. This trial also accepted the testimony of experts, to establish the mental state of the defendant. Clearly, the decision as to whether a defendant was not guilty by reason of insanity is a legal decision, but the judgement as to whether the defendant was insane at the time of the act, should rightly lie with expert witnesses.

The forensic psychologist, and more often, the forensic psychiatrist, are most often called upon to make judgements as to whether an act was the product of 'mental disease or defect'. The term 'forensic' originates from the Latin *forensis*, referring to the Roman Forum, and therefore pertains to their role in court, although this meaning has been broadened in recent years. These expert judgements often have to be made retrospectively, working on the known circumstances of the act, the present state of the defendant, and estimates of their mental state at the time. There is room for disagreement here, which if not resolved by experts (an inquisitorial approach) may be battled out between defence and prosecution (an adversarial approach), with the final decision being a purely legal judgement.

For many years, a relationship between the mental state and the actual offence committed needed to be established. In England following the Mental Health Act of 1959, no such link was required. This act and its 1983 revision make reference to 'mental illness, arrested or incomplete development of the mind, psychopathic disorder and any other disorder or disability of the mind'. Psychopathic disorder is associated with criminal acts (see chapter 10), and is often used in the case of homicide. This disorder creates unique problems for the laws governing the mentally disordered offender. It has vague criteria and has been used as a catch-all term for persistent violent offenders. As it is listed as a personality disorder, the law assumes it can be treated. However, the 1975 Butler report recognised that psychopathic individuals were being imprisoned because they were not treatable and recommended that 'psychopathy' be removed from legal and diagnostic classifications.

Guilty but insane. Allowing insanity as a defence could be seen as being 'soft' on crime. Thus, there is the question of what should happen to the mentally abnormal offender. They may avoid a prison sentence, but the alternative has become less of a 'soft option'. A hospital order can be imposed by a court to have the offender detained in hospital for treatment. They can be detained until treated, or under a 'restriction order' until judged fit for discharge by a Mental Health Review Tribunal.

In Britain about 200 offenders are sent to maximum security hospitals, or Special Hospitals, such as Rampton. About 70 per cent of the patients in these hospitals have committed serious offences. During the 1970s a lack of facilities for such patients led to the setting up of Regional Secure Units (RSU). These units are headed by a forensic psychiatrist, but employ a number of clinical psychologists, and liaise closely with the courts and other agencies.

Diminished responsibility. The 1957 Homicide Act introduced the concept of diminished responsibility for murder. In this case, rather than removing the responsibility for the crime by reason of insanity, the responsibility is reduced, as is the sentence.

Prevalence of the insanity defence. Cases of violent crimes involving disturbed offenders usually make the newspaper headlines. This over-reporting of such cases greatly distorts their prevalence, which is in fact quite low. The defence is used in around two per cent of cases, and is successful in less than half of these. A notorious case illustrates the difficulty in securing this kind of conviction. Peter Sutcliffe, the 'Yorkshire Ripper', was declared insane by four psychiatrists; however, the jury decided this was not sufficient to diminish his responsibility for the crimes and sentenced him to prison for murder. Three years later, he was transferred to a Special Hospital for his illness.

Competency to stand trial

The mental health requirements for an individual to stand trial are rather similar to other medical requirements in being fairly minimal. This decision is independent of the defendant's mental state at the time of the offence and is restricted to the time of the trial only. It is easier to determine diagnosis as this is diagnosis at the time rather than a retrospective decision. It is recognised that mental state can change in the long period between the act and the trial, hence the independence of these decisions. The basic requirements for competency to stand trial are that the defendant can understand the charge and participate rationally in the court process. This has often been found to be acceptable even when the defendant has been suffering from a psychotic condition.

Competency for trial can be misused as a delaying tactic by the defence council. During the period between being declared unfit for the trial process and the trial, the defendant may be held in custody 'until deemed fit'. In some cases, until deemed fit is unlikely to ever occur, for example in the case of mental retardation. A further issue is that of the use of medication in order to achieve competency for trial. This is generally acceptable as it would be in routine medical situations.

Involuntary commitment

About seven per cent of patients in Britain are now compulsorily detained. There are a complex set of sections of the 1983 Mental Health Act which are numbered. When referring to compulsory commitment to psychiatric care, it is often the case that it is referred to by the section number of the Act relevant to that particular type of detainment. This has often been reduced to simply stating that the patient had been 'sectioned'. The main sections regarding compulsory admissions are as follows.

Section 2. Admission for assessment

For this, the patient must have a disorder and be detained for their own or others' safety. Treatment can also be carried out under this section which can last up to 28 days. An application for this section can be made by a social worker or the patient's nearest relative and medical recommendations from two doctors (one officially approved for this purpose).

The patient has rights of appeal over this process which must be made within the first 14 days. The Mental Health Review Tribunal receives these appeals and will make a decision. It is this tribunal that will receive further applications for the patient's release as being fit.

Section 3. Admission for treatment

This detention lasts up to 6 months and is subject to review at the end of that period and may be renewed. Decisions here have to be made with regard to the patient's ability to care for themselves when discharged.

Section 4. Emergency admission

This section is to avoid the delay possible when applying for a Section 2 order. This recommendation can be made by any one doctor and the application by a nearest relative or approved social worker. This only lasts 72 hours but can be converted to a Section 2 order.

Clearly in the case of these kinds of powers, especially when recommendations may come from relatives of the patient, the potential for abuse or infringement of civil rights is both possible and recognised. Safeguards are in place both to protect the patient from wrongful detention and inappropriate treatment, and if that treatment is necessary, the patient still has the right of appeal and the right to be treated with decency and in good conditions. Other sections of the Act cover more specific circumstances, for example Section 35 covers a court order to remand an accused person awaiting trial to hospital for a report.

Dangerousness

The Home Office and DHSS (1975) Committee on Mentally Abnormal Offenders published a definition of dangerousness including the words 'a propensity to cause serious physical injury or lasting psychological harm'. Difficulties arise with this concept as with the notion of psychopathy mentioned earlier. As with psychopathy, psychiatrists may be called upon to estimate an individual's likelihood of being a danger to others. Prior history of violence and mental state are primary considerations in making this judgement. However, there is a universal tendency for both courts and expert witnesses to overestimate a defendant's potential for harming others. This has often been represented as detaining three offenders for every one who could be dangerous to others. In practice, those actually found to commit harm on discharge is a smaller figure still. These figures are usually arrived at as a result of court decisions, and it is heartening to find that psychiatrists and psychologists are usually more accurate than this in their own predictions. Compulsory detention and treatment have always been viewed critically both by professionals who admit it is necessary, and the public, who often do not understand the complexity of such decisions. The image of wrongful detainment and treatment used in punitive ways portrayed in the film *One flew over the*

Cuckoo's Nest, can leave a lasting impression with the public, who may view occupational therapy as forced labour and also see aversion therapy and token economies in an equally negative way. A realistic view of the current situation is that the number of beds available in secure settings is so restricted as to make the discharge of those not suitable for life in the community a greater probability.

Prevention and community care

Compared with the focus on individuals who are so greatly in need of detention and treatment that this has to be imposed by law, prevention would seem a more logical area in which to invest. Currently a topic of heated debate, the concept of caring for existing patients in the community rather than behind the doors of an institution would also seem a sound proposition. However, there are great difficulties in funding, organising and implementing both of these.

Prevention

Clinical psychologists tend to be involved with assessing and treating patients who are already ill. Community psychiatric nurses carry out a similar function but tend to go out to visit the patients in the community in their own homes. Community services to prevent or reduce the factors in society which may precipitate or increase the chance of mental illness are wide-ranging. These involve specific approaches such as primary healthcare teams which may comprise GPs and health visitors in addition to community psychiatric nurses. Such a specific approach targets those at risk, hopefully avoiding the onset of a disorder, or relapse in the case of an existing condition. Less specific approaches would be aimed at the health of society as a whole and the general living conditions of those in it. For example, health education, which includes such mental health related information as stress management and other areas of health psychology. Promotion of the use of community services and education on mental disorders are also generally aimed at communities. These could be seen as 'levels' of prevention.

Levels of prevention

Different approaches of care and prevention are usually grouped into three levels, as follows:

Tertiary prevention. This is concerned with the prevention of relapse in patients who have been treated for a disorder and discharged as fit to live in the community. The processes involved here, or after-care programmes, involve such stepping stones as half-way houses, in which patients may adjust to the demands of the world outside the institution while still under some supervision.

Secondary prevention. This is carried out at the stage of early detection of problems before they become disorders, or outreach. The main aim here is to target those who are at risk or perhaps give early treatment or prophylactic treatment, not waiting for the patient to seek help.

Primary prevention. This examines the psychological disorders of whole communities rather than an individual's and, as mentioned earlier, involves a very disparate set of preventative approaches.

In many countries in the world, there has been a move towards tertiary prevention as an alternative to admitting patients into hospital settings. There has been a vast increase in the number of individuals receiving out-patient treatment with a consequent drop in the number of institutionalised patients. This has been a planned and deliberate move which has gone under the title of 'The Care in the Community Programme'.

Care in the community

During the first half of this century, long-stay psychiatric patients were kept in large psychiatric hospitals, which had routines and facilities very different from those experienced by those patients who returned to their own homes following a shorter episode of illness. Both sets of patients faced problems, although of a different nature.

Institutionalisation

Long-term institutionalisation was seen as necessary at this time, especially for patients with mental retardation or chronic schizophrenia. With the advent of neuroleptics in the 1950s, many patients who had been in hospital for years had their psychotic symptoms made manageable and were theoretically ready for discharge. However, they had become, to a greater or lesser degree, institutionalised, that is, their behaviour and expectations were adapted to institutional life and skills for living in the outside world were lacking. Some patients had little idea of how to cook a meal, let alone run a household, get a job and keep domestic accounts. Many patients had a great deal done for them and were suffering from learned helplessness, some others had become agoraphobic.

Discharge into the community

Patients who avoided institutionalisation by recovering relatively rapidly also faced problems. They were very vulnerable to the pressures of life, many suffering relapse, accident or suicide once outside the supervision and protection of the hospital ward. The stigma of having been a mental patient still creates difficulties in the form of social prejudice and discrimination in employment. This only added to the stresses faced by the ex-patient.

Scull's Dilemma

Clearly the discharge of institutionalised patients involved more and more intractable problems. The choice presented here would seem to be one of progressive institutionalisation or release into uncertainty and possible danger. This has been referred to as 'Scull's Dilemma', the basic argument of which is, 'if it is wrong to get patients out of institutions, and wrong to keep them in, what are we to do with them?' Scull is a sociologist, who is well-acquainted with the intricate problems of the psychiatric institution. In the 1960s, when this issue was becoming a wide concern, sociologists were beginning to comment on the plight of patients, and the 'anti-psychiatry movement' was being well received by a radical academic and youth movement. The combined pressures of the Scull's Dilemma issue, and criticism of the orthodox methods of psychiatry, led to the consideration of the mental patient's right to be treated as any other normal person, the therapeutic idea here being that if the patient was treated normally and in normal settings, they would behave in a more normal manner.

De-institutionalisation in Italy

At the time when radical movements were at their most popular, treating patients as normal individuals was attempted with severely psychotic patients living in special groups where psychiatrist and patient were virtually indistinguishable. Although the results of this type of 'experiment' were interesting, the practical outcomes were usually restricted to a few self-selecting and able patients in private care. Meanwhile, other work with similar motives was progressing within mainstream medicine, which had more practical ambitions. The concept of 'Care in the Community' was seen by many to be the answer to the problems outlined above. This minimised the time spent in institutions, provided services for after-care, 'halfway houses' and other support services enabling the planned discharge of vulnerable patients.

A more radical approach to community care began with the work of Franco Basaglia in Gorizia in the 1960s and Trieste in the 1970s. Basaglia's work within his own institution was supplemented by the political pressure he encouraged in others towards the aim of not only establishing care in the community but emptying the institutions altogether. Eventually this aim was represented in Italy by 'law 180' in 1978. This law prevented the admission of new patients and enforced the review of all existing patients with a view to discharge.

The problems that followed this radical move should have served as a warning to those interested parties in other countries. Rather than seeing this move as an opportunity to provide a long-lasting and effective network of services for these patients, and others, in the community, political interest lay in the vast savings to be made in terms of wages for psychiatrists and other staff, as well as from the sale of the many large institutions. The result was protest from these unemployed health professionals and the police who had the job of coping with the growing numbers of patients living on the streets as a result of inadequate provision of care in the community. This, and many anecdotal accounts of former patients dying of neglect, has led to something of a reversal of this policy. Politicians see such an outcome as a failure of theoretical aims, whereas professionals would see this as an example of the failure to adequately fund the implementation of these aims.

Community care in Britain and other countries

The move to keep patients supported in the community rather than in hospitals has been ongoing in a number of countries, including Britain and the USA, since the 1960s. This became a far more radical move, especially with regard to psychiatric patients during the 1980s. Although greater consideration to providing services *before* the mass discharge of patients has been taken, especially in the USA, some of the negative effects of the transition to the community are unarguably evident on the streets of both countries today. The growing number of homeless individuals on the streets of British cities contain an unknown proportion of psychiatrically-disturbed individuals receiving little care in the community. In addition, there have been a number of tragic incidents, reported in the media, where patients in the community have harmed themselves or others. Amongst these, the public were disturbed to see Ben Silcock climb into a compound of lions whilst refusing to take his medication, and after being refused admission to a hospital, another patient tragically stabbed an innocent passer by.

A further difficulty in implementing a move to care in the community has been referred to as the 'NIMBY' phenomenon, or 'not in my back yard'. Public sympathy for the plight of patients is clearly evident, but in many cases disappears if plans to open a half-way house for the mentally disturbed are suggested for their particular neighbourhood.

Although there have been many problems of underfunding and co-ordination in implementing care in the community for the mentally ill, the benefits following its potential success are still seen as worthy of the transition process. The *Audit Commission Report* (1986) in Britain identified weaknesses of co-ordination, planning and implementation of services for the long-term mentally ill. Two years later, the Griffiths Report, *Community Care – an Agenda for Action* made recommendations for the reorganisation of services for a wide range of disabled individuals. In this, social care was separated from health care, and made the responsibility of the local authorities, rather than the health authorities, who were responsible for health care.

The future of mental health care in the community

There have been a number of subsequent DHSS publications, which attempt to identify structures in the service provision for the community and the patterns of co-ordination between the voluntary and state-provided services.

In the USA, cases of hospital closure have been halted as it has been found that large hospitals still play a vital role in a community care scheme. In Britain the value of an efficient residential care unit, such as a large hospital, can be seen in the quality and organisation of the community-based services established from it. Clearly, a poorly equipped residential hospital would not provide the rehabilitation necessary for a patient to then be supported in the community. The presence of the central residential hospital services also leaves community based residential units free to respond to other local needs.

An important function of community-based services is the ease of access to treatment for patients. This ease of access is important for the patient to gain treatment quickly, but also in a manner which permits the patient to maintain family and other social support contacts.

There are many specific and general issues of concern when examining the future of community care. A number of these are addressed in the HMSO white paper (1989), *Caring for People: Community Care in the Next Decade and Beyond* in a very optimistic manner. There are worrying issues which also need to be resolved, not least of which is the tendency to use families of patients as replacements for residential care. This is difficult to avoid as it is a direct consequence of the move to the community. However, as it states in the white paper, the intention is to 'help people to lead, as far as possible, full and independent lives; not merely shifting their dependence from state to family.

SUMMARY

Since 1843 when the McNaghten case in England established insanity as a defence against a criminal charge, there have been a number of cases that have extended and clarified the rights if the mentally ill.

Forensic psychologists and psychiatrists have been involved in the courtroom process as expert witnesses. One of their main duties is to assess individuals to four differing ends.

They are asked to estimate if an individual was suffering a mental disease or defect at the time of a criminal act. This is difficult as the judgement is retrospective and has to he ascertained from various sources of information such as the details of the act itself. The Mental Health Act of 1959 and its 1983 revision clarified some aspects of this task, for example, not requiring a direct link between the illness and the act committed. Courts could, on this advice, consider the individual guilty but insane and have the option of compulsorily detaining them in a Special Hospital or Regional Secure Unit under the various sections of the Mental Health Act. Such an order may also impose treatment, providing various safeguards protecting the patient's rights are fulfilled.

Forensic psychiatrists may also be called upon to advise a court as to whether a defendant was sufficiently disturbed at the time of a homicide as to warrant a plea of diminished responsibility. Rather than removing the defendant from the normal penalties this may mean a lesser sentence or reduced charge.

Such expert witnesses may also be called upon to judge a defendant fit to stand trial. This is an easier judgement as it involves assessing the defendant's current state, and the requirements to stand trial are less demanding than those required for insanity at the time of the act.

Psychiatrists and psychologists may also be required to estimate the risk to the public of an individual, usually referred to as 'dangerousness'. There is a tendency to overestimate this risk and the issue becomes even more complex if a diagnosis of 'psychopathy' is involved.

In the last 30 years there has been a move away from keeping the chronically mentally ill in large institutions and maintaining them in the community. This process has had a chequered history involving the work of those who oppose the orthodox methods of psychiatry. The experience of emptying institutions in Italy led to difficulties for the discharged patients when the provision for them in the community was less than adequate. In

Britain this process is ongoing and although there are similar problems, a network of co-ordinated services has been established in the community.

The patient's best interests are thought to be served by their remaining in the community with easy access to treatment with more resources going to the prevention of mental illness and its relapse.

FURTHER READING

HMSO. 1989. *Caring for People: Community Care in the Next Decade and Beyond.* London: HMSO.

Jones, K. 1982. Scull's Dilemma. *British Journal of Psychiatry,* 141: 221–226.

Jones, K. & Poletti, A. 1985. Understanding the Italian Experience. *British Journal of Psychiatry,* 146: 341–347.

Newton, J. 1994. *Preventing Mental Illness in Practice.* London: Routledge.

Oliver, J. *et al.* 1995. *Quality of Life and Mental Health Services.* London: Routledge.

Pilling, S. 1991. *Rehabilitation and Community Care.* London: Routledge.

Prins, H. 1995. *Offenders, Deviants or Patients?* London: Routledge.

Williams, K. 1994. *A Textbook on Criminology* (2nd ed) London: Blackstone Press Ltd.

19 Research in Abnormal Psychology

Human behaviour, even behaviour that varies from the norm, is something everyone can claim some knowledge of. Based on their own experiences and the casual observations that everyday living provides, people have their own notions about the causes of human behaviour and, perhaps, especially about the causes of abnormal behaviour. As indicated in chapter 1, those notions are often off the mark. Casual observation is an unreliable way of arriving at an accurate knowledge of normal or abnormal behaviour.

Over the years, the study of abnormal behaviour has adopted the rigour and controls of scientific methodology. This chapter examines the characteristics, requirements, and vocabulary of scientific research. It then describes the research designs most frequently used in the study of abnormal behaviour. Along the way, it describes basic concepts of statistical analysis.

Research on abnormal behaviour is subject to limitations imposed by ethical considerations and practicality. An intervention introduced into an experiment in physics is a matter only of its usefulness in completing the experiment; an intervention in studying abnormal behaviour must take into account any negative effects on the subject and must consider also any unrelated and confounding reactions it might arouse in those whose behaviour is being studied, both control and experimental groups.

The goals of scientific study

There are three goals of scientific study: description, prediction and understanding.

Description

In pursuit of describing a psychological phenomenon, the basic activity of the scientist is *observation*. Scientific observation requires special training. To give scientific significance to their activities, scientists usually limit their observations to the areas of their training and competence. Astronomers observing people's behaviour would miss much of significance in the behaviour of those they were observing, and psychologists would be equally handicapped in observing the celestial bodies.

On the basis of trained observation, scientists are able to describe the phenomena under study in great detail. They group similar phenomena into named categories and seek to discover relationships among the categories. They use various means to clarify their observations and make them more precise. Psychologist-researchers make their observations many times (when they can), sometimes of the same person; at other times, by observing many people, frequently people in different settings. They use 'instruments', such as psychological tests, questionnaires, rating scales, or checklists. They magnify their observations by viewing them with the help of electroencephalograms, or brain scans. The use of such supplements to observation increases the reliability (dependability) and comparability of repeated observations.

To make their observations as precise as possible, scientists define variables under study in *operational terms* by quantifying them. They describe results of their research and make comparisons in statistical values, such as measures of central tendency (means, modes, or medians), and measures of scatter or distribution, such as the standard deviation. To identify relationships between variables, they use coefficients of correlation. They compare or contrast the quantitatively expressed results of their observations by a process called *statistical inference*. In that process, when they have taken two sets of measurements that differ from each other, they compute ratios to tell them whether or not such differences were a matter of chance variation or the result of 'true' differences between the two phenomena that had been measured.

Prediction

The result of scientific observation and statistical treatment of measured observations is a statement that may lead to the prediction of future behaviour or events, for example, a prediction of the likelihood of later development of criminal behaviour.

Prediction is usually based on a comparison with chance guessing. For example, correctly guessing heads or tails on one toss of a coin does not show much predictive power, but correctly predicting ten heads in a row would not seem to be a chance occurrence. In abnormal psychology, the occurrence of schizophrenia in members of one's close family would lead to a prediction of increased risk for the disorder in one's lifetime.

Understanding

This goal of scientific research means being able to identify a cause-and-effect relationship between two phenomena or events. Establishing a causal relationship requires that three conditions be met:

1 If one event is said to cause another, the two events must vary together, that is, for example, when one is absent, the other is absent; when one changes, the other changes.
2 The stated cause must exist or occur before the stated effect.

3 There must be no other reasonable alternative cause for the perceived relationship between the two events.

The third condition is usually the most difficult to establish. An example of an early failure to meet the condition occurred in early studies of the schizophrenias. Researchers hypothesised that there might be measurable differences in the blood or urine chemistry of schizophrenics and non-schizophrenics. To test their hypothesis, they compared blood and urine in two sample populations, a group of hospitalised schizophrenics and a non-hospitalised normal population. They did find notable differences, but those differences resulted from a *confounding effect:* the difference between a hospital diet and an uncontrolled diet. The differences had nothing to do with schizophrenia.

Confounding effects and internal validity

To draw a conclusion about causality, the two populations compared must differ significantly only in the variable under study. There cannot be more than one variable that could have caused the reported effect. When that condition has been established (and this is not always easy to accomplish), the study is said to have *internal validity.*

External validity

The external validity of judgements about causation may be established by the conclusion's 'generalisability', that is, does the same covariation occur when different groups are studied, in different situations, usually with different researchers? Establishing generalisability is possible only when the populations under study are representative of the universe they are designated to represent. If, for example, causal factors in the development of a conversion disorder (hysteria) are hypothesised only on the basis of patients seen in psychoanalytic therapy, drawn from the upper classes of a highly specific culture (Freud's practice), the sample on which the conclusion is based could hardly be considered representative of people generally, and the conclusions reached, without further research, might not be truly generalisable. Its *external validity* would therefore not have been established.

Sampling of subjects

The representativeness of a sample of individuals partaking in a study depends on the method of selection and the larger population from which they are to be selected. A truly random sample is usually impossible. You rarely have the opportunity to randomly select from the complete population that the study generalises its results to, for example, all known individuals with schizophrenia. Even if you could, one refusal to partake in the study would make the sample less than perfect. Thus sampling must be a compromise between the availability of participants, ethics and being able to select on a truly random basis. The last point tends to mitigate against another requirement of studies, that the sample size should also be large enough for the statistical procedures to be carried out.

Research designs

There are six basic ways in which psychologists attempt to study abnormal behaviour in a scientific way:

- descriptive studies
- correlational studies
- developmental or longitudinal studies
- experimental research designs
- analogue experiments
- experiments of nature.

Descriptive studies

The most basic design is one in which the researcher gathers data in such a way as to describe the phenomena under study. The researcher may want to describe the history of a phenomenon, that is, the events leading up to the present state of affairs, in which case the psychologist and associated psychiatrist, social worker, medical doctor, relatives and friends, gather or provide the information that goes into a case history. The researcher may wish to describe the current state of affairs, principally the prevalence and distribution of one variable, for example, psychiatric illness, in a large, described population, in which case the survey method is used.

Case history

The earliest psychiatric disorders were based on the life stories and current symptomatologies of patients in therapy. Such a history begins with the present and goes back to the earliest years that can be recalled by the patient or other knowledgeable persons. The patient's own interview account of those years is frequently supplemented by reports of friends, relatives, school and medical records, and whatever sources of information are available about the individual's life. Today, the case history usually includes a battery of psychological tests.

In a case history, the clinician or researcher may seek an understanding of a particular individual's illness, or, from a number of case histories of the same illness, the clinician may hope to understand the etiology of the disease itself and possible treatment approaches.

Kraepelin, principally on the basis of case studies, was able to provide the framework for a classification of psychiatric disorders that is still used today. Bleuler, in taking the case histories of a number of psychiatric patients, drew the conclusion that schizophrenia was not one but at least two quite different disorders.

Evaluation of the case history

As a scientific method, the case history has both advantages and serious limitations.

Advantages of the case study. The case history offers three advantages:

1 The case history provides a description in its natural setting as the individual experienced it. In this way, it has some advantage, for example, to the experiment which introduces many artificialities not characteristic of real life.
2 The case history explores types of human behaviour that, because of their rarity, cannot often be studied by other methodologies, for example, the survey or experiment.
3 The case history, thoughtfully considered, is a source of worthwhile hypotheses subject to future study and verification.

Disadvantages of the case study. There are three disadvantages of the case study:

1 Selectivity. The patient's recall of life experiences is not total. Memory, attitudes, the patient's expectations about what the therapist wants to hear, all may cause the patient to be highly selective in what he or she includes in the case history. The described experiences are retrospective and coloured by all that followed in the patient's life. The description of a childhood experience 20 years after it happened may not closely resemble the reality of the experience.
2 A life history is a one-time event. The experience of gathering it cannot be repeated in exactly the same way. A clinician's practice is ordinarily a varied one, embracing patients with a variety of illnesses. Repeatability (or replication) is ordinarily a requirement of the scientific method. It is a practical impossibility in using the case history. A clinician's practice cannot be drawn from a representative sample, not even a representative sample of all people suffering from the same psychiatric disorder. As has been described previously, Freud's patients, for example, were drawn from a very narrow cultural base: middle- and upper-class members of Viennese society during the Victorian period. Even when clinicians gather the case histories of many individuals, those histories would not be selected randomly. They are what might be called an 'opportunistic sample' whose characteristics were influenced more by the nature of the clinicians's practice than by random selection.
3 It is never possible, when constructing a case study, to exclude the possibility of other influential causes that have not been revealed by the patient. To find compelling evidence of causation, we would have to know that one event, the cause, was always followed by a described effect, and that when an effect was present, it had always been preceded by the hypothesised cause. But even many case histories may not provide that information.

The survey

A survey is essentially a large-scale quantification of occurrences, for example the number of people in inner London who are suffering from unipolar depression, or the psychiatric disorder that accounts for the largest number of hospital admissions. The information is gathered from public records or from brief front door or telephone interviews with a sample population. Information that can be gathered in that way is valuable in planning mental health resources, but it tells us very little about aetiology or effective treatment. However, it may lead to the development of hypotheses.

Characteristics of the survey. H. B. Murphy (1968) provides an example of survey results that led him to an hypothesis about an environmental condition that possibly contributed to the development of schizophrenia. He summarised the results of a number of surveys, tallying the cases of schizophrenia by socioeconomic class. Murphy reported a disproportionately high rate of schizophrenia in the lower socioeconomic classes throughout much of the Western world. From this, he hypothesised a relationship between schizophrenia and poverty. The limitation in the survey method is indicated in his statement that from the data the direction of a causal relationship could not be determined.

He states, 'It is not altogether clear what is the direction of causality in this relationship; whether the conditions of life of the lowest social classes are conducive to the development of schizophrenia, or schizophrenia leads to a decline in social class position.'

Survey research is of two types:

1 Reactive surveys, in which subjects are required to answer questions in an interview or on a printed questionnaire.
2 Non-reactive surveys, in which a survey uses available records, without seeking any reaction from members of the population being surveyed. The example cited above exemplifies a non-reactive survey. Non-reactive surveys use hospital, school, or other public records.

In survey research, a representative sample of the population to be described is critical. Without representativeness of sample, survey results are meaningless. Scientific surveys carefully describe procedures used to obtain a random sample. In addition, they set the size of the sample required for reliable descriptions in accordance with statistical formulae for such purposes. In reporting results, they usually indicate the margin of error in their results. The larger the sample, the smaller the probable error.

Advantages of the survey method. The principal advantages are as follows:

1 They provide useful information on the incidence (number of new cases by time period, for example, annually) and its prevalence (number of cases in a described population).

2 Since a survey usually relates the psychiatric disorder to other information about the individual, the information provided helps identify individuals at risk and increases our understanding of point of onset and future course of the illness.

3 Statistical relationships uncovered in a survey often suggest hypotheses as to possible aetiology.

4 Surveys are able to identify victims of particular disorders, not yet in therapy, who can be referred for treatment.

Disadvantages of the survey method. There are two possible hazards in survey research. They are as follows:

1 As the value of a survey is dependent totally upon the representativeness of the sample. To assure that participants have been selected randomly, researchers have to state in advance how they will be selected so that each member of the population under study will have an equal chance of being selected.

2 In reactive surveys, the social desirability of an answer sometimes causes the respondent to give that answer rather than one that more accurately states the facts. Many adult individuals, for instance, might not be willing to state that they frequently have nightmares or often feel depressed. The researcher can often phrase questions in too forceful a way. The problem with doing so is that it might produce too many inaccurate positive answers.

Correlational studies

In studying abnormal behaviour, psychologists often go beyond simple descriptive studies, such as those provided by the case history or the survey, to consider how two aspects of the individual's behaviour are related. They ask the question, for example, how do divorce and the presence of a psychological disorder correlate with each other? Or the psychologist may seek to test the hypothesis that poverty influences juvenile delinquency by recording delinquency rates and the prevalence of poverty in different sections of an urban community. He or she might then correlate those two prevalency levels. If the two correlated (varied together), one could say that poverty and delinquency were associated. On the basis of such a relationship, it would be premature to say that one caused the other.

The coefficient of correlation

The coefficient of correlation is the statistical ratio used to assess the degree to which two events or conditions vary together. A coefficient of correlation may be positive (expressed in a positive number) and thus indicate that as one variable increases (a factor under study), the second variable also increases. A perfect relationship, in which each variable increased to the same degree as the other, would be expressed by a coefficient of 1.00. Such a finding rarely, if ever, occurs when measuring human characteristics. The coefficient of correlation may be negative (expressed in a negative number), indicating that as one variable increases, the other decreases. For example, research reports that there is a negative correlation between time spent studying and failure rate. Some hard-working students may be disappointed to discover that the negative relationship is not minus 1.00, indicating a perfect negative relationship. Some students, despite hard work, still fail.

Correlation and causality

There is a temptation with covariation to believe a causal relation exists between the two variables. An important caveat is in order here: covariation does not demonstrate causality. Determining a causal relation demands more careful study than simply identifying a correlation between the two variables. For one thing, the time order between the two variables has to be considered. In Murphy's study (discussed above), the unanswered question was which came first, the poverty or the schizophrenia? Did the presence of the disorder lead to impoverishment, or did living in poverty increase the likelihood of schizophrenia?

Beyond that, the researcher must consider the possible presence of an independent third variable influencing or confounding both other variables. An example of this would be to note that there is a relationship between schizophrenia and the time of year one is born. Before making claims for astrology, it would be prudent to first examine a possible third variable, which in this case, turns out to be the increased incidence of birth complications leading to brain abnormalities and hence an increased risk of schizophrenia. That third variable is likely to be the independent, confounding cause of the correlation between the two variables. In studies of abnormal behaviour, non-causal correlations may often be found and conclusions drawn that ignore the presence of a third common influence on the two variables being studied.

Researchers attempt to eliminate the presence of a contaminating or confounding variable by matching the subjects under study in as many characteristics as possible. There are two problems with doing so: such matching sometimes results in the groups becoming so highly selected as to be unrepresentative. An example illustrating the danger, cited by Bootzin (1988) follows: 'Matching senior citizens and college students on general health would lead to a most unrepresentative group of senior citizens since so many of them have health problems as they age.'

Major advantages of the correlational method.

1 A principal advantage of the method is that it allows the study of naturally existing groups when ethical or practical considerations would rule out the more rigidly structured experimental approach (to be discussed later). For instance, in studies of depression, it might be desirable to discover the relationship between dreaming and intensity of depression. The correlational method lends itself readily to such a study without undue interference in the life of the patient. Both variables, extent of night-time dreaming and level of depression, are measurable. Obtaining a coefficient of correlation would at

least demonstrate covariation between the two and lend preliminary encouragement to further study of the possibility that there might be a causal relationship.

Study of such a relationship might, in the first instance, be performed on natural groups in the population, for example, college students. Researchers label such studies *correlational research design.*

2 The correlational method provides a precise measurement of the covariation of any two measurable variables. There are many occasions in abnormal psychology when obtaining such a measurement would be helpful.

3 Correlational studies are free of the artificiality of laboratory research.

Disadvantage of the correlational method. As indicated previously, the correlational study does not allow the research to draw any definitive conclusions about causal relations. To counterbalance that disadvantage, it does encourage (or discourage) further research efforts to test out a speculative hypothesis.

Developmental or longitudinal studies

Following the course of an individual's development over many years offers many advantages, the principal one of which is establishment of a time-order relationship between life-time crises and psychiatric disorder, for example, in phobic reaction or depression. The methodology is essentially a variation of the correlational design and is subject to its limitations. The sequence of events, one event following upon another, by itself does not establish a causal relationship.

Problems in longitudinal studies

The developmental method has certain problems. Attrition of the population under study is one of them. A beginning population of 100 subjects, over a period of five to ten years, because of the difficulty of maintaining contact with subjects, might become so small as to become unreliable for statistical analysis.

When the developmental study becomes a retrospective recall of early development on the part of the patient, it resembles the case study method. Such retrospective recall, as has previously been suggested, is highly unreliable.

A more scientific approach is to keep individuals under study through many years, preferably beginning at an early point in their life. Most often in abnormal psychology, a longitudinal study is likely to begin when the individual first comes to the attention of a clinic because of early signs of psychological difficulty. Such studies are called *high-risk research strategy.*

There have been a number of studies of children with conduct disorder in childhood, who on investigation later in life are found to have committed a number of criminal offences. Here the connection is overtly apparent and the continuity of such behaviour through life has led to the inclusion of conduct disorder in childhood as one of the criteria for anti-social personality disorder in adults.

Less intuitively obvious was the relationship established by John Bowlby, between separation from a significant carer before the age of six and delinquency in adolescence. However, this research was based on retrospective data and no information was gathered about such early separations in the general population.

The cross-sectional study

A variation of the longitudinal or developmental research design is the cross-sectional study. A typical longitudinal study follows the same group of children over several years. In a cross-sectional study, at a single point in the study, groups of children representing a cross section of different ages are compared to trace the development of certain behavioural patterns. A study conducted by Jersild and Holmes in 1975 is a good example of a cross-sectional study. They identified children's fears at three periods, from ages one to six, and then attempted to relate them to specific developmental changes.

This method is more economical of time and effort than the longitudinal study. It has, however, more value in tracing developmental sequences than in identifying aetiological factors in psychiatric disorders. But as with correlational studies, it tends to build (or weaken) hypotheses under consideration but does not crucially test them. Its weakness is that it ignores the effect of varying (and unmeasured) life experiences among the children studied, and it also tends to compare groups brought up in different historical periods, when health provision may have varied. Its rationale for doing so is the assumption that a large enough sample will 'wash out' individual differences.

The experimental research design

A well-conducted experiment is an ideal model of the scientific method. As with all experiments, experimental research in abnormal behaviour begins with a hypothesis. The experimenter's hypothesis usually relates to speculation about possible causes of a psychiatric disorder or possible therapies. It may have been formed on the basis of other research, tentative but suggestive. Such hypotheses grow out of findings in case studies or in correlational studies, sometimes even from surveys. Since the two most important goals of research in abnormal psychology are the identification of causes and the testing of hypotheses for effectiveness of treatment, hypotheses usually relate to those questions.

In all experimental research, there are two variables whose relationship is the prime concern of the researchers: an independent variable and a dependent variable. The independent variable is the hypothesised cause of a particular phenomenon; in abnormal psychology, for example, a specific form of therapy might be hypothesised as a cause of improvement in some psychiatric disorders, such as phobic disorder. In such cases, providing the therapy or not would be the independent variable.

A dependent variable is one where the occurrence is dependent on whether or not the independent variable preceded it. The most rudimentary experimental design may be illustrated as follows: pre-test – experimental treatment – post-test condition of the patient, usually with some objective measure of this. Here the experimental treatment is the independent variable; the dependent variable is any change between pre-test and post-test. The experimental treatment might be an hypothesised therapy, described in specific, preferably quantitative, terms. A requirement of a good experiment is that both variables be operationally defined, that is, there should be a quantified or measured statement of the independent and dependent variables.

The design described here is a single-subject design in which the before-and-after comparison serves as a control. There are relatively few conclusions. This design is often referred to as a quasi-experimental design, as it lacks a true control situation. In most experiments, two groups are set up, one known as the experimental group, the other as the control group. Such a two-group experiment may be diagrammed as follows:

Experimental group:
    Pre-test → Experimental treatment   → Post-test
Control group:
    Pre-test → No experimental treatment → Post-test

If subjects in such an experimental design have been assigned randomly to each group so that each group is representative of the population being studied, and if the number of subjects is large enough to produce statistically reliable results, the researchers may conclude that any difference between the experimental group and the control group in the post-test would have been caused by the experimental treatment.

We can best illustrate the various steps in experimental research by describing a well-controlled experiment reported by Vogel in the *Archives of General Psychiatry* (1975). Here are the steps the researchers took:

Step 1. Developing an hypothesis. The researchers were aware of two critical pieces of information. First, they knew that depressed patients who missed several nights of sleep, contrary to the way most of us would feel, felt less depressed. Secondly they knew that the medications regularly taken by the patients (which were helping their depression) tended, as a side effect, to reduce the amount of dreaming experienced by the individual. In a speculative leap, they hypothesised that reducing dream activity itself would lighten the depression. They then proceeded to test the hypothesis in an experiment.

Step 2. Operationally defining the independent variable. They described it as follows: in each of three weeks for three or four consecutive nights, the subjects in the experimental group were awakened whenever it was observed that they were dreaming, a fact that could be determined by observing the rapid eye movement (REM) that accompanies dreaming.

Step 3. Measuring the dependent variable. The dependent variable in this experiment was level of depression, which was measured on a rating scale before and after the experimental treatment (all the circumstances of which had been described to the subjects before the experiment was attempted).

Step 4. Setting up a control group. Other depressed patients, selected to represent different types of depression but matched on other critical variables, experienced the same nocturnal awakenings in the same fashion as the experimental subjects, except that they were awakened during non-dreaming periods (determined by the absence of rapid eye movement). Experimental and control groups, it may be confidently assumed, differed only in the amount of dreaming they did during a three-week period; only the presence of the independent variable distinguished the control and experimental groups.

Step 5. Drawing a conclusion. In an experiment, the critical finding is a statistically significant difference between the control and the experimental groups in their post-experimental treatment results. In the described experiment, only the endogenously depressed (a depression not caused by a life crisis) members of the experimental group showed a reduction in depressive symptoms. The authors concluded that dream deprivation lightens depressive symptoms in endogenously depressed patients; there was no evidence that it has a positive effect on other types of depression.

Special experimental controls

There are two special precautions researchers take in running an experiment. They use what has become known as an ABAB research design, which seeks to measure the effectiveness of an experimental treatment by showing that the individual's behaviour changes in opposite directions with alternating conditions of experimental treatment and no experimental treatment. A second requisite precaution is to eliminate both subject and experimenter bias by keeping both 'blind' as to which are the experimental subjects and which the controls.

The ABAB design. This design uses only one group of subjects. Instead of using an experimental and a control group, the experimenter sets up two experimental conditions, one with the experimental treatment and the other without. An ABAB research design can be diagrammed as follows:

Determination of baseline → Experimental treatment → Measurement of change
A return to baseline   → No treatment   → Measurement of change

Measurement of any change

If there is a change (alleviation of symptoms) after treatment, but no such change without treatment, the experimenter can conclude that the experimental treatment produced the change. Such a result when the experiment is a test of a specified therapy would cause experimenters to consider the treatment effective for the condition studied. The ABAB design is frequently called a reverse design experiment because any improvement in behaviour after Condition I (with treatment) is likely to be reversed after Condition II (without treatment).

Here is an example of an ABAB design testing the effectiveness of a specific drug. During Condition I, for a three-week period, a number of depressed patients are given daily doses of the drug to be tested. At the end of the three-week period, the presence of depressive symptoms is rated by neutral and uninformed observers. A period of three weeks is allowed to elapse, and patients' symptoms return to their previous level. For a second period of three weeks, each day the subjects are given a placebo (a useless substance with the same external features as the actual drug). Again, at the end of the period, the researchers assess the depressive symptoms. If there has been improvement in the depression after Condition I but not after Condition II, the experimenter can judge the drug to be an effective agent for relieving depressive symptoms.

The double-blind experiment

Frequently described as an elegant design, the double-blind experiment is typically used in all major drug therapy research. In the double-blind experiment, some subjects (the experimental group) are given dosages of the drug under study; others (the control group) are given a placebo. In the experiment, both subjects and experimenters are kept 'blind' as to which group individuals belong to until the experiment has been completed. Only after the results are completed are the control and experimental groups officially identified. The double-blind design eliminates any interfering effects from suggestibility in subjects and possible bias by experimenters.

Analogue experiments

An experimenter may attempt to reproduce in a group of normal subjects behaviour and feelings analogous to those that might be found in psychiatrically ill individuals. Although similar to the feelings and behaviour seen in psychopathology, for ethical reasons the reactions produced must be milder than in a real illness and only of short duration. The condition produced can be considered the independent variable, the effect of which on future reactions of the subjects (the dependent variable) is then carefully observed and measured.

Analogue experiments, although they have their limitations, are especially helpful in research on abnormal behaviour because it is infrequent that researchers have an opportunity of placing psychiatrically ill persons into the rigidities of an experimental design.

We describe here an example of a typical experiment conducted by Heroto and Seligman in 1975. Two groups of matched college students were initially given quite different experimental tasks. Each group was encouraged to feel that success in solving problems was a significant indicator of the individual's general ability. The control group first worked on a number of solvable problems; the experimental group faced a situation in which their failure was guaranteed. They were given a set of unsolvable problems on which to work. Naturally enough, they left that experience feeling at least discouraged, and probably mildly depressed. Their assigned task left them feeling helpless and ultimately hopeless. It was apparent that they felt quite differently about themselves than did the control group. The researchers set as the independent variable that difference in the feelings of the two groups. The experimental subjects were given self-feelings analogous to but much milder than the feelings of depressed patients.

The hypothesis the experimenters were testing was: depression is related to a learned form of helplessness. In the literature search leading to their hypothesis, they had learned that depressed patients did poorly in solving problems.

What was the experimenter's reasoning in testing their hypothesis? They began by defining the experimental condition (that is, having no success in solving problems under conditions of strong motivation) as 'learned helplessness'. If that state of mind caused the experimental group to do poorly on a second group of solvable problems when compared with the control group (which, indeed, turned out to be the case), they would therefore be showing signs of depression; that is, inadequate performance. With those findings, the experimenters could conclude that 'learned helplessness' causes depression.

Since the disappointment in not solving experimental problems was trivial when compared with the intense suffering faced by pathologically depressed patients, the results can be considered only suggestive, possibly confirmatory, of other similar findings. Standing alone, it could not be considered the definitive establishment of a causal relationship between learned helplessness and depression.

Evaluation of analogue experiments

Analogue experiments have one principal advantage and one almost completely neutralising disadvantage. They allow experimental conditions that could not ethically be imposed on psychiatric patients. To discourage and deflate the egos of a normal group of college students is allowable, especially if they were briefed about experimental conditions soon after the experiment, as they were.

Their disadvantage is that the analogous state produced by the experiment, of necessity, has to be a very pale version of the real illness. The basic criticism of the analogue experiment is that it is only analogous to, not identical to, real life. The intellectual leap from analogy to reality is a big one, and may not be justified in all cases.

Animal research offers a different kind of analogy, from animal to human. Although there are ethical and humane limits placed on animal research, many valuable insights into human behaviour have been suggested as a result of using animals analogously in experimental designs in ways that would not be acceptable if the subjects had been human.

Experiments of nature

Natural events, more often than not catastrophic events, such as floods, earthquakes, disastrous storms, and other such traumatic occurrences such as rape, aeroplane accidents, and military combat, provide occasions for studying certain types of abnormal behaviour. Such unfortunate events have, for example, provided the basis for describing the onset of post-traumatic stress disorder, its symptomatology, possible therapies, and even possible preventive measures. After such studies, the fully-developed diagnostic criteria for that disorder were first presented in DSMIII (1980).

With such traumatic events, the striking, extreme, and all-encompassing nature of the event allows the researcher to conclude that any significant departure from previous levels of functioning can legitimately be considered an effect of the trauma.

That conclusion is a broad, global one, which does not specify what it is about the occurrence that causes the breakdown. There are many possibilities: suddenness, immediate threat of death, guilt about personal survival while relatives and friends did not survive. These are all psychologically disruptive experiences, possibly causative of a psychiatric breakdown. Psychological opinion suggests that the specific causal agent varies with the nature of the trauma.

In a sense, such catastrophic events can be labelled experiments of nature. From that point of view, the catastrophe is the independent variable and, for example, post-traumatic stress disorder would be the dependent variable. The psychological literature provides many examples of how studying the effect of natural catastrophes or other trauma increases our understanding of abnormal behaviour. There have been many examples of traumatic events where individuals have been studied for long-term reactions such as the Gulf War and the Hillsborough football ground disaster in Sheffield.

Overall evaluation of the experimental design

Two strong advantages of the experimental design, particularly since it can be conducted in a laboratory setting, have been identified by Rosenhan and Seligman (1989). To quote those authors, the experiment 'is the foremost method for isolating causal elements'. The careful control built into the experiment, which largely limits the operation of extraneous variables, is the principal factor giving the experiment that capability.

The second advantage is its repeatability; almost all significant experiments are replicated, sometimes on different populations, to test the generalisability of the experiment's conclusions.

A crucial limiting disadvantage of the experiment is its artificiality. The circumstances of the experiment signal to the subjects that they are a 'special' group under study for scientific purposes. Attitudes created by that knowledge can cause them to behave in unnatural ways.

As society's interest in protecting the individual's rights increases, more limits are being placed on what can be done experimentally on humans and increasingly, as well, on animal subjects. For example, the early experiment performed by Watson and Rayner in 1920, in which they created a phobia in an eleven-month-old child whose parents unwisely allowed the research, would now be forbidden by law and by ethical considerations.

Because of an experiment's artificiality and the social and ethical limitations placed on certain types of experimentation, the study of abnormal behaviour will continue to use correlational studies and experiments of nature, and we will continue to look towards the case study as a source of promising hypotheses.

SUMMARY

Abnormal psychology shares the goals of all science. Those goals are description, prediction, and understanding. The basic activity of the scientist is observation refined by special training and aided by the use of instruments. The abnormal psychology examples of instrumentation are psychological tests, rating scales, electroencephalography.

Research in abnormal psychology is principally interested in describing the individual's symptoms, understanding the causes of mental disorders and learning what therapies are helpful.

The basic requirements for scientific research in abnormal psychology are the absence of 'confounding effects'; they are extraneous factors that may influence the results (internal validity); generalisability to other populations by other researchers (external validity) and the representativeness of the sample, that is the extent to which the sample is truly a good example of the population being described.

There are six basic research designs in abnormal psychology. They are descriptive studies, developmental or longitudinal studies, correlational studies, experiments, analogue experiments, and 'experiments' of nature.

DESCRIPTIVE STUDIES. There are two types. They are the case history and the survey.

DEVELOPMENTAL OR LONGITUDINAL STUDIES. Such studies may observe changing patterns of behaviour in individuals or, in the cross-sectional study, observe behaviour in a cross-section of different age groups.

CORRELATIONAL STUDIES. Here the researcher attempts to discover whether two types of behaviour tend to be associated, that is, do they tend to vary together? The measure of that variation is the coefficient of correlation.

THE EXPERIMENT. Here the observation takes place in a laboratory setting in which the experimenter is able to control all significant variables. The experiment is set up so that the researcher can evaluate the effect of the independent variable (the variable under his or her control) on the dependent variable, that factor which, it is hypothesised, is dependent on the influence of the independent variable, which in an experiment must always precede the dependent variable.

There are five quantifying steps in experimental research. They are developing a hypothesis; quantifying the independent variable, that is providing an operational definition of it; setting up a control group, that is, one free of any influence from the independent variable; measuring the dependent variable for the experimental and control groups; drawing a conclusion.

ANALOGUE EXPERIMENTS. Here the experimenter will attempt to reproduce in a group of normal subjects behaviour and feelings similar to those that might be found in psychiatrically ill individuals. The use of animal research also illustrates analogous experimentation.

EXPERIMENTS OF NATURE. Here the researcher studies the impact of some catastrophic natural occurrence (considered the independent variable) on the behaviour of the surviving victims of the disaster (the dependent variable).

Each of the six research designs has specific advantages and disadvantages. Ethical and practical considerations frequently determine which design will be chosen.

FURTHER READING

Banister, P. *et al.* 1994. *Qualitative Methods in Psychology: A Research Guide*. Open University Press.

Cronbach, L. 1990. *Essentials of Psychological Testing* (5th ed). HarperCollins.

Fava, M. & Rosenbaum, J. 1992. *Research Designs and Methods in Psychiatry.* Elsevier Science Publishers.

Graziano, A. & Raulin, M. 1993. *Research Methods*. HarperCollins.

Harris, P. 1986. *Designing and Reporting Experiments*. Open University Press.

Hart, E. & Bond, M. 1995. *Action Research for Health and Social Care: A Guide to Practice.* Open University Press.

Kazdin, A. 1992. *Research Design in Clinical Psychology* (2nd ed.). Allyn & Bacon.

20 The Diagnostic and Statistical Manual of Mental Disorders (DSM-IV)

Originally issued in 1952 by the American Psychiatric Association the most recently published manual, familiarly known as DSM-IV, was published in 1993.

It provides a means of classifying all recognised psychological disorders and evaluating their severity. The manual uses five axes to enable clinicians to be precise about diagnosis and evaluation, as follows:

Axis I lists all recognised clinical syndromes except the personality disorders and adult mental retardation which are classified under Axis II.

Axis III asks the clinician to identify any physical conditions that might affect psychological functioning and any treatment.

Axis IV asks the clinician to rate the severity of any psychological stressors in the individual's life.

Axis V asks the clinician to rate the highest level of the individual's earlier functioning.

(The listing of clinical syndromes is reprinted from DSM-IV with permission of the American Psychiatric Association.)

NOS = Not Otherwise Specified.

An x appearing in a diagnostic code indicates that a specific code number is required.

An ellipsis (. . .) is used in the names of certain disorders to indicate that the name of a specific mental disorder or general medical condition should be inserted when recording the name (eg. 293. 0 Delirium due to hypothyroidism) . . . . .

Numbers in parentheses are page numbers.

If criteria are currently met one of the following severity specifiers may be noted after the diagnosis:

Mild
Moderate
Severe

If criteria are no longer met one of the following specifiers may be noted:

In partial remission
In full remission
Prior history

Disorders Usually First
Disorders Usually First Diagnosed in Infancy, Childhood, or Adolescence (37)

MENTAL RETARDATION (39)

Note: These are coded on Axis II.

317	Mild Mental Retardation (41)
318.0	Moderate Mental Retardation (41)
318.1	Severe Mental Retardation (41)
318.2	Profound Mental Retardation (41)
319	Mental Retardation, Severity Unspecified (42)

LEARNING DISORDERS (46)

315.00	Reading Disorder (48)
315.1	Mathematics Disorder (50)
315.2	Disorder of Written Expression (51)
315.9	Learning Disorder NOS (53)

MOTOR SKILLS DISORDER

315.4	Developmental Coordination Disorder (53)

COMMUNICATION DISORDERS (55)

315.31	Expressive Language Disorder (55)
315.31	Mixed Receptive–Expressive Language Disorder (58)
315.39	Phonological Disorder (61)
307.0	Stuttering (63)
307.9	Communication Disorder NOS (65)

PERVASIVE DEVELOPMENTAL DISORDER (65)

299.00	Autistic Disorder (66)
299.80	Rett's Disorder (71)
299.10	Childhood Disintegrative Disorder (73)
299.80	Asperger's Disorder (75)
299.80	Pervasive Developmental Disorder NOS (77)

ATTENTION-DEFICIT AND DISRUPTIVE BEHAVIOUR DISORDERS (78)

314.xx	Attention-Deficit/ Hyperactivity Disorder (78)
.01	Combined Type
.00	Predominantly Inattentive Type
.01	Predominantly Hyperactive– Impulsive Type
314.9	Attention-Deficit/ Hyperactivity Disorder NOS (85)
312.8	Conduct Disorder (85) *Specify type:* Childhood-Onset Type/Adolescent-Onset Type
313.81	Oppositional Defiant Disorder (91)
312.9	Disruptive Behaviour Disorder NOS (94)

FEEDING AND EATING DISORDERS OF INFANCY OR EARLY CHILDHOOD (94)

307.52	Pica (95)
307.53	Rumination Disorder (96)
307.59	Feeding Disorder of Infancy or Early Childhood (98)

TIC DISORDERS (100)

307.23	Tourette's Disorder (101)
307.22	Chronic Motor or Vocal Tic Disorder (103)
307.21	Transient Tic Disorder (104) *Specify if:* Single Episode/ Recurrent
307.20	Tic Disorder NOS (105)

ELIMINATION DISORDERS (106)

—.—	Encopresis (106)
787.6	With Constipation and Overflow Incontinence
307.7	Without Constipation and Overflow Incontinence
307.6	Enuresis (Not Due to a General Medical Condition) (108)

Creutzfeldt–Jakob disease on Axis III) (150)

294.1   Dementia Due to . . . (*Indicate the General Medical Condition not listed above) (also code the general medical condition on Axis III*) (151)

—.—   Substance-Induced Persisting Dementia (*refer to Subtance-Related Disorders for subsance-specific codes*) (152)

—.—   Dementia Due to Multiple Etiologies (*code each of the specific etiologies*) (154)

294.8   Dementia NOS (155)

AMNESTIC DISORDERS (156)

294.0   Amnestic Disorder Due to . . . (*Indicate the General Medical Condition*) (158)
Specify if: Transient/Chronic

—.—   Substance-Induced Persisting Amnestic Disorder (*refer to Substance-Related Disorders for substance-specific codes*) (161)

294.8   Amnestic Disorder NOS (163)

OTHER COGNITIVE DISORDERS (163)

249.9   Cognitive Disorder NOS (163)

Mental Disorders Due to a General Medical Condition Not Elsewhere Classified (165)

293.89   Catatonic Disorder Due to . . . (*Indicate the General Medical Condition*) (169)

310.1   Personality Change Due to . . . (*Indicate the General Medical Condition*) (171)
Specify type: Labile Type Disinhibited Type/Aggressive Type/Apathetic Type/Paranoid Type/Other Type/Combined

Type/Unspecified Type

293.9   Mental Disorder NOS Due to . . . (*Indicate the General Medical Condition*) (174)

Substance-Related Disorders (175)

---

[a]*The following specifiers may be applied to Substance Dependence:*
With Physiological Dependence/
   Without Physiological Dependence
Early Full Remission/Early Partial
   Remission
Sustained Full Remission/ Sustained
   Partial Remission
On Agonist Therapy/In a Controlled
   Environment

The following specifiers apply to Substance-Induced Disorders as noted: [i]With Onset During Intoxication/[w]With Onset During Withdrawal

ALCOHOL-RELATED DISORDERS (194)

Alcohol Use Disorders

303.90   Alcohol Dependence[a] (195)
305.00   Alcohol Abuse (196)

Alcohol-Induced Disorders

303.00   Alcohol Intoxication (196)
291.8   Alcohol Withdrawal (197)
         Specify if: With Perceptual
         Disturbances
291.0   Alcohol Intoxication Delirium
         (129)
291.0   Alcohol Withdrawal Delirium
291.2   Alcohol-Induced Persisting
         Dementia (152)
291.1   Alcohol-Induced Persisting
         Amnestic Disorder (161)
291.x   Alcohol-Induced Psychotic
         Disorder (310)
    .5   With Delusions[i,w]
    .3   With Hallucinations[i,w]
291.8   Alcohol-Induced Mood

Disorder[L,W] (370)

291.8 Alcohol-Induced Anxiety Disorder[L,W] (439)

291.8 Alcohol-Induced Sexual Dysfunction[I] (519)

291.8 Alcohol-Induced Sleep Disorder[L,W] (601)

291.9 Alcohol-Related Disorder NOS (204)

AMPHETAMINE (OR AMPHETA-MINE-LIKE)-RELATED DISORDERS (204)

Amphetamine Use Disorders

304.40 Amphetamine Dependence[a] (206)

305.70 Amphetamine Abuse (206)

Amphetamine-Induced Disorders

292.89 Amphetamine Intoxication (207)
   Specify if: With Perceptual Disturbances

292.0 Amphetamine Withdrawal (208)

292.81 Amphetamine Intoxication Delirium (129)

292.xx Amphetamine-Induced Psychotic Disorder (310)
   .11 With Delusions[I]
   .12 With Hallucinations[I]

292.84 Amphetamine-Induced Mood Disorder[L,W] (370)

292.89 Amphetamine-Induced Anxiety Disorder[I] (439)

292.89 Amphetamine-Induced Sexual Dysfunction[I] (519)

292.89 Amphetamine-Induced Sleep Disorder[L,W] (601)

292.9 Amphetamine-Related Disorder NOS (211)

CAFFEINE-RELATED DISORDERS (212)

Caffeine-Induced Disorders

305.90 Caffeine Intoxication (212)

292.89 Caffeine-Induced Anxiety Disorder[I] (439)

292.89 Caffeine-Induced Sleep Disorder[I] (601)

292.9 Caffeine-Related Disorder NOS (215)

CANNABIS-RELATED DISORDERS (215)

Cannabis Use Disorders

304.30 Cannabis Dependence[a] (216)

305.20 Cannabis Abuse (217)

Cannabis-Induced Disorders

292.89 Cannabis Intoxication (217)
   Specify if: With Perceptual Disturbances

292.81 Cannabis Intoxication Delirium (129)

292.xx Cannabis-Induced Psychotic Disorder (310)
   .11 With Delusions[I]
   .12 With Hallucinations[I]

292.89 Cannabis-Induced Anxiety Disorder[I] (439)

292.9 Cannabis-Related Disorder NOS (221)

COCAINE-RELATED DISORDERS (221)

Cocaine Use Disorders

304.20 Cocaine Dependence[a] (222)

305.60 Cocaine Abuse (223)

Cocaine-Induced Disorders

292.89 Cocaine Intoxication (223)
   Specify if: With Perceptual Disturbances

292.0 Cocaine Withdrawal (225)

292.81 Cocaine Intoxication Delirium (129)

292.xx Cocaine-Induced Psychotic Disorder (310)
   .11 With Delusions[I]
   .12 With Hallucinations[I]

292.84 Cocaine-Induced Mood Disorder[L,W] (370)

292.89 Cocaine-Induced Anxiety
Disorder[I,W] (439)

292.89 Cocaine-Induced Sexual
Dysfunction[I] (519)

292.89 Cocaine-Induced Sleep
Disorder[I,W] (601)

292.9 Cocaine-Related Disorder NOS
(229)

**HALLUCINOGEN-RELATED
DISORDERS** (229)

Hallucinogen Use Disorders

304.50 Hallucinogen Dependence[a]
(230)

305.30 Hallucinogen Abuse (231)

Hallucinogen-Induced Disorders

292.89 Hallucinogen Intoxication
(232)

292.89 Hallucinogen Persisting
Perception Disorder
(Flashbacks) (233)

292.81 Hallucinogen Intoxication
Delirium (129)

292.xx Hallucinogen-Induced
Psychotic Disorder (310)

.11 With Delusions[I]

.12 With Hallucinations[I]

292.84 Hallucinogen-Induced Mood
Disorder[I] (370)

292.89 Hallucinogen-Induced
Anxiety Disorder[I] (439)

292.9 Hallucinogen-Related
Disorder NOS (236)

INHALANT-RELATED DISORDERS
(236)

Inhalant Use Disorders

304.60 Inhalant Dependence[a] (238)

305.90 Inhalant Abuse (238)

Inhalant-Induced Disorders

292.89 Inhalant Intoxication (239)

292.81 Inhalant Intoxication Delirium
(129)

292.82 Inhalant-Induced Persisting
Dementia (152)

292.xx Inhalant-Induced Psychotic
Disorder (310)

.11 With Delusions[I]

.12 With Hallucinations[I]

292.84 Inhalant-Induced Mood
Disorder[I] (370)

292.89 Inhalant-Induced Anxiety
Disorder(439)

292.9 Inhalant-Related Disorder
NOS (242)

NICOTINE-RELATED DISORDERS
(242)

Nicotine Use Disorder

305.10 Nicotine Dependence[a] (243)

Nicotine-Induced Disorder

292.0 Nicotine Withdrawal (244)

292.9 Nicotine-Related Disorder
NOS (247)

OPIOID-RELATED DISORDERS (247)

Opioid Use Disorders

304.00 Opioid Dependence[a] (248)

305.50 Opioid Abuse (249)

Opioid-Induced Disorders

292.89 Opioid Intoxication (249)
Specify if: With Perceptual
Disturbances

292.0 Opioid Withdrawal (250)

292.81 Opioid Intoxication Delirium
(129)

292.xx Opioid-Induced Psychotic
Disorder (310)

.11 With Delusions[I]

.12 With Hallucinations[I]

292.84 Opioid-Induced Mood
Disorder[I] (370)

292.89 Opioid-Induced Sexual
Dysfunction[I] (519)

292.89 Opioid-Induced Sleep
Disorder[I,W] (601)

292.9 Opioid-Related Disorder NOS
(255)

PHENCYCLIDINE (OR) PHENCYCLIDINE-LIKE RELATED DISORDERS (255)

Phencyclidine Use Disorders

304 .90 Phencyclidine Dependence[a] (256)

305.90 Phencyclidine Abuse (257)

Phencyclidine-Induced Disorders

292.89 Phencyclidine Intoxication (257)
Specify if: With Perceptual Disturbances

292.81 Phencyclidine Intoxication Delirium (129)

292.xx Phencyclidine-Induced Psychotic Disorder (310)
.11 With Delusions[1]
.12 With Hallucinations[1]

292.84 Phencyclidine-Induced Mood Disorder[1] (370)

292.89 Phencyclidine-Induced Anxiety Disorder[1] (439)

292.9 Phencyclidine-Related Disorder NOS (261)

SEDATIVE-, HYPNOTIC-, OR ANXIOLYTIC-RELATED DISORDERS (261)

Sedative, Hypnotic, or Anxiolytic Use Disorders

304.10 Sedative, Hypnotic, or Anxiolytic Dependence (262)

305.40 Sedative, Hypnotic, or Anxiolytic Abuse (263)

Sedative-, Hypnotic-, or Anxiolytic-Induced Disorders

292.89 Sedative, Hypnotic, or Anxiolytic Intoxication (263)

292.0 Sedative, Hypnotic, or Anxiolytic Withdrawal (264)
Specify if: With Perceptual Disturbances

292.81 Sedative, Hypnotic, or Anxiolytic Intoxication Delirium (129)

292.81 Sedative, Hypnotic, or Anxiolytic Withdrawal Delirium (129)

292.82 Sedative-, Hypnotic-, or Anxiolytic-Induced Persisting Dementia (152)

292.83 Sedative-, Hypnotic-, or Anxiolytic-Induced Persisting Amnestic Disorder (161)

292.xx Sedative-, Hypnotic-, or Anxiolytic-Induced Psychotic Disorder (310)
.11 With Delusions[I,W]
.12 With Hallucinations[I,W]

292.84 Sedative-, Hypnotic-, or Anxiolytic-Induced Disorder[I,W] (370)

292.89 Sedative-, Hypnotic-, or Anxiolytic-Induced Anxiety Disorder[W] (439)

292.89 Sedative-, Hypnotic-, or Anxiolytic-Induced Sexual Dysfunction[1] (519)

292.89 Sedative-, Hypnotic-, or Anxiolytic-Induced Sleep Disorder[I,W] (601)

292.9 Sedative-, Hypnotic-, or Anxiolytic-Related Disorder NOS (269)

POLYSUBSTANCE-RELATED DISORDER

304.80 Polysubstance Dependence[a] (270)

OTHER (OR UNKNOWN) SUBSTANCE-RELATED DISORDERS (270)

Other (or Unknown) Substance Use Disorders

304.90 Other (or Unknown) Substance Dependence[a] (176)

305.90 Other (or Unknown) Substance Abuse (182)

Other (or Unknown) Substance-Induced Disorders

292.89 Other (or Unknown) Substance Intoxication (183)
        Specify if: With Perceptual Disturbances

292.0   Other (or Unknown) Substance Withdrawal (184)
        Specify if: With Perceptual Disturbances

292.81 Other (or Unknown) Substance-Induced Delirium (129)

292.82 Other (or Unknown) Substance-Induced Persisting Dementia (152)

292.83 Other (or Unknown) Substance-Induced Persisting Amnestic Disorder (161)

292.xx Other (or Unknown) Substance-Induced Psychotic Disorder (310)
   .11 With Delusions[I, W]
   .12 With Hallucinations[I, W]

292.84 Other (or Unknown) Substance-Induced Mood Disorder[I,W] (370)

292.89 Other (or Unknown) Substance-Induced Anxiety Disorder[I, W] (439)

292.89 Other (or Unknown) Substance-Induced Sexual Dysfunction[I] (519)

292.89 Other (or Unknown) Substance-Induced Sleep Disorder[I,W] (601)

292.9   Other (or Unknown) Substance-Related Disorder NOS (272)

Schizophrenia and Other Psychotic Disorders (273)

295.xx Schizophrenia (274)
The following Classification of Longitudinal Course applies to all subtypes of Schizophrenia.

Episodic With Interepisode Residual Symptoms
        (*Specify if:* With Prominent Negative Symptoms)/Episodic with No Interepisode Residual Symptoms
Continuous (*specify if:* With Prominent Negative Symptoms)
Single Episode In Partial Remission
        (*Specify if:* With Prominent Negative Symptoms)/Single Episode In Full Remission
Other or Unspecified Pattern
   .30 Paranoid Type (287)
   .10 Disorganised Type (287)
   .20 Catatonic Type (288)
   .90 Undifferentiated Type (289)
   .60 Residual Type (289)

295.40 Schizophreniform Disorder (290)
        Specify if: Without Good Prognosis Features/With Good Prognostic Features

295.70 Schizoaffective Disorder (292)
        Specify Type: Bipolar Type/Depressive Type

297.1   Delusional Disorder (296)
        Specify Type: Erotomanic Type/Grandiose Type/Jealous Type/Persecutory Type/Somatic Type/Mixed Type/Unspecified Type

298.8   Brief Psychotic Disorder (302)
        Specify if: With Marked Stressor(s)/Without Marked Stressor(s)/With Postpartum Onset

297.3   Shared Psychotic Disorder (305)

293.xx Psychotic Disorder Due to . . . *[Indicate the General Medical Condition]* (306)
   .81 With Delusions
   .82 With Hallucinations
   —·— Substance-Induced Psychotic Disorder (refer to *Substance-*

Related Disorders for substance-specific codes) (310)
Specify if: With Onset During Intoxication/With Onset During Withdrawal
298.9 Psychotic Disorder NOS (315)

Mood Disorders (317)

Code current state of Major Depressive Disorder or Bipolar I Disorder in fifth digit:

1 = Mild
2 = Moderate
3 = Severe Without Psychotic Features
4 = Severe With Psychotic Features
   Specify: Mood-Congruent Psychotic Features/Mood-Incongruent Psychotic Features
5 = In Partial Remission
6 = In Full Remission
0 - Unspecified

The following specifiers apply (for current or most recent episode) to Mood Disorders as noted:

[a]Severity/Psychotic/ Remission Specifiers/[b]Chronic/[c]With Catatonic Features/[d]With Melancholic Features/[e]With Atypical Features/[f]With Postpartum Onset

The following specifiers apply to Mood Disorders as noted:

[g]With or Without Full Interepisode Recovery/[h]With Seasonal Pattern/[i]With Rapid Cycling

DEPRESSIVE DISORDERS

296.xx Major Depressive Disorder (339)
   .2x Single Episode[a,b,c,d,e,f]
   .3x Recurrent[a,b,c,d,e,f,g,h]
300.4 Dysthymic Disorder (345)
   Specify if: Early Onset/Late Onset
   Specify: With Atypical Features
311 Depressive Disorder NOS (350)

BIPOLAR DISORDERS

296.xx Bipolar I Disorder (350)
   .0x Single Manic Episode[a,c,f]
      Specify if: Mixed
   .40 Most Recent Episode Hypomanic[g,h,i]
   .4x Most Recent Episode Mixed[a,c,f,g,h,i]
   .6x Most Recent Episode Mixed[a,c,f,g,h,i]
   .5x Most Recent Episode Depressed[a,b,c,d,e,f,g,h,i]
   .7 Most Recent Episode Unspecified[g,h,i]
296.89 Bipolar II Disorder[a,b,c,d,e,f,g,h,i] (359)
   Specify (current or most recent episode):
   Hypomanic/Depressed
301.13 Cyclothymic Disorder (363)
296.80 Bipolar Disorder NOS (366)
293.83 Mood Disorder Due to . . . *[Indicate the General Medical Condition]* (366)
   Specify type: With Depressive Features With Major Depressive-Like Episode/With Manic Features/With Mixed Features
—.— Substance-Induced Mood Disorder *(refer to Substance Related Disorders for substance specific codes)* (370)
   Specify type: With Depressive Features With Manic Features With Mixed Features
   Specify if: With Onset During Intoxication/With Onset During Withdrawal
296.90 Mood Disorder NOS (375)

Anxiety Disorders (393)

300.01 Panic Disorder Without Agoraphobia (397)

300.21 Panic Disorder With Agoraphobia (397)

300.22 Agoraphobia Without History of Panic Disorder (403)

300.29 Specific Phobia (405)
Specify type: Animal Type/ Natural Environment Type/ Blood-Injection-Injury Type/Situational Type/Other Type

300.23 Social Phobia (411)
Specify if: Generalised

300.3 Obsessive-Compulsive Disorder (417)
Specify if: With Poor Insight

309.81 Posttraumatic Stress Disorder (424)
Specify if: Acute/Chronic
Specify if: With Delayed Onset

308.3 Acute Stress Disorder (429)

300.02 Generalised Anxiety Disorder (432)

293.89 Anxiety Disorder Due to . . . *[Indicate the General Medical Condition]* (436)
Specify if: With Generalised Anxiety/With Panic Attacks/With Obsessive-Compulsive Symptoms.

——.—— Substance-Induced Anxiety Disorder *(refer to Substance-Related Disorders for substance-specific codes)* (439)
Specify if: With Generalised Anxiety/With Panic Attacks/ With Obsessive-Compulsive Symptoms/With Phobic Symptoms
Specify if: With Onset During Intoxication/With Onset During Withdrawal

300.00 Anxiety Disorder NOS (444)

Somatoform Disorders (445)

300.81 Somatization Disorder (446)

300.81 Undifferentiated Somatoform Disorder (450)

300.11 Conversion Disorder (452)
Specify type: With Motor Symptom or Deficit/With Sensory Symptom or Deficit/ With Seizures or Convulsions/ With Mixed Presentation

307.xx Pain Disorder (458)

.80 Associated With Psychological Factors

.89 Associated With Both Psychological Factors and a General Medical Condition
Specify if: Acute/Chronic

300.7 Hypochondriasis (462)
Specify if: With Poor Insight

300.7 Body Dysmorphic Disorder (466)

300.81 Somatoform Disorder NOS (468)

Factitious Disorders (471)

300.xx Factitious Disorder (471)

.16 With Predominantly Psychological Signs and Symptoms

.19 With Predominantly Physical Signs and Symptoms

.19 With Combined Psychological and Physical Signs and Symptoms

300.19 Factitious Disorder NOS (475)

Dissociative Disorders (477)

300.12 Dissociative Amnesia (478)

300.13 Dissociative Fugue (481)

300.14 Dissociative Identity Disorder (484)

300.6 Depersonalisation Disorder (488)

300.15 Dissociative Disorder NOS (490)

Sexual and Gender Identity Disorders (493)

SEXUAL DYSFUNCTIONS (493)

The following specifiers apply to all primary Sexual Dysfunctions:

Lifelong Type/Acquired Type/ Generalised Type/Situational Type Due to Psychological Factors/Due to Combined Factors

Sexual Desire Disorders

302.71 Hypoactive Sexual Desire Disorder (496)

302.79 Sexual Aversion Disorder (499)

Sexual Arousal Disorders

302.72 Female Sexual Arousal Disorder (500)

302.72 Male Erectile Disorder (502)

Orgasmic Disorders

302.73 Female Orgasmic Disorder (505)

302.74 Male Orgasmic Disorder (507)

302.75 Premature Ejaculation (509)

Sexual Pain Disorders

302.76 Dyspareunia (Not Due to a General Medical Condition) (511)

306.51 Vaginismus (Not Due to a General Medical Condition) (513)

Sexual Dysfunction Due to a General Medical Condition (515)

625.8 Female Hypoactive Sexual Desire Disorder Due to . . . *[Indicate the General Medical Condition]* (515)

608.89 Male Hypoactive Sexual Desire Disorder Due to . . . *[Indicate the General Medical Condition]* (515)

607.84 Male Erectile Disorder Due to ... *[Indicate the General Medical Condition]* (515)

625.0 Female Dyspareunia Due to . . . *[Indicate the General Medical Condition]* (515)

608.89 Male Dyspareunia Due to . . . *[Indicate the General Medical Condition]* (515)

625.8 Other Female Sexual Dysfunction Due to . . . *[Indicate the General Medical Condition]* (515)

608.89 Other Male Sexual Dysfunction Due to . . . *[Indicate the General Medical Condition]* (515)

——.— Substance-Induced Sexual Dysfunction *(refer to Substance-Related Disorders for substance-specific codes)* (519)

Specify if: With Impaired Desire/With Impaired Arousal/ With Impaired Orgasm/With Sexual Pain

Specify if: With Onset During Intoxication

302.70 Sexual Dysfunction NOS (522)

PARAPHILIAS (522)

302.4 Exhibitionism (525)

302.81 Fetishism (526)

302.89 Frotteurism (527)

302.2 Pedophilia (527)

Specify if: Sexually Attracted to Males/Sexually Attracted to Females/Sexually Attracted to Both

Specify if: Limited to Incest

Specify type: Exclusive Type/Nonexclusive Type

302.83 Sexual Masochism (529)

302.84 Sexual Sadism (530)

302.3 Transvestic Fetishism (530)

Specify if: With Gender Dysphoria

302.82 Voyeurism (532)
302.9   Paraphilia NOS (532)

GENDER IDENTITY DISORDERS (532)

302.xx Gender Identity Disorder (532)
   .6   in Children
   .85   in Adolescents and Adults
     Specify if: Sexually Attracted
     to Males/Sexually Attracted to
     Females/Sexually Attracted to
     Both/Sexually Attracted to
     Neither
302.6   Gender Identity Disorder
     NOS (538)
302.9   Sexual Disorder NOS (538)

Eating Disorders (539)

307.1   Anorexia Nervosa (539)
     Specify type: Restricting Type;
     Binge-Eating/Purging Type
307.51 Bulimia Nervosa (545)
     Specify type: Purging
     Type/Nonpurging Type
307.50 Eating Disorder NOS (550)

Sleep Disorders (551)

PRIMARY SLEEP DISORDERS (553)
Dyssomnias (553)
307.42 Primary Insomnia (553)
307.44 Primary Hypersomnia (557)
     Specify if: Recurrent
347   Narcolepsy (562)
780.59 Breathing-Related Sleep
     Disorder (567)
307.45 Circadian Rhythm Sleep
     Disorder (573)
     Specify type: Delayed Sleep
     Phase Type/Jet Lag Type/Shift
     Work Type/Unspecified Type
307.47 Dyssomnia NOS (579)

Parasomnias (579)
307.47 Nightmare Disorder (580)
307.46 Sleep Terror Disorder (583)
307.46 Sleepwalking Disorder (587)
307.47 Parasomnia NOS (592)

SLEEP DISORDERS RELATED TO ANOTHER MENTAL DISORDER (592)
307.42 Insomnia Related to . . .
     [Indicate the Axis I or Axis II
     Disorder] (592)
307.44 Hypersomnia Related to . . .
     [Indicate the Axis I or Axis II
     Disorder] (592)

OTHER SLEEP DISORDERS
780.xx Sleep Disorder Due to . . .
     [Indicate the General Medical
     Condition] (597)
   .52 Insomnia Type
   .54 Hypersomnia Type
   .59 Parasomnia Type
   .59 Mixed Type
——.— Substance-Induced Sleep
     Disorder *(refer to Substance-*
     Related Disorders for sub-
     stance-specific codes) (601)
     Specify type: Insomnia Type/
     Hypersomnia Type/
     Parasomnia Type/Mixed Type
     Specify if: With Onset During
     Intoxication/With Onset
     During Withdrawal

Impulse-Control Disorders Not Elsewhere Classified (609)

312.34 Intermittent Explosive
     Disorder (609)
312.32 Kleptomania (612)
312.33 Pyromania (614)
312.31 Pathological Gambling (615)
312.39 Trichotillomania (618)
312.30 Impulse-Control Disorder
     NOS (621)

Adjustment Disorders (623)

309.xx Adjustment Disorder (623)
- .0 With Depressed Mood
- .24 With Anxiety
- .28 With Mixed Anxiety and Depressed Mood
- .3 With Disturbance of Conduct
- .4 With Mixed Disturbance of Emotions and Conduct Unspecified
- .9 Unspecified

Specify if: Acute/Chronic

Personality Disorders (629)

Note: These are coded on Axis II.

301.0 Paranoid Personality Disorder (634)
301.20 Schizoid Personality Disorder (638)
301.22 Schizotypal Personality Disorder (641)
301.7 Antisocial Personality Disorder (645)
301.83 Borderline Personality Disorder (650)
301.50 Histrionic Personality Disorder (655)
301.81 Narcissistic Personality Disorder (658)
301.82 Avoidant Personality Disorder (662)
301.6 Dependent Personality Disorder (665)
301.4 Obsessive-Compulsive Personality Disorder (669)
301.9 Personality Disorder NOS (673)

Other Conditions That May Be a Focus of Clinical Attention (675)

PSYCHOLOGICAL FACTORS AFFECTING MEDICAL CONDITION (675)

316 ... *[Specified Psychological Factor]* Affecting ... *[Indicate the General Medical Condition]* (675)
Choose name based on nature of factors:
Mental Disorder Affecting Medical Condition
Psychological Symptoms Affecting Medical Condition
Personality Traits or Coping Style Affecting Medical Condition
Maladaptive Health Behaviours Affecting Medical Condition
Stress-Related Physiological Response Affecting Medical Condition
Other or Unspecified Psychological Factors Affecting Medical Condition

MEDICATION-INDUCED MOVEMENT DISORDERS (678)

332.1 Neuroleptic-Induced Parkinsonism (679)
333.92 Neuroleptic Malignant Syndrome (679)
333.7 Neuroleptic-Induced Acute Dystonia (679)
333.99 Neuroleptic-Induced Acute Akathisia (679)
333.82 Neuroleptic-Induced Tardive Dyskinesia (679)
333.1 Medication-Induced Postural Tremor (680)
333.90 Medication-Induced Movement Disorder NOS (680)

OTHER MEDICATION-INDUCED DISORDER

995.2 Adverse Effects of

Medication NOS (680)

RELATIONAL PROBLEMS (680)

V61.9 Relational Problem Related to a Mental Disorder or General Medical Condition (681)

V61.20 Parent-Child Relational Problem (681)

V61.1 Partner Relational Problem (681)

V61.8 Sibling Relational Problem (681)

V62.81 Relational Problem NOS (681)

PROBLEMS RELATED TO ABUSE OR NEGLECT (682)

V61.21 Physical Abuse of Child (682)
(*code 995.5 if focus of attention is on victim*)

V61.21 Sexual Abuse of Child (682)
(*code 995.5 if focus of attention is on victim*)

V61.21 Neglect of Child (682)
(*code 995.5 if focus of attention is on victim*)

V61.1 Physical Abuse of Adult (682)
(*code 995.81 if focus of attention is on victim*)

V61.1 Sexual Abuse of Adult (682)
(*code 995.81 if focus of attention is on victim*)

ADDITIONAL CONDITIONS THAT MAY BE A FOCUS OF CLINICAL ATTENTION (683)

V15.81 Noncompliance With Treatment (683)

V65.2 Malingering (683)

V71.01 Adult Antisocial Behaviour (683)

V71.02 Child or Adolescent Antisocial Behaviour (684)

V62.89 Borderline Intellectual Functioning (684)
Note: *This is coded on Axis II.*

780.9 Age-Related Cognitive Decline (684)

V62.82 Bereavement (684)

V62.3 Academic Problem (685)

V62.2 Occupational Problem (685)

313.82 Identity Problem (685)

V62.89 Religious or Spiritual Problem (685)

V62.4 Acculturation Problem (685)

V62.89 Phase of Life Problem (685)

Additional Codes

300.9   Unspecified Mental Disorder (nonpsychotic) (687)

V71.09 No Diagnosis or Condition on Axis I (687)

799.9   Diagnosis or Condition Deferred on Axis I (687)

V71.09 No Diagnosis on Axis II (687)

799.9   Diagnosis Deferred on Axis II (687)

Multiaxial System

Axis I   Clinical Disorders
          Other Conditions That May Be a Focus of Clinical Attention

Axis II   Personality Disorders
          Mental Retardation

Axis III General Medical Conditions

Axis IV Psychosocial and Environmental Problems

Axis V   Global Assessment of Functioning

21 The International Classification of Mental and Behavioural Disorders (ICD-10)

The ICD system covers medical as well as psychiatric disorders, the latter forming chapter 5 of the manual. Although it was first issued around 100 years ago, mental disorders were first added in version 6 of the ICD system (World Health Organisation, 1948). The early versions were based on Kraepelin's original descriptions of these disorders.

The most recent edition of this system is the ICD-10 (WHO, 1992) which contains 458 categories of psychiatric disorder in its fifth chapter. It has been field tested in 39 countries and is expected to remain in use for around 20 years.

This chapter gives the main categories of the disorders listed in ICD-10 with their reference numbers.

List of Categories

F00–F09
Organic, including symptomatic, mental disorders

F00 Dementia in Alzheimer's disease
   F00.0 Dementia in Alzheimer's disease with early onset
   F00.1 Dementia in Alzheimer's disease with late onset
   F00.2 Dementia in Alzheimer's disease, atypical or mixed type
   F00.9 Dementia in Alzheimer's disease, unspecified

F01 Vascular dementia
   F01.0 Vascular dementia of acute onset
   F01.1 Multi-infarct dementia
   F01.2 Subcortical vascular dementia
   F01.3 Mixed cortical and subcortical vascular dementia
   F01.8 Other vascular dementia
   F01.9 Vascular dementia, unspecified

F02 Dementia in other diseases classified elsewhere
F02.0 Dementia in Pick's disease
F02.1 Dementia in Creutzfeldt–Jakob disease
F02.2 Dementia in Huntington's disease
F02.3 Dementia in Parkinson's disease
F02.4 Dementia in human immunodeficiency virus (HIV) disease
F02.8 Dementia in other specified diseases classified elsewhere

F03 Unspecified dementia

A fifth character may be added to specify dementia in F00–F03, as follows:
.x0 Without additional symptoms
.x1 Other symptoms, predominantly delusional
.x2 Other symptoms, predominantly hallucinatory
.x3 Other symptoms, predominantly depressive
.x4 Other mixed symtoms

F04 Organic amnesic syndrome, not induced by alcohol and other psychoactive substances

F05 Delirium, not induced by alcohol and other psychoactive substances
F05.0 Delirium, not superimposed on dementia, so described
F05.1 Delirium, superimposed on dementia
F05.8 Other delirium
F05.9 Delirium, unspecified

F06 Other mental disorders due to brain damage and dysfunction and to physical disease
F06.0 Organic hallucinosis
F06.1 Organic catatonic disorder
F06.2 Organic delusional (schizophrenia-like) disorder
F06.3 Organic mood (affective) disorders
.30 Organic manic disorder
.31 Organic bipolar disorder
.32 Organic depressive disorder
.33 Organic mixed affective disorder
F06.4 Organic anxiety disorder
F06.5 Organic dissociative disorder
F06.6 Organic emotionally labile (asthenic) disorder
F06.7 Mild cognitive disorder
F06.8 Other specified mental disorders due to brain damage and dysfunction and to physical disease.
F06.9 Unspecified mental disorder due to brain damage and dysfunction and to physical disease

F07 Personality and behavioural disorders due to brain disease, damage and dysfunction

F07.0 Organic personality disorder

F07.1 Post-encephalitic syndrome

F07.2 Post-concussional syndrome

F07.8 Other organic personality and behavioural disorders due to brain disease, damage and dysfunction

F07.9 Unspecified organic personality and behavioural disorder due to brain disease, damage and dysfunction

F09 Unspecified organic or symptomatic mental disorder

F10–F19
Mental and behavioural disorders due to psychoactive substance use

F10 - **Mental and behavioural disorders due to use of alcohol**

F11 - **Mental and behavioural disorders due to use of opioids**

F12 - **Mental and behavioural disorders due to use of cannabinoids**

F13 - **Mental and behavioural disorders due to use of sedatives or hypnotics**

F14 - **Mental and behavioural disorders due to use of cocaine**

F15 - **Mental and behavioural disorders due to use of other stimulants, including caffeine**

F16 - **Mental and behavioural disorders due to use of hallucinogens**

F17 - **Mental and behavioural disorders due to use of tobacco**

F18 - **Mental and behavioural disorders due to use of volatile solvents**

F19 - **Mental and behavioural disorders due to multiple drug use and use of other psychoactive substances**

Four- and five-character categories may be used to specify the clinical conditions, as follows:

F1x.0 Acute intoxication

.00 Uncomplicated

.01 With trauma or other bodily injury

.02 With other medical complications

.03 With delirium

.04 With perceptual distortions

.05 With coma

.06 With convulsions

.07 Pathological intoxication

F1x.1 Harmful use

F1x.2 Dependence syndrome

.20 Currently abstinent

.21 Currently abstinent, but in a protected environment

.22 Currently on a clinically supervised maintenance or replacement regime (controlled dependence)

.23 Currently abstinent, but receiving treatment with aversive or blocking drugs

.24 Currently using the substance (active dependence)

.25 Continuous use

.26 Episodic use (dipsomania)

F1x.3 Withdrawal state

.30 Uncomplicated

.31 Convulsions

F1x.4 Withdrawal state with delirium

.40 Without convulsions

.41 With convulsions

F1x.5 Psychotic disorder

.50 Schizophrenia-like

.51 Predominantly delusional

.52 Predominantly hallucinatory

.53 Predominantly polymorphic

.54 Predominalntly depressive symptoms

.55 Predominantly manic symptoms

.56 Mixed

F1x.6 Amnesic syndrome

F1x.7 Residual and late-onset psychotic disorder

.70 Flashbacks

.71 Personality or behaviour disorder

.72 Residual affective disorder

.73 Dementia

.74 Other persisting cognitive impairment

.75 Late-onset psychotic disorder

F1x.8 Other mental and behavioural disorders

F20–F29
Schizophrenia, schizotypal and delusional disorders

F20 Schizophrenia

F20.0 Paranoid schizophrenia

F20.1 Hebephrenic schizophrenia

F20.2 Catatonic schizophrenia

F20.3 Undifferentiated schizophrenia

F20.4 Post-schizophrenic depression
F20.5 Residual schizophrenia
F20.6 Simple schizophrenia
F20.8 Other schizophrenia
F20.9 Schizophrenia, unspecified

A fifth character may be used to classify course:

.x0 Continuous
.x1 Episodic with progressive deficit
.x2 Episodic with stable deficit
.x3 Episodic remittent
.x4 Incomplete remission
.x5 Complete remission
.x8 Other
.x9 Period of observation less than one year

F21 Schizotypal disorder

F22 Persistent delusional disorders

F22.0 Delusional disorder
F22.8 Other persistent delusional disorders
F22.9 Persistent delusional disorder, unspecified

F23 Acute and transient psychotic disorders

F23.0 Acute polymorphic psychotic disorder without symptoms of schizo-phrenia
F23.1 Acute polymorphic psychotic disorder with symptoms of schizo-phrenia
F23.2 Acute schizophrenia-like psychotic disorder
F23.3 Other acute predominantly delusional psychotic disorders
F23.8 Other actue and transient psychotic disorders
F23.9 Acute and transient psychotic disorders unspecified

A fifth character may be used to identify the presence or absence of associated acute stress

.x0 Without associated acute stress
.x1 With associated acute stress

F24 Induced delusional disorder

F25 Schizoaffective disorders

F25.0 Schizoaffective disorder, manic type
F25.1 Schizoaffective disorder, depressive type
F25.2 Schizoaffective disorder, mixed type
F25.8 Other schizoaffective disorders
F25.9 Schizoaffective disorder, unspecified

F28 Other non-organic psychotic disorders

F29 Unspecified non-organic psychosis

F30–F39
Mood (affective) disorders

F30 Manic episode
F30.0 Hypomania
F30.1 Mania without psychotic symptoms
F30.2 Mania with psychotic symptoms
F30.8 Other manic episodes
F30.9 Manic episode, unspecified

F31 Bipolar affective disorder
F31.0 Bipolar affective disorder, current episode hypomanic
F31.1 Bipolar affective disorder, current episode manic without psychotic symptoms
F31.2 Bipolar affective disorder, current episode manic with psychotic symptoms.
F31.3 Bipolar affective disorder, current episode mild or moderate depression
  .30 Without somatic symptoms
  .31 With somatic symptoms
F31.4 Bipolar affective disorder, current episode severe depression without psychotic symptoms
F31.5 Bipolar affective disorder, current episode severe depression with psychotic symptoms
F31.6 Bipolar affective disorder, current episode mixed
F31.7 Bipolar affective disorder, currently in remission
F31.8 Other bipolar affective disorders
F31.9 Bipolar affective disorder, unspecified

F32 Depressive episode
F32.0 Mild depressive episode
  .00 Without somatic symptoms
  .01 With somatic symptoms
F32.1 Moderate depressive episode
  .10 Without somatic symptoms
  .11 With somatic symptoms
F32.2 Severe depressive episode without psychotic symptoms
F32.3 Severe depressive episode with psychotic symptoms
F32.8 Other depressive episodes
F32.9 Depressive episode, unspecified

F33 Recurrent depressive disorder
F33.0 Recurrent depressive disorder, current episode mild
  .00 Without somatic symptoms
  .01 With somatic symptoms

F33.1 Recurrent depressive disorder, current episode moderate
.10 Without somatic symptoms
.11 With somatic symptoms
F33.2 Recurrent depressive disorder, current episode severe without psychotic symptoms
F33.3 Recurrent depressive disorder, current episode severe with psychotic symptoms
F33.4 Recurrent depressive disorder, currently in remission
F33.8 Other recurrent depressive disorders
F33.9 Recurrent depressive disorder, unspecified

F34 Persistent mood (affective) disorders
F34.0 Cyclothymia
F34.1 Dysthymia
F34.8 Other persistent mood (affective) disorders
F34.9 Persistent mood (affective) disorder, unspecified

F38 Other mood (affective) disorders
F38.0 Other single mood (affective) disorders
.00 Mixed affective episode
F38.1 Other recurrent mood (affective) disorders
.10 Recurrent brief depressive disorder
F38.8 Other specified mood (affective) disorder
F39 Unspecified mood (affective) disorder

F40–F48
Neurotic, stress-related and somatoform disorders

F40 Phobic anxiety disorders
F40.0 Agoraphobia
.00 Without panic disorder
.01 With panic disorder
F40.1 Social phobias
F40.2 Specific (isolated) phobias
F40.8 Other phobic anxiety disorders
F40.9 Phobic anxiety disorder, unspecified

F41 Other anxiety disorders
F41.0 Panic disorder (episodic paroxysmal anxiety)
F41.1 Generalised anxiety disorder
F41.2 Mixed anxiety and depressive disorder
F41.3 Other mixed anxiety disorders
F41.8 Other specified anxiety disorders
F41.9 Anxiety disorder, unspecified

F42 Obsessive - compulsive disorder
F42.0 Predominantly obsessional thoughts or ruminations

F42.1 Predominantly compulsive acts (obsessional rituals)

F42.2 Mixed obsessional thoughts and acts

F42.8 Other obsessive – compulsive disorders

F42.9 Obsessive – compulsive disorder, unspecified

F42 Reaction to severe stress, and adjustment disorders

F43.0 Acute stress reactions

F43.1 Post-traumatic stress disorder

F43.2 Adjustment disorders

.20 Brief depressive reaction

.21 Prolonged depressive reaction

.22 Mixed anxiety and depressive reaction

.23 With predominant disturbance of other emotions

.24 With predominant disturbance of conduct

.25 With mixed disturbance of emotions and conduct

.28 With other specified predominant symptoms

F43.8 Other reactions to severe stress

F43.9 Reaction to severe stress, unspecified

F44 Dissociative (conversion) disorders

F44.0 Dissociative amnesia

F44.1 Dissociative fugue

F44.2 Dissociative stupor

F44.3 Trance and possession disorders

F44.4 Dissociative motor disorders

F44.5 Dissociative convulsions

F44.6 Dissociative anaesthesia and sensory loss

F44.7 Mixed dissociative (conversion) disorders

F44.8 Other dissociative (conversion) disorders

.80 Ganser's syndrome

.81 Multiple personality disorder

.82 Transient dissociative (conversion) disorders occurring in childhood and adolescence

.88 Other specified dissociative (conversion) disorders

F44.9 Dissociative (conversion) disorder, unspecified

F45 Somatoform disorders

F45.0 Somatisation disorder

F45.1 Undifferentiated somatoform disorder

F45.2 Hypochondriacal disorder

F45.3 Somatoform autonomic dysfunction

.30 Heart and cardiovascular system

.31 Upper gastrointestinal tract

.32 Lower gastrointestinal tract

.33 Respiratory system

.34 Genitourinary system

.38 Other organ or system
F45.4 Persistent somatoform pain disorder
F45.8 Other somatoform disorders
F45.9 Somatoform disorder, unspecified

F48 Other neurotic disorders
F48.0 Neurasthenia
F48.1 Depersonalisation – derealisation syndrome
F48.8 Other specified neurotic disorders
F48.9 Neurotic disorder, unspecified

F50–F59
Behavioural syndromes associated with physiological disturbances and physical factors

F50 Eating disorders
F50.0 Anorexia nervosa
F50.1 Atypical anorexia nervosa
F50.2 Bulimia nervosa
F50.3 Atypical bulimia nervosa
F50.4 Overeating associated with other psychological disturbances
F50.5 Vomiting associated with other psychological disturbances
F50.8 Other eating disorders
F50.9 Eating disorder, unspecified

F51 Non–organic sleep disorders
F51.0 Non-organic insomnia
F51.1 Non-organic hypersomnia
F51.2 Non-organic disorder of the sleep–wake schedule
F51.3 Sleepwalking (somnambulism)
F51.4 Sleep terrors (night terrors)
F51.5 Nightmares
F51.8 Other non-organic sleep disorders
F51.9 Non-organic sleep disorder, unspecified

F52 Sexual dysfunction, not caused by organic disorder or disease
F52.0 Lack or loss of sexual desire
F52.1 Sexual aversion and lack of sexual enjoyment
.10 Sexual aversion
.11 Lack of sexual enjoyment
F52.2 Failure of genital response
F52.3 Orgasmic dysfunction
F52.4 Premature ejaculation
F52.5 Non-organic vaginismus
F52.6 Non-organic dyspareunia
F52.7 Excessive sexual drive

F52.8 Other sexual dysfunction, not caused by organic disorders or disease

F52.9 Unspecified sexual dysfunction, not caused by organic disorder or disease

F53 Mental and behavioural disorders associated with the puerperium, not elsewhere classified

F53.0 Mild mental and behavioural disorders associated with the puerperium, not elsewhere classified

F53.1 Severe mental and behavioural disorders associated with the puerperium, not elsewhere classified

F53.8 Other mental and behavioural disorders associated with the puerperium, not elsewhere classified

F53.9 Puerperal mental disorder, unspecified

F54 Psychological and behavioural factors associated with disorders or diseases classified elsewhere

F55 Abuse of non-dependence-producing substances

F55.0 Antidepressants

F55.1 Laxatives

F55.2 Analgesics

F55.3 Antacids

F55.4 Vitamins

F55.5 Steroids or hormones

F55.6 Specific herbal or folk remedies

F55.8 Other substances that do not produce dependence

F55.9 Unspecified

F59 Unspecified behavioural syndromes associated with physiological disturbances and physical factors

F60–F69
Disorders of adult personality and behaviour

F60 Specific personality disorders

F60.0 Paranoid personality disorder

F60.1 Schizoid personality disorder

F60.2 Dissocial personality disorder

F60.3 Emotionally unstable personality disorder

    .30 Impulsive type

    .31 Borderline type

F60.4 Histrionic personality disorder

F60.5 Anankastic personality disorder

F60.6 Anxious (avoidant) personality disorder

F60.7 Dependent personality disorder

F60.8 Other specific personality disorders

F60.9 Personality disorder, unspecified

F61 Mixed and other personality disorders
F61.0 Mixed personality disorders
F61.1 Troublesome personality changes

F62 Enduring personality changes, not attributable to brain damage and disease
F62.0 Enduring personality change after catastrophic experience
F62.1 Enduring personality change after psychiatric illness
F62.8 Other enduring personality changes
F62.9 Enduring personality change, unspecified

F63 Habit and impulse disorders
F63.0 Pathological gambling
F63.1 Pathological fire-setting (pyromania)
F63.2 Pathological stealing (kleptomania)
F63.3 Trichotillomania
F63.8 Other habit and impulse disorders
F63.9 Habit and impulse disorder, unspecified

F64 Gender identity disorders
F64.0 Transsexualism
F64.1 Dual-role transvestism
F64.2 Gender identity disorder of childhood
F64.8 Other gender identity disorders
F64.9 Gender identity disorder, unspecified

F65 Disorders of sexual preference
F65.0 Fetishism
F65.1 Fetishistic transvestism
F65.2 Exhibitionism
F65.3 Voyeurism
F65.4 Paedophilia
F65.5 Sadomasochism
F65.6 Multiple disorders of sexual preference
F65.8 Other disorders of sexual preference
F65.9 Disorder of sexual preference, unspecified

F66 Psychological and behavioural disorders associated with sexual development and orientation
F66.0 Sexual maturation disorder
F66.1 Egodystonic sexual orientation
F66.2 Sexual relationship disorder
F66.8 Other psychosexual development disorders
F66.9 Psychosexual development disorder, unspecified

A fifth character may be used to indicate association with:
.x0 Heterosexuality

.x1 Homosexuality
.x2 Bisexuality
.x8 Other, including prepubertal

F68 Other disorders of adult personality and behaviour
F68.0 Elaboration of physical symptoms for psychological reasons
F68.1 Intentional production or feigning of symptoms or disabilities, either physical or psychological (factitious disorder)
F68.8 Other specified disorders of adult personality and behaviour

F69 Unspecified disorder of adult personality and behaviour

F70–F79
Mental retardation

F70 Mild mental retardation

F71 Moderate mental retardation

F72 Severe mental retardation

F73 Profound mental retardation

F78 Other mental retardation

F79 Unspecified mental retardation

A fourth character may be used to specify the extent of associated behavioural impairment:
F7x.0 No, or minimal, impairment of behaviour
F7x.1 Significant impairment of behaviour requiring attention or treatment
F7x.8 Other impairments of behaviour
F7x.9 Without mention of impairment of behaviour

F80–F89
Disorders of psychological development

F80 Specific developmental disorders of speech and language
F80.0 Specific speech articulation disorder
F80.1 Expressive language disorder
F80.2 Receptive language disorder
F80.3 Acquired aphasia with epilepsy (Landau–Kleffner syndrome)
F80.8 Other developmental disorders of speech and language
F80.9 Developmental disorder of speech and language, unspecified

F81 Specific developmental disorders of scholastic skills

F81.0 Specific reading disorder
F81.1 Specific spelling disorder
F81.2 Specific disorder of arithmetical skills
F81.3 Mixed disorder of scholastic skills
F81.8 Other developmental disorders of scholastic skills
F81.9 Developmental disorder of scholastic skills, unspecified

F82 Specific developmental disorder of motor function

F83 Mixed specific developmental disorders

F84 Pervasive developmental disorders

F84.0 Childhood autism
F84.1 Atypical autism
F84.2 Rett's Syndrome
F84.3 Other childhood disintegrative disorder
F84.4 Overactive disorder associated with mental retardation and stereo-
typed movements
F84.5 Asperger's Syndrome
F85.8 Other pervasive developmental disorders
F85.9 Pervasive developmental disorder, unspecified

F88 Other disorders of psychological development

F89 Unspecified disorder of psychological development

F90–F98
Behavioural and emotional disorders with onset usually occurring in childhood and adolescence

F90 Hyperkinetic disorders

F90.0 Disturbance of activity and attention
F90.1 Hyperkinetic conduct disorder
F90.8 Other hyperkinetic disorders
F90.9 Hyperkinetic disorder, unspecified

F91 Conduct disorders

F91.0 Conduct disorder confined to the family context
F91.1 Unsocialised conduct disorder
F91.2 Socialised conduct disorder
F91.3 Oppositional defiant disorder
F91.8 Other conduct disorders
F91.9 Conduct disorder, unspecified

F92 Mixed disorders of conduct and emotions

F92.0 Depressive conduct disorder

F92.8 Other mixed disorders of conduct and emotions

F92.9 Mixed disorder of conduct and emotions, unspecified

F93 Emotional disorders with onset specific to childhood

F93.0 Separation anxiety disorder of childhood

F93.1 Phobic anxiety disorder of childhood

F93.2 Social anxiety disorder of childhood

F93.3 Sibling rivalry disorder

F93.8 Other childhood emotional disorders

F93.9 Childhood emotional disorder, unspecified

F94 Disorders of social functioning with onset specific to childhood and adolescence

F94.0 Elective mutism

F94.1 Reactive attachment disorder of childhood

F94.2 Disinhibited attachment disorder of childhood

F94.8 Other childhood disorders of social functioning

F94.9 Childhood disorders of social functioning, unspecified

F95 Tic disorders

F95.0 Transient tic disorder

F95.1 Chronic motor or vocal tic disorder

F95.2 Combined vocal and multiple motor tic disorder (de la Tourette's syndrome)

F95.8 Other tic disorders

F95.9 Tic disorders, unspecified

F98 Other behavioural and emotional disorders with onset usually occurring in childhood and adolescence

F98.0 Non-organic enuresis

F98.1 Non-organic encopresis

F98.2 Feeding disorder of infancy and childhood

F98.3 Pica of infancy and childhood

F98.4 Stereotyped movement disorders

F98.5 Stuttering (stammering)

F98.6 Cluttering

F98.8 Other specified behavioural and emotional disorders with onset usually occurring in childhood and adolescence

F98.9 Unspecified behavioural and emotional disorders with onset usually occurring in childhood and adolescence

F99
Unspecified mental disorder

F99 Mental disorder, not otherwise specified

Glossary

A

adjustment disorder A disorder characterised by difficulty adapting to a stressful event.

adrenaline This hormone is released in reaction to stress, resulting in a variety of physiological changes.

aetiology The determination of the causes of disease.

affect A person's feelings or emotions.

agnosia A disorder in which a person fails to recognise common items.

agoraphobia An irrational and intense fear of public or open spaces.

alcoholism A physical and psychological addiction to alcohol which results in impaired functioning.

Alzheimer's disease A type of dementia which results in progressive intellectual deterioration and memory impairment.

amnesia Loss of memory, either total or partial, that can result from physiological or psychological causes.

amniocentesis A test performed on pregnant women in which amniotic fluid is tested for chromosomal abnormalities.

amphetamines A central nervous system stimulant that produces a feeling of well-being and increased energy.

anorexia nervosa An eating disorder characterised by an irrational fear of obesity and an extremely limited intake of food.

antisocial personality disorder A chronic personality disorder characterised by impulsivity, superficial interpersonal relationships and an inability to accept responsibility.

anxiety A nonspecific, unpleasant feeling of apprehension and fear coupled with physiological arousal.

anxiety disorder This *DSM IIIR* classification encompasses panic disorders, phobic reactions, generalised anxiety disorder, and obsessive-compulsive disorder.

aphasia A language disorder resulting from brain injury in which the ability to communicate or to understand communication is impaired.

assertiveness training This cognitive–behavioural technique teaches a person to express his feelings and cognitions in an effective, nonaggressive manner.

attention-deficit hyperactivity disorder A behavioural disorder in children in which the child's ability to function is impaired by inattention, impulsivity and hyperactivity.

attribution This theory, from social psychology, deals with the way people assess and explain their behaviours.

autistic disorder This childhood disorder, classified as a pervasive developmental disorder in the *DSM-IV*, is marked by severe communication difficulties, an inability to develop appropriate social relationships, and, frequently, cognitive impairment.

autonomic nervous system The part of the nervous system that regulates the internal environment including the endocrine glands, stomach, heart and intestines.

aversion therapy This type of behavioural treatment attempts to modify behaviour by pairing an unpleasant stimulus, such as electric shock, with the behaviour that is to be changed.

avoidant personality This disorder is characterised by extreme sensitivity to social rejection, poor self-esteem and social withdrawal.

B

barbiturate A drug that acts to depress many of the functions of the central nervous system. These types of sedatives can be physically and psychologically addictive.

baseline This term, used in behaviour therapy, represents a person's level of response before any intervention is attempted.

behaviour therapy This type of therapy focuses on overt behaviour and attempts to modify this behaviour through the use of classical and operant conditioning principles.

benzodiazepines A family of drugs used to decrease anxiety. Two of the most common are Librium and Valium.

biofeedback A system that allows a person to monitor certain physiological reactions and to achieve limited voluntary control over these reactions.

bipolar disorder This term replaced the term manic-depressive disorder and refers to a condition characterised by mood swings from mania to depression. This term can also be used to refer to a condition of mania without depression.

bisexual A person whose sexual orientation involves both heterosexual and homosexual activity.

borderline personality disorder This personality disorder is marked by unpredictable and unstable behaviour.

British Psychological Society (BPS) In Britain this society oversees practice of, and education in psychology, setting guidelines for others and the criteria for membership of the society.

bulimia This eating disorder is marked by uncontrollable binges during which enormous amounts of food are eaten.

C

case study An encompassing study of a single individual that utilises observation and biographical information.

castration anxiety This term, central to Freud's Oedipus complex, refers to a fear in males of losing their penis as a punishment for their desires.

catastrophic misinterpretation This is the misinterpretation of bodily function changes (eg. increased heart rate) as a sign of impending death or severe panic, precipitating the panic by this reaction.

catharsis The release of emotional tension linked to childhood traumatic events through verbal expression.

cerebral cortex The surface layer or grey matter of the cerebrum.

cerebrum The largest part of the brain, the cerebrum regulates motor activities and is the centre of learning and memory. It is divided into two hemispheres.

chlorpromazine The generic name for the antipsychotic medication marketed under the name Thorazine.

chronic This term refers to a long-lasting, often degenerative condition.

classical conditioning A basic learning theory,

first developed by Pavlov, in which a neutral stimulus is coupled with a response-producing stimulus. After many pairings, the neural stimulus will elicit the same response by itself.

clinical psychologist A type of psychologist who has been trained at the doctoral level, and who specialises in the assessment and treatment of abnormal behaviour.

cocaine This drug, derived from the cocoa plant, acts as a stimulant to the central nervous system and produces feelings of euphoria and extreme self-confidence. It can also be used to relieve pain.

cognition This term refers to the act of thinking and perceiving, and to the way in which we arrange our thoughts and attitudes about our environment.

cognitive–behavioural therapy A treatment modality which focuses on modifying behaviour by changing faulty or maladaptive thoughts and beliefs.

community care The idea of treating patients whilst they are living in the community as opposed to being inpatients in hospital. Intended to avoid the effects of institutionalisation.

community psychology The branch of psychology that recognises the importance of environmental conditions on mental health and focuses on preventive intervention in the community rather than individual treatment.

compulsion The need to act in a repetitive, often senseless fashion in order to reduce feelings of anxiety.

concussion A brain injury, resulting from a blow to the head, that does not cause any permanent damage. Symptoms include mild confusion and short-term memory loss.

conduct disorder A type of disruptive behaviour disorder of childhood that is characterised by a disregard for the rights of others and for the rules of society.

confabulation A false and often unlikely story that an individual will use to cover gaps in his memory. The individual believes these stories are accurate accounts.

confidentiality A guiding principle of many professions that makes it unethical for the professional to divulge information about his client to anyone else without the client's permission.

confounding effect An effect in an experiment that results from causes other than the independent variable.

congenital A condition present at birth but not as a result of heredity.

control group The group in an experiment who are not subjected to the experimental condition but in all other ways are similar to the experimental groups.

controlled drinking A behavioural treatment method that attempts to teach alcoholics to drink in a limited, controlled manner.

conversion disorder This disorder, formerly known as hysteria, results in impaired motor or sensory functioning even though no physical reason for this impairment can be found.

coping skills A cognitive–behavioural technique that teaches individuals a variety of ways to manage the stresses of everyday life.

correlational research A study that evaluates the relationship between two or more variables without explaining the causal relationship between these variables.

counter-transference The feelings an analyst experiences toward a patient that are a result of the therapist's past experiences.

covert This term is used to describe behaviour that is not readily observable and may include emotions and cognitions.

covert sensitisation A cognitive–behavioural technique in which distressing imagery is paired with an unwanted behaviour to decrease the occurrence of that behaviour.

cyclothymic disorder An affective disorder characterised by mood swings of a less serious nature than those experienced in bipolar disorder. This disorder tends to be chronic.

D

decompensation A condition that occurs when an individual can no longer deal effectively with environmental stresses.

defense mechanism A psychoanalytic term that describes the unconscious process by which the ego prevents unacceptable anxiety-provoking conflicts from becoming conscious.

deinstitutionalisation An approach that focuses on moving mental patients out of large institutions and maintaining them in the community.

delusions Inaccurate beliefs that are firmly held, even in the presence of factual and contradictory evidence.

dementia An impairment of cognitive functioning which results from a deterioration of brain tissue.

denial A psychoanalytic defense mechanism that prevents distressing realities from becoming conscious.

dependent personality disorder This disorder is marked by poor self-esteem and an inability to assume responsibility for one's life. These people cannot tolerate being alone for any extended period of time.

dependent variable The part of an experiment that is supposed to change as a result of the application of the independent variable.

depression This affective disorder, which is a common psychological difficulty, involves overwhelming sadness, loss of interest in previously enjoyable activities, poor self-esteem, and social withdrawal.

detoxification Medical process that seeks to remove all alcohol from a person's body.

developmental disorder A series of disorders in which a child's functioning is impaired. This impairment can be in many areas or may be limited to a very specific area of development.

diagnosis The assessment and classification of specific behavioural disorders.

diathesis-stress model Theory that explains abnormal behaviour as a result of the combination of physical or psychological predisposition and environmental stress.

diazepam The generic name for the antianxiety medication marketed as Valium.

disorientation A confused cognitive state in which a person is unsure about his own identity and about time and place.

displacement A psychological defense mechanism in which feelings about a person or object are shifted to a different, more acceptable person or object.

disruptive behaviour disorders A group of childhood disorders that includes attention-deficit disorder, oppositional-defiant disorder, and conduct disorder.

dizygotic twins Fraternal but not identical twins who are the product of two separate eggs.

dopamine A neurotransmitter substance that, when abnormalities are present, has been linked to the development of schizophrenia and Parkinson's disease.

Down's syndrome A type of mental retardation resulting from an individual being born with 47 chromosomes.

dyslexia A type of learning disorder which impairs the ability to read.

dysthymia An affective condition marked by chronic, moderate depression.

E

echolalia The automatic repeating of the words and sounds of others.

ecstasy A synthetic stimulant with hallucinogenic effects much used in the UK dance culture. Usual chemical name is methylenedioxymethamphetamine (MDMA).

ego A term from psychoanalytic theory, Freud saw the ego as part of a person's personality that is mostly conscious and manages the demands of the id, the superego and reality.

ego-dystonic Thoughts, ideas or values that are not acceptable to the ego.

ego-syntonic Thoughts, ideas or values that are acceptable to the ego.

electroconvulsive therapy Also known as ECT, this treatment involves applying electric current to the patient's brain in order to produce a convulsion. This treatment is most frequently used with severely depressed patients who are a high risk for suicide.

empathy The ability to comprehend the feelings, needs, and desires of someone else.

empirical The use of experiments or observation to gather information.

encephalitis An acute inflammation of the brain commonly resulting from a viral infection.

encopresis A habit disorder involving loss of sphincter control and inappropriate bowel movements after the age of three.

endogenous Resulting from within a person rather than from external events.

endorphins Naturally occurring opiates, produced in the brain, that function as neurotransmitters and reduce pain.

enuresis A habit disorder, occurring most commonly in children, in which a person fails to achieve bladder control at a developmentally appropriate age.

epilepsy A nervous disorder marked by impaired consciousness sometimes accompanied by seizures.

erogenous zones Those areas of the body that are sexually responsive.

exhibitionism An abnormal sexual disorder in which a person receives gratification by exposing his genitals in public.

existential therapy A treatment approach that focuses on an individual's right to freely determine the course of his or her life and to accept responsibility for those choices.

exogenous Attributable to external causes, this term is frequently used to describe a type of depression.

experiment The basis for much scientific study, this investigative technique seeks to test a hypothesis by actively manipulating a variable under controlled conditions and observing what occurs.

external validity A measure of the ability of experimental results to be generalised to other situations and populations.

extinction A term used in behaviour modification in which reinforcement is removed to weaken or eliminate the acquired response.

F

factitious disorder A self-limiting physical or psychological condition which is used to receive attention.

family therapy A group treatment approach which aims to facilitate communication among family members and to modify dysfunctional behaviour.

foetal alcohol syndrome (FAS) This disorder results from an infant being exposed to alcohol during the mother's pregnancy. Characteristics include impaired cognitive functioning, restricted growth and physical abnormalities.

fetishism A sexual disorder marked by the need to include an inanimate object in sexual activity in order to achieve arousal.

fixation A psychoanalytic term which describes an individual's inability to progress beyond a certain developmental stage.

flat affect An inability to experience a normal emotional response.

flooding A behavioural technique in which the client is subjected to a fear-inducing stimulus to decrease his conditioned response.

free association A psychoanalytic technique in which the patient says whatever comes to mind with no restrictions.

free-floating anxiety Generalised feelings of anxiety that cannot be attributed to a specific source.

functional disorder Any abnormal disorder for which there is no known organic basis.

G

galvanic skin response A measure of the changes in electrical resistance of the skin.

gender identity disorder A disorder marked by a conflict between an individual's physical characteristics and sexual identity.

general adaptation syndrome A three-stage reaction to stress, postulated by Selye, characterised by a physiological alarm reaction, defensive responses and exhaustion.

generalisation An operant conditioning term in which a response will occur in the presence of a stimulus similar to the conditioned stimulus.

generalised anxiety disorder Anxiety experienced in situations in which there is no apparent anxiety-inducing stimulus.

genetic counselling One means of preventing the passing on of disease causing genes to the next generation is by not having children of one's own. This form of counselling gives advice on the risks involved.

genetic linkage When the genetic make-up of an individual is being formed, there is a tendency for genes close together on chromosomes to stay together. Thus, when trying to locate the gene for a disorder, a marker or linked gene for an easily identified characteristic may help to indicate the presence of the unidentified gene.

genital stage The psychosexual stage of development when an individual develops the capacity for mature sexuality.

genotype The part of a person's characteristics that can be attributed to genetic factors.

gerontology The field of scientific study which focuses on the aging process and the interests and needs of older individuals.

gestalt therapy A humanistic model of treatment that emphasises current concerns and the individual's perception of himself and his environment.

GP In England the family doctor is referred to as a General Practitioner (GP).

grand mal The most serious type of epileptic seizure during which an individual suffers extreme convulsions and loss of conscious functioning.

group therapy A treatment modality utilised by therapists of various orientations, in which two or more individuals are treated at the same time.

H

halfway house A temporary home provided for recently discharged psychiatric patients to ease their transition back to the community.

hallucination A false sensory perception that frequently is of a visual nature.

heredity An individual's characteristics that can be attributed to genetic makeup.

heroin An opiate which is derived from morphine and is addictive.

heterosexual Sexual preference for the opposite sex.

hierarchy of needs Theory developed by Maslow that postulates that an individual's basic needs must be met before higher level needs, such as self-actualisation, can be addressed.

histrionic personality Disorder marked by excessive displays of emotion, dependency, self-centred behaviour and unstable sexual relationships.

homosexuality Sexual preference for a member of one's same sex.

humanistic perspective The view that emphasises an individual's free will and responsibility to choose his or her own direction in life.

hypertension Abnormal high blood pressure which is frequently a result of psychological stress.

hypnosis A highly relaxed condition resembling a trance during which an individual is very open to suggestion.

hypochondriasis A chronic disorder marked by unfounded and excessive concerns about becoming ill.

hypothesis An unproved explanation for behaviour which is evaluated in a psychological experiment.

hysteria The development of a physical problem which is not attributable to an organic factor.

I

id This Freudian concept is identified as the part of the personality structure which is governed by instinctual impulses and biological drives.

identification A psychoanalytic concept by which an individual achieves a higher state of development by accepting the values and viewpoints of the same-sexed parent.

incest Sexual contact between family members.

independent variable The part of an experiment that is controlled by the investigator to determine its effect on the experimental subjects.

indoleamine A monoamine neurotransmitter linked to an organism's emotional state.

informed consent Guideline that requires that a patient be provided appropriate information before undergoing any treatment or experimental procedure.

insanity defense A legal manoeuvre by which a defendant admits to committing a crime but pleads innocent because of mental disease.

insight therapy A treatment modality that focuses on having the patient better understand the underlying reasons for their behaviour.

insomnia A disorder characterised by problems in falling asleep and staying asleep.

instrumental learning A process in which a subject is reinforced for performing a designated response so that the frequency of this response will increase.

intellectualisation The repression of unacceptable emotions and the replacement of these emotions with a dry, intellectual explanation.

intelligence test A standardised measure, usually administered by a psychologist, of evaluating an individual's level of intellectual functioning.

intermittent reinforcement A method of reinforcing responses at periodic rates rather than after every response.

internal validity The changes that occur in an experiment which can be attributed to the independent variable.

International Classification of Diseases (ICD) This is an international system of classification based in Geneva and produced by the World Health Organisation. It is in its tenth revision ICD-10, in which the fifth chapter is dedicated to mental disorders.

intrapsychic conflict A Freudian term that describes the attempt by one area of the personality structure to resist thoughts, feelings or impulses from a different area.

introjection Freudian term for the process by which an individual accepts and internalises the values of another person or group.

isolation Psychoanalytic concept in which the ego as a defense mechanism represses the emotions associated with a situation but not the memory of the situation.

in vivo treatment A treatment technique that takes place in the actual situation.

irrational beliefs Thoughts that rational-emotive therapists feel are self-defeating and lead to unproductive emotions and behaviours.

K

kleptomania An abnormal condition in which an individual steals impulsively, even though there may be no need for that which is stolen.

Korsakoff's syndrome A psychotic condition resulting from long-term alcoholism that is characterised by severe cognitive impairment.

L

lability An unstable emotional state.

latency period The development stage, as defined by Freud, during which sexual impulses are not important to an individual.

learned helplessness The belief, developed in response to previous experiences, that one has no control over what occurs in life and is therefore helpless to make changes.

learning disabilities Difficulties learning arithmetic and reading, as well as speech problems, which can not be attributed to level of cognitive ability, physical impairment or psychological factors.

libido Freudian term for the sexual and instinctual drives harboured in the id.

Librium The trade name of chlordiazepoxide, an antianxiety medication.

lithium carbonate A medication, composed of chemical salts, which is used to control the symptoms of bipolar disorder.

lobotomy An outdated method of treating severe mental disease in which nerve fibres in the brain are surgically severed.

locus of control Theory that suggests that people view situations in one of two ways; either they believe they have the ability to control the outcome of a situation or that they are powerless to control the outcome.

logotherapy A form of existential treatment, developed by Victor Frankl after his experiences in a concentration camp during World War II, that focuses on an individual's need to create a life that is productive and meaningful.

longitudinal study Method of investigation and research that focuses on observing and evaluating the same individuals over an extended period of time.

Luria-Nebraska Neuropsychological Battery A group of standardised tests which are used to evaluate brain damage and determine its location.

M

magical thinking A belief, common in young children, that thoughts and behaviours can affect situations in ways that cannot be explained by the laws of nature.

magnetic resonance imaging A relatively recent technique that detects low-level resonance to provide information about the functioning of the brain.

mainstreaming An educational concept aimed at providing handicapped students maximum exposure to a regular class setting.

major depression An affective disorder in which a person experiences severe depressive episodes but does not experience manic episodes.

major tranquilizers Medications used to treat psychosis.

maladaptive behaviour Behaviour that does not meet the demands of one's environment in an adequate manner.

malingering Faking a physical or mental disorder for personal gain.

mania A state of unfounded euphoria coupled with heightened cognitive and motor activity marked by pressured speech, poor judgment and impulsiveness.

masochism Disorder in which sexual gratification is achieved by being degraded or by having pain inflicted upon you.

medical model An approach to the diagnosis and treatment of psychological disorders based on the approach medicine takes to physical disease.

monoamine oxidase (MAO) inhibitor Group of antidepressant drugs that are effective with some depressed individuals.

N

narcissistic personality A disorder marked by extreme self-involvement and an inflated sense of self-worth.

negative reinforcement A behavioural technique in which the cessation of a noxious condition, such as electric shock, will increase the likelihood that a behaviour will occur.

neo-Freudians Theorists who accept many of the basic tenets of psychoanalysis but who have altered Freud's ideas in significant ways.

nervous breakdown A general term used to describe a person's inability to maintain an adequate level of functioning in response to the stresses of the person's life.

Neurology The branch of science that studies the central nervous system.

neuropsychological assessment A battery of tests designed to measure brain damage and its location.

neurotransmitter A group of substances produced by the body that function within the central nervous system to enable the passing of impulses between neurons.

O

object relations The internalised important relationships of the past that influence present social functioning.

obsessive–compulsive disorder A disorder characterised by intrusive, unpleasant thoughts and irrational ritualistic behaviours.

Oedipal conflict Psychoanalytic term that describes a young boy's sexual desire for his mother and his wish to replace his father.

operant conditioning Theory that posits that learning takes place when new behaviours are reinforced.

oppositional-defiant disorder A conduct disorder of childhood characterised by argumentative and angry behaviour directed mainly toward authority figures.

oral stage One of the earliest stages of development, according to Freud, in which the infant's pleasures are focused on the mouth and feeding activity.

organic psychosis An extreme cognitive disorder that results from actual physical impairment.

outpatient In the context of psychological treatment, a patient who resides outside of the treatment centre but makes visits to receive continued care.

overanxious disorder An anxiety disorder of childhood marked by irrational fears, performance anxiety, and an excessive need for reassurance.

overt behaviour Behaviour that can be readily seen by an observer.

P

paedophiliac A person who achieves sexual excitement through physical contact with children.

panic disorder An anxiety disorder in which a person experiences overwhelming fear and believes that he or she may go crazy or suffer a heart attack.

paranoid schizophrenia A form of schizophrenia in which delusional ideation is prominent.

paraphilias Sexual behaviour in which unusual objects of scenarios are necessary to achieve sexual excitement.

parasympathetic nervous system The part of the nervous system that controls bodily functions when the body is at rest.

Parkinson's disease Disease caused by an inability of the brain to produce sufficient dopamine. Symptoms include muscle rigidity, lack of facial expression and tremors.

passive–aggressive personality disorder Disorder in which underlying hostile impulses are expressed indirectly through the use of procrastination, forgetfulness and complaining.

perseveration The act of persisting in a line of thought or activity when it is no longer functional or appropriate.

pervasive developmental disorder A serious childhood disorder in which there is impaired functioning across many areas of development.

petit mal epilepsy A mild type of epileptic disorder in which short periods of loss of consciousness take place.

phallic stage The stage of development, according to Freud, during which the genitals are the focus of curiosity and pleasurable activity.

pharmacology The study of drugs and their effects.

phobia A fear for which there is no basis in reality.

placebo effect A change or effect that takes place because a person believes and expects it will take place.

pleasure principle The principle, according to Freud, that there are instinctual needs that strive to be gratified without concern about reality.

positive reinforcer A reinforcer, in operant conditioning, that increases the likelihood that a behaviour will occur.

posthypnotic suggestion The suggestion proposed while the client is in a trance to be acted on after the trance is over.

post-traumatic stress disorder Disorder in which a person experiences impairing symptoms resulting from an earlier distressing situation.

predictive validity The extent to which a test can predict future performance.

premature ejaculation Sexual dysfunction in which the male is unable to control ejaculation, so that it occurs before satisfying sexual relations can take place with his partner.

premorbid Term that describes a person's level of functioning before psychological problems develop.

prognosis Diagnostician's prediction on the direction an illness will take in the future.

projection Psychoanalytic defense mechanism in which a person rejects thoughts or desires he is experiencing and attributes them to someone else.

projective tests Measurement instruments composed of purposely ambiguous material that attempts to uncover an individual's unconscious thought processes.

psychoanalysis Therapeutic technique, developed by Freud, that focuses on uncovering unconscious material as a way of understanding one's behaviour.

psychomotor epilepsy A form of epilepsy in which the person engages in behaviour that is outside of his or her conscious control.

psychopathic personality Personality disorder characterised by amoral behaviour and superficial, exploitive social relationships.

psychopathology The area of psychology that is concerned with deviant behaviour.

psychopharmacology The study of medications and their effects on psychological disorders.

psychophysiological disorders Physical disorders that result in part from psychological causes.

psychosis Extreme psychological disturbance in which thought processes are severely impaired and personality integration is disrupted.

psychotherapy The systematic treatment of personality disorders or mental illness by psychological methods.

R

rape An act of violence in which sexual intercourse takes place through the use of force.

rational–emotive therapy (RET) Therapeutic techniques, developed by Albert Ellis, that focus on changing a patient's irrational beliefs.

reaction formation A psychoanalytic defense mechanism in which a person replaces an unacceptable impulse with its opposite.

reality principle A psychoanalytic term that describes the ego's efforts to meditate between the demands of the id and of the real world.

reinforcement In operant conditioning, the technique of following a response with a stimulus that will change the strength of the response.

reliability The ability of a test to consistently measure what it is designed to measure.

repression Psychoanalytic defense mechanism in which unacceptable thoughts or impulses are forced out of conscious awareness.

resistance A term from psychoanalytic therapy that describes the tendency of patients to avoid working on issues in treatment that make them anxious.

retrospective study A form of research that focuses on a subject's history when conducting an investigation.

Ritalin A stimulant drug that has the paradoxical effect of reducing hyperactive symptoms in children with attention-deficit disorder.

Rorschach test A projective test composed of ten bisymmetrical inkblots. The subject is asked to describe what the inkblots look like.

S

sadism Aberrant sexual behaviour in which sexual excitement is achieved by inflicting pain upon one's partner.

schizo-affective disorder A severe psychotic disorder that combines symptoms of schizophrenia with depression or elation.

schizoid personality disorder Personality disorder in which a person is socially withdrawn, emotionally aloof and indifferent to the feelings of others.

schizophrenia A severe disorder characterised by unusual behaviour, distortion of reality, cognitive disorganisation and inappropriate affect.

school phobia A disorder of childhood in which a child becomes panicked at the thought of attending school.

seasonal affective disorder (SAD) Disorder characterised by the onset of depression in the Autumn and the remission of this depression in the Spring.

secondary gain The increased attention and other benefits that one receives when ill.

self-actualisation Term, developed by Maslow, that describes a person functioning at his or her full capability.

sensate focus A technique of sexual therapy in which a couple is guided through a series of non-threatening sexual activities leading to mutually satisfying sexual intercourse.

separation anxiety disorder A childhood disorder in which a child is extremely fearful of being separated from his family.

sexual dysfunction Any impairment of a person's ability to desire sexual contact, to become sexually aroused or to achieve orgasm.

shaping An operant conditioning technique in which a complex response is taught by rewarding an incremental series of similar but less complex responses.

single-blind experiment A type of experiment in which the subject is unaware of whether he has received a placebo or the experimental condition.

social phobia Extreme anxiety about being observed in social situations.

somatoform disorder Disorder in which a person experiences physical symptoms that result from psychological rather than physiological causes.

statistical significance A statistical analysis that determines the probability of an experimental result occurring by chance.

statutory rape Sexual intercourse, usually consensual, with a legal minor.

stimulants A class of drugs that act upon the central nervous system to produce feelings of elation, confidence and agitation.

stress A person's internal response to the demands of the environment.

stroke Impairment to the central nervous system resulting from blockage or total rupture of the blood vessels supplying nutrients to the area.

Subjective Unit of Discomfort (SUD) scale This is a hierarchy of fear provoking situations used in systematic desensitisation.

sublimation A psychoanalytic defense mechanism in which psychic energy is directed away from unacceptable outlets and directed toward socially desirable ones.

suicidal ideation Obsessive thoughts about ending one's life.

superego The part of the personality structure, according to Freudian theory, that has internalised the ethical and moral values learned from parents and other important people.

sympathetic nervous system That part of the nervous system that controls important bodily functions during times of stress.

systematic desensitisation A behavioural therapy technique that utilises relaxation training to reduce the anxiety evoked by certain situations.

T

Tardive Dyskinesia A side effect of phenothiazine medication that results in neuromuscular impairment.

test–retest reliability The extent to which a test, given to the same individuals at different times, will produce consistent scores.

thematic apperception test (TAT) A projective test in which the subject is asked to create stories about ambiguous pictures.

therapeutic community The structuring of a hospital setting so that all events and activities have a therapeutic value for the patient.

tic An involuntary muscle twitch, usually in the area of the face.

token economy A behavioural technique, frequently employed in residential settings, in which targeted behaviours are rewarded with tokens that can be used to purchase reinforcing objects or activities.

Tourette's syndrome An uncommon but severe disorder characterised by tics and involuntary verbalisations.

tranquilisers Medications that are used to alleviate anxiety and as antipsychotics.

transference A tendency on the part of a patient, according to Freudian theory, to imbue the therapist with the qualities of significant people in their life.

transsexualism A psychosexual dysfunction in which an individual identifies with the opposite sex.

transvestism Sexual dysfunction in which an individual achieves sexual excitement by dressing as a member of the opposite sex.

tricyclic antidepressants A group of medications used to treat depression by prolonging the activity of neurotransmitters.

Turner's syndrome Abnormality in which females are born with one X chromosome instead of two X chromosomes. These girls do not develop sexually at puberty and have specific cognitive deficits.

type A personality Personality type characterised by aggressiveness, hostility and an excessive drive to achieve. Some medical research links this personality type to an increased risk of heart disease.

U

unconditioned response A response to a stimulus that occurs naturally and without being taught.

unconditioned stimulus A stimulus that produces an unlearned, unconditioned response.

unconscious The part of a person's psychological makeup, according to Freud, that stores repressed thoughts, memories and impulses.

unipolar disorder An extreme emotional disorder characterised by depression without manic episodes.

V

validity The ability of a test to accurately measure what it is designed to measure.

vicarious conditioning Conditioning that takes place by observing the consequences of the behaviour of other people.

voyeurism A sexual dysfunction in which sexual excitement is achieved by watching people undress or participate in sexual behaviour.

W

Wechsler intelligence scales Standardised intelligence tests for preschoolers to adults that provide verbal and performance scale scores and a general IQ score.

word salad An incoherent, disorganised speech pattern that is often observed in psychotic patients.

X

xenophobia An irrational fear of any stranger.

Z

zeitgeist Denotes the 'spirit of the time' or that expected of the historical context.

zoophilia A sexual dysfunction in which sexual excitement is achieved by sexual contact with animals.

zoophobia An irrational fear of animals.

Index